SURVIVING
THE
COLLEGE
ADMISSIONS
MADNESS

KEVIN ROBERT
MARTIN

Additional Resources, Publications, and Social Media

Your Ticket to the Forty Acres: The Unofficial Guide for UT Undergraduate Admissions (2017): https://www.amazon.com/dp/B0721C2Z4S

Getting into Texas Universities: Create your Perfect Apply Texas and UT-Austin: https://get-into-ut-austin.teachable.com/p/getting-into-texas

Applications Admissions Madness Blog: https://admissionsmadness.com/blog

Admissions Madness YouTube channel: https://youtube.com/c/admissionsmadness

UTAdmissions Guy YouTube channel: https://youtube.com/c/utadmissionsguy

The Unofficial Blog for UT-Austin Admissions: https://texadmissions.com/blog

Facebook: https://facebook.com/admissionsmadness

Reddit usernames: https://reddit.com/user/BlueLightSpcl/ and https://reddit.com/user/ADMISSIONSMADNESS

Instagram: https://www.instagram.com/kevinrobertmartin/

LinkedIn: https://www.linkedin.com/in/kevin-martin-5917bb55/

Kevin with Cats: https://kevinwithcats.com

For my parents
Who love and accept me,
Even when they
Misunderstand me.

"If a problem can be solved at all, to understand it and to know what to do about it are the same thing. On the other hand, doing something about a problem which you do not understand is like trying to clear away darkness by thrusting it aside with your hands. When light is brought, the darkness vanishes at once."

- Alan Watts, *The Wisdom of Insecurity:*
  A Message for an Age of Anxiety

Disclaimer: Are you a college applicant applying to a handful of affordable universities where you will realistically gain admission? Are you excited to attend most of your options? Do you enjoy writing, get a good night's sleep, block out the expectations of others, and limit your time on social media? Congratulations! You're the rare soul for whom this book is unnecessary, although it may still be of interest. For the remainder of we mortals who experience anxiety, self-doubt, and fear of the unknown, buckle up. I welcome you on a tour of our mad, mad college admissions world.

This book contains references to politics, alcohol use, mental illness, suicide, and horse meat consumption.

Surviving the College Admissions Madness

Argument

Almost every college admissions book follows a similar formula: They explain what you should do rather than avoid. Authors identify best practices for "getting into your dream school." Bloggers write how-to's for navigating the SAT, refining your college essays, and visiting campus. The *Essential College Admissions Handbook* promises a stress-free path to college acceptances in easy-to-follow steps. Others offer comprehensive playbooks or "essential information" that will somehow uncover the missing bit of data to solve all your worries.

If college applications were so simple, why do tens of thousands of families lose sleep and agonize over them each year? These guidebooks are fine places to begin your admissions journey. But they miss deeper truths about human behavior and the higher education system. This book challenges conventional college admissions wisdom.

When I first started to notice deeply troubling higher education trends, I assumed they were recent developments. Instead, I've come to learn, questions about how universities admit their applicants and who deserves spaces are a central theme in American history. Students applying for America's top-50 colleges and universities compete in a system whose rules they didn't choose. Nor did their parents' nor even their grandparents' generation invent.

The earliest mention of elite college admissions comes from a 1907 *New York Times* critique by Carnegie Mellon's eventual second president, Thomas Stockham Baker. His headline may sound shockingly familiar: "'Getting Into College' Has Become a Very Serious Problem; The Vagaries of the Necessary Requirements for Admission to Leading Institutions Becoming More Pronounced Every Year—A Consideration of the Baneful Effect of Chaotic Conditions."[1]

An article written nearly six decades later in 1965 by Fred E. Crossland in the *Phi Delta Kappan* raises the same concerns I present in this book. "Because of our collective failures in both secondary and higher education, we have come close to making access to our colleges and universities a shambles (sic). For tens of thousands of our young people, *we have made college admissions a traumatic experience.* We may have seriously damaged the senior year in high school. We have created unnecessary tensions. *We have been wasteful of our national human resources* (emphases mine)."[2] NYU Professor Scott Galloway observes that today's elite universities have created "the most thorough and arduous job-interview process in modern history."[3]

Reading source material from generations ago aligns with observations from my decade spent inside and around college admissions, first as an undergraduate admissions counselor and application reader for UT-Austin. What's changed in the past half-century is the much more comprehensive range of students applying for highly selective universities and the inescapable virtual landscapes that amplify anxieties and unhealthy comparisons with one another. College admissions is intriguing because it captures so many fundamental themes concerning history, culture, economics, politics, and identity. It's a fascinating lens through which to view society.

A first-generation college client of mine, attempting to transfer from their community college to elite computer science bachelor's programs, asks the right question: "Peoples' careers, income stability, respect, and reputation are affected when and where they do or don't get into college. How can the admissions process be so unaccountable for something everyone takes so seriously?"

My cynical response: **Elite universities do not care about you.**

My thesis proposes that the entire college admissions system maximizes institutional control and power at the expense of student flexibility and well-being.

Inelastic demand for the elite university experience means that elite universities will always receive tons of applications. Application numbers skyrocket while freshmen class sizes remain the same. Whatever barriers the universities erect for applying, families will find a way to overcome. Universities are not incentivized to provide adequate customer service or be accountable to the public. They act like unscrupulous internet or utility monopolies who know that you have no alternative but to put up with their nonsense—a trend laid bare due to inadequate and botched COVID reopenings. Tax-exempt universities neglect their responsibilities to the American public.

Power disparities between universities and families remain the fundamental reason why the admissions process is so stressful and exasperating. Universities possess a near-monopoly on information regarding their admissions review processes, statistics, and enrollment priorities. Most elite universities fall short of the transparency required to be an informed applicant, leaving the public in the dark regarding their methods and statistics. Akin to luxury brands rather than a public good, they are primarily responsible for increasing wealth inequality in the United States instead of serving as part of the solution. Universities prioritize generating revenue over a genuine commitment to diversity and access.

Holistic review that aims to "get to know the whole student" is one of the many half-truths or outright lies that hypocritical universities promote. Individual admissions officers likely care about your well-being, but the bureaucracies don't. To your professors, you're a butt on a seat or a face on Zoom. Even at universities that love to promote low student-to-faculty ratios, admissions offices and enrollment managers consider you as nothing more than Excel cells on spreadsheets that track financial, demographic, academic performance, and projected graduation rates.

I argue that a tangled web of bad incentives among society, university administrators, enrollment managers, and admissions counselors produce unintended consequences culminating in America's mad, mad college admissions system. Still, no single architect or organization constructed the machinery responsible for the collective college applicant suffering, yet the College Board, the Ivy League, and other elite institutions play a role.

The confusions, misunderstandings, and occasional mental breakdowns associated with college admissions are primarily the fault of irresponsible, unaccountable, and opaque institutions. University bureaucracies alienate applicants from their humanity and sense of self. Reading essay advice blogs might help you get in, but they won't help you stay sane. Surviving and even thriving depends on digging deep into your beliefs and understanding your behaviors within the broader context of society.

This book is the first genuine attempt in the crowded admissions genre to integrate applicant psychology with the sociology and economics of higher education. Many authors write for a general audience, whereas I'm speaking directly to students and families navigating their applications. I'm not in an air-conditioned box seat commenting on the admissions fight from afar. Instead, I'm cleaning your cuts ringside.

Students and families, remember this: *The madness isn't your fault.*

Elite universities are highly sought after not only for perceptions of prestige and the attendant esteem of enrolling at a luxury brand school. They also add considerable value to a student's lifetime earnings and future opportunities. Universities don't operate in a free or efficient marketplace. Instead, higher education resembles an exclusive if informal cartel that fixes prices and standard operating procedures between its members.

They collectively possess a near-monopoly on educational services and credentials required for elite graduate studies. Regional accreditation agencies, which universities depend on for legitimacy, rarely if ever boot members nor easily allow new institutions to provide higher education services.[4] For-profit universities have overwhelmingly failed to deliver quality educations, so there is little possibility for market disruptions.

Moreover, most professional licenses and certification boards depend on degrees from accredited universities, so the "piece of paper" one receives at graduation is a prerequisite for many careers. Earning a bachelor's degree became the new minimum credential starting in the 1990s. A high school education isn't a ticket to gainful middle-class employment anymore. Employers rely on accreditation to impose minimum requirements that filter applicants; pursuing alternative training isn't practical for most students. You can't Udemy your way to an accounting license.

Passing through the college admissions gatekeepers is a necessary evil for wealthy families aiming to maintain their elite social status and for first-generation college students seeking upward mobility. Wealthy families secure their standing in society through intensive educational investments. A lack of educational opportunities for families living in poverty or even in the middle class is a near-guarantee that their children will not ascend to the upper class. Rising inequality is both a cause and effect for who can access elite college degrees.

Admissions decisions reflect a student's wealth and privilege more than individual efforts and possessing sincere interests, a symptom of American society's Meritocracy Madness that I unpack further in chapter 10. Failing to earn a four-year degree makes joining the contemporary knowledge and information economy and securing a living—let alone lucrative—wage significantly less likely. Many families are acutely aware of what's at stake, imposing added pressure on their children. Few high school students enter their senior year and exit the admissions system better off physically and psychologically.

College admissions screws over students (in different ways for varied reasons) who are privileged or marginalized, rich or poor, black or white, rural or urban, first-time freshman or transfer, domestic or international.

Even though almost everyone is screwed, college admissions by holistic review overwhelmingly favors the savviest families from the most privileged backgrounds. I used to subscribe to journalist Frank Bruni's prescription that *Where You Go Is Not Who You'll Be*. To a point, I agree that a college doesn't need to define you. Your success is mostly up to the efforts you make once you arrive on campus, regardless of which university you attend. It remains true that you can get an excellent education at less popular universities outside of the *US News* top 100, but Bruni's sentiment rings hollow. Given America's intractable wealth inequality, a poor student entering college and exiting with debt is more likely to remain poor regardless of which university they attend. That raises the stakes for broadening access at elite universities for students living in poverty.

Yale admissions counselor John Yi reminded applicants in 2016 that "it's important for students to keep in perspective the fact that there are so many different schools out there."[5] *Easy for him to say*, a skeptical student might protest. John has a Yale degree.

John is like the first kid in the neighborhood to get a PlayStation 5. His friends are rightly suspicious when he reassures them that their PlayStation 4s are good enough. "There are plenty of games for it, and they're cheaper!" he insists.

Dammit! I want a PS5, too!

And with good reason. A superior good isn't a substitute for an inferior if adequate one, especially when your classmates post about their new luxury good on social media. Sooner than later, the PS4 will become obsolete, locking out those console owners from new games or outdated networks. Figuratively speaking, we're becoming a society of those with PS5s who play with others who have PS5s, while those with older generation consoles are left behind. Segments of the population who desperately want, yet know that they can never afford, a PS5 build up resentment between haves and have-nots. Early adopters who can afford a PS5 will be the first in line for the next-generation PS6.

To John and the other tone-deaf if well-intentioned gatekeepers insist their elite education isn't a big deal: Fewer families than ever have a realistic chance of gaining admission to Ivy League universities. Increasing inequality squeezes out the middle class, and you're partly to blame. Aggressive recruitment that drives application numbers higher and higher makes your claims that you can get a good education anywhere hold less weight.

Freshman class sizes have not expanded much in decades because elite universities assert it would diminish their education quality; a plausible claim, especially for STEM education. In reality, if Harvard or Princeton enrolled thousands more first-year students each year, it would dilute their perceived prestige and scarcity. A Rolex maintains its luster because few people can afford them. An Ivy League degree is elite in part because universities themselves impose artificial scarcity on their services. On the other hand, Rice University announced a 20 percent larger freshmen class over the next four years, accommodating 800 more undergraduate students.[6] Still, without more dramatic increases in enrollment spaces, most students cannot access elite university educations.

Institutional promotion of diversity and inclusion seems disingenuous when students at mediocre public schools cannot reasonably expect to secure a coveted space. Elite universities founded mainly by and for Christian white men *de facto* predominantly serve wealthy white families, despite nominal equality guaranteed by post–Civil War constitutional amendments and civil rights legislation. Holistic review, a development in the 1960s along with the civil rights movement, started with good intentions. I discuss the origins of holistic review as a response to segregation in chapter 5.

Nowadays, holistic review further marginalizes the underserved communities that elite universities purport to seek. Asian American and affluent international families who can afford the highly specialized training and education requisite to getting in and full-pay tuition are gaining admission to and enrolling at historically white universities. Although they make up an increasingly large presence on elite college campuses, Asian Americans aren't the "people of color" universities have in mind, despite many being first- or second-generation immigrants. Asian students come from a wide variety of backgrounds, mother tongues, and ancestral homes. They're treated like monoliths by the dominant white culture and are largely excluded from conversations regarding diversity.

Asian Americans experience racism in their daily lives, especially in elite high schools and college campuses where white students perceive them as a threat to their hegemony. Bigotry has become increasingly normalized following COVID-19 and rhetoric like "the China virus" or Trump's "Kungflu." Hate crimes against Asian Americans reached record levels in 2020 and continue into 2021.[7]

The Supreme Court case *Korematsu v. the United States* upheld the internment of 120,000 Japanese Americans during World War II. *Korematsu* remained legal precedent until a 2018 repudiation by Chief Justice John Roberts in *Trump v. Hawaii*, overturning Trump's Middle East travel ban. Elite universities can take for granted that Asian students will apply in record numbers, so they largely fall outside recruitment efforts targeting diverse populations. Elite universities do not care about most of their students, but they care about Asians the least. I discuss how the new religion of antiracism excludes Asian Americans and Asian diaspora students from conversations about diversity and inclusion, a controversial topic I discuss in chapter 9, "Rethinking Diversity."

What is the scope of the admissions madness? How many families are applying for America's top 50 or so universities? What do I mean by an "elite university"?

When I generalize about elite universities, I have in mind the campuses for whom it is the majority of their applicants' first choice. When admitted students decide to enroll, that is the "yield" in admissions jargon. Most top 50 universities yield 40–50 percent of their applicants. The average yield rate for Ivy League universities is 64 percent. The most in-demand universities such as Harvard and Stanford might enroll 75–80 percent of their admitted students.

Highly selective doesn't always mean elite. Some universities, such as Miami and Tulane, might accept less than 25 percent of their students, qualifying them as highly selective. However, their yield rates are also low, somewhere between 20 percent and 30 percent. A lower yield rate suggests that these are not the dream schools for most of their admitted students. Selective universities with lower yield rates contribute to the madness, but they're usually a second or third choice for most applicants.

There are many college ranking systems, and debates about what qualifies as "elite" remain an open question and one that may shift over time. It's challenging to derive precise statistics because there is no national clearinghouse or public database of how many applications the median applicant submits. In chapter 7, "Avoiding Application Mistakes," I dive much deeper into finding the right fit and value universities and how rankings and prestige are not everything.

For now, I propose a working definition of "elite" that means the campuses with rising application numbers at a much higher rate than the national average. They occupy a central fixture in family conversations and social media. They're the campuses that vaguely constitute some "top 50," even if notions of a "top school" aren't about any particular ranking system or "best of" list. Although I shine a light on questionable admissions review and recruitment practices of less-selective and non-elite universities, they are not the focus of this book.

I've tallied the admissions and enrollment statistics for 45 of the most in-demand public and private universities, broadly defined, during the Fall 2020 pre-pandemic admissions cycle. I consider 27 private universities of varying sizes, 7 of the top small liberal arts colleges, and 11 of the most sought-after public research universities. (The list can be found in this endnote.[8])

Approximately 1.6 million applications were submitted for 279,000 acceptance offers. These 45 colleges and universities enroll approximately 116,400 first-year students each year. The average admissions rate for public and private elite universities was 17 percent, with the average admitted applicants receiving 2.4 offers. In my dataset, the 34 private universities have an average admissions rate of 9.5 percent compared with 28 percent for the top public universities. Coveting these scarce spaces drives the admissions madness.

If each student submits between four and six applications, between 270,000 and 400,000 families are navigating the elite college admissions cycle each year. There are approximately 4.5 million seniors at American high schools each year, so, broadly speaking, most of the 1.6 million applications to elite universities are submitted by students ranking within the top quarter of their schools. They overwhelmingly come from affluent suburbs. At a minimum, competitive applicants pursue Advanced Placement or International Baccalaureate curricula. They make mostly A's and score over 1400 on the SAT, which puts them within the 95th percentile of test takers worldwide. Tens of thousands of international families also compete for these 116,400 spaces, so the admissions madness is a global phenomenon.

Many of the approximately 350,000 applicants will not receive any offers from top-50 universities, forcing them to enroll at their second and third choices, such as Tulane, Miami, or their state's public flagship university. The possibility of rejection from everywhere means it's critically important that all students have safety schools and at least one "security" school where they're 100 percent guaranteed admission. Students who apply mainly or exclusively to top-50 universities risk rejection from all of them, adding further humiliation when they enroll at their ninth-choice university.

Conversely, universities seek and compete for the top 5 percent of the applicants aiming for elite universities, representing around 13,000 to 20,000 of the most outstanding students worldwide. An even more rarified tier of 1,000 or so of the most exceptional students will have considerable national and international level achievements and a unique story; they may get into some or all of the highly selective universities to which they apply.

The problem is that no student knows in advance if they are in the top 1,000. Without any admissions guarantees, they apply to fifteen or twenty universities alongside their less competitive peers. One client of mine gained admission to over a dozen universities in the US News top 50, including a few full-ride merit scholarship offers. They gained admission to MIT yet were rejected by comparatively less-selective USC, so it is impossible to know in advance where one might gain admission. Neither of us realized the strength of their profile until the results arrived. Each positive outcome left them feeling exhilarated with a twinge of guilt for taking admissions spaces from others. Attracting these highest-tier applicants is why even top-ten universities spend tens of millions of dollars each year on glossy brochures and annoying mailing list sequences, which I expand upon in chapter 8, "Questionable Enrollment and Recruitment Practices."

An average of 2.4 elite university acceptances per applicant is misleading because most students will receive zero offers. In contrast, a small pool of exceptional students will earn most of the admissions spaces. Said another way, there are approximately 22,000 Ivy League admissions offers. However, there are far fewer than 22,000 individual students occupying those spaces. If elite universities care about any of their applicants—and I propose that they don't—these highest tiers concern their admissions counselors and not the other 95 percent of good but not great students.

Celebrating students who gain admission to all eight Ivy League campuses yet can enroll only in one takes a few of those admissions offers away from great but not exceptional students who are excluded from elite universities altogether. One problem with college admissions is that a decentralized system permits students to submit as many applications as they desire. That produces an inefficient system where spaces are not distributed evenly to everyone who might enroll, which I discuss in chapter 5.2.

If one student could only gain admission to a single elite university, a broader pool of students would occupy the approximately 279,000 elite university admissions offers. Reforms that decrease the ratio of admissions offers to enrollment spaces, currently at 2.4 per applicant, would signal a more efficient and potentially fair system. A plausible remedy for the inefficient distribution of spaces is admissions by partial lottery, a possibility I discuss in chapter 10.2.

The Fall 2021 admissions cycle isn't complete at the time of writing, so the COVID admissions portrait is unclear. What is evident is that the madness is accelerating. Applications submitted to highly selective universities have skyrocketed. Colgate has doubled their application numbers from the previous year, and Harvard received 57,000 applications, an increase of 17,000 from the last cycle. Nevertheless, Harvard intends to enroll a freshmen class of 1,700 despite most of their student body attending Zoom University.

A January 26, 2021 *Chronicle of Higher Education* article provides early insight into the COVID admissions cycle.[9] Overall applications submitted to at least one of the 900 participating Common App universities are up 10 percent from the previous year, at 5.58 million distributed among almost one million unique applicants. The average Common App student submits around 5.5 applications, but because not all universities use the Common

App, the average number of applications per student remains unknown. I estimate students aiming for top-50 universities submit on average eight to ten applications each.

These application gains concentrate at elite universities with declines at the Cal State University and State University of New York (SUNY) systems that historically serve middle- and working-class or nontraditional students. Widespread adoption of test-optional policies and fee waivers for qualifying low-income students has not notably increased the number of first-generation students applying to college. Test-optional policies appear to be benefitting mediocre students at affluent high schools rather than increasing access for marginalized communities. The total number of applications submitted comes mostly from students living in college-going communities. Despite intensive recruiting and outreach efforts, elite universities have failed in expanding the pool of potential applicants beyond predominantly wealthy families.

Students from affluent families and the top high schools continue to crowd out spaces for everyone else. Common Application administrators have issued "alarm bells" at the rising gap between who applies to and gains admission at elite universities. It may be true that you can earn a good education at many of America's 4,000 colleges and universities, most of which aren't especially selective. They aren't the primary culprits of the admissions madness that I investigate.

Yale law professor Daniel Markovits wrote *The Meritocracy Trap*, which examines the origins and persistence of economic and educational inequality in the United States. He cites research that the achievement gap between rich and poor students today is more extensive than between white and black students in the early 1950s during segregation. Families with wealth outside of the top 5 percent are increasingly left behind. Wealthy states such as Connecticut spend more than double on public education than poorer states such as Mississippi.

Private schools spend on average six times more per pupil and employ twice as many—and often more experienced and highly qualified—teachers than their public counterparts. Less than 2 percent of American students attend private schools, yet they occupy a quarter of the enrollment spaces at Ivy League universities. Some private schools send up to 50 students each year to Harvard. Caitlin Flanagan of the *Atlantic* sums up the division between elite private schools and public schools in underserved communities. "Many schools for the richest American kids have gates and security guards; the message is *you are precious to us.* Many schools for the poorest kids have metal detectors and police officers; the message is *you are a threat to us* (emphasis hers)."[10]

The number one question students ask is: Which factors matter most in my admissions chances? The answers they have in mind are their essays, academics, or resume. Those matter, but what matters most is your zip code.

Harvard Professor Michael Sandel cites research that an applicant from the top 1 percent is 77 times more likely to gain admission to an Ivy League school compared with a student from the bottom 20 percent.[11] Although universities are much more accessible for students from diverse gender, racial, and cultural backgrounds than at any time in history, the Ivy League and its equivalents collectively enroll more students from the 1 percent of American society than the bottom half. Financial-aid guarantees matter little if few low-income or first-generation students gain admission. It's ironic that British aristocracy's traditional champions Oxford and Cambridge now enroll more socioeconomically diverse student bodies than their diversity-evangelizing American peers.

Access to substantially more resources gives wealthy students considerable advantages, the least of which is intensive exam preparation. Markovitz writes in the *Atlantic*, "Only about one in two hundred children from the poorest third of households achieve SAT scores at Yale's mean."[12] The gap between wealthy and middle-class children is growing substantially faster than between the middle class and families living in poverty. Middle-class families who don't make enough money or have the financial stability to save for college are increasingly priced out of elite educations. Yet, they earn too much to benefit from need-based aid schemes.

More now than ever, reaching the highest tiers of American professional life requires an elite degree. Corporate hiring practices and elite graduate schools use a bachelor's degree as a front-end filter, ignoring applicants from lesser universities. One in four Yale Law School students received bachelor's degrees from Harvard, Princeton, and Yale. Daniel Markovits writes, "Meritocratic education now predominantly serves an elite caste rather than the general public…. Middle-class workers, without elite degrees, face discrimination all across the labor market that increasingly privileges elaborate education and extravagant training."[13] The gap between the rich and middle class is accelerating faster than the gap between middle and lower classes in part because of access to elite undergraduate educations.

Middle-class millennials were the first generation in American history less likely to make more money than their parents. Gen Z seems to be following the same trajectory as they begin and graduate college during a global pandemic. In theory, Markovits argues, meritocracy is supposed to make us more equal. Meritocracy isn't obviously unjust in the way that aristocracies transfer wealth between generations or governments that decide leadership based on family pedigree.

In practice, the American Dream is an illusion and the original sin of the meritocracy gospel.[14] The United States is two to three times less socially mobile than "socialist" countries such as France, Germany, Sweden, Canada, Finland, Norway, and Denmark. If you're born outside of the top quintile of wealth in America, there is an overwhelming chance you will die earlier and with the same or less wealth than your parents. Generation Z works harder than perhaps any cohort of teenagers. Yet, society fails to provide them with adequate job prospects or pathways to earn college degrees that don't entail a lifetime of debt. Harvard Professor Michael Sandel summarizes the lack of social mobility bluntly: "Relatively few children of the poor rise to affluence, and relatively few children of affluence fall below the ranks of the upper middle class."[15]

College students are both the customer and the commodity. They pay not just for academics, skills, and social networks but also for the quintessential "American college experience." Even during the pandemic, students shelled out tens of thousands of tuition dollars for Zoom University classes lest they be left behind in our meritocratic rat race. Alternatives such as online learning or trade schools may help some consumers, especially from non-college-going communities. Online learning is highly unlikely to displace entrenched brick-and-mortar universities whose appeal endures despite the pandemic. Ambitious high school students have little choice but to apply to and be consumers of elite universities' services.

Although the wealthiest students attending the best schools have overwhelming advantages compared to the low-income students they often tutor to bolster their college resume; they buckle under the extreme pressures expected of them. Lack of sleep has become a virtue, "busyness" the default mode of living, panic attacks an unwelcome occurrence disrupting their rigid schedules. Adulthood seeps deeper into adolescence.

Paradoxically, digital-native teens, deprived of unstructured time and glued to their devices, are less prepared than ever to enter an increasingly complex adult world. Nevertheless, the competition within the top 1 percent and America's best high schools is intense, and admission spaces zero-sum. One can get ahead only by dominating those below. Poor students don't have a spot at the admissions dinner table, whereas rich kids take most of the seats and politely fight over the food. Middle-class students scramble for the crumbs.

Elite universities are composed mainly of the winners from the cutthroat admissions competition. Higher education economics demands that an ever-increasing supply of full-tuition-paying students receive their degrees to make space for the next cohort. Because wealth concentrates in fewer families than in previous generations, affluent students are highly sought-after commodities. They subsidize need-based financial aid for the few low-income students on elite college campuses.

A shrinking middle class pressures universities to recruit and graduate a dwindling supply of full-tuition students. Recruiting wealthy students who are primarily white or Asian comes into conflict with many institutions' commitment to increasing education access for first-generation and low-income students who are often, but not always, black, Hispanic, or Native American.

Most universities are less interested in student health than getting you in and out as quickly as possible. Increasing education delivery efficiency is essential to maintain freshman retention and four-year graduation rates. It's more convenient and less of a hassle to push students through with easy A's than to enforce rigor. Federal aid such as Pell Grants depends on universities maintaining a certain graduation rate threshold. Their budgets depend on granting you a degree, creating pressures to diminish curricula quality for myriad reasons. A higher percentage of Pell-eligible student enrollment boosts a university's ranking, further entangling the web of incentives that drives the admissions madness.

Excellence matters more than well-being, reflected in mental health crises and binge drinking cultures affecting virtually all elite college campuses. Campuses confront pressures to meet their medical school placement metrics, research grants acquired, and their graduates receiving prestigious fellowships such as Fulbright and Rhodes Scholars. Excellent students become advertisement fodder in recruitment brochures targeting prospective students. Universities commoditize student experiences, and thus the recruitment-to-graduation pipeline continues indefinitely.

UT-Austin published and promoted my undergraduate achievements to attract future students in various articles and outlets, sometimes without my consent. One headline regarding my research abroad read, "Some students go to Cancun. This Liberal Arts undergraduate went to Bosnia and Rwanda." Idiotic in its own right and ironic because I read the article while I was literally in the Yucatan near Cancun, pursuing an English teaching certificate.

College admissions involves fundamental questions of who deserves what. How does a society distribute a scarce number of spaces for a large pool of qualified candidates?

Questions about justice and fairness encompass culture and politics. Universities themselves are battlegrounds for ideology and public policy. An honest college admissions book must confront troubling aspects of American history and our highly unequal contemporary society. Understanding our past can help frame conversations around poverty, race, and who can or cannot access a high-quality college education. I make no apologies for engaging directly with cultural and political issues or the criticisms I level against both the political right and left.

I attempt to unpack why the American admissions system is absurd and inefficient. I'm less interested in offering policy recommendations to unaccountable politicians. Proposing admissions reforms will not resonate with nonresponsive university bureaucracies. However, throughout I provide ample possible solutions to remedy the system-wide madness. Most of my suggestions boil down to

- fewer essays and application requirements such as recommendation letters, interviews, Subject Tests, and letters of continued interest,
- diminishing or eliminating the role of holistic review at less-selective universities,
- more transparent and accountable admissions standards, i.e., publishing what's required to be competitive,
- consistent enrollment management policies that don't exploit students as consumers with a decreased emphasis on aggressive marketing and recruitment,
- putting the applicants' needs on par with university budgets, and
- removing the tax-exempt "charity" status for elite universities unless they serve broader swaths of society.

I make a serious proposal endorsing a partial admissions lottery in this book's conclusion. Universities are highly resistant to change because they are unwilling to sacrifice an iota of control or lose any recruiting or admissions edge relative to their peer institutions.

I contend that no professionals affiliated with institutions or education consulting firms are willing or able to provide such a comprehensive takedown of the admissions system. They're either overly concerned about their professional reputations or

their institutions hamstring their freedom of speech. Other counselors simply choose to do nothing or fail to acknowledge their
complicity in aggravating hundreds of thousands of families each
year. They talk amongst themselves at conferences and private
Facebook groups where I lurk, yet the public remains mostly in
the dark regarding higher education and college admissions policy
debates. Their conversations behind closed doors are out of touch
with the lived realities and primary concerns of the families they
supposedly serve.

Since 2015, I've served as an independent college consultant
through my self-employed business, Tex Admissions. When I
worked for UT, I was genuinely unaware of the agony families
experience. Admissions professionals are necessarily detached
from their prospective students and society in general. Working
independently, rather than for a university, opens my eyes to the
broader admissions landscape. I see the applicants' deliberations,
hesitations, and worries that rarely revealed themselves during
high school visits, college fairs, and admissions presentations on
behalf of UT.

In 2017, I published *Your Ticket to the Forty Acres: The
Unofficial Guide for UT Undergraduate Admissions*. My book has
undoubtedly helped many families navigate UT-Austin's byzan-
tine admissions system and improve their applications to national
universities. Rather than clutter Amazon with yet another essay
tips catalog or a "definitive guide," I want to share with you here
the cognitive biases and distortions that produce systematic errors
for many highly selective university applicants most of the time.

I enjoyed writing *Your Ticket* and appreciate that it remains
relevant years later. However, *Surviving the College Admissions
Madness* is the book I've always wanted to write because my life's
purpose is to question conventional wisdom and speak truth to
power. I've also had a ton of fun reflecting on and calling into

question the higher education system beyond Texas. (See this endnote for an opinion piece by Frank Bruni with a similar title unaffiliated to this book.[16])

The unfortunate reality for many soon-to-be college students is that their troubles are just beginning when they enroll at elite universities. High school insecurities and anxieties about the future intensify as the competition becomes fiercer. The success funnel narrows at each step. Prestigious law schools are filled with the most ambitious bachelor's degree recipients. Earning a position at a prominent firm requires attending a top-12 law school. Promotion from lawyer to associate before becoming a partner requires working longer billable hours and sacrificing more than their colleagues. The law firm partner finds time to have kids who are expected to march to the same tune of meritocratic excellence at all costs. On and on, the cycle continues unless an incredibly forward-thinking and heroically self-aware parent allows their child space to grow and flourish on their own terms and reconsider whether the prestige madness is worthwhile.

Conversations regarding current college students are essential yet outside this book's scope. However, in chapter 4, I touch on how enrolling at your dream school may not be the panacea you imagine. The dream school Heaven that they imagine resembles a hellish life for many.

There are volumes published on failures regarding college student mental health; runaway tuition inflation, crippling debt, and a decrease in higher education funding; the watering down of college curricula and the lowering of grading standards; the McDonaldsification of universities as degree mills;[17] the corporatization of university administrations; exploitation of underserved populations by malicious for-profit universities; overreliance on poorly compensated, temporary adjunct professors; inadequate resources or job prospects for graduate students; and the priority of college athletics over academics accompanying absurd "student-athlete" designations.

Division I college football players are the most extreme example of universities leveraging near-total control over a person's autonomy by limiting profiting from their namesake or changing universities without penalty. College football players aiming for the NFL, like aspirants to the nation's top medical schools or Wall Street firms, have no choice but to play by rules written against their best interests. Few college football players make it to the NFL, and even the "successful" ones finish their football careers with brain damage and numerous injuries. It's not unlike highly paid corporate lawyers or management consultants who earn seven-figure salaries yet experience midlife crises and failed marriages following two or three decades of 60- to 100-hour workweeks without a vacation.

I hope that some find my book a partial remedy to the admissions madness. College admissions is one page among many life chapters for ambitious people seeking entry into society's highest echelons. I was a first-generation college student who submitted a single college application to UT-Austin, where state law guaranteed me admission. I and many like me are often wholly unaware that this elite universe exists.

Regardless of your background, understanding and surviving the admissions system now will help you later in life. The definition of insanity is doing the same thing over and over and expecting different results. College application pitfalls will reoccur when you apply for internships, graduate schools, or fellowships. For some, I hope my book begins a process of critical thinking that will help you lead a more balanced and fulfilling life long after graduating from high school and college.

My qualitative analysis offers perspectives from history, pop culture, behavioral economics, cognitive psychology, philosophy, and the social sciences to shed light on the higher education system in which you're unwittingly participating.

Working in and around college admissions makes me realize that it's highly undemocratic. It bears a closer resemblance to entry into medieval priesthoods than a level playing field open to all comers. It isn't a coincidental turn of phrase that we call admissions reviewers "gatekeepers." Christianity's Saint Peter is the apocryphal keeper of the keys. He alone possesses the book of names granting souls admission to Heaven's pearly gates or descent into Hell. In the Gospel of Matthew 16:19, Jesus offers to Peter, "I will give you the keys of the kingdom of heaven, and whatever you bind on Earth shall be bound in heaven, and whatever you loose on Earth shall be loosed in heaven."[18]

Peter must be accountable for his actions; he has skin in the game. He understands the gravity of his decisions and what's at stake. If he allows dastardly souls into Heaven, he risks catastrophe.

In our admissions story, universities face few if any consequences for their behavior. They lack accountability, and praying to them doesn't do any good. Souls seeking entrance to Heaven have the benefit of knowing who's potentially sending them to Hell. They can look Peter in the eye if otherworldly beings permit such a thing.

College admissions doesn't have an equivalent to Jesus the Son of God anointing carefully chosen gatekeepers to decide the fates of hundreds of thousands of teenage souls. Admissions gatekeepers seem omniscient and all-powerful to their applicants, but they're not. Most of the few thousand professionals at America's top universities stumbled into their admissions jobs. Turnover rates are high, with most first-time counselors exiting the profession within two years. Many campuses outsource their admissions file review to noncounselor readers paid $15–20 an hour.

No high school student dreams of enrolling at college to work in the office that makes admissions decisions. I've yet to read or assist with a college essay that declares working in admissions is their dream job. There is no typical academic major that leads to an admissions position, so it isn't an obvious career choice.

When UT-Austin released their heavily downvoted official freshman Fall 2021 YouTube video announcing record application numbers and, therefore, record rejections, a disembodied voice breaks the devastating news, overlayed with serene scenes of happy, ethnically diverse students.[19] Rather than a soothing Morgan Freeman, the audience receives a middle manager reading from a script heavily vetted by the university's communications and public relations team. Viewers don't know who is speaking, and because comments are disabled, it isn't possible for students to ask questions or vent their frustrations. The video comes not from the Office of Admissions but "UT Enrollment and Student Management Success." It's unclear at many universities who is actually in charge and making the admissions decisions.

Elite universities have traded the pre-twentieth-century doctrine of admission by your family's pedigree for a more insidious gospel of meritocracy supposedly open to anyone demonstrating sufficient talent. Merit-based holistic review distorts incentives for students to pursue their genuine interests. A distorted value system paradoxically makes it more difficult for universities to select for the very qualities they purport to seek: sincerity, curiosity, and internal motivation. Yale Professor Daniel Markovits warns that "meritocracy traps entire generations inside demeaning fears and inauthentic ambitions: always hungry, never finding, or even knowing, the right food."[20]

Like religion, a holistic review meritocracy mandates that prospective applicants' beliefs, behaviors, and decisions flow into a single point: *Am I pleasing the admissions gods?*

Students who don't know the rules or refuse to play the credentials-accumulation game and spend their time freely will not be rewarded for their efforts. Parents sometimes apologize to me because their children play too many video games, the implicit assumption being that their hobby is a missed opportunity to build their college resume. Even video games are emerging as a pathway to college admissions and scholarships as the eSports industry booms. Unstructured play and hobby time without adult supervision or college admissions consequences are increasingly rare or nonexistent in affluent communities.

Ambitious applicants who ordinarily have concerns for social justice push aside their ethics for a chance at communing on Ivy-rimmed campuses. They're willing to lie and cheat to get ahead even if they're not liars and cheaters in other situations, which I discuss further in chapter 6.4, "Cheaters Often Win."

Adherents bow down to the admissions regulations and surrender themselves to whatever it takes to enter the hallowed grounds of Harvard Yard. They prostrate themselves to multi-billion-dollar institutions in 650 words or less for the honor of incurring five- and six-figures debt. Substituting the eucharist's wine for M&Ms and Diet Coke, admission gatekeepers are modern-day high priests who deliberate on Zoom and around closed-door conference tables. Their pulpit is your mailbox and inbox, and their holy texts are a catalog of glossy brochures and spammy emails.

Like the Pope appearing on Easter Sunday, the admissions high priests dust off their Doritos Cool Ranch finger dust, rise from their Excel sheets, and press Run Program.

Behold! Your admissions decisions!

And the applicant masses scramble to make sense of the latest revelations.

Admissions high priests take themselves so seriously, but when you take a more detached view of their gospel and rituals, you realize how it's absurd, silly, ridiculous, bizarre, nonsensical, and downright wacky. Laughter can often be the best medicine. It might also be your only option for preserving your sanity.

Taking a step back, rolling your eyes, and mocking your college applications might help reframe the anxiety and indirectly improve your admissions chances. I used to believe college admissions memes shared among students were immature and unproductive, but I understand now that they give expression to fears and offer catharsis. Memes and mockery are a powerful form of resistance.

I make light of college admissions practices in part because we have a **humor bias** and are more likely to remember and share funny tidbits than boring bib-bobs. I also joke because the powerful fear laughter. If we laugh at their stories, it makes them harder to believe. But not everything in this book is light or funny. We will deal with serious subjects that, for some, are matters of life and death. I discuss what's at stake in chapter 4.3 as part of a broader conversation about identifying and addressing the root causes of suffering caused by college admissions.

Many families believe these fictions, accepting blindly that what the admissions high priests say gives them their power at the expense of your independence of thought. Universities claim to seek innovative thinkers and community disrupters, yet applicants are expected to have unquestioned faith in a highly unfair admissions system. You're less likely to question the rules and pay the application fees if you perceive their expectations as legitimate and the rules fair. Their reassurances of fairness are nothing except public relations speak to cover for their revenue-generating agendas.

Elite universities do not care about you.

I equip you, applicants and parents, with the vocabulary, frameworks, and tools to make sense of America's broken higher education system, starting with the admissions gatekeepers. I want to help you avoid mistakes and identify the sources of your discontent. I challenge you to step off your Peloton and think about the machine revolving underneath rather than staring at the screen and spinning your legs mindlessly. A focus exclusively on *how to* apply to college blinds families to seeing *why our college application system is broken.*

There is no secret piece of advice or six-easy-steps that will build a bridge over rivers of anxiety leading to lands of contentment and prosperity. No amount of "chancing" or combing Naviance Scatterplots will decrease the inherent uncertainty, which I discuss in chapter 6.10. I prefer not to patronize my readers by promising them that college applications are *so simple if they just follow my advice.*

I'm writing for families and high school educators who want a deeper understanding of the truth rather than wasting tens of hours on Reddit's Applying to College or College Confidential. Online forums are populated with the blind who lead the blind and snap at anyone who attempts to see things reasonably. Even though students and parents aren't the primary causes of the college admissions madness, I bring attention to some of their most absurd excesses.

I wager that at least some people are starving for original ideas that slice through the nonsense. My book assumes a certain degree of background knowledge and direct college application experience. Consider my inquiries the equivalent of an upper-division college course rather than Admissions 101.

I left America seven years ago and have achieved financial security through my college consulting business, Tex Admissions. I already have more client inquiries than I can accommodate. I have no reputation to preserve, employees to pay, or a boss who tells me what I can and cannot say. I am self-publishing to have freedom from traditional publishers' editorial preferences or rights to my content.

A lifetime of book royalties will never recoup the tens of thousands of dollars required to put this project together; I'm not publishing this book for the money. My YouTube and blog content are always ad-free, so I don't worry about pandering to sponsors or producing click-bait material. I share anecdotes from my personal life because independent education consulting isn't something I do as a side gig; it constitutes much of who I am. I'm not a journalist merely passing through or a late-career professional looking to cash in on the admissions madness.

I expect my ideas to be highly unpopular with some audiences, yet I'm accountable to nobody except the families I assist, to nothing except the truth. I prefer fierce adoration or animosity from a few people than to be generally well liked by many. On the other hand, if someone reads my book and agrees 100 percent with what I've written, I've failed in my task of being sufficiently thought provoking.

Universities and universe share the same Latin root word *universus*, meaning whole, or turned into one. Collectively, the higher education system and their high priest gatekeepers perceive themselves as the center of the universe. Universities know that you have few alternatives but to believe their sales pitches and tolerate their unfriendly practices. The college admissions madness persists because of widespread acceptance of the gospel of elite universities securing esteem and fortune, what behavioral economists call the **availability cascade**. Society reiterates these admissions stories, and they're accepted as fact without further consideration.

And what is a religion if not a collection of stories that enough people believe without question? Bureaucrats convince themselves they're serving society while hoodwinking the masses into believing that the sun rotates around the Earth. Whether they realize it or not, admissions counselors are complicit in a system that strips teenagers of their dignity. I proclaim that universities should revolve around ideals of fairness and accountability rather than occupying the center of and dominating our collective consciousness. Consider my book as a call to action against an unfair system rigged against you.

A significant disconnect between universities and applicants is that reviewers skim most student files in only eight to ten minutes despite applicants dedicating dozens of hours agonizing over their applications. Admissions offices justify admissions by "student-centered" holistic review to "get to know the whole student." That's bullshit. They want to read your application in the shortest amount of time that allows them to translate your life into acronym jargons and spreadsheet metrics.

The first Big Question we will explore asks why do elite undergraduate programs require many varied prompts that far exceed requirements for medical, law, and graduate schools? What seems patently absurd in one area is accepted without question in another. Let's begin our admissions critique by exposing numerous travesties of that quintessential American institution: The College Essay.

1. College Essay Madness

Essay tips and example books such as *Conquering the College Essay in Ten Easy Steps* pose similar problems as the college handbooks mentioned in the introduction, but for different reasons. Students never see the tens of thousands of essays that didn't get applicants into Harvard or even the hundreds of mediocre ones that did, dubbed the **survivorship bias**. (Throughout, I bold cognitive biases and distortions.)

Essay guides neglect a presentation of the brainstorming, drafting, and intermediate revision and rewriting steps that produce a final submission, something I've tried to correct with my Teachable course and YouTube channel.[21] Reading amazing essays paralyzes many students from even beginning, which contributes to procrastination. Just as the Harvard Crimson staff presents their 50 best samples, so, too, I offer on my blog only a handful of the most exceptional essay submissions from my clients. Nobody would read or ever see "50 Mediocre but Still Good Enough for Harvard Essays."

A transfer client I Zoomed with today shared they felt discouraged after reading the examples on my blog. "How can I ever write something that good? Those essays don't sound like me either. I don't have anything unique or special about myself." All valid concerns, yet I've never worked with a student who couldn't develop and polish interesting, high-quality essays unique to them.

Still, reading essay samples can do more harm than good. Guides often publish only the most extreme stories, making most applicants with relatively unremarkable lives feel insecure, assuming that hardships and "sob stories" are prerequisites to gaining admission. Nevertheless, essay examples are my most popular posts by far, so I would be foolish not to supply the content. I try to offer a wide variety of themes, particularly those that make engaging otherwise mundane life experiences.[22] Even with a mountain of college essay examples online, most students submit crappy essays.

1.1 Most college essays are not very good

The reality is that most application submissions everywhere are not very good. Even academically perfect students with stellar resumes who attend the nation's top high schools submit inadequate responses. Many still manage to gain admission despite poor essays. One problem with holistic review as a tool for assessing talent and character is that mostly mediocre essays aren't useful indicators for much of anything. Imagine the number of books admissions professionals could read or write if not for the hundreds of millions of crappy essays they review each year.

I know most essays aren't very good because I used to read them when I was an admissions counselor for UT-Austin. I worked in an era when people still asked, "do they really read all the essays?" We read them all, our sanity be damned. Perhaps a dozen out of 2,000 essays were worth sharing with colleagues. Maybe another hundred wouldn't embarrass the applicant if they reread them years later. The remaining 90 percent of submissions ranged from unremarkable to downright awful, including my own shoddy, last-minute UT application essays that "got me into UT honors."

I got into honors, not due to my above average at best grades and mediocre ACT score, but because I happened to be born at a time when spaces in prestigious programs were challenging but not unattainable. I discuss the roles of luck and privilege in college admissions in this book's conclusion.

The most popular online community for students applying to and discussing college admissions is Reddit's Applying to College (A2C), with over 250,000 members. Whenever topics around essay quality arise, current and former admissions counselors chime in with universal agreement that most applications aren't very good. Admitted students love to self-report their essays as 8 or 9/10, but these assessments are prone to **the better-than-average fallacy/placement bias.**

Almost all students assume their essays are much better than other applicants. Statistically speaking, half of all applicants must be below average. There is a sub-genre for beating the college essay that clocks in at over 4,000 books because doing even a little bit better than the median mediocre can give you an edge. College essays are also arguably the highest-stakes writing assignments that the applicant will ever complete, which command high consulting fees from people like me. Independent undergraduate admissions consultants may be the highest-paid copyeditors and writing coaches in the world.

If most essays aren't very good, why do they play such a prominent role? The gatekeepers' gospel leads us to believe that the college essay is an essential tool in deciding each applicant's fate. Admissions offices claim that essays allow students to provide context to their transcript and resume; supply background information about their home environment; share about their identity; and discuss their ambitions and dreams, or anything else not easily quantifiable. Admissions readers "get to know" their applicants, never mind that few essays are read closely. They're certainly not being critiqued and red-penciled like an AP English Literature assignment. Entire applications are usually skimmed in less than ten minutes.

Essays are necessary, selective universities claim, to separate a crowded applicant pool of the academically perfect and extracurricularly outstanding. In a 2019 National Association of College Admissions Counseling (NACAC) survey of 220 universities, 24 percent rated essays are of "considerable importance," second only to a student's transcript and standardized test scores. With the ACT and SAT falling out of favor, the essays occupy an even more critical role. Contrast the weight on essays with only 6.4 percent of universities weighting extracurricular activities as considerably important, less important than demonstrated interest and recommendation letters.[23]

The undergraduate college essay is, frankly, a terrible tool for filtering incoming undergraduate students. It may also be the least lousy tool available for universities such as MIT, which denies 90 percent of applicants who score in the top 1 percent on the ACT/SAT math sections. A skeptic might argue that essays are critical for the US News top 100 schools. They assert that the vast majority of America's more than 4,000 colleges and universities require nothing more than a transcript to apply. I respond that may have been true 20 years ago, but the college applications' landscape has changed. More universities than ever require essays, something I discuss later in chapters 1.3 and 1.4.

The 2019 NACAC survey reports that 36 percent of applicants submit over seven applications, more than doubling the number since 2005 and almost four times as many as 1990 applicants. Rising application loads mean more essay submissions.

A common approach on Reddit's Applying to College is to "shotgun" as many as 30 applications, hoping one of the pellets hits the target at a single highly selective university. Shotgunners acknowledge they are highly likely to get rejected almost every-where. Worldwide demand for spaces at the top 50 American universities far outstrips the available spaces, which have remained steady for decades. Obsession over the Ivy League and their equivalents is an extreme example of **the bandwagon effect** where the most luxurious university brands become increasingly popular.

It's not unheard of for some applicants to submit upward of 50 essays for their varied admissions, honors, and scholarship applications. Students who apply for nationwide universities likely work anywhere from 100 to 200 hours, if not more, on their applications, not accounting for distractions.

Fred Crossland, mentioned earlier, who critiqued college admissions in 1965, makes the same point. He laments how "millions of dollars are wasted on application fees… millions of man-hours are wasted on recruitment… millions of anxious student-hours are wasted on unnecessary and redundant testing and filling out of forms; that precious time should be spent in learning and experiencing the joys of intellectual growth." Technological innovations such as the Common Application that replaced paper applications promised streamlining and time-saving efficiencies. Instead, high school students work more than ever on their college applications.

1.2 Students—the madness isn't your fault

When I used to review applications, it was tempting to blame the students for their banality and flawed prose. Some essay-writing factors remain within the applicant's control, such as not procrastinating, rewriting or revising or at least making an effort to read through their first drafts, and having someone look at their work before they submit.

The typical essays I reviewed at UT look nearly identical to my Tex Admissions clients' early drafts, which we work on for four to six weeks before they're as good as they're going to get. My favorite "first drafts" clients send me are those they've already rewritten a few times and received revisions from a trusted teacher. Their revised drafts are usually slightly better than average, but most of them still aren't ones they would want to publish on their social media or Reddit. Receiving honest, constructive feedback in any domain from competent people willing to offer their time is incredibly difficult to find, even when you're open to their comments.

Who else could be responsible for poor essays if not the student (or their parent)? Over time, I've realized that the problems run much deeper, in part, because most people, regardless of age, background, or native language, write poorly. One theory a colleague proposed to me is that a preponderance of text messaging produces essays entirely free of capitalized letters and coherent syntax.

An applicant's seeming lack of writing ability or capacity to express themselves adequately isn't primarily their fault. Their English classes mistake literary analysis for writing in the real world. Silicon Valley visionary and hacker-philosopher Paul Graham penned my all-time favorite piece about writing: "The Age of the Essay." I reread it at least once a year. Like the twentieth-century invention of the modern Business School, few universities had English departments before the middle of the nineteenth century.

Graham notes that Harvard hired their first English Literature professor in 1876 and Oxford in 1885. His research suggests that expectations for research professors also to teach classes produced unintended consequences for teaching English Literature. Psychology professors or chemists can conduct original research, but he asks, "how do you do research on composition?" English professors imitated classical scholars from centuries before who studied ancient texts, but two problems arose. "An expert on literature need not himself be a good writer, any more than an art historian has to be a good painter, and (b) the subject of writing now tends to be literature, since that's what the professor is interested in."[24]

His observation partially explains why I receive student drafts revised by their English Literature teacher that show little sign anyone edited it at all. Essays edited by an English teacher are often dull and always impersonally written in the passive voice. Likewise, it may come as a surprise, but English teachers aren't always the best recommendation letter writers. Many high school English teachers haven't learned the mechanics of writing anything beyond literary analysis.

English Literature as a high school subject became widespread at the turn of the twentieth century. It has evolved into the primary medium for teaching students to write even though it's completely divorced from any practical, real-world skills. Graham writes, "It's no wonder if [literary analysis] seems to the student a pointless exercise, because we're now three steps removed from real work: the students are imitating English professors, who are imitating classical scholars, who are merely the inheritors of a tradition growing out of what was, 700 years ago, fascinating and urgently needed work."

When students consider majoring in English Literature because "they want to learn how to write," I nudge them toward degrees like UT's Rhetoric and Writing that provide practical skills valuable in the real world. Or I suggest Creative Writing programs for the budding novelist or poet because they teach fiction writing for an audience besides their English teacher. Communications majors, particularly those related to journalism and media, also teach practical writing and storytelling skills. Like the "College Essay Mentor" Chris Hunt, some of the best independent admissions consultants worked as professional journalists, not English Literature PhDs or former high school English teachers.[25] When hiring an independent college consulting firm, be wary if their editing staff is composed mainly of people with English degrees.

After my sophomore year, I dropped AP English while the teachers I snubbed commented to my face that I "would be a failure" and "never amount to anything." I made sure to email the doubters when I was the only student from my school who scored a five on AP English Language. I didn't study or even know about the new "Evidence-Based Arguments" until the exam morning. I learned how to play the AP exam game, giving the impression in my responses that I knew what I was talking about when, frankly, I was an excellent bullshitter. English classes mainly teach you how to bullshit rather than write precisely and clearly.

Although we did little by way of actual work or writing, junior year regular English with Mrs. Kimbrell was the first time I felt unconditionally loved and accepted by any teacher. I took senior year non-honors English with Mrs. Richard. She had three gold teeth and stomped thunderously to punctuate her arguments. She always referred to herself in the third person, and her favorite saying was, "We don't play no games in Mrs. Richard's House."

Mrs. Richard had a finely calibrated bullshit detector. She didn't tolerate misbehavior or the kind of nonsense writing that passes for quality work in AP courses. She was the first adult to tell me I wasn't a very good writer. And she was right. She provided concrete tips for writing concisely. She didn't care that I had been the best student in Pre-AP English. The only C I ever earned in high school came in Mrs. Richard's House. Her class taught me that I had significant room for improvement.

Unsurprisingly, students are unequipped to tell stories, write in the first person, or communicate their hopes and ambitions with reference to their specific experiences and interests. They don't know how to construct arguments or, in the case of college admissions, supply reasons why they deserve a place at their desired universities. They don't have a Mrs. Richard providing honest, critical, and constructive feedback.

Parents, when have you ever used allegory, allusion, or alliteration in a job cover letter or an e-mail to your clients? Has any college student outside of the English Literature or Creative Writing departments ever used the tools taught in high school English? Students earning the highest grades in AP English deploy the loftiest metaphors and run-on sentences. Persuasive college essays require clarity, precision, word economy, and honesty. Consequently, the average college essay is a vague, rambling mess indistinguishable from any other.

Most of my clients are accustomed to making straight A's in English, which they mistake as validation for their writing competency. The **Law of the Instrument** – the "to the hammer, everything is a nail" fallacy – means students rely on familiar methods that work in AP classes and ignore or undervalue alternative approaches. I'm confident they would not fare well in Mrs. Richard's House.

Graham concludes his piece with the single best piece of advice that I share with my clients: Whatever you write, *avoid being boring*. Graham's message is the same as my book: Think for yourself and have the courage to disobey the status quo. "Don't believe what you're supposed to. Don't write the essay readers expect; one learns nothing from what one expects. And don't write the way they taught you to in school."

The most unproductive yet popular advice given to students is to "find their voice." Mrs. Richard would have undoubtedly responded to recommendations for "finding your voice" with a hearty, gold-toothy laugh. What most students need to hear is the truth: They're not very good writers.

They lack both the initial training and years of craftsmanship to have a "voice." Well-meaning advice to "find your voice" makes students more resistant to identify and correct their glaring writing errors and bad habits. Their "voice" reads like daydreams transcribed into streams of consciousness that make little sense to anonymous readers. They have no idea how to recognize "voice" because they're trained to write in the third person and passive voice about existential themes in Sartre rather than first-person expositions about their summer away from school.

High school Speech and Debate did more to develop my writing and communication skills than anything else in high school. In college, I learned writing mechanics and argumentation, not from English literature classes but by following intensive feedback from my various humanities and social sciences professors. My professors equipped me with the tools to help me start finding my voice.

I've filled over twenty-five handwritten journals, published two books, and written many millions of words while receiving intensive feedback over the years. I'm just now starting to "find my voice" following years of focused practice and experimentation. My style continues changing depending on what I'm reading or where I am in the world. Prolific bestseller Stephen King wrote the book *On Writing*. If he concedes that his style and voice continue to evolve and that his early drafts require intensive editing, so, too, do you and I need feedback.

It comes as an unexpected shock when I gently point out many specific content and writing mechanics errors to students, suggesting room for improvement. I identify specific examples of what they are doing well and suggest they try to do more of it. Most respond well to constructive criticism, rise to my rigorous editing standards, and improve their writing over time. In short, they start to "find their voice" by experimentation, trial and error, and having a mentor who can help hone their craft.

Their responsiveness gives me faith that they're more durable and resilient than society (or their parents and teachers) provide them credit. Working together may be the first and only time that they have an opportunity to receive concrete suggestions on multiple versions of the same essays. At best, our high school and university instructors return our papers marked up once, with few subsequent comments. Formal education offers few opportunities to improve. My clients work for three to five revision rounds before arriving at the end.

What frustrates me most is the College Essay is almost always a missed opportunity for growth. Writing doesn't need to be like having your teeth drilled. Most students just want their college applications to end, like how most of us long for the moment when the dentist lets us rinse our mouth and hands us tiny toothpaste samples.

In rare instances, I have clients who enjoy and even occasionally *have fun* writing their essays. They're not necessarily the students who think of themselves as gifted writers. On the contrary, enjoying writing or perceiving oneself as a "good writer" doesn't correlate with who thrives during the college essay crafting process. The primary criteria for enjoying college essays are the students who have an earnest curiosity to know themselves and the world around them.

Parents often comment to me, "I love researching undergraduate majors! There's so much cool stuff out there that was unavailable to me as a college student." Some take their excitement a little too far, mistaking themselves as the ones going off to college, but they understand the world for some students is ripe with possibilities. College essays offer opportunities for introspection, discovery, and a medium to explore how you came to be and what that might mean for your future. Part of my role as an independent counselor is to challenge students to think deeply about themselves. Much of my initial feedback boils down to "tell me more" about this thing or that. Like a Hollywood director coaching a highly talented yet reserved actress, I aim to extract the student's best performance.

1.3 You get an essay! And you get an essay! Everybody gets an essay (requirement)!

A common observation among higher education critics is that the admissions madness is confined only to America's most elite universities. Alia Wong of the *Atlantic* reassures its readers that "College-Admissions Hysteria Is Not the Norm." She rightly observes that the vast majority of college applicants will enroll at one of the many hundreds of less-selective universities that admit the majority of their applicants. "Roughly 3 percent of the country's bachelor's-degree candidates were enrolled at a four-year university that accepts fewer than a quarter of undergraduate applicants."[26] Therefore, she might argue, the college admissions madness I criticize isn't something most students will confront.

One straightforward rebuttal is that 3 percent of the approximately 10.8 million bachelor's degree seekers is still over 300,000 students subject to the whims of the admissions madness. Students at elite universities are not evenly distributed throughout society. Instead, they come overwhelmingly from wealthy suburbs and cosmopolitan cities, the sorts of families more inclined to subscribe to the *Atlantic*.

High concentrations of elite college applicants mean college admissions is a genuine problem for affluent Bay Area or Manhattan families, even if it's not on the radar of most rural students living in the Midwest or Great Plains. Students living in communities that send few graduates to four-year universities face an even steeper uphill climb to gain entry at elite universities, even if they're less exposed to the pressures of growing up in affluent communities.

A second response is that 3 percent of the total enrollment of elite universities doesn't mean there aren't many more students aiming for these schools but who had to settle for less-selective universities. A comprehensive census of how many students apply to which universities and where they eventually enroll doesn't exist. My conservative estimate in the introduction is that 300,000–350,0000 students attempt applications to at least one top-50 university each year. Every student who takes the PSAT will inevitably be flooded with college promotional materials. There is no avoiding the admissions marketplace even if a given student chooses not to participate. The percentage of students attempting to gain admission at elite universities affects a sizeable segment of high school graduates nationwide.

Still, Alia Wong misses the point entirely. A more alarming concern is how essay requirements proliferate at less-selective campuses such as Auburn, Kentucky, and Oklahoma that admit 75 percent or more of their applicants. Many students aren't worried about getting denied outright to everywhere they apply. They justifiably complain about the efforts required to jump through the varied hoops necessary for most colleges on their list.

Twenty years ago, less-selective universities admitted applicants based exclusively on their grades and SAT/ACT scores. Essays infiltrate application processes to an ever-increasing number of schools, adding to the overburdened student's workload and sources of stress. Safety schools don't necessarily imply less work, as they did a generation ago. When parents share, "I don't ever remember me or anyone I knew having to write a single college essay, let alone three dozen," they're probably recalling their generation's admissions landscape accurately.

Consider non-selective Loyola University in New Orleans that admits 94 percent of their applicants. Loyola admissions still requires the Common Application essay "to demonstrate your creativity and ability to organize and express your thoughts."[27] Are essays really necessary when one in 20 applicants *won't* gain admission? Suppose you're a Louisiana student applying exclusively in-state for universities that require no essays, such as LSU, Louisiana Tech, or Louisiana Lafayette. Essay-free alternatives may tempt you not to bother with Loyola University's essay requirement.

Non-selective Houston Baptist University acknowledges the intuition that "more essays means fewer applicants." Their marketing materials advertise in bold print "a special advantage" of applying: They have no essay requirements. I used to conduct application workshops in low-income schools as a UT counselor—schools that were our highest priority to recruit "students from diverse backgrounds." Time after time, I watched students deliberately not apply to UT as soon as they saw the essay requirement, even though their class rank guaranteed them automatic admission by state law. I even suggested submitting a blank essay—they would get in regardless—but that didn't sit right with them or me. I can't say I blamed them for applying at less-selective universities.

A critic might counter, "If they're too lazy or unwilling or unable to write college essays, maybe they're not UT material." That point may be misguided psychologically if valid rationally. After all, universities want to recruit students who can communicate. But why should the willingness to submit an essay be a front-end filter to a university where they're guaranteed admission by law based on their class rank? College essays signal little to admissions committees other than students' ability and fortitude to overcome pages and pages of paperwork. Many countries worldwide have simple applications and admit their undergraduate students without any application essays, which I discuss more in chapter 5.

It was sufficient a generation ago for most universities that a student merely graduate high school on a college-preparation curriculum and take the SAT or ACT. What's changed, and why?

It's almost unavoidable that, unless a student enrolls at an open-enrollment community college, they are likely to encounter at least one college essay. That's a problem if you're a university that claims to want to include diverse students in your applicant pool and on campus. It's also an issue to a university's bottom line if full-tuition-paying students may be inclined to apply at universities with fewer required application items or supplemental essays.

Centralized application portals, such as the Common and Coalition Application that attempt to standardize essay requirements, provide no guarantees that member universities will adhere to them. The University of Kentucky, which admits over 90 percent of its applicants, requires everyone to discuss a challenge or setback instead of permitting students to submit the Common App essay. Almost every college applicant will already have a Common App essay written on one of the seven available topic options. Limiting the submission option to a single choice almost guarantees more work for students. Kentucky also requires a second, very specific essay for honors and scholarships, whose issues for diversity recruitment I discuss in chapter 9.[28]

Some less-selective flagship schools, such as Missouri, Montana, Nebraska, Maine, and Arkansas, do not require any essays. These campuses "assure admission" to applicants based on academic minimums that they publish clearly on their admissions pages. At Montana, for example, students with a 2.5 GPA or

1120 on the SAT gain admission without further consideration.[29] Students outside these academic cutoffs can submit an essay to promote their candidacy, which seems fair to me.

However, an applicant to assured admissions Kansas (93 percent acceptance rate) might mistakenly believe they can move on with their lives after completing their application until they're invited to apply for the separate honors program.[30] Surprise! You get more than 2,000 words' worth of essay requirements.

Moreover, the University of Wyoming is a renegade cowboy bucking the assured admissions trend. Despite admitting 94 percent of their applicants, in addition to the 650-word Common Application essay, they require a 250-word response: "Why Wyoming?" Why, indeed.

Higher education professionals congratulate each other when one of their peer institutions forgoes the SAT/ACT requirement. I've yet to see a thread on the admissions professionals Facebook groups celebrating a dropped essay requirement. I contend that the simplest way for less-selective universities to promote inclusion and decrease barriers to applying is to forgo any essay requirements. Eliminating essays will also help universities collect more application fees and reduce the labor required to review applications. Fewer essays will also decrease the workload of high school counselors. I fail to see the upside of adding essays when universities can enroll nearly every applicant based on their academics alone.

It's often challenging to identify what's even required in advance of creating an application. Some universities publish precisely which essays or supplementals are required on a single webpage, but many don't. A Redditor tipped me off about Kentucky's absurd essay requirements, but I failed to find them after searching their website for 15 minutes. Clicking "dream boldly" on Kentucky's admissions page redirects you to "apply." Under apply, the next click-through button reads, "we make it easy!" That link directs you to a page consisting solely of redirects to the *three* different applications they accept despite removing the Common Application's seven options and permitting only the obstacle/ setback prompt. Allowing for multiple applications puzzles applicants; they wonder if one is secretly preferable to the others.

Like many universities recently, Kentucky trades slick branding at the expense of sharing upfront precisely what's expected and required. Most universities are more concerned about selling themselves than informing the public. If I can't find an essay requirement—and I've been working in college admissions for a decade—what hope do first-generation college students have? There's no mention of any essay requirements or precisely what materials are necessary until you've created and made considerable progress on your application. The only way I could find the essay topics without adding Kentucky to my Common Application account was from a College Vine tips post.[31] *So easy, Kentucky.*

Universities often add essays or change requirements even after the application opens. Texas A&M added a surprise essay on diversity without updating their website or notifying applicants—more on diversity-themed essays in chapter 9. They snuck the prompt in for transfer applicants in a later cycle and still hadn't updated their website. The prompt is nearly identical to UT-Austin's "how will you enrich the learning environment" question yet different enough to confuse. I instruct students to offer the same essay response for both universities, and none have been rejected.

In 2018, UT-Austin added a fourth short-answer topic concerning diversity in the first week of August, after the application had already opened. They subsequently removed the requirement on their official admissions page. It disappeared without an announcement or clarification. But the question still appeared on the Apply Texas portal for thousands of students who followed the universal advice to begin their applications early, causing immeasurable confusion. Applicants wondered, was the fourth short answer on diversity required or not? UT never said.

Similarly, for Fall 2021, Rice removed their "Residential Colleges" diversity essay for a few days. Then, like a magician's sleight of hand, they mysteriously reinserted it into the Common Application.[32] Neither campus offered public apologies or explanations.

When I criticize the college essay, in part, I'm condemning universities that admit almost every student but still practice holistic review admissions. Holistic review everywhere is bullshit for reasons I detail in chapter 6, but it's especially silly at universities that admit more applicants than they reject. Maybe the movement toward holistic admissions offers the pretense that they're more selective or "inclusive." Holistic review serves as a kind of virtue signaling. Many less-selective yet "holistic review" universities still admit students within a week of receiving their applications, presumably because their grades and test scores well exceed unpublished but internally practiced academic minimums. I'm confident that elite universities read and review the entire application, however quickly. But at less-selective schools with fewer resources or counselors, I suspect they don't read the essays at all, especially for applicants with stellar academics who would gain admission under any circumstance.

1.4 Introducing a new measurement unit for essay length: a Princeton

More universities than ever require essays. Each university requires more essays on average than a generation ago. Essay requirements have spiraled out of control. Allow me to introduce a new unit of measurement to quantify the college essay madness: a Princeton.

Essay requirements measured in Princetons are a useful rule of thumb for when a university has excessive essays or a questionable commitment to college access and inclusion. A Princeton equals approximately 1000 words in supplemental essays, not including the main Common Application essay that students will submit to all their Common Application schools.

If your program is substantially less selective and requires more writing than Princeton, you're doing it wrong. The more Princetons requested of an applicant, the less time they can spend on other applications or their limited free time in general. More Princetons equals more admissions madness.

Consider the UT-Dallas McDermott Scholars application. In addition to the Apply Texas essays, they required ten unique essays totaling 5,000 words. They discontinued the program during the pandemic for "insufficient human resources" and funding, presumably, in part, because reading a single application must take half an hour even at skimming speed.

UTD McDermott clocks in at five Princetons, not to be outdone by Penn State Honors programs. Applying for the combined Penn State Schreyer Honors requires nine essays totaling nearly 5,000 words, including gems like "what is effective followership?" and reflect on the statement "get comfortable with being uncomfortable." Honors applicants applying to the BS/MBA dual degree must submit an additional nine essays that add an additional 1,500 words to an already stratospheric 6.5 Princeton quotient. That's 20 essays, not accounting for an optional 500-word essay for regular admissions.

Consider an academically outstanding applicant to UT-Austin applying for Architecture, Plan II Honors, and the Forty Acres full-ride scholarship. Like all first-time freshman applicants, they must tell their life story in a UT-specific 500–700 words and answer three questions in 250–350 words concerning their major choice, leadership experiences, and diversity (~1,700 words total). There is an optional special circumstances short answer. Architecture requires a 250–300-word response about creativity and a request to upload three photos to "describe what you are trying to evoke with these images" in 50–75 words each. Plan II requires a 250-word essay about an issue of importance and five quirky sentences to assess their "Plan II-ness." Forty Acres is an entirely separate Texas Exes scholarship portal with slightly different word limit parameters where the applicant must reinsert everything submitted on Apply Texas. Our Forty Acres applicant must answer three essays of 250–300 words whose content won't be useful for any other college application. In total, that workload amounts to one long essay, seven short ones, and four shorter responses for an estimated 3,000 words, or three Princetons.

It's common for Architecture programs to have a rigorous and extensive essay and portfolio requirement because they generally have much fewer spaces than more popular majors such as Business or Engineering. They also want applicants with specific technical competencies and artistic abilities, not unlike Fine Arts programs auditioning vocalists or violin players. But I'm unsure what highly selective Rice University admissions is attempting to accomplish with their Architecture requirements. All students must submit short responses that answer why they're applying to Rice irrespective of their major. They must submit two additional essays that answer why they're pursuing their major and a lengthy response on diversity.

Rice Architecture applicants must submit an additional response of 250 words: "Why are you determined to study architecture? Could you please elaborate on your past experiences and how they have motivated you to apply to Rice University and the School of Architecture in particular?" A second Rice Architecture prompt requires further redundancies: "Please expand on relevant experiences and motivations outside of your academic trajectory that have inspired you to study architecture, focusing on aspects that are not accommodated by other prompts in the application."

To summarize, Rice Architecture applicants need to write three essays addressing their varied reasons for pursuing their major in addition to discussing why they're applying to Rice across two prompts. No other Rice major or program has such repetitious requirements. There are undoubtedly ways to supply different angles to each Rice prompt, but anyone less than the savviest and most privileged applicant is likely to stumble.

At least Rice Architecture publishes upfront on their website what they require. The University of Southern California is a notable offender of hidden "major-specific requirements" where additional requirements appear depending on what you study. All applicants must submit two 250-word essays and answer a dozen "list" questions such as your life's theme song, who is your dream roommate, and which TV series you will binge-watch next. Almost all majors require additional materials that students only realize once they make their Common Application account and select their desired majors in the USC-specific tab. Students sometimes draft the USC essays before filling in their major selection on Common App, so I have to remind them every time to double-check the requirements. USC Marshall's World Bachelor in Business requires a video introduction and four additional essays whose requirements you only learn after making the Common Application because the topics aren't listed on their website.

One question for USC's Dornsife school gives students the challenging task of writing in 250 words about a hypothetical *ten-minute* speech if they "had the attention of a million people," disregarding that a ten-minute speech amounts to 1,500 words or more. Why not just ask what your TED Talk would be?

One Reddit A2C post titled "the USC Dornsife Supplement is slowly killing me" shares their frustrations. "I've been trying to find examples for the USC Dornsife supplements, but I just found out that they started it THIS CYCLE (added more pressure sheesh)… I've had no motivation to do it for the past couple of weeks, I just wanna sleep already [shaking my head]." Applicants to Computer Science and Engineering must submit two additional essays. Prospective students to USC's Iovine and Andre Young Academy must write a different essay and film a one-minute video. Consequently, applicants who select Dornsife and the Iovine Academy programs as their first and second majors need to submit materials for all of the above, around three Princetons.

Georgia Tech took the peculiar approach during the pandemic, in the name of "increasing access," as one of the only selective universities I know to *not* require the Common Application essay. Still, all students must write their two Georgia Tech–specific supplements, which possess even greater weight without the student's main essay that usually supports supplemental responses. An unintentional consequence is that students are more likely to *overthink* Georgia Tech's application now that critical information is missing, rather than them considering it a favor. Moreover, how many Georgia Tech applicants are truly applying solely to their campus on their Common Application? I could be mistaken, but I assume more than 95 percent of students applying to schools of Georgia Tech's caliber have already written at least one 650-word essay for other universities.

Then, in a reversal toward the end of the admissions cycle, they allowed students the option to submit their Common App essay or not, adding another layer of confusion. Before the change, students who submitted their applications wondered if they could update their application with their Common App essay.

The sensible approach to decrease barriers would be to require the Common App essay and omit the supplements from the very beginning rather than a hokey-pokey approach that further undermines the accessibility of their university.

Illinois Urbana-Champaign has always required a supplemental essay to discuss why you selected your first-choice major in 400 words—fair, especially for their highly competitive Computer Science program. This year, despite the pandemic, they've felt it necessary for students to write an equally lengthy essay for their *second* major. More than one of my clients has struggled with this expectation as each of their preferred majors are often nearly identical. Another concern is whether the second-choice essay is read if they're almost certain to gain admission to their first choice.

Measuring Princetons isn't always easy because there is no standardized unit of college essay measurement. Supplement requirements often depart from word limits and ask for "one and a half to two pages" or similar vagaries without specifying single- or double-spaced or font size. They fail to acknowledge that international applicants might have different page dimensions beyond the standard United States A4. Some universities ask applicants to upload a document file rather than copy and paste their responses directly into the application. Hence, the potential for unintentionally tripping a wire by choosing the wrong font size is a real cause for concern.

Sometimes, applicants don't even know how many words are required for an essay because the university arbitrarily decides to list "character limits" rather than word limits. Apply Texas schools require essay lengths at a maximum of "80 lines of 120 characters each," or 9,600 characters. That creates confusion for UT-Austin applicants who are "recommended" to submit essays of 500–750 words when the application portal permits over 1,000 words. It's unclear whether there is a hard word limit, especially since UT also allows uploading an essay to your application portal later on, which can truly be of any length.

Moreover, word limits don't mean the same thing depending on the application. Many universities accept both the Coalition and Common apps. The Coalition Application has soft essay length recommendations and allows upward of 1,000 words, whereas the main Common Application essay cannot be a single word over 650. Clever students with long essays can work around the Common Application by simply using Coalition where possible, giving a subtle advantage to those who know how to bend the rules.

The University of Michigan has word limit requirements for first-time freshmen, yet they inexplicably have character limits for prospective transfers even though the topics are largely the same. Michigan admissions doesn't list any length limits on their website. It's only until the transfer applicant makes a Common Application account that they're greeted with four essays: two of 1,500 characters, one of 2,750 characters, and a personal statement between 1,250 and 3,250 characters. A monosyllabic writer might be able to squeeze 800 or 900 words into their personal statement. A voracious consumer of polysyllabic SAT words might work in half that many. Determining Michigan's Princeton quotient is beyond my limited mathematical abilities.

Similarly, a science summer program at the University of Washington stipulates for their three questions that "there is a character limit in each of the essay questions of 1200 characters. This is approximately 250 words but use a character count if you are unsure." In reality, 1,200 characters are more like 160–180 words because most words have more than five letters on average. The applicant is left wondering how many words are allowed and whether character limits include or exclude spaces.

Character limits are also not intuitive. Estimating how many characters you type is like trying to guess the number of jelly beans in a jar. Because word processors default to listing the word count and not characters, applicants waste time manually toggling constantly to check if they're within the character limit. Inconsistent phrasing and nonstandardized submission of essays among universities and programs perpetuate an insidious time-suck for applicants.

Essay topics are also becoming increasingly absurd. Pomona invites applicants to share, in 50 words, their favorite way to eat a potato. The University of Virginia requests that students discuss their favorite word in 250 words. If no favorite word comes to mind, maybe you can try your luck with alternative prompts such as "UVA students paint messages on Beta Bridge when they want to share information with our community. What would you paint on Beta Bridge and why is this your message?" Or perhaps you prefer "we are a community with quirks, both in language and in traditions. Describe one of your quirks and why it is part of who you are."

One client sums up the UVA options perfectly: "These prompts SUCK."

Texas A&M presents a truly bizarre 250-word prompt for Engineering Honors guaranteed to produce a mountain of awful responses. "Describe the internet to somebody from the 19th century and how it is useful to address something you care about. Include who you are telling and why you decided to share the information that you did." Without any better alternatives, one of my clients began his prompt with "Dear Great-Great-Grandpa in some random Sri Lankan village…" Another time-traveled *Back to the Future*-style to meet Samuel Morse. A third student typed to Thomas Jefferson with "kind regards from the future" that messages send quicker nowadays. With the internet, Jefferson could broadcast the Louisiana Purchase instantaneously. For good measure, the applicant provided a cheerful update that American settlers did indeed reach the Pacific and achieve Manifest Destiny. Jefferson and Morse are undoubtedly resting better thanks to Texas A&M Engineering Honor's commitment to stupid essay topics.

Similarly, the University of Chicago makes a tradition of predictably quirky "extended essay" topics chosen by current students and alumni. "Each year, we email newly admitted and current college students and ask them for essay topics. We receive several hundred responses, many of which are eloquent, intriguing, or *downright wacky*" (emphasis mine).

How fun! Downright Wacky College Admissions was an alternative book title I considered.[33]

Since at least the early '90s, prospective applicants know to anticipate U Chicago's unconventional application and decide whether to apply at all.

- Who does Sally sell her seashells to? How much wood can a woodchuck really chuck if a woodchuck could chuck wood? Pick a favorite tongue twister (either originally in English or translated from another language) and consider a resolution to its conundrum using the method of your choice. Math, philosophy, linguistics... it's all up to you (or your woodchuck).
- "Do you feel lucky? Well, do ya, punk?"—Eleanor Roosevelt. Misattribute a famous quote and explore the implications of doing so.
- The seven liberal arts in antiquity consisted of the Quadrivium—astronomy, mathematics, geometry, and music—and the Trivium—rhetoric, grammar, and logic. Describe your own take on the Quadrivium or the Trivium. What do you think is essential for everyone to know?[34]

◆ In the spirit of adventurous inquiry (and with the encouragement of one of our current students!) choose one of our past prompts (or create a question of your own). Be original, creative, thought provoking. Draw on your best qualities as a writer, thinker, visionary, social critic, sage, citizen of the world, or future citizen of the University of Chicago; take a little risk, and *have fun*! (emphasis mine)

A top comment on one Reddit A2C thread elicited an honest response. "My UChicago essay was a hot piece of pseudo-intellectual trash."[35] Essay garbage in, arbitrary admissions decisions out.

Reading a few of these U Chicago Fall 2021 downright wacky questions, my Dutch girlfriend asked, "why do the students have to write this stuff?" I don't know, *liefje*.

At least the University of Georgia acknowledges the admissions madness when their supplement requirement prefaces: "The college admissions process can create anxiety. In an attempt to make it less stressful, please tell us an interesting or amusing story about yourself from your high school years that you have not already shared in your application (200–300 words)." Let's set aside the suspect utility of the question itself and what reviewers hope to learn from an amusing story. Under the pretense of making the process less stressful, UGA increases the workload of students. Most students can recycle and repurpose already-polished essays regarding common topics such as their major choice, leadership experiences, volunteering, or diverse backgrounds. Precisely zero other universities have this "amusing story" topic. Therefore, applicants must write yet another original response or forgo UGA entirely.

If you're feeling bold at your next college fair or campus visit, politely ask the representative to justify their silly and vague essay topic or clarify inconsistent application guidelines. Don't let them get away with their crimes against general sensibility and your well-being. It'll almost certainly be a more interesting conversation than the usual banalities that counselors are accustomed to, who answer the same questions over and over at college fairs. Pushing back might even help your admissions chances by impressing your representative when you ask *why* things are the case. Of the questions that I used to receive as a UT-Austin admissions counselor, 99 percent were exclusively concerned with applying and getting *in*.

1.5 Not-optional optional options

Less-selective Texas Tech University starts offering scholarships to Texas residents ranking in the top 10 percent and scoring a 19 or higher on the ACT. For Fall 2021 applicants, they presented five "optional" scholarship essays exceeding 1,500 words, or 1.5 Princetons. It's ridiculous for a university that makes admissions decisions—and most scholarship offers—based solely on academics to have essays at all. Texas Tech doesn't explain how these essays are used or why they're offered.[36] The essays simply appear on Apply Texas without further comment. I learned about them only when students started asking if they were *really optional* or not. I didn't have an answer.

The University of California application allows an optional 550-word special circumstances essay. Still, they suggest "*this shouldn't be an essay*, but rather a place to explain unusual personal or family circumstances…" A befuddled nonnative English–speaking client rightly wondered, "How to understand the sentence 'This shouldn't be an essay?' If it's not an essay, what form of writing will it be?" I have no idea.

Students inevitably feel pressure to submit "optional" items because ambiguity around admissions vocabulary requires families to read between the lines. Or they visit the misinformation machine College Confidential to divine what universities *really* want. "Optional" essays, beyond requesting if applicants have any special or exceptional circumstances, only add to their overburdened workload. Students constantly worry about whether they're doing the right thing. My colleague Janine Robinson is headed in the right direction with her "Escape Essay Hell" branding. Students, maybe for your next AP Literature assignment, you can discuss how college essays deserve a special place somewhere among Dante's nine circles.

The pandemic exposes the uncertainty around whether "test-optional" schools genuinely are indifferent to whether you submit the standardized exams or might low-key penalize you for opting out. Universities leave open to interpretation whether extracurriculars and leadership matter even more, and if so, how they're weighted in place of the SAT.

How is an applicant supposed to make sense of this waffling test-optional language on Texas Tech's scholarship page? "While students may select test-optional for admission purposes, students may submit test scores for scholarship consideration." Do applicants need or not need test scores for scholarship consideration? I have no idea, and I'm a college whisperer for a living.

Georgetown got into hot water over the pandemic summer for not riding the test-optional tide before begrudgingly changing course. Sarah Weber announced Georgetown's adoption of their test-optional policy in the *Georgetown Voice* on September 27, 2020. I've italicized the qualifications and hedging language that obscures exactly what Georgetown expects and how test-optional applicants may be evaluated:

> "While Georgetown *still encourages* students to submit test scores as part of their application, the admissions

process will not penalize students who do not submit SAT or ACT scores. In addition to the *flexible approach* to standardized testing, Georgetown *will allow AP test scores to cover the previously optional,* although *highly recommended,* submission of SAT subject test scores. As with SAT and ACT scores, applicants are *asked to submit scores from any SAT subject test* scores they took *prior to the pandemic,* though *it is not required.*" (emphasis mine)[37]

Combining unrelated discussions about AP scores and Subject Tests further obscures how Georgetown might evaluate students who, for example, opt out of the ACT yet choose to submit SAT Subject Tests. Does "asked to submit scores from any SAT subject test scores" mean they're required, recommended, or optional? Is there a practical difference or an unspoken set of expectations between *recommended* and *optional*?

The press release adds further confusion with the caveat "prior to the pandemic." When exactly did the pandemic begin? February or March in the northeast US, but not nationwide until the fall. As of writing in late November 2020, Vermont and Hawaii appear largely spared from the worst. Did the pandemic begin in December 2019 with China? Are applicants living in China expected to submit Subject Tests taken *after* their pandemic ended? How do we account for students living in Taiwan, Vietnam, or New Zealand who experienced brief or no lockdowns and life continues as usual? Do applicants from COVID-free Thailand need to submit their SAT Subject Tests? Might they be penalized for opting out of the SAT if Bangkok offered test sittings in Summer or Fall 2020?

We're not out of the weeds yet, patient reader. Georgetown's announcement spends a few paragraphs summarizing the test-optional debate and whether test scores reflect wealth or academic aptitude. Near the bottom of the press release, they write, "Supporters of standardized college admissions tests argue while testing is flawed and can exacerbate disparities along racial and economic lines, *it also provides an objective measure of a student's intelligence*" (emphasis mine). Well, Georgetown, which is it? Do you believe standardized exams correlate with wealth *or* intelligence?

It's disingenuous to present "both sides" of the debate and not take a decisive stand on how they consider standardized exams' utility. Peer institutions are left wondering whether Georgetown's commitment to inclusion is sincere or not. Their post-pandemic testing policies answer the question for us. "Georgetown's stipulation that ACT and SAT scores *will still be required for applicants post-pandemic* indicates that the university will continue to consider standardized test scores as a part of its holistic admission process." They reassure future applicants that they will have *ample* opportunity to prepare and be rewarded for scheming future exams.

Can you make any sense of what they're expecting for pandemic-era applicants? Their corporate-speak reassurances do not persuade me: "Rest assured that the widespread cancellation of ACT and SAT dates will not affect their ability *to apply* to Georgetown." Their announcement communicates nothing about how they will *assess* test-optional applicants. Except that almost everyone already knows how to apply, Georgetown. What families and guidance counselors want to know is what in the hell it all means! How does test-optional affect holistic review?

Even after the College Board discontinued the administration of Subject Tests starting Winter 2021, Georgetown doubled down. They issued a statement requesting any previously taken Subject Test scores still be submitted. Predictably, applicants who no longer have access to SAT Subject Tests wonder if their chances are jeopardized. For students without scores, they "recommend (not require)" AP scores as a substitute. It's perfectly fine for Georgetown to require standardized exams during the pandemic, even if it's unpopular and subject to predictable backlash. They're a private university free to do what they want for the most part. What's infuriating is their equivocation that muddies what they expect from applicants. George Orwell himself couldn't have composed a better double-speak press release.

A reasonable applicant may conclude that Georgetown's not-optional optional messaging expects you to submit a test score. You may further worry if you have the financial means to do so, even if it requires flying across the country to an open testing center, as many have (against COVID travel advisory warnings). College Board was overloaded with emails and phone calls. Families struggled to receive consistent information about finding testing centers and sitting for the exam, not even considering their role in admissions. Only the most determined, privileged, and savvy families successfully navigated standardized testing during the pandemic.

It's implausible that Georgetown "actively seek[s] out and recruits highly talented, motivated students from all walks of life and diverse backgrounds," as their multicultural recruitment office claims. Simultaneously, communicating ambiguous testing policies that robust research findings suggest disadvantages students from low-income households and rural families further obscures their positions on equity and inclusion.[38]

If university communications officials with advanced degrees are unable or unwilling to write clearly, what hope do their applicants have? Parents ask me daily, "what do the universities *really* want?" Like a timid cat hesitating at the backyard door, unsure whether it wants to remain inside or go outside, universities don't seem to know what they want. They're the cat who comes inside before crying to go back out.

Setting aside Georgetown's downright wacky press release, an unintended consequence of the test-optional movement is that admissions offices have one fewer metric to measure their applicants. Test-optional universities nationwide struggle to communicate to the public the substantive admissions review differences between test submitters and those who opt out. In a bizarre turn, the University of California campuses have opted to go "test blind" for the next few admissions cycles, but only for California residents. The SAT and ACT are test-optional for everyone else. They intend to implement a proposed UC-specific standardized exam by Fall 2025.[39] Only a tone-deaf bureaucrat can delude themselves that the solution to flawed examinations is yet another test. Watch as a cottage industry of test preparation consultants materializes to meet the demand.

For test-optional applicants who do not meet the GPA requirements, the less-selective University of Houston requires essays for the first time in their history—topics different from UT-Austin, Texas A&M, or other Apply Texas schools. They're also longer, at 1,000 words, an entire Princeton, rather than 500–700 words for every other Texas public university that requires essays.

Additionally, Fall 2021 University of Houston Honors Program applicants received a surprise email. UH Honors isn't especially selective. Half of their admitted students score between 1300 and 1400 on the SAT and 31 percent rank outside of the top 10 percent of their class, which is below average for non-honors admission to UT-Austin and Texas A&M. Consideration for UH honors requires an atypical essay without further explanation, a deadline, or submission instructions. It's unlike any requirement for honors programs or regular admissions requirements at any Texas university. They ask for "a full-length academic writing sample: 3–5 page literary analysis paper with a central thesis and strong supporting arguments." Never mind that most research papers that students submit for AP English Language or Literature are often longer than five pages or are much shorter, sloppy "timed writings" to prepare for AP exams. What, precisely, does Houston Honors mean by "full length?"

A client of mine who submitted a literary analysis of a Shakespearean play between three and five pages received an email from UH Honors staff that it was too short and needed to be longer, adding additional stress to the applicant. Her font size was 14 instead of 11 or 12 despite those parameters not having been specified in the application. She added another page and a half of fluff. UH Honors' other problems are that STEM students may be less strong in literary analysis, and international applicants may not have a ready-made sample.

A test-optional UH Honors applicant will submit upward of five Princetons' worth of essays. I'm confident UH Honors can admit a strong class of students without sneaky hoops for applicants to jump through, especially during an already-disruptive pandemic. Without an onerous "literary analysis" requirement, they would undoubtedly receive more applications and perhaps have a larger pool of talent to select from. Honors staff could save a substantial amount of time by not having to skim so many research papers.

What's the point in having an application common to all Texas universities if member institutions and specific programs are free to add or subtract requirements from year to year, and even within admissions cycles, as their whims see fit? Institutions are not incentivized to surrender some of their control and standardize requirements among one another. UH Honors making up bullshit busy work as the semester progresses reflects a broader failure of universities nationwide to adequately open or educate their students. Students and families suffer due to bureaucratic incompetence.

Universities do not care about you.

1.6 Authenticity and many other institutional values

Universities love for students to share their *authenticity*, that slippery word much derided by students on Reddit's A2C. More than 100,000 applicants to New York University write responses to the supplement "why do you want to study at NYU?"

I'm waiting for the day that will never come when an applicant writes a *sincerely* honest response. Given that 34 percent of NYU undergraduates report binge drinking—below the national average, LiveWellNYU reassures—and 65 percent engage in sexual intercourse, it would be unfair to penalize our hypothetical applicant's *authenticity*.

> "I'm going to be real with you. I'm here to party hard and 'collaborate' with a *tremendous* diversity of cute classmates and seductive strangers in the City that Never Sleeps! I researched your website and saw 'Learning' listed as a Value. I'm glad we're on the same page when you write underneath: 'We recognize that students will make mistakes and poor decisions. Oftentimes, these missteps are opportunities for growth and development.' I can assure you I will manage my time *very* wisely with *ample* opportunities for growth and development." [40]

That response will never be written because college essay questions have an implicit **courtesy bias**. Students give a more polite opinion and disguise their true feelings so as not to offend. At least when you're writing an AP Government paper for a teacher with strong political views, you know your audience and exactly how to flatter. College admissions adds a layer of complexity because your reader is almost always anonymous. I've only had one client ever admit in private that partying was what they were most excited for in college. That's remarkable given many of us who attended universities spent much of our time doing exactly that, including me. I wager that there's a non-zero possibility your alumni interviewer or admissions reviewer might be sipping a glass of wine or two while piling through their record number of applications.

The pandemic exposes the disconnect between what students write in their essays and the realities of young adults living away from home. It's comical, if disheartening, even tragic, when universities nationwide haphazardly opened for in-person classes for Fall 2020. Many reversed their policies days or weeks after students arrived on campus, sending students home to Zoom U or live under lock and key in dorms. Rather than reflecting on their policies and rethinking the entire summer they had to prepare; many deluded administrators pointed fingers at college students. Students are doing what they've done since at least Prohibition and the advent of the modern fraternity a century ago: party without adult interference or oversight. Universities need butts in the seats and "student-athletes" on the field to sustain their business model. The admissions madness must continue uninterrupted.[41]

I acknowledge and am readily aware of the harmful consequences of alcohol on the developing brain, such as an increased tendency for risky behavior, correlation with drug usage, and myriad other social problems. Risky behavior hasn't done my own neurology many favors. NYU and most universities are doing and should do more to curb a binge drinking culture, especially during the pandemic. Yet the point remains. Admissions offices expect polished, totally unrealistic presentations of teenagers still forming their sense of self.

These implicit expectations force students to adopt **illusory superiority**, where they overestimate their desirable qualities and underestimate undesirable attributes relative to other people. There is an added pressure for applicants to present themselves as the absolute best at whatever it is they're doing, whether their portrayal reflects reality or not. I see resumes with Model UN descriptions that could give former American Ambassador to the UN and current USAID Director Samantha Power a run for her money. The college essay format forces students who already don't write well to fit their still-evolving life experiences to match lofty ideals. Unrealistic expectations incentivize students to hyperbolize their accomplishments while sidestepping their (many) flaws.

Consider these virtues and values incorporated into various university Vision Statements, in no particular order: authenticity, grit, tenacity, zest, courage, curiosity, integrity, dignity, entrepreneurial, critical thinking, artistic rigor, risk-taking, self-awareness, empowerment, globally engaged, discovery, grace, honor, ambition, balance, creativity, intellectual breadth, excellence, purpose, accountability, adaptability, equity, conscientiousness, self-control, compassion, charity, empathy, social justice, citizenship, sportsmanship, maturity, kindness, faith, reverence, wisdom, tolerance, and humility. Or whatever else the university's public relations team can cook up, such as a word that I'm pretty sure the big brains at Stanford concocted: interdisciplinarity.[42]

Like the courtesy bias and illusory superiority, admissions expectations produce a **social desirability bias**. Students overreport their desirable behavior and underreport their undesirable characteristics. I've helped students tailor their stories to every one of those criteria—including, it turns out, interdisciplinarity—lest some incredibly ambitious students feel overwhelmed trying to address the glossary of human virtues in 650 words (or fewer). A secondary consequence is the pressure students feel to link everything they're writing into their major or connect their major into pro-social values such as service or philanthropy. These pressures produce a sea of Computer Science or Finance majors writing difficult-to-believe essays about how search engine optimization or credit default swaps will save the world.

YouTuber Jack Liu presents his admissions file acquired from the Michigan Ross business school. One of his admissions readers criticized him because "he never mentions any desire to make a positive impact through business." In contrast, another reader offers a glowing recommendation because "he has a very clear interest in business."[43] At least Michigan Ross subjects students to multiple readers to limit bias and scoring inconsistency. It isn't sufficient, it seems, for the admissions high priests to enjoy or want to major in something for its own sake. Everything must be presented from a socially desirable angle.

Any decent college essay guide will suggest visiting the Vision Statement to see what a university claims to value so that you can adjust your varied essays accordingly. What's a prospective student-athlete applying to Kenyon College supposed to do when presented with fourteen compound phrases and at least two dozen virtues?[44] Universities might counter that they're *unique* in their values and which applicants they seek. I accept that different universities have varied cultures and environments.

But why does a given school's *unique* personality require multiple essay topics to find those that fit their purported value system? The resume and transcript may be a better reflection of interests, skills, and hobbies. Law schools have a wide range of personalities, values, specialties, career pipelines, etc. However, they do just fine to identify well-fitting students for their programs without onerous essay requirements.

Vague question parameters that bias whitewashing of flaws produce awkward essays that marry an Instagram confessional to a job cover letter from someone who's never applied for a job. (Working at your dad's hedge fund or corporate real estate entity doesn't count.) A recent satirical rejection letter written in *McSweeny's* by Amelia Tate captures this perfectly: "We Are Unable to Offer You a Place at Yale Because Your Essay Read Like the Closing Narration of a Teen Rom-Com."

Ever-evolving topics with more universities requiring additional essays for admissions and scholarships is great for my business. Each essay change is another opportunity to write a blog post and field inquiries from anxious families. It's an absurdity when you take a step back and wonder what Auburn gains from asking high school students how they feel about Mondays. Just how many applicants tip the admissions scales in their favor at the University of Southern California with their killer response to "what's your favorite snack?"

It's an understandable temptation to dismiss the entire system as a farce when Lori Laughlin and Mossimo Giannulli "donated" enough money to supply every USC undergrad with a pack of Oreo Minis every day for 70 days—assuredly a few hundred applicants' favorite snack—to get their unqualified kids into the university. Laughlin's daughter Olivia Jade, who regularly uploaded videos to her 1.8 million followers about how much she disliked school, had already developed a successful cosmetics line and probably shouldn't have enrolled at university. Their briberies are a modern form of Medieval-era "indulgences" where a wealthy patron could pay the Catholic Church to ensure their soul's passage to Heaven. Some corrupt people and occasional silly essay questions are symptoms of a deeply diseased higher education system that begins with college admissions whose madness predates World War I.

Critiquing admissions, unfortunately, yields few practical or straightforward remedies. There is personal value and admissions outcome utility to you for understanding the bull you're wrangling. After every admissions cycle, I ask myself: Does anybody else think this process is completely insane? Have we lost our collective minds? More concretely, I wonder

- if the college admissions and application process is easily solved with step-by-step formulas, why do tens of thousands of students and families lose sleep, worry endlessly, and suffer?
- why the process is so stressful, and in what ways do anxieties arise? What, if anything, can be done to alleviate the college application pressure?
- has admission to prestigious American universities always been so subjective, arbitrary, and high stakes?
- what application mistakes and cognitive errors should students recognize and avoid?
- what role do elite universities play in society?
- how do universities balance enrolling full tuition–paying, academically stellar students with their commitment to including underrepresented, diverse populations?
- how do early deadlines, deferrals, waitlists, and appeals disadvantage applicants?
- do university practices that claim to promote diversity do more harm than good?
- have applicants to prestigious universities always written essays?

- do interviews and recommendation letters make a difference, and are they a worthwhile allocation of time and resources?
- do other countries practice a similar college admissions madness?
- what might holistic admissions look like in ten or 20 years?
- might there be other ways to select for and define talent, such as an admissions lottery?
- should some students delay college enrollment or forgo a university education entirely?
- who's to blame? Is anyone in charge?

2. Can Anything Stop the Madness?

College admissions is rife with a **bias for the status quo**. We exhibit an implicit preference for a system whose alternatives are impossible to imagine, also known as **system justification**. Parents with multiple children start to suspect something is off once their youngest finishes applying. By then, they've moved on to other concerns, such as badgering professors to give their child the A they perceive their expensive tuition entitles. Politicians and society's elite are not incentivized to reform a system where the rules are stacked in favor of their offspring and family friends. If anything, elites push back against efforts to enroll more diverse classes and lobby to maintain practices such as legacy admissions, large donations, and spaces for recruited athletes playing obscure sports, which I highlight in chapter 6.7.

Universities likewise implement changes at a glacial pace because they fail to coordinate. One positive step was discontinuing the deeply flawed ACT/SAT "writing section" experiment introduced in the mid-2000s, which eventually took over a decade for universities to terminate. There was an interim period in the early 2010s where some universities phased out the writing section whereas others declared that valid exams *must* have the writing; this inconsistent messaging produced untold confusion and unnecessary exam sittings for unaware students. Applicants today wonder whether they *need* the additional (and more expensive) writing section alongside juggling which universities do and don't Superscore (taking the highest sections from different dates), a practice that incentivizes sitting for many exams.

Administrators understand students will apply in record numbers regardless of how arduous the requirements. Why bother with transparency when public relations consultants suggest that they can simply make a button on their website, like Kentucky does, that assures you it's easy? Unless there is a substantial decrease in demand for elite university degrees, which I don't forecast happening, then the runaway admissions train will continue barreling along its tracks. Reforms arise only after widespread public outcry, as in the Varsity Blues scandal, or when a critical mass of their peer institutions moves first. Since Bowdoin was America's first elite university to go test-optional, half a century and a global pandemic later, a plurality of elite universities have rightfully questioned the utility of the SAT/ACT and dropped the requirement.

SAT Subject Tests, which were often required or "recommended," were always a College Board moneymaking farce. Most campuses concede they play little to no role in their admissions review process, even when many required them in the past. Subject Tests added a disproportionate burden on applicants relative to their importance as an admissions factor.

UT-Austin and no Texas public university have ever required or even accepted Subject Tests—it's against state law to require a test beyond the ACT/SAT—but that doesn't stop students from submitting them anyway. Again, medical schools can field qualified candidates competent enough to become physicians and specialists with a single exam, the MCAT. Why do we expect students to take and retake the ACT and SAT and Math II and Chemistry after many will have already taken the equivalent AP or IB exam? Applicants still ask me whether they need to take the Subject Tests and question my answer even though not a single university requires them anymore. MIT was the final campus to drop the requirement, and College Board has finally discontinued Subject Tests entirely.

Finally, students aren't incentivized to take collective action. Like an 18-year-old advocating for lowering the drinking age, that issue becomes irrelevant the day they turn 21. People over 21 don't want to reduce the drinking age to allow a bunch of teenagers to crowd their favorite spots.

I served as Reddit's Applying to College community's first moderator responsible for cultivating an inclusive and sane atmosphere. It was almost impossible to retain student moderators because they understandably lost interest in college admissions a year or two after high school. Some moved on to medical or law school admissions online communities. Of the moderators I recruited in 2017, zero remain, and as of March 2021, no current moderator has held the position for over a year. Consequently, there is little continuity between admissions cycles as high school sophomores and juniors replace the cohort of graduating high school seniors.

Low-effort posts and memes on Reddit drown out efforts to lessen the occasionally sane voices calling for a stress reduction to the admissions madness. Anxious students consume "admissions decision reveal" and "how I got into my dream school" viral videos. Rather than uniting around a shared struggle to resist an unjust system, envious users drag down one another. Jealousy and resentment on college admissions forums and social media produce a **crab mentality** of "if I can't have it, neither can you." If crabs in a bucket cooperated, each one could climb on top of one another to freedom. Developing a collective consciousness among applicants is the only viable solution for reform coming from outside of politics or universities. Instead, Redditors act like crabs at the bottom of a bucket who pull down those at the top: Every crab fights and none escapes. College admissions unintentionally divides and conquers.

In a community currently exceeding 250,000 members, trolls and insecure know-it-alls run off and even "dox" the private information of experienced, well-intentioned admissions professionals and high-quality posters. Teenagers are especially prone to the **egocentric bias**, where they rely too heavily on their perspective or have a higher opinion of themselves relative to their experiences. A2C is a tidal wave of the **Dunning-Kruger Effect** where Ivy League college students or other pseudo-authorities overestimate their abilities and knowledge. Content quality is a race to the bottom. It only takes one malicious post to cancel out the feel-goods from ten positive comments.

High-quality or even mediocre posts become the exceptions rather than the rule, not unlike our broader political discourses on social media and YouTube comments. The larger an online community, the more likely it is to fail, absent heavy moderation and an overwhelming majority of members participating in good faith. Condescension from anonymous teenagers who would never talk to their teachers or me as such in-person persuades me that online communities can't curb the madness.

I stopped participating on A2C in 2017—then a fifth of its current size—when I received backlash and even threats of violence for a benign post. In response to threads from students reporting they were "denied from their safety school," which by definition isn't a safety, I suggested a new category. I advised that maybe, just maybe, it's a good idea to include a "security school" on your list where you're 100 percent guaranteed admission based on your grades and SAT/ACT scores. Rejecting that and other reasonable-seeming suggestions capture the **system justification**

bias. Students embrace the current state of affairs and disparage alternatives at the expense of their individual and collective self-interest. Rather than sources of high-quality information or mobilization against an unjust higher education system, online college admissions communities become a torrent of doubts, anxieties, and insecurities. Redditors, you're your own worst enemies.

2.1 A brief overview of admissions anxieties and worries

Suppose change and reform can't or won't come from students, parents, universities, or the elite. In that case, we're left with the recreated email exchange to open my book concerning UT-Austin's admissions process, *Your Ticket to the Forty Acres*. It's the kind of anxious message I receive almost every day. Parents and students report application burnout, anxiety about the unknowable, and an existential concern for a future yet to occur.

Just this week, one parent emailed me five times with the same question written in different ways: Is my child going to gain admission? Five times I responded in slightly different ways that, yes, she has got a good chance. On the fifth time, I reminded them that my assessment hadn't changed since she completed her application two months ago. Still, I counseled that she needs to prepare for the possibility things might not work out and be okay with her (still favorable) second- or third-choice universities where she's already admitted. And in the end, the student ended up getting multiple full-ride offers to her top choices! All that worrying and lost sleep was for naught.

Another well-meaning parent took the opposite approach. They remind their daughter every day—to the point of discouragement and insecurity—that she better not get her hopes up even though she has a more than 95 percent chance of getting into her top choice. That's a recipe for resentment and arguments at the dinner table. I wonder why families with students who are almost certain to gain admission would still hire me. I can only conclude that it's to assuage these underlying worries. I reassured the daughter that she's an academically perfect student with thoughtful interests who would contribute greatly to her dream school, which helped alleviate some stress and tension.

I often find myself moderating family disputes, finding the silver linings in each party's perspectives or complaints. I'm sincerely grateful I've never had an office. I work entirely remotely and accept calls only on scheduled Zoom appointments. I'm not sure I could absorb the collective anxieties of dozens of families in-person each year. High school counselors at elite private schools have my sympathies and respect. Some students and parents are a breeze to work with, and they depart the admissions process with their sanity intact. They're excited to enroll at whichever university is lucky enough to welcome them, even if it's their second or third choice. But most families stumble.

When I worked in the Office of Admissions for my alma mater, I failed to appreciate just how much stress the admissions process causes families. I spoke with prospective students for a minute or two behind my table at college fairs, not realizing they had prepared their questions for hours. I did not see the dozens or sometimes hundreds of hours that went into the essays alone. I reviewed their applications in tidy packages, read them for ten or 12 minutes, and scored them before moving on to number 48 for the day.

Only when students were rejected did I receive weeks' worth of emails and phone calls in February and March from understandably disgruntled parents. I thought their anger was merely the disappointment of rejection, but then I realized the perceived failure of a lifetime's planning culminated in arriving short of their child's admissions goal. They wanted an answer to a question neither I nor nobody else in UT's admissions bureaucracy could answer: Why did you reject my child? It's exceedingly rare at a selective university for a single person to decide a student's fate, which diffuses responsibility throughout the bureaucracy. Every bureaucrat is complicit, yet nobody is accountable.

Even though I wasn't "the one" responsible for rejecting their child, receiving abuse felt like being one half of an unhappily married couple that never discusses their problems. Until, one day, the simmering pot boils over, and kitchen dishes explode against the wall with a spouse moving out. For many, it's the first time they've ever been told no without recourse. To the meanest parents, I had to hold my tongue not to say what I felt. *Glad they're going to Texas A&M or Texas State and not UT!* Part of me appreciates the reckoning college admissions imposes where no amount of money, connections, or complaining will reverse most decisions.

The most frustrating complaint I receive, usually from parents but sometimes students, is "my child's school is so competitive! It's impossible to make straight A's/earn leadership positions/rank high. Why doesn't such and such university give preference to their top-100 nationally ranked high school? Should we move schools?" Never mind that a student attending a top 5 percent high school has more resources, better-qualified teachers, smaller class sizes, more counselors, and fewer social problems, a "Meritocracy Madness" that I discuss in chapter 10.

I dedicate a portion of my book *Your Ticket to the Forty Acres* to unequal access to education resources. The complaint implies that their academically average student deserves admission over top students at resource-poor high schools. This **group attribution error** tends to incorrectly assume that you are also a great student by merely attending a great high school, even if your transcript strongly suggests otherwise. Universities aren't especially interested in mediocre students attending excellent high schools.

When I worked for UT, this error manifested when middling students from small private schools felt the state's automatic admissions top 6 percent law was grossly unjust toward their already highly privileged demographic.

It's additionally frustrating to academically outstanding students who still got denied while trying to make sense of their many lower-academic classmates who gained admission to the same program. Some results surprised even me. How could that top 2 percent class rank 1550 SAT student get denied to UT's McCombs School of Business when I've never seen a student with such strong academics not get in? For especially persistent parents, I would break the script given to us by senior management and ask, "Did you even read your child's essay?" They never called back. It's troubling that outstanding essays are no guarantee of admission. As an independent consultant, I can share honestly with these befuddled families after the fact that I'm confident their poor essays sank the application.

2.2 Parents are not the primary problem

The two biggest mistakes I see parents make are underestimating the competition level of admissions at highly selective universities or over-involving themselves in planning their child's life from the womb to pass through admissions gatekeepers. When I worked as a UT-Austin admissions counselor, time and again, parents shared sentiments like, "it didn't used to be like this when I was an applicant. Anyone with decent grades and 1200 on the SAT could enroll." And their observations are correct. Admission to flagship public universities nationwide have become substantially more competitive in the past four decades. UCLA admitted 74 percent of its applicants in 1980 and projects to accept only 10 percent for Fall 2021.

Much of my job involved explaining how and why the competitive admissions landscape has evolved. However, many parents are delusional about their child's prospects for Ivy League universities and their equivalents. They either underestimate that MIT rejecting 90 percent of their applicants with perfect Math SAT scores means that their middling test score student has a chance, or they overinflate their own child's credentials. Having near-perfect academics is necessary but not sufficient for admission to top universities.

Most days on Reddit involve threads with students explaining to their resistant parents that Harvard and Princeton aren't likely options if they scored 1250 on the SAT and made mostly B's in their classes. Almost every parent of Harvard's 57,000 applicants thinks they're the most remarkable creatures on the planet. To admissions counselors, they're one application among a "sea of sameness," or a data point on an Excel spreadsheet. Harvard can only admit 5 percent of students whose parents think they're the most exceptional students, athletes, and musicians in their communities.

Parents impose unrealistic expectations on their children, adding to the pressure to excel. Students tie their self-worth to admissions outcomes for fear of disappointing their parents. They set themselves up for failure and disappointment. Often, students are not offered admission not because of anything within their control but simply because there are too few spaces for too many qualified applicants.

Behind the scenes, I've come to learn, students from ambitious families plan their child's college applications for years. Rather than underestimating the admissions landscape, they're acutely aware of the elite admissions challenge. Parents begin preparing for college enrollment from the womb by consuming foods and crafting environments that optimize intrauterine development.

The madness for some families begins with preschool. Some preschools begin enrolling toddlers at age two and charge more than $40,000.

Brooklyn's Horace Mann nursery and kindergarten school admits less than 10 percent of their applicants, comparable to Dartmouth. Their application requires an independently assessed exam, a child interview, a separate parent interview, an additional parent statement, and, if the child is already enrolled in a program, a teacher's reference. Preschool admissions consultants charge thousands of dollars, and families might apply to as many as ten schools.

Elite families secure private sports and music lessons, enroll in gifted and talented elementary programs, move school districts or even states, and attend pricey summer camps. Some families hire college professors at thousands of dollars per hour for private tutorials. Parents appear to spend most waking moments grooming their children to pass through the first of many gatekeepers en route to securing their space among the American elite.

I refuse to participate in the "resume planning" services that some consultants specialize in because I'm not going to dictate what a student needs or doesn't need to do with their interests. I still subscribe to the old-fashioned notion that a person's internal motivation and curiosity should dictate how they spend their time rather than an exclusive focus on external factors such as the demands of college admissions. Because I don't traffic in resume planning, I deter the families most intent on gaming the system and attracting those with sincere interests and hobbies.

There is a constellation of expensive summer camps, non-substantive internships with brand name corporations, and "research" opportunities that allow students to become supposed coauthors or principal investigators in high-profile labs. Independent counselors connect students with prestigious-seeming opportunities that will pad their resume and give the impression they're pursuing sincere and interesting experiences. Some wealthy families—particularly international applicants whose high schools don't have extracurricular resources common to American schools—pay upward of six figures for "background advancement" services. Related firms help students set up certified 501c3 nonprofits to glorify what is merely an occasional park cleanup or tutoring commitment.

These services are discrete and rarely publish their offerings, so it isn't something you can easily google. They spread by word of mouth within elite community networks, just like Varsity Blues ringleader Rick Singer's Key Worldwide Foundation and The Edge College & Career Network. Universities or research labs in need of funding sell their names or offer their facilities for lucrative prices to high school families hoping to gain an edge. Admissions reviewers claim they can tell authentic pursuits from disingenuous ones, but I'm skeptical. They're not omniscient admissions gods. If pay-to-play programs didn't provide tangible admissions benefits, families wouldn't shell out tens of thousands of dollars to inflate their resumes and provide ammunition for future college essays.

Inflated credentials attempt to dress up the proverbial emperor without clothes. Less-affluent students or those without professional family networks rightly wonder how a YouTuber or their classmate has four internships and three coauthor publications before getting their driver's license. Internally motivated, curious applicants pursuing interests for their own sake pay the price because reviewers might mistake them for their inauthentic counterparts. When my clients cold-call companies for internships or secure positions technically reserved for college students or graduates, I always tell them to contextualize their initiative in their resume and essay. What's on the resume matters as much, if not less than, how you received the opportunity. Providing the context of their initiative distinguishes them from the students whose parents secured the opportunities for them. Concerns about sincerity are potentially one reason why MIT requests how you found the opportunity for their optional "discuss a research project" prompt.

Still, helicopter parents are less a root problem than a symptom of their environment. Lori Laughlin and the other Varsity Blues admissions scandal cheaters and convicted felons are merely extreme instances of the admissions madness taken to its logical conclusion. Parents create fake Instagram accounts to portray their unathletic child as tennis's next Naomi Osaka. They arrange for 20-somethings to take the SAT for their child without their knowledge or consent. Desperation makes people act irrationally and illegally.

It's unimaginable to some families that their unexceptional if capable child may need to attend a less-prestigious university. Families respond to a college admissions arms race where, if some fencers or baritones gain an advantage, it comes at the actual or perceived cost of their child's future opportunities: the **zero-sum bias**. I don't think it's coincidental that the rise in helicopter parenting in the late '80s correlates with a dramatically more competitive college admissions landscape. I continuously remind myself that parents have good intentions and try their best to support their children, even when their hovering is counterproductive.

Nevertheless, overparenting corrupts their child's sense of what matters. In a 2014 Harvard survey of 10,000 middle and high school students, 80 percent answered that they believe their parents care more about achievement and good grades than caring for others. Likewise, the same percentage of students report that their teachers communicate the same priorities. In the same survey, 96 percent of parents say they want to raise ethical, caring children. Yet there is a disconnect "between what adults tell children they should value and the messages we grown-ups actually send through our behavior."[45] When in conflict, excellence matters more than character, which creates an unintended epidemic of academic dishonesty that I discuss in chapter 6.4, "Cheaters Often Win."

Early on in my independent consulting career, I used to be critical of my clients for regularly emailing me after midnight. I realize now that, for many, their regimented lives are scheduled to the hour every day of the year. Also, I'm less judgmental of parents who seem like their child's manager because, for some students, there isn't enough time in the day for one person to attend to their myriad tasks. Living in Bali and New Zealand matches my time zones perfectly with my night owl students (and parents). The only time they can fit in essays is in the wee hours of the morning or on the rare weekend when they don't have extracurricular or volunteer commitments.

Educational and extracurricular planning starting from the womb won't come as a shock to many of my readers. It surprised me because neither of my parents went to college, and I come from a working-class community, Mesquite. My dad drove bread trucks for forty years before driving school buses today. He's the sort of essential worker invisible to elite society.

Few of my former classmates have earned degrees, nor did most of us have two parents, let alone wealthy ones who could connect us with internships or volunteer opportunities abroad. My hometown has other problems, such as unplanned pregnancies, undocumented immigration status, domestic violence, crime, and hunger. I consider my older brother something like a saint for spending his 15+ year career teaching at our old high-need high school in a district unwilling to provide PPE or other safety measures during the pandemic.

However, our hometown isn't impoverished enough for well-meaning white families in Highland Park or Preston Hollow to build Habitat for Humanity houses or stock food banks. Affluent families reserve their philanthropy for urban Dallas neighborhoods such as Oak Cliff and Pleasant Grove. Could you imagine the inverse where inner-city black students instruct suburban whites and Asians? Can anyone plausibly think the admissions playing field is level in a divided society where wealthy students tutor impoverished pupils "on the other side of town?"

Finally, affluent families hire consultants like me to help their children cross the finish line. I acknowledge my role in the admissions juggernaut. I find meaning in alleviating the suffering of others. The liberal left likes to demonize the top 1 percent and their attendant white privilege in ways that I sympathize with. More so than systemic racism, widening wealth inequality is arguably America's most pressing issue. I work mainly with white and Asian students not because of their ethnicity but because they happen to be the demographics who can afford my services. I argue in chapters 9 and 10 that class rather than race is the predominant cleavage dividing America into two castes of haves and have-nots.

But critics make a mistaken assumption equating wealth and opportunity with a life free from suffering. I've come to learn that a Gucci bag or Harvard degree doesn't free someone from their physiology. Some of the most miserable people I've met are also the wealthiest. We're all struggling to make sense of our place in the world and navigating our fears, doubts, and uncertainties. Rich and poor people alike live with suffering, even if the magnitude and reasons vary. Driving intersectionality wedges between groups of people diminishes the possibility of finding common ground. What binds humanity together is our never-ending discontent—more on our psychology in chapter 4.

The ideal parents to work with are those who understand it is their child writing the essays and earning their future degree, not them. Student-centered parents provide resources for their children to succeed without forcing them to pursue extracurriculars or classes they don't enjoy or have time for, encourage their children that it is okay to walk away from a commitment that isn't serving them, and help them feel agency to choose what is or isn't in their best interests. They support their child's areas of interest or future majors without pressuring them into STEM or medicine that may not be a good fit academically. One of the highest compliments a teen can offer of their parents is that they're "pretty chill."

Responsible parents openly discuss family finances so their child doesn't have unrealistic expectations about what they can afford. Conscientious parents limit college application discussions to a few times a week at most rather than asking multiple times a day if they have finished their essays and applications or have reconsidered their decision not to apply to Harvard. They have confidence that they've raised their child well and that their child will be happy and successful regardless of which university they attend.

Students who email me almost exclusively—with their parents checking in from time to time—signals an ideal balance between the division of roles and responsibilities within a family. For students and parents who request feedback on their progress and behavior, I answer honestly, even if the truth is uncomfortable. That also means my compliments weigh more. I love telling parents they're doing a good job when it's deserved, because raising a teenager is an unimaginably difficult task, especially nowadays. And if your kid is anything like me as a teenager...

I enjoy helping students achieve their goals. My professional objective is to get students into their top choices and trust that the university will help develop them into conscientious adults and contributors to society. Families think they're hiring me to give their students an edge at gaining admission to their dream school, which is partly the case but much less so than the hidden value I add. I spend less of my time during the admissions season on writing mechanics or where to apply. I share whatever knowledge or skills I've acquired over my decade in college admissions and my rigorous education as an honors UT-Austin liberal arts graduate. More importantly, most of my professional services involve putting out endless worry fires. Dealing with others' constant stress puts me in a sometimes-awkward position because what some students need isn't a mentor or coach but a professionally licensed therapist, which I'm not.

2.3 Independent educational consultants are also not the primary problem

I hypothesize that the independent college consulting industry proliferates less to address nuts-and-bolts admissions questions. Instead, consultants, test preparation agencies, immigration agents, and resume planning specialists occupy the collective, underlying anxiety void created by highly selective American universities. They provide some degree of certainty and comfort in a highly uncertain world.

I mistakenly thought a global pandemic might temper the admissions madness and clamoring for spaces at Zoom U. As I write in late November 2020, the University of Georgia reports a 27 percent *increase* in nonbinding Early Action applications. Their communications team places a reminder at the bottom of their corporate-speak press release to "please be patient, be nice and be courteous."[46]

Brown University's Admissions Dean Logan Powell boasts a 16 percent *increase* in binding Early Decision applicants for

Fall 2025 while in the same paragraph claiming to "be passionate about broadening access [for underrepresented students] to Brown."[47] Their Fall 2021 regular decision admissions rate was less than 4 percent. His sentiment ignores that Early Decision overwhelmingly advantages the most privileged families, which I discuss in chapter 8.1. NYU Professor Scott Galloway further counters Dean Powell with an apt analogy. "A university president bragging about rejecting 90 percent of applicants is tantamount to a homeless shelter taking pride in turning away 90 percent of the needy that arrive each night."[48] You can't plausibly maintain a scarcity of spaces that favors wealthy students while promoting diversity and inclusion in the same paragraph. I will discuss the disconnect between ever-increasing selectivity and enrolling diverse classes in chapter 9.

University admissions officials love to wag their fingers at expensive independent education consultants as if we're the engine driving society's increasing inequality. We're not the engine propelling the madness. Instead, we're exhaust fumes emerging from a much larger machine. Elite universities bear most of the responsibility for the admissions madness. However, criticisms of the unregulated college consultant industry by university administrators have some merit. Politicians don't have an incentive to regulate because they depend on our services.

Most consultants aren't worth what they charge or shouldn't be operating at all, in my experience. I offer a "second opinion" service to students who've hired someone else and are getting ready to submit their applications. The last thing I want to do is add to the anxiety or diminish a student's months' hard work by recommending that they need to start over. Most of the time, their edited essays are fine and require minor corrections. Some are even quite good and are ready to submit without reservation, leading me to believe the consulting industry isn't completely hopeless. I can glance at essays, like a seasoned mechanic opening your car hood, and diagnose whether significant repairs are required.

A few clients every year fire their former overpromising-and-underdelivering counselor and hire me instead. Some with younger children retain me. It takes a lot of faith to hire a second person after being burned by the first. If we lived in an entirely fair world with university spaces evenly and transparently distributed throughout society, my job and industry would cease to exist overnight. I'm not describing a utopia because some countries make a decent effort at achieving equity without causing tremendous stress for their applicants or creating the environment for a thriving multibillion-dollar consulting industry, which I discuss in chapter 5.1.

Unqualified service providers are especially abundant in China, India, and other emerging markets. They take advantage of desperate families less familiar with the American admissions and immigration systems. It's a lucrative market for bad actors to take advantage of anxious families.[49] Even the charlatans and hucksters respond to a need in the marketplace rather than create its market conditions. SAT tutors charging $600 an hour couldn't command such high rates if not for the importance of high-stakes standardized exams. However, the test-optional movement and pandemic may diminish that industry.[50]

Even if nobody alive remembers how or why the admissions madness started, reforms begin with the universities. They who live in their Ivory Towers ought not to cast the first stone. They're so high up that they're bound to miss anyway.

Independent consulting is not free of questionable ethical considerations, but neither is any job. No career path is pure, but some industries are more problematic than others. The danger comes from failing to acknowledge one's professional moral dilemmas and conflicts of interest. I provide a service, and people know precisely where their money goes: to me. Universities go to great lengths to justify lucrative head football coach salaries or yet another flashy campus amenity on the backs of pitiful adjunct professor salaries and the exploitation of graduate student labor.[51]

Their motives must appear pure, whereas I can be an unapologetic if considerate capitalist. Students pay tuition, and it evaporates into bloated administrator salaries and lazy river amenities. Consider that I'm writing a book where, if administrators considered my criticisms seriously and diminished the importance of the college essay, the sheer number required, or standardized their processes, I would be out of work. In the words of *Black Swan* author Nassim Taleb's most recent popular book, I have *skin in the game*.

Universities adding or changing requirements make it easier for me to justify raising my prices. Wealthy families' consulting fees subsidize my many dozens of ad-free videos and high-quality blog posts on Tex Admissions for students anywhere who cannot afford my services to help them make sense of our incomprehensible admissions systems. I try to respond to every email within reason, regardless of whether the family hires me. My ethic is in response to many students who can't get answers from official sources.

Here is a message from today from an already-admitted student wondering about taking a gap year. "I have emailed the UT admissions people, but I have not heard back. I was wondering if you could please answer my question. I would truly appreciate your help." I offer my UT admissions guide free and discount my course to any students who ask. I undoubtedly reach orders of magnitude more students and families independently than I did when working for a university. Most importantly, I can be a lot more honest and transparent. I revisit the ethics of providing services to wealthy families in chapter 9.2.

2.4 My intentions

I'm much less interested in providing a measured list of policy recommendations or reforms to university bureaucrats subject to the **status quo bias** resistant to reform. Let them have their national conferences and planning meetings with lots of talk and breakout sessions that produce little meaningful change. The "big" admissions innovation of the previous decade was to create yet another unnecessary application: Coalition. I'm not optimistic for substantive reform any time soon. I've tried unsuccessfully to challenge the admissions system from the inside, which I detail in chapter 8.3 Dashboard and the dark side of big data.

I'm tired of talking about college admissions with career bureaucrats. They simply don't listen. For any new or junior admissions counselors reading this book, take note. You're unwitting participants in a much larger machine that purports noble values regarding social mobility and opportunity, whereas the reality is much more complicated. You're conditioned into a dogmatic high priesthood. Admissions people are often so deluded by their varied institutionalized diversity and "college access" campaigns that they fail to recognize they're a primary agent driving social inequality in the United States.

Admissions professionals prefer to pat each others' backs at exclusive conferences and virtue signal superficial support for marginalized demographics on social media and woke press releases. Even the best collection of the world's most thoughtful and conscientious higher education professionals and admissions counselors participating in a broken admissions system will still produce unintended consequences that damage society more than they help. Despite their considerable admissions powers, they receive mediocre salaries, work long hours, and were likely average college students themselves.

If two-thirds of an Ivy League campus's graduates begin careers in consulting or finance, and most others attend graduate school, who do you think constitutes the remaining people who work in their admissions offices? Careers in college admissions do not attract a university's most talented graduates. Some veteran counselors wouldn't have gained entry to their alma maters if they were applying today, including me to UT-Austin Freshmen Honors. Yet, they collectively decide the fate of millions of applications. Many of their future students are already more brilliant and accomplished than the middling gatekeepers rendering their verdicts. Most college applicants will never know who adjudicated their decision, whether they received a fair hearing, or why an outcome went one way or the other.

Higher education journalist Jeffrey Selingo reminds his readers in his recent popular book *Who Gets in and Why* that "While many people initially enter the admissions profession to serve the needs of students, they soon find out that selling the college is a necessity in an increasingly competitive industry."[52] Admissions counselors are like proselytizing missionaries who are more interested in your tithes than anything else. Increasingly, admissions counselors are becoming salespeople at the expense of their primary responsibility, selecting the most desirable applicants. Perverse incentive structures preclude heroic acts by individuals seeking change. Individuals may do great and important work, yet it is impossible to undermine financial and budget incentives determined by senior university administrators. Tuition dollars and athletics revenues will always supersede student well-being. The only way to stimulate reform is from the outside, which partially explains why the best college admissions books don't come from universities or current admissions counselors.

Who Gets in and Why is one of the best pieces written on college admissions. Spending a year inside Emory, Davidson, and the University of Washington at Seattle, Selingo lifts the hood on questionable college recruitment and enrollment management practices. He humanizes the process by profiling well-intentioned admissions professionals and families hoping to secure their slice of the American Dream.

His investigations expose what everyone suspects: admissions decisions are arbitrary, and universities wield a near-monopoly of power over students. He writes in the introduction, "It's messier than I realized, with no one pass at an applicant necessarily the final one. It's more arbitrary. It includes deeper and wider pools of qualified applicants than any one person can imagine. It's driven by money and agendas from so many directions."[53] Unlike Selingo's, most admissions books promise simple solutions, and expensive firms offer precise admissions chances and guarantees. They're inaccurate at best and exploitative at worst.

Selingo is part of a larger bibliography of admissions exposes written by journalists, like Jacques Steinberg's 2003 work *The Gatekeepers*. My criticism is that they write for a general-interest audience. Although each author provides helpful albeit unoriginal advice, they're of the "if you had to explain college admissions to an alien visiting from outer space" genre. On paying for college, Selingo states the obvious: "The pressure that families feel to pay huge sums for what they see as the 'right college' is real."[54] *You don't say!*

His readers may or may not have kids nearing college entrance or are educators who help their students navigate the admissions process. Much of what he observes regarding admissions review and enrollment management are trends that haven't changed materially over the years. They're merely a difference in degree and an acceleration of the intensity of the admissions madness. But his arguments are largely unoriginal and have been thoroughly covered by previous works. Many educators or savvy families with multiple college-going children respond to his investigations with *duh, we already knew this.*

He is an outsider peeking in, whereas I spent the beginning of my career working inside UT-Austin admissions. Some have criticized me that I haven't worked inside an admissions office since late 2013, yet the same concern isn't raised about journalists who are briefly passing through and merely observing admissions practices. Assisting families over the past six years as an independent counselor gives me a deeper appreciation of the college application anxiety and stress than when I worked for a university. I write directly to people already engaging with the college application process and know that the process is confusing and stressful. Selingo's polite criticisms and reasonable suggestions for reform don't go far enough in calling for a radical reconsideration of the entire college admissions apparatus. I reference his work throughout and pick up where he leaves off.

I wrote a 300-page book about a single university, UT-Austin. However, much of UT admissions remains shrouded in mystery because of their opacity and unpredictable admissions practices. UT's admissions page is typical for universities everywhere. It provides a textbook example of supplying as little helpful information as possible. Some UT applicants exceed the words written in their essays compared with the total number of words published on their leading admissions pages. UT used to have an extensive FAQs page and biographies for every counselor to humanize the process somewhat. A push for form-over-substance branding removed those more personalized sections in favor of sleek corporate marketing. UT is not unique but part of a larger trend among elite universities to diminish their accountability to the public.

Does UT really need to spend millions on marketing to promote themselves? I'm confident the university will receive more than enough qualified applicants to fill their available spaces even if they didn't spend a dime on marketing or admissions outreach. Most UT applicants will apply regardless of font schemes or photos portraying diverse students.

During my first year in 2011, we conducted information sessions that were 80 percent information and 20 percent sales pitch. The proportion reversed in subsequent years. Rather than answering actual questions, I found myself pitching to families already desperate to get into their dream school. It's a strange feeling to sell something that people would pay any price for, only for us to decline their money with an admissions rejection. Imagine attending a 90-minute presentation of hard-selling holiday timeshare accommodations only for the presenters to deny your purchase months later. There is an information asymmetry between my hundreds of thousands of words and videos I've published on UT-Austin admissions and what's available on their website.

At UT-Austin, the system constrained me heavily as to what I could or couldn't say, and understandably so. Bureaucracies need everyone on the same page and communications with the public consistent. Inconsistent messaging leads to rumors and misinformation necessary to dispel when I worked as a counselor and now as an independent consultant.

The **continued influence effect** is the tendency to believe previously learned misinformation even after it has been corrected. The same rumors, such as attending Austin Community College helps increase one's UT-Austin transfer admissions, or how it's critical to apply on August 1, persist year after year. Online message boards and community gossip drills an infinitely deep well of misinformation, but universities rarely participate in these online spaces to cut off nonsense at the source. Valuing consistency and limiting information to the minimum required by state and federal laws comes at the consequence of empowering staff to adapt their styles to diverse populations or advocate for reform within their bureaucracy. Strict policies made us admissions robots, not counselors.

Following a weekend college fair hosted by a North Texas–area Chinese American community, the organizers invited me to write a "College Admissions 101" article in the English section of their Mandarin-medium newspaper. My boss forwarded the request to the senior staff, who granted their permission. I diligently wrote and revised the uncontroversial and non-UT-specific 5,000-word essay, only to have the permission rescinded without explanation a few weeks after submitting it for review. I subsequently "lost face" with the event organizers for reneging on the commitment. UT's "limitless opportunities" vision statement seems not to extend to its admissions officers.

Bureaucracies are highly risk averse. They don't want anything in writing that isn't thoroughly vetted by the communications team. If you visit nearly any college admissions page and wonder why there is such little content, risk-aversion helps explain the lack of transparency and paucity of clear answers to frequently asked questions. Even university-sponsored admissions blogs—a step in the right direction toward greater transparency—are finely manicured to share a lot while saying little. The emergence of unhelpful chatbots increases distances between universities and society.

Some people criticized my book *Your Ticket to the Forty Acres* because they advise families to listen *only to official sources*. What if official sources are unable or unwilling to discuss their intentions and processes? There were exact parameters around what we could and couldn't tell families, creating the impression that UT had something to hide. Universities have overwhelmingly transitioned from *informing* the public to *persuading* you to apply and enroll.

Check UT admissions Twitter @bealonghorn or the social media presence of most other universities, and its 90 percent sales pitch sprinkled with glib reminders about deadlines. Their public relations teams create superficial YouTube videos or podcast episodes to give the impression they're informing, although they're providing little substance. Nowadays, I'm often a resource of last resort for students who email universities and don't receive a response. Like so many themes of this book, the problem about inconsistent communications with the public isn't new or specific to any particular campus. It's a system-wide, intractable problem.

Private school counselor Marguerite L. Jackson comments in March 1965 on the emergence of dedicated college counselors who try to "provide realistic and sensible information for the student to facilitate the process of choosing a college. And yet the counselor [themselves] are operating under very hazy notions, half-perceptions, and misperceptions. The reason again seems lodged in the gap between the high school counselor and the college admissions officer."[55] Harvard fought tooth and nail to prevent lifting the hood on their admissions review "trade secrets" in recent litigation regarding alleged Asian American discrimination.

After a deluge of requests that were successfully granted initially, UT-Austin recently shut down efforts for their enrolled students to seek their admissions files through open records requests. UT requested the state's Attorney General's office to invoke an obscure statute to deny further requests by their enrolled students.[56] A lack of transparency diminishes institutional accountability and creates the space for rumormongering.

I'm not arguing that individual admissions counselors, university administrators, or the bureaucracies are nefarious actors intent on causing harm and suffering. Instead, individuals simply don't matter much in the aggregate outcome of profound suffering inflicted on tens of thousands of families each year.

One of my favorite aspects of working for UT, and one of the very (very) few things I miss about conventional employment, is working alongside well-intentioned and conscientious professionals representing dozens of universities. They may not have been straight-A honors students in college, but most were decent and kind. It upsets me when I see Redditors insulting specific admissions counselors and university officials, the **hostile attribution bias**. At worst, I can assure you that a university is utterly indifferent to you or your application and isn't out to get you. Like the students, admissions professionals are abiding by rules they didn't create nor have the power to change. We're humans, too.

The broader higher education ecosystem supplies both causes and effects of the madness. Universities respond to perverse incentives in society to the detriment of students' well-being. There isn't some grand conspiracy or a College Board New World Order pulling strings. On the contrary, the highly decentralized and non-uniform requirement system is a primary culprit for the admissions madness. Undergraduate admissions lacks any entity like the (flawed) American Medical Association or State Bar Associations that provide checks on the supply of medical and law degrees. Like addressing climate change, it's almost impossible to point your finger at a single source in such a complex ecosystem and exclaim, "There! That's the problem!" Although Exxon and the College Board come pretty close for each.

One of the many things I love about my current professional position is complete independence from institutions. I can write so provocatively and honestly because I don't have to worry about offending a boss that I don't have or a high school or university that I don't represent. I'm not a journalist who needs to please his employer. I'm self-publishing without concern for maximizing profits or censoring myself at a publishing house. I acknowledge that my book is controversial and may be highly unpopular with admissions professionals. Some of them I consider friends who make sacrifices for their students and do essential work. I'm unafraid of burning bridges.

Bureaucrats and even former colleagues will assuredly insist that I've got everything wrong, especially the third rails I touch in chapter 9, "Rethinking Diversity." They will mock me and toe the party line that their institution really does care about students, especially those who are most marginalized. The bureaucrats will mistake their own sincere concern for student wellness with that of their soulless institution's naked greed, exposed yet again most recently by risking mostly black athletes' health by forcing a college football season during COVID.

It's me they will point at, the privileged white male independent consultant providing services to wealthy families who is the problem. I'm a symptom of the multibillion-dollar college consulting industry that does not exist in a more equitable, centralized, and transparent system such as Germany, the Netherlands, and New Zealand. In fact, the only college consulting firms in New Zealand cater to students wishing to study at elite American universities.

To the hypocritical bureaucrats, I will laugh and hold up a mirror. You're the problem. Despite my provocative and occasionally hostile tone, I remain open to dialogue. If there are any (courageous) university administrators out there permitted by their bureaucracies to have challenging conversations conducted in good faith, I invite you to join an uncensored and edit-free conversation on my YouTube channel. Come prepared because I won't hold back if I detect any bullshit.

In the corporate-speak of elite universities, my book practices a genuine "student-centered" approach to equip families with clear-seeing insights. We're living in a system with the wrong incentives producing unintended consequences that optimize for a university's bottom line. Corporate employment pipelines need elite degrees for convenient human resources filters at the expense of students and their families' health and well-being.

It's no accident that 40 percent of Harvard graduates funnel into top management consulting and Wall Street firms. I assume many budding analysts never wrote Common Application essays about the finer points of sub-prime mortgage collateralized debt obligations or admiring the Bobs from Office Space. Although college admissions sucks, hundreds of thousands of students have gone before you. My message is that many of them turn out alright long term, and you probably will, too. I wish the system as practiced wasn't so, but there is little that you can do as an applicant besides taking ownership of what's within your control.

This book attempts to address the Bigger Questions and, in the jargon of college admissions, to *empower* students, families, and high school educators to have a reference point when suffering surfaces and you're unsure why. I offer a vocabulary that gives context to the feeling "this process totally sucks" when you're losing sleep to work on an essay you may or may not have anticipated. The next chapter reframes college admissions through metaphor. I also share this book's origin story.

3. A College Essay

Common metaphors describe college applications as a "journey." But college admissions is less flying a plane with an exact destination and step-by-step instructions and more like stepping through a minefield without a minesweeper.

The likelihood of misstepping is high even if you make baby steps to avoid the mines directly underneath your feet. You know that you need to get to a university on the other side, but the path is highly uncertain. My book is the minesweeper that allows you to lift your head and look further afield to anticipate what's coming. I want to help you open your eyes to see the mines more clearly so that you don't cause harm to yourself and the other tens of thousands of applicants tiptoeing through the college admissions equivalent of the Korean Demilitarized Zone.

Avoiding metaphorical landmines is often how I feel about traveling the world, which I've been doing continuously since 2014. I started Tex Admissions from my friend's apartment in Guatemala City and have provided my services while rarely stepping foot in America. For over four years, I didn't remain in a single location for more than a month, usually moving every few days. I've worked from airplanes, bus stops, humid hostels, and even broken down by the side of rural roads. I have to buy a new computer every two years because constant jostling, dust, and humidity decays their components quickly. One computer died the day before I flew from Dallas to Barbados to begin 2017, forcing me to make a late-night Best Buy run to buy a new one.

Traveling is continually humbling because it forces me to accept that I don't know what I don't know. Over time, I've acquired an extensive catalog of possible dangers to anticipate. Still, I'm frequently caught off guard. Once, a freak electrocution accident at a Tongan guesthouse nearly severed my right second toe and led to a Kafkaesque experience at Tonga's national public hospital.

It's challenging to plan a month ahead when I rarely know where life will take me next week or even later that day. I accept the reality that life never proceeds neatly from A to B to C, no matter how much I plan and anticipate. Providing a glimpse into my unconventional lifestyle will help frame my admissions perspectives. Thousands of travelers have gone before me, just like the hundreds of thousands of college applicants who have gone before you. We're each the heroes of our own stories who need to learn tough lessons firsthand to learn and grow. If you can learn from others' mistakes or receive the wisdom of experienced mentors, you might save yourself a lot of pain.

The following story offers lessons in acknowledging unfamiliar circumstances, adapting under pressure, hoping my mistakes don't cost me too dearly, and accepting that much in life is outside our control. It could be a response to Washington and Lee's Johnson Scholarship program: "Reflect on a time when your path was not as simple or direct as anticipated. How did you manage, and what did you learn?"

It's also in a format you may recognize: the college essay.

3.1 Where's Bobina?

Exiting the airport at 4 a.m. in Kazakhstan's capital, formerly known as Astana, I tried to find my taxi driver. Snow fell even though it was only late September in 2017. I still wasn't feeling well following Oktoberfest excesses in Munich the week before. He spotted me first, easy because I was the only passenger on the mostly empty Belavia flight from Minsk, Belarus, carrying a traveler's backpack.

Opening the door to his LADA Granta and pushing aside the baby seats, he introduced himself as the hostel's owner. I wrote in my journal: "I'm relieved that the hostel is so comfortable. I left a review as it was one of the best I'd ever stayed." You never know what to expect when arriving in a new country, especially in the former Soviet Union. Clean sheets, centralized heating, and individual power outlets were an improvement on cold showers and sharing a twelve-bed dorm with snoring migrant laborers the previous year in Kyiv, Ukraine.

I woke up starving "and a little disoriented. I staggered out and walked down the road for an hour to find food—unsuccessful." I converted my dollars and Euros to a bundle of Kazakh Tenge and spotted a McDonald's in the distance. It seemed closed and under construction, only for me to learn later that it was open. Even the Golden Arches look a little sadder in Central Asia. I shivered, not so much because Astana was cold but because it was windy. It's the only place in the world I've visited that's flatter and drearier than Lubbock and the Permian Basin.

Like Texas, everyone drives in Astana. Distances on Google Maps don't align with the roads, so I consistently underestimated how long it took to walk somewhere across their weirdly wide divided-lane streets. I worked up the courage to go out a second time. I found a bag of Russian-branded chips at a second магазин (*magazin*) corner store—that word at least I recognized—because the first shop didn't have small notes to break 2,000 Tenge (~$5 USD). I never eat Doritos, but in that moment, I would have killed for something familiar.

I texted my friend Anthony set to arrive in a few days from Amsterdam. "Dude, seriously, why did you talk us into coming to Kazakhstan? It's cold and strange." Anthony graduated with me from UT-Austin's Moody College of Communications in 2011, majoring in communications, but we met only later in 2014 when he moved to Yangon. He successfully started Myanmar's first independent public relations firm, ERA. He has remained there throughout the 2021 military coup and popular uprisings.

He reminded me to keep an eye on the prize, about which I was completely indifferent: a concert with his favorite artist in high school, the obscure Russian trance DJ named Bobina. His hits include *Flying Kitten* and *Go Get Vodka*. Knowing that I'm his only friend foolish enough to book a spontaneous last-minute ticket to Central Asia, I agreed to meet Anthony first in Astana. We planned to attend the concert and take a 24-hour overnight train to Kazakhstan's other city, Almaty, for Bobina's second performance.

All the while, I'm in the thick of college admissions season working as an independent consultant for college applicants and their families for my solo-venture Tex Admissions. I served as an undergraduate admissions counselor for UT-Austin from 2011 until the end of 2013, responsible for reading hundreds of admissions files and serving dozens of schools in Dallas and Collin counties. I've since worked with hundreds of families independently, with students gaining admission to prestigious universities and full-ride scholarships nationwide.

On January 1, 2014, I left America permanently when I completed a Fulbright grant teaching English in Malaysia before traveling the world ever since. I've visited more than 115 countries. In the spirit of USC's "what's essential about understanding you?" I respond that most of my clients don't know that my life's possessions fit in the backpack that I still live out of. I spent part of 2020 living in a converted 1998 Mitsubishi Chariot minivan. I wrote part of this book while fasting for five days, isolated in a remote cottage. My perspectives on college admissions are as unconventional as my lifestyle.

When Anthony arrived in Astana, we went for lunch. We ate thinly sliced horse filets grilled at our table, a horrifying and—please don't judge me too harshly here—unexpectedly tasty Kazakh delicacy. (We didn't try camel meat or milk, nor did we attend a camel shaving class, unfortunately. Anthony attended the 2018 World Nomad Games on a subsequent Central Asia trip, featuring competitions such as arm wrestling, eagle hunting, and horseback archery.[57] I recently passed on an invitation to eat dog at a wedding in Tonga in the South Pacific.)

It wasn't like I woke up that day deciding to eat what many cultures revere as pets; it just happened. In admissions speak, I *adapted* to my environment and *experienced* a *diverse* culture. Anthony getting food poisoning from the horse and me somehow avoiding it didn't deter us from Mission Bobina. You might say we *overcame adversity* and had the *grit* to persist.

We checked Bobina's site, which left us confused because it listed the concert but no portal to buy tickets. We shrugged and accepted the middling DJ's wisdom to grab a bottle of Stolichnaya...on a Wednesday. Hostel staff wrote a note for us in Kazakh "we need tickets" while we transferred our remaining liquid courage to an empty water bottle.

Catching Ubers in Kazakhstan, which had just introduced ridesharing to the country a few months before, was never straightforward. Drivers came from the countryside and rented cars that Uber was rumored to subsidize, so many of them didn't know how to drive, let alone interpret a GPS. Still, we coaxed Bobina onto his Bluetooth radio to set the mood. Following a few wrong turns, we made it to the country's largest indoor stadium.

Low key and anonymous is my preferred way to travel, but we tossed aside subtlety on that night. I wrote in my journal: "We barged into the security area and evidently bought two tickets from girls who happened to have extra. We never did find our assigned seats." After unsuccessfully trying to weasel our way into the ground floor pit, we settled for the upper deck.

"Anthony, why is there an old fat guy in a yellow tracksuit going on and on about something? He's talking more than playing music."

He said, "Either Bobina has let himself go, or that isn't Bobina."

We looked around our section and passed the "water" bottle back and forth. Almost everyone was middle-aged women in groups. We gestured and pointed. "Where's Bobina? Who is this guy? What's going on?"

The Kazakhs who we didn't terrify glanced at us and shrugged. We figured the *banditi* on stage was the opening act for what we could only assume was Astana's most important concert in their history. The tracksuit guy walked off stage, and the audience sat down. Bobina finally appeared on stage and played a few songs. At the same time, everyone else remained seated except for Anthony and me, who were practically falling over ourselves, to the mounting annoyance of our neighbors. But then our hero exited stage left. The crowd rose and cheered for the imposter with the expanding waistline and ample gold chains.

A woman finally took pity on us and spoke English with the clipped consonants that I've learned not to misinterpret as rudeness from native Russian speakers. "I don't know what is this Bobina you speak, but this Sergey Zhukov concert…"

"Anthony, who in the hell is Sergey Zukhov, and where's Bobina?"

We googled and learned that he was the Justin Timberlake of an American-inspired '90s pop band *Hands Up!* following the fall of the Soviet Union. Sergey Zukhov explained the crowd's middle-aged women demographics and why we couldn't find tickets online. We needed to google the "Sergey Zukhov" concert and not Bobina's. Appearing past his prime, Sergey didn't quite have his adolescent voice or agile moves that post-Soviet teenage girls presumably used to admire. He settled for what appeared to be political commentary, *Russki* this, *Amerikansky* that.

Defeated, we ordered and canceled a few wayward Ubers before hitchhiking home. We arrived in Almaty two days later following a very hungover, lurching overnight train ride.

A Kazakh acquaintance of ours set us up for a boy's day at the spa. When a giant woman entered wearing a beekeeper's outfit, we knew we were in trouble. She took turns beating us with the broad leaf of a banyan tree in a steam sauna before plunging us into an ice-cold swimming pool.

Refreshed if mildly terrified, we messaged Bobina on Instagram to ask why he only played a few songs. We were shocked that he actually responded. He even apologized that he was merely the intermission for who we took to be a has-been artist cashing in on post-Soviet nostalgia. He declined our request to hang out. It was too bad for him because another seedy acquaintance, Sergey, taught me the trick for getting into any exclusive Kazakhstan club: speaking Spanish to and confusing the bouncers. Sergey "led by example" that it's okay to walk through the Almaty McDonald's drive-through at 5 a.m. as long as you mime that you're a car.

With Almaty a bust, Anthony returned to Myanmar a few days later.[58] I didn't have any outbound plane tickets or plans. I looked at the map and saw Bishkek, Kyrgyzstan, just over the Tien Shan mountains five hours away. I ate a greasy doner kebab at the bus station for breakfast and took a standing-room-only Soviet-era *marshrutka* minibus, reporting in my journal: "everything went surprisingly smoothly except that bus mix-up and delay on the border."

I no longer recall that particular mix-up because land crossings in the developing world are rarely without at least some confusion. Few if any tourists cross land borders in out-of-the-way regions. Once, while crossing the border from Swaziland to Mozambique, I stamped into the country without issue, even though the visa took almost a month to secure. After exiting the office, a teenage border guard took my passport and called over every other officer.

At a border crossing notorious for corruption, at first, I was afraid of arrest or worried that I would need to pay a bribe. Ten or so guards, a few without shoes, simply wanted to flip through my passport's many pages and stamps. I gathered with my broken Portuguese that some of them had never seen a real American passport. They handed it back with a smile.

On the minibus, I met Muzi, a smooth-talking Liswati diamond smuggler wearing Gucci crocodile-scale shoes, out of place in a crowd mainly wearing flip-flops, including me. We passed the time drinking warm beers in a tin shack while waiting for the bus to take us to Mozambique's dusty capital, Maputo. He opened his backpack to let me peek inside. I realized only much later that hanging out with someone carrying a backpack full of illicit foreign currency maybe wasn't a good idea. After arriving in Maputo, he hopped out of the taxi we were taking in the middle of a busy intersection and ran straight to a bank without saying goodbye.

I spent my days in Bishkek, Kyrgyzstan treating myself to excellent restaurants in one of the world's least expensive cities (no horse this time). I treated myself to daily, high-quality $10-hour massages from not-beekeepers-with-banyan-leaves. Soaking up the oddly warm and not windy weather at sunny cafes, I sketched out the framework for the book that you're currently reading. At that time, I labeled it "48 Mistakes College Applicants Make" before letting it rest during the intervening years. Another working title was "Admissions Meditations," not in the mindfulness sense but along the lines of Marcus Aurelius's philosophical *Meditations.*

Never having intended to go to Central Asia the month before, I found myself in an even more obscure if pleasant country that, unbeknownst to me, was confronting a critical democratic crossroads. Arriving at an almost-full hostel with young Europeans after staying at empty ones in Belarus and Kazakhstan confused me.

The other guests were election observers for the Organization for Security and Co-operation in Europe (OSCE). They warned me about the upcoming presidential election. Around the same time, I journaled: "In a bizarre coincidence, I've signed my first ever Kyrgyz-American client," who was delighted when I sent photos of his ancestral homeland. It's fun for me that, more often than not, when an international student emails me, I've visited their country or city. I'm disappointed to report that I've yet to take an Indian Classical or Bollywood dance class that many of my clients write about, although it's on the bucket list.

I opted out of a possible Tajikistan visit due to unrest in the disputed Ferghana Valley. Instead, I booked an Aeroflot plane ticket scheduled to leave in a week for Baku, Azerbaijan. I hired a Kyrgyz driver to take me around picturesque Issyk-Kul Lake in the country's remote east. On our way back to Bishkek, we got pulled over at a speeding checkpoint. He gestured and shrugged. *Don't worry! Don't worry! Happens all time! No problems!*

He paid a 150 Kyrgyz Som (~$2) bribe tucked between his palm and driver's license to get out of a speeding ticket. I bought us dinner to balance the ledger. Afterward, we passed miles and miles of parked eighteen-wheelers and freighter trucks leading north to the Kazakh border that I had crossed a few days before. Drivers milled around, and vendors sold food. Kazakhstan had closed its borders and begun amassing troops, preparing for a rumored invasion if "their" candidate, former Prime Minister and billionaire Ömürbek Babanov, lost the election.

Tensions rose dramatically at the Bishkek hostel. The election observers warned something could erupt. Up until that moment, no Central Asian country had ever experienced a free and fair election or a transfer of power that didn't involve the death of a sitting leader or a revolution. I knew from time spent during civil unrest in Thailand in 2014 and in Central Mexico's Oaxaca and Guatemala in 2015 that airports are often the first targets for occupation. Protestors barricade airports to prevent politicians or corrupt officials from fleeing. *The Dictators Handbook* by Bruce Bueno de Mesquita and Alistair Smith references one of my all-time favorite social science findings: The straightest roads and shortest distances between a presidential palace and the airport correlate with corruption and authoritarianism.[59]

The election results arrived. The ruling party's Sooronbay Jeenbekov won by a wide if competitive margin. The staff listened to Kyrgyz-language radio to follow any reports of unrest. I double-checked my travel insurance (I wasn't covered) and prepared possible alternative plans if the airport was closed or my flight was canceled. I woke up at 4:30 a.m. the following morning and met my driver from the previous days.

Had anything happened? No, he replied with surprise, his neck leaning forward, eyes wide and glaring in the dashboard dome light, hands upturned as if to balance invisible plates. His neck and hands moved in unison to emphasize the point.

Normal! It is normal! No worries!

Setting aside my momentary concerns about the relative standards of "normal" in Kyrgyzstan, I gathered that no politicians had to take a midnight charter flight to Astana or Moscow. We breezed to the airport, and I transited through Moscow to Baku without issue except for a stern warning by the Azeri immigration official to *never* visit Armenia. I visited Armenia six weeks later anyway.

The election I didn't know was happening the week before turned out to be Central Asia's and Kyrgyzstan's only fair and conflict-free election ever. Exactly three years later, for a week during the October 2020 parliamentary election, Bishkek experienced widespread protests with occupations of the president's house, Supreme Court, and looting that caused over a thousand injuries and widespread property damage. President Jeenbekov subsequently resigned.

Leaving Kyrgyzstan two weeks after arriving in Central Asia was one of the most prominent "non-events" of my life despite my foolishness's best self-sabotaging efforts. Often, that which fails to happen is more significant than things that do. Rejection from every internship I applied for while a UT student opened other, more promising doors, for example.

That week was also not noticeably different from many over the previous seven years. Only in retrospect and writing out stories like this do I realize that they're far from typical. The weekend before I launched Tex Admissions in early April 2015, my friends and I were detained at gunpoint by Guatemalan federal military police on my first night in the country. Scared shitless at the time, it already seemed like water under the bridge the next morning, grateful we weren't in prison, happy to continue the party through the morning and afternoon from the safe confines of the hostel commons room. I met a girl that afternoon and changed around all my travel ideas to spend a few months together in Guatemala and Mexico.

Worrying about my travel lifestyle upending itself catastrophically is not unlike students who spend their teenage lives worrying about getting into college. Many report back to me as current students or graduates that "I have a hard time seeing why that process made me so upset." And without skipping a beat, they share their current anxieties about applying for an upcoming internship or preparing for a job interview. The cycle of worry continues, unbroken.

College admissions playbooks might offer a map to success. But the reality of the terrain is much more complicated with issues difficult to anticipate, just like how Google Maps or Uber in Kazakhstan doesn't quite match with every other time I've used the apps. I'm not usually so clueless, even after four years abroad before arriving in Central Asia. I've learned to resign to circumstances as a stranger in foreign countries.

On the one hand, being a well-off white American offers me many privileges abroad, but I'm at the mercy of unwritten cultural mores. I don't even pretend to know what's going on most of the time. It annoys me when Westerners become belligerent with locals and say things like, "this isn't how we do it back home!" Or they haggle endlessly to save a few cents on bananas or transportation. I try to learn from travelers who came before me to limit my errors. Making mistakes becomes the norm when you can't take for granted necessities such as finding food, clean drinking water, or predictable law and order. Each setback helps me learn for the next time I might need to attend a concert in a post-Soviet country.

Anthony and I arrived in Kazakhstan on the confused assumption that we needed to search for Bobina tickets rather than Sergey Zhukov. We didn't know what question to ask. We didn't know what we didn't know: the same critical blind spot experienced by most college applicants and their families. Trying to salvage one misadventure led me to another, but that's life. My life tends to progress at a much more accelerated pace than is typical.

Anthony laughed when I told him that I include our story in my book. Every mediocre college essay concludes with a quote, so here's Anthony's response. "A cautionary tale for some, an entire philosophy of life for others."

4. Stoicism and the Gap Theory of Happiness

When I dreamed about traveling the world, I imagined a perpetual state of excitement with exotic places, unfamiliar foods, beautiful women. And there was plenty of that, but I envisioned some mythical endpoint where my dream life would be complete. Unsurprisingly, that moment never arrives.

I reminisced about my shorter stints abroad during college in Eastern Europe and Rwanda that never exceeded the honeymoon phase. The novelty of near-constant movement, however, wears off over time. I meet tons of travelers who are away from six months to a year, but almost none travel continuously for more than 18 months. Most honest backpackers will admit that the 74th waterfall just doesn't offer quite the same rush as their second.

Meaningful long-term travel requires striving toward higher purposes, or you risk burnout, just like any other endeavor. Midlife-crisis adults who I regularly meet abroad have quit their unfulfilling careers. They mistakenly believe a year jaunting around the world or seeking spirituality in Bali will automatically raise their baseline happiness. Many often experience feelings oddly reminiscent of their corporate burnout because they think running away from their problems will somehow solve them.

I meet a lot of miserable people in paradise. Most of the self-help industry caters to reaching some mythic happiness endpoint. They promise a life free from suffering or desire if the reader can only secure their dream job, leave their toxic relationship, or find their life's passion. That endpoint is elusive if not unreachable. Only a dedicated commitment to a lifetime of prayer or meditation can domesticate our impulses and cravings. My mental states are still far from domesticated.

One of the most robust findings by behavioral economists such as Daniel Kahneman is that we're terrible forecasters of what will make our future selves happy. **Affective** or **hedonic forecasting** is a cognitive bias that asserts we're poor forecasters of our future happiness. Affective forecasting has implications in every realm of human behavior, especially for students applying to college.

When Sam Harris asks Kahneman in episode #150 of the Making Sense podcast if his academic understanding of the sum of human errors has helped him make better decisions in his daily life, Kahneman responded, "Not much." The takeaway from the Nobel Prize-winning behavioral economics pioneer isn't to throw your hands up and surrender. The first step to taking back control of your life is recognizing your cognitive blind spots and admitting, like Kahneman, that there is much about yourself and the world that you do not understand.

Kahneman's findings aren't new. Ancient philosophers and religious traditions possess a deep understanding of human behavior. A key framework that helps us make sense of the root suffering of college admissions and discontentment for humans everywhere throughout history is the practice of Stoicism. Stoicism instructs domesticating destructive emotions, practicing self-discipline, and confronting life's challenges with equanimity. The late Senator John McCain, for example, credits Stoic teachings for helping him endure more than five years as a POW in North Vietnam.

Similarly, Buddhist meditation training, *dhyāna,* preaches an awareness that neither fortune nor catastrophe is inherently good or bad. Our reactions to external events dictate how we respond to life's ups and downs. Most people have heard of Roman Stoic philosopher-king Marcus Aurelius from the 2000 film *Gladiator*. Russell Crowe plays the titular protagonist trying to stop Aurelius's corrupt son, Commodus, played by Joaquin Phoenix, from taking the throne.[60] His still-popular *Meditations* and recent adaptations in books such as Ryan Holliday's *The Obstacle is the Way* help millions of people today practice equanimity in the face of adversity.

Fewer people are aware that Aurelius received much of his wisdom from Epictetus, a second-century AD Greek philosopher born a slave to wealthy property owners. After earning his freedom, he taught philosophy in Rome before his subsequent banishment back to Greece. His student Arian transcribed his lectures in *The Discourses*. Epictetus teaches that freedom and happiness occur only when we "cease worrying about things which are beyond our power or will." Elsewhere, he writes, "Circumstances don't make the man, they only reveal him to himself." College admissions is a mirror that reveals the character of students and families.

A contemporary adaptation of Stoic teachings comes from philosophy professor and Stoicism practitioner William B. Irvine, who puts forward the "Gap Theory of Happiness." He identifies that the roots of unhappiness are simply the gap between what you have and what you want.

I highly recommend subscribing to Sam Harris's Waking Up meditation app to listen to Irvine's Stoic Path lectures. If you cannot afford the app, Harris offers it free to anyone, no questions asked.[61] Spending a few hours with Irvine is the single best practice I've found to reframe not just college admissions but life more generally.

In Irvine's Stoic meditation introduction, he offers a challenge. Consider a goal in recent months or years that you worked hard and desired greatly to achieve, for example, earning a perfect SAT score, qualifying for a state- or national-level tournament, or saving up enough money to buy a new phone. Did the acquisition bring you everlasting happiness? Or did your desires move on to something else days or weeks later? If you're like every human on the planet, the answer is yes. He says:

> "You want something, you work to get it, and you finally do get it. For a while, you're happy, but then the problem is you get used to the thing you have, and you're no longer happy. You don't live happily ever after the way you thought you would. You end up at pretty much the same position you were at before all of that trouble. And you find yourself wanting newer new things.... If you're currently unhappy, it's proof that you have never in your life succeeded in doing something that would let you live happily ever after. Yet the dream persists.... It turns out that the 'get happy by getting what you want' strategy provides you with a recipe not for having a good life, but one filled with dissatisfaction. By adopting this strategy, you unwittingly place yourself on a 'hedonic treadmill' on which happiness is like water vanishing as a mirage in the desert."

I'm no better than anyone else at forecasting what will make me happy. When I worked for UT Admissions, I had to swallow my own admissions medicine when I applied for a prestigious Fulbright Fellowship that required a lengthy interview, a UT faculty endorsement, and passing multiple gatekeepers. It took almost two years from beginning the application and gaining admission before I moved to Malaysia to teach English. I saw the fellowship as my first step toward achieving my dream life of traveling the world. I even obsessively checked updates on a neurotic message board called the Grad Café, no different than College Confidential. Fulbright applicants on the Grad Café were concerned almost exclusively about getting in rather than what the actual fellowship might entail. I had recently received a CELTA English Teaching certification and wanted to connect with other potential teachers excited to move abroad.

Instead, Grad Café members and I fantasized about receiving admission. From that community, I learned that admitted emails contain (P) in the title. I remember the precise time and place when I received the (P), 9 a.m., just after arriving at the admissions office on April 4, 2013. A flood of emotions overwhelmed me, but not entirely positive ones as I imagined in my dreams. I shouted, cried, and mostly wondered what would come next. A dirty secret of receiving admission to your dream school is it's unlikely to bring you the euphoria you imagine.

My boss wisely counseled me to keep it a secret from upper management until the last minute. There was a bureaucratic tendency to turn over staff they knew were lame ducks so that they could hire someone new. I didn't share the news with anyone except my closest friends and family. My girlfriend and I separated for a time before sharing an awkward final six months knowing I would leave for a year without the intention to return to full-time living in America. She surprised me on my last day in America by announcing her plan to move to Colombia to teach English. All along, we had similar long-term ambitions, yet my short-term goals clouded imagining or even discussing a future together.

My life changed forever, for better or worse. Teaching English in a rural, homogenous, religiously conservative fishing village proved the most challenging year of my life. Within weeks of arriving, I realized I had made a colossal mistake. I felt like life was almost entirely outside of my control. It was a struggle to wake up most mornings, and I escaped on as many weekends and holidays as possible.

The actual "teaching" I did at an impoverished school was almost a total waste of time. I felt adrift and without purpose. The dream I thought I wanted instead turned into a nightmare for reasons outside the scope of this book. I couldn't wait to complete my contract and move on with my life. When people see Fulbright on my biography and ask about it, I bristle at even acknowledging the credential, although I understand how it signals my competence.

The most positive thing I can say about my year is that I limped across the finish line and didn't terminate my contract early. My experience is an example of the downsides of "grit." I regularly reassure students that it's okay to quit an extracurricular activity they don't enjoy or an AP course that requires way too much time. I experienced significant trauma, some of which I'm still processing more than six years later. Difficulties in Malaysia motivated me to construct a radically different life.

Encountering setbacks and obstacles boosted what Irvine calls "the psychological immune system" or what Nietzsche phrased as "what doesn't kill you makes you stronger." My Malaysian nightmare prepared me for my eventual chaotic life of perpetual travel. I'm less afraid of failing than I am about never trying at all, which is one motivation for writing this book. I'm grateful to say that I've been living my dream life ever since that year spent walking a false path. There is nothing I desire that money can't buy, nor are there many places left I want to visit. Rather than waiting until retirement, I'm thankful to have already experienced much of the world in light of the pandemic. I feel like Epictetus is speaking to me when he counsels:

"Now is the time to get serious about living your ideals. How long can you afford to put off who you really want to be? Your nobler self cannot wait any longer. Put your principles into practice—now. Stop the excuses and the procrastination. This is your life! You aren't a child anymore.... The longer you wait, the more you'll be vulnerable to mediocrity and feel filled with shame and regret, because you know you are capable of better. From this instant on, vow to stop disappointing yourself. Separate yourself from the mob. Decide to be extraordinary and do what you need to do—now."

Am I any happier day to day now compared with when I lived and worked in Texas? In some ways, yes. I rarely have days that I perceive as bad. I sleep eight to ten hours a night, even during the busy admissions season. I rarely work more than eight hours a day. Once I began making sufficient money through Tex Admissions to live and travel without worry starting in 2018, I quickly realized that increasing sums of money don't yield greater happiness. Nowadays, I don't have to worry about paying the bills, and I buy whatever food or drink I desire. I have enough savings and investments to cover multiple emergencies.

My life is largely worry free, yet I'm far from living in a persistent state of contentedness, let alone happiness. I'm thankful that my depressive cloud lifted as soon as I left Malaysia because I wondered if I might remain in a permanent state of despair and melancholy. Only through genetic luck do I possess a brain and hormonal system that isn't prone to clinical depression or other mental illness. I discuss Moral Luck in chapter 10.1.

When I do have down moments, I remind myself that they pale compared to my worst days in Malaysia. One memory that remains with me is taking an early morning minibus, hungover and dehydrated, in the Philippines shortly after completing my Fulbright grant. Sitting in the aisle on a small wooden box with my knees to my chest and my backpack under my chin was one of the happiest memories of that year. I was no longer accountable to the US and Malaysian governments, free to choose my own discomforts. My worst days living on my terms are better than my best days earning paychecks from someone else or representing institutions whose policies I almost certainly disagree with.

The total of my life experiences and skills are ideally suited for independent college consulting. Six months of the year, when students aren't applying, I have few professional obligations. I spend that time boosting my "psychological immune system" by taking calculated risks, such as writing portions of this book in solitude while fasting or traveling to the South Pacific during cyclone season. I do what I want and, more importantly, avoid that which doesn't serve me. I get many of the small questions wrong, for example, hiring a shady search engine optimization firm, but I've gotten a few of my big questions right.

I'm acutely aware that I have one of the best lives possible by most objective measures, especially currently living safe and sound in COVID-free New Zealand and Australia. It isn't accidental that I live here but a strategic choice born from years on the road. I started paying close attention to COVID after Wuhan shut down in early January. While much of the world has experienced profound suffering and disruptions, 2020 was arguably my best year ever. I credit my UT-Austin liberal arts and social sciences training for equipping me with the media literacy and critical thinking skills to thrive in a chaotic, globalized world.

Nevertheless, for the most part, my baseline happiness hasn't changed much from high school. I value living meaningfully rather than chasing happiness. With each new achievement, country visited, or client acquired, I feel a momentary serotonin hit before reverting to the median. And I'm okay with that.

Asked, "Who is the rich man?" Epictetus replied, "He who is content." It would be tempting for me to chase ever-higher material goals, such as earning a million-dollar revenue, expanding my business to encompass many offices and employees, or commoditizing my digital nomad lifestyle on Instagram for internet cred. I might unintentionally become a millionaire someday, but that isn't the goal. I view growth as inward-oriented toward being a more loving, conscientious, and compassionate person rather than outward obsessions with money, website clicks, or YouTube subscribers.

I'm writing this book and its related content because I'm curious if I can build something new. I have doubts about whether Tex Admissions or *Your Ticket to the Forty Acres* makes me a one-trick pony. I'm sharing the kinds of ideas I've always wanted to write but didn't have the courage or experience to do. Rather than chasing the next accolade, I try to practice (very imperfectly) William Irvine's advice from ancient Stoic philosophers to live with contentment.

> "Learn how to want the things that you already have, to love the life that you happen to be living…. [You will be] vastly better off than the millionaire who, despite living in a mansion, is convinced that he would be lastingly happy if only he replaced his Ferrari with a newer model…. This millionaire will likely be envied by many people. They will imagine that if only they could be living his life, they would at last be happy, and at last their problems will disappear. "

My message isn't that you should live your life like mine. I wish we lived in a world where everyone could explore their creativities and find their ideal academic and professional fits. Sadly, we don't. I'm not an Instagram influencer or a YouTube guru. I'm not a life coach who hosts seminars on positive thinking your way to your dream life, nor am I a mentor for the many adults I meet in transition periods.

Adults, in general, can be exhausting to talk with because they see their life options much more narrowly than teenagers and undergraduates unafraid to dream big. Many are burnt out from an intense meritocratic competition against other elites. Some are downright unbearable to be around, but it's hard to blame them when we live in a system that obliterates our sense of self. Daniel Markovits in *The Meritocracy Trap* writes, "The most successful students and workers also become the least secure, as smaller differences in performance produce greater differences in rewards at the top than anywhere else. Elite insecurity begins almost at birth and never ends—especially at the meritocratic ladder's very highest rungs."[62]

However, some of my favorite types of people to meet are the rare souls in or nearing retirement who continue to reinvent themselves and find meaning in their later years. They've either opted out of or reframed the academic and corporate rat race to live with something resembling balance and sanity.

I'm a pragmatic adult living out my dreams hatched during my undergraduate years and refusing to settle for small-mindedness. I rarely talk about my unconventional personal life with admissions clients unless they ask, and it's usually the parents who are more interested in what I'm up to abroad. The students are too focused on the immediate goals of completing their applications and getting into their dream school.

On the contrary, I deter people who mistake my life as their dream because my way is a highly uncertain, risky, and sometimes dangerous path. My path and lifestyle aren't for everyone.

Instead, to quote Nietzsche, I've found my way. What is yours?

4.1 A few cognitive traps and distortions to avoid

I assume almost everyone gaining admission to and enrolling at Ivy League universities and their equivalents viewed it as their dream come true, a validation of their life's work and their parents' sacrifices. Even within this figurative millionaire's club, there are still hierarchies. Harvard looks down on Yale while Brown and Cornell are on the losing end of many Ivy League jokes. A Yale reject attending Cornell has the envy of applicants shut out entirely from the Ivy League. Even MIT and Caltech practice friendly rivalries.

Some Texas State Bobcats wish they were A&M Aggies, both of whom might dream of being Texas Longhorns. Community college students often wish they were at any four-year university, and severely disabled people might wish they could leave their homes unassisted. Epictetus counsels, "He is a wise man who does not grieve for the things which he has not, but rejoices for those which he has."

There is a hierarchy of desires that leave students wishing for more. As a UT honors student, many of my classmates were envious of their high school friends who enrolled at Ivy League universities. Non-honors students envied our positions. Unless you're the second coming of John von Neumann, Marie Curie, or Albert Einstein, it's almost certain that someone in your MIT math and science classes will be more knowledgeable and accomplished than you. Somebody almost certainly gained admission to a program or earned a scholarship that you coveted.

It's been years since I met someone who has visited more countries than me, but I know there are more prolific travelers and adventurers out in the world getting more off the grid than me. My adventures pale compared to someone like Ed Stafford, who is the only person to have walked the entire Amazon river from source to sea, an 860-day journey.

There will always be a gap between what you have and what you want. "If I can just get into computer science or my dream school," you might reason, "then I will be satisfied." Getting denied from your desired programs leads to devastation. A damaged ego prevents you from seeing your second- or third-choice universities in a favorable light. Since Daniel Kahneman and Amos Tversky coined the term **loss aversion**, subsequent robust findings in behavioral economics conclude that the pain produced by losing $100 is greater than the pleasure derived from winning the same amount. Getting rejected sucks, even if rationally you understand everything is likely to turn out alright.

Achieving your college admissions goals seems less about the satisfaction of getting in and more about avoiding the pain of rejection. Students who apply to more than a dozen universities and honors programs where admissions chances for everyone are highly unlikely set themselves up for repeated failure. Loss aversion motivates my plea for students to apply to more match universities where they're more likely to gain admission or scholarships to avert the inevitable pain of constant rejection. It's predictable when students pander to reviewers by writing about resiliency and grit yet crumble under their unfavorable admissions decisions.

Interestingly, many students report being content and even enjoying their backup schools after they transition and give it a few months. As soon as UT releases their large rejection batch, usually in late January, I receive literally hundreds of inquiries about transferring as quickly as possible. I instruct them to get in touch with me once they've acquired sufficient college hours. I receive comparatively far fewer over the summer and fall once they move onto campus and their classes begin.

One error in reasoning that helps alleviate anxiety is the **choice-supportive bias**, where we remember chosen options as having been better than rejected options. We're experts at making the most out of most situations while convincing ourselves we made the right choice all along. Adjusting to the new situation manifests in phenomena like "A&M is my favorite school ever!" when, six months ago, their bedroom was covered in burnt-orange Texas Longhorn decorations.

Just as we're poor at forecasting our happiness, we also overestimate the duration of negative emotions following setbacks. Have you ever offered your heartbroken friend the advice that things will get better with time? Then you're aware of the **fading affect bias** where emotions associated with unpleasant memories fade more quickly than emotions associated with positive events—time heals all wounds.

Conversely, we're prone to **chronological snobbery**, where we overestimate the significance of the present. Indeed, your college choice is almost certainly the most significant decision up until high school graduation, but it's merely the first of many lifetime crossroads and possible setbacks. I counsel distraught students and families to give themselves a few days or weeks to work through the five stages of grief before making such an important decision about where to enroll. The storm passes, and life moves on.

College applicants regularly fall prey to the **Just World Fallacy**. We live in an unfair world subject to randomness, coincidence, and arbitrary outcomes, both positive and negative. Positive thinking doesn't always produce positive results. I discuss in chapter 6.10 how it's impossible to assess admissions chances accurately or explain most results after the fact. For many, college admissions is the first time they've fallen short of their goals and been told no. Parents say, "It isn't fair that my daughter didn't gain admission and her classmate with lower grades did!" Families complain about state laws outside of their control, such as Texas's top 10 percent guaranteed admission or Supreme Court rulings regarding affirmative action and race in admissions.

Students wish ill on their alumnus interviewer or assigned admissions counselor. They respond with disbelief when a classmate who everyone knows cheats gets into their dream school. It won't be the first time in your life that a cheater or a bully obtains an unfair or undeserved advantage over you, and they may become your boss someday. Cheaters often win, a reality I discuss in chapter 6.4.

On the contrary, applicants admitted to their dream school may receive compliments like "you deserved it" or "it's only fair that you've gotten in given how much adversity you've experienced." If a given student *deserved* a positive outcome, as many well-wishers claim, it's nonsensical to suggest a rejected student deserved it, too. Many equally qualified applicants subject to severe hardships may get unlucky. There are also not enough elite admissions spaces to go around for too many deserving applicants.

Just because you perceive that the world *ought* to be a certain way doesn't mean that it *is* that way in practice: the **is/ought fallacy**. The world *should be* fair, but it *is not*. Conversely, just because the world is unfair doesn't justify continued injustices. Acknowledging this simple truth will help not tying your ego and self-worth to admissions outcomes because life entitles you to *nothing*. Suppose your first impulse to explain something admissions related is an appeal to a sense of justice or fairness. In that case, it may help instead to reframe your response as gratitude and appreciation.

It's possible to frame unfavorable and favorable outcomes the same. "It hurts to be rejected, but I'm thankful for this setback so I can learn and grow. I'm glad that I tried my best on my essays. I will make the most out of my next opportunity." To your admitted friend or sibling, it may be more considerate to share neutral sentiments like "I'm sincerely happy for you, and I wish you the best." Removing language around fairness can help remedy the fallacy that we live in a world where only good things happen to deserving people or its opposite.

What explains the roots of Irvine's persuasive Gap Theory of Happiness? How does it provide a framework for examining the anxiety inherent in college admissions?

The root causes of application anxiety, especially for affluent families whose basic needs are met, are almost entirely outside our control—our neurology. Reading Ray Dalio's *Principles* helped me reconcile the paradox between the powerlessness experienced, particularly by the highest-achieving and most-privileged students, who say they understand not to fixate on a dream school yet obsess anyway. He premises human psychology and relationships on physiology and the brain's many structures.

His frustrations running Bridgewater, one of the most successful hedge funds in history, echoes how I sometimes feel working with students and families. He writes, "While I used to get angry and frustrated at people because of the choices they made, I came to realize that they weren't intentionally acting in a way that seemed counterproductive; they were just living out things as they saw them, based on how their brains worked."[63] Accepting people as they are and modifying my approach and expectations has improved my professional services and personal relationships over time.

He divides our neurology into higher and lower selves. Our higher, conscious self responsible for planning, imagination, and learning resides in our brain's outer layers, the neo- and prefrontal cortex. Our lower, subconscious, "more primitive" self responsible for emotions, habits, and fears is located primarily in the amygdala. The amygdala is one part of the larger limbic system that helps regulate emotions and process and store memories. "[It] is deeply embedded in the cerebrum, which is one of the most powerful parts of your brain...

> ...When something upsets us—and that something could be a sound, a sight, or just a gut feeling—the amygdala sends a notice to our bodies to prepare to fight or flee: the heartbeat speeds up, the blood pressure rises, and breathing quickens.... Your conscious mind (which resides in the prefrontal cortex) can refuse to obey its instructions.... For most people, life is a never-ending battle between these two parts of the brain.... The biggest difference between people who guide their own personal evolution and achieve their goals and those who don't is that those who make progress reflect on what causes their amygdala hijackings." (Dalio, p. 220)

Desires and fears residing in the amygdala produce an unquenchable thirst for more, which provides the neurological basis for *The Gap Theory of Happiness*. Neuroanatomy supports the wisdom of the ancient Stoics and yogis. British-born Zen Buddhist practitioner Alan Watts spent his life synthesizing Eastern and Western religious traditions and spiritual practices. He understood neuroscience before it became a discipline. "The brain is much more concerned about the future than the present. It considers future happiness as the guarantee of an indefinitely long future of pleasures."

The prefrontal cortex (PFC) is primarily responsible for emotional regulation, abstract thought, and long-term planning, among other functions. It continues developing well into our twenties. The flighty impulses of our amygdala often override the PFC. A fully developed PFC later in life helps check impulses and overrides risk-taking behaviors. Although more resilient to change than later life stages when the brain develops connections more slowly, developing brains are more sensitive to stress and lack of sleep.

College applications take away from opportunities for a good night's sleep, compounded by early school start times and homework from full course loads that often don't align with the typical teen's circadian rhythms. Society expects teenagers to adapt to the modern adult world before their brains are ready. And that's not even considering the whirlwind of hormones circulating during the teenage years that further complicate living with balance. Children who grow up in poverty or abusive families subject to adverse life experiences degrade their capacity to cope and mature.

Ambitious teenagers from affluent families often experience high levels of persistent psychological stress. Neuroscientist Daniel Levitin in *The Changing Mind* traces our modern conception of stress to the 1960s, coincident with the beginning of the college admissions madness. Stress is "the psychological tension we feel from *anticipating* adverse events, and the biological correlates of them (emphasis mine)." Applying to college is rife with anticipating all the things that may go wrong.

Levitin observes that our various biological systems aim for homeostasis. The body adjusts blood sugar levels, heart rate, core body temperature, blood pressure, and so on to avoid *allostasis*. Painful or unpredictable situations trigger an allostatic response that disrupts our body's equilibrium. He identifies two main types of stress hormones, catecholamines and glucocorticoids. We call these hormones colloquially our fight-flight-freeze system.

When our environment consistently triggers these stress hormone releases, it destabilizes our insulin, glucose, lipid levels, and neurotransmitters. Destabilized hormonal systems impair our immune, digestive, and reproductive systems in addition to our cardiac and mental health. Levitin notes that prolonged high allostatic loads lead to mood swings, irrational or self-destructive behavior, and an increased likelihood of a host of chronic illnesses. Students living in poverty or who experience adverse life circumstances are even more at risk for suffering from chronic stress and the attendant antisocial behavior. Remember, you never know what battles your classmates might be fighting at home.

College admissions is perfectly suited to hijacking our lower-level amygdala and limbic system emotional centers that override PFC's higher-order logical reasoning systems. Many students feel an increased allostatic load that knocks the body and mind out of equilibrium. In response, they seek out more information to alleviate their stress, often unsuccessfully.

Levitin notes that our brains crave certainty. The **information paradox** is our tendency to consume more information and admissions statistics to satiate the need to clarify uncertainties, yet more information often produces less genuine knowledge. Overconsumption of information leads to second-guessing. A classic example is trying to estimate admissions chances based on Naviance Scatterplots. Information bias pressures people into asking the same questions repeatedly; they fail to realize more information isn't going to address their anxiety. I remind myself that the worried parent's amygdala is motivating their latest 2 a.m. emails inquiring if their daughter will gain admission. Their cortisol stress hormones are kicking into overdrive, no doubt compounded by their lack of sleep and other anxiety sources.

Identifying the biological correlations of stress and anxiety helps reframe the problem as less about personal or character failures. Levitin refers to hormones as "the hidden strings that pull our bodies," but your mindset isn't entirely outside your control. Becoming aware of and having the frameworks to describe stressful emotions is the first step toward reclaiming power of your life. Acknowledging that there are many layers of consciousness responsible for your emotional states might help untangle why a particular Reddit post or Instagram story triggers unpleasant feelings.

Dalio's *Principles* is worth reading in full because he provides practical tips and references for choosing your habits well and learning to harness the power of your subconscious, lower-level neurological systems outside the scope of this book. His formula "pain + reflection = progress" represents the only constructive calculation for reframing the college admissions madness. Reflection is the opposite of rumination or brooding. Locking yourself in your room and refusing to talk to anyone may feel good, but it isn't healthy or helpful. Experiencing at least some college application pain is unavoidable. Dwelling on pain gets to the roots of suffering. Stress provides opportunities for developing resiliency, as the Stoics instruct.

Levitin concludes with the same recommendations that I practice in my daily life: exercise, practice good sleep hygiene,[64] listen to music, spend time in nature, have a supportive social network, meditate, develop hobbies for their own sake, or seek Cognitive Behavioral Therapy (CBT) if you cannot manage your anxieties alone.

He also warns that "not all social support is healthy. Talking to a friend who helps you to catastrophize, obsess, and co-ruminate increases stress hormones." The same goes for posting on Reddit or other social media channels that reinforce the "amygdala-cortisol-negative emotions-information seeking" feedback loop. Your parents and teachers are correct when they advise maintaining positive relationships and deflecting unnourishing friendships. Maintaining good habits and healthy relationships is a lifetime's journey; it is never too early or late to start from scratch or begin again.

4.2 Less-obvious anxiety sources

I'm continually reminding students (and particularly parents) that everything is going to be okay. Let's set aside typical sources of stress around course scheduling, preparing for standardized exams, applying for summer programs, and building the resume prior to applying. Consider a few non-obvious but common examples *after* finishing their essay drafts and applications that I confront each week of how stress manifests itself into counterproductive behavior.

Students break already-polished essays by "trying to make better" something that didn't need changing. Their essays become a convenient punching bag to project their uneasiness. If they can just find that perfect semicolon placement, their emotional brain reasons, then it will *finally be complete*. No college essay or any piece of writing will ever be perfect. Perfectionist writing tendencies are an extension of a fear of not meeting society's impossibly high expectations.

Students often continue reinserting unrealistic colleges onto their list last-minute, a practice I call **application creep**. They succumb to their parents' pressure, whose family friends post online and gossip about where their child is applying. In his landmark book *The Paradox of Choice* (2004), Barry Schwartz argues that having as many as 4,000 colleges and university options produces the counterintuitive effect of making us miserable. Access to so many choices produces anxiety and suffering because applicants want to find the perfect fit and fear missing out if they choose incorrectly. Because students are often unable to limit their search to four or five schools, some apply to 20 or 30 under the mistaken assumption that more options will make them happier.

After students submit their applications, they stress even more because the decisions are now entirely outside of their control. There is no action they can take to "improve their chances," and some may be inclined to email their admissions counselors obsessively. Students refresh their emails and application portals, reread and scrutinize already-submitted essays, and sift through hundreds of daily posts of other stressed-out students in online communities such as Reddit's Applying to College (A2C) or College Confidential (CC).

A recent A2C thread reads, "I stressed about not receiving an interview from Yale. Now, I'm even more worried that they've offered me one." Two other A2C posts plucked at random today capture the irrationalities of worries translating into time management inefficiencies. "When you check A2C and realize you've seen all of the hot posts already so you just sorta scroll through everything from today mindlessly" and "A2Cers be like 'I'm so stressed and have no time to write these essays' but then spent thirty minutes a day checking up what's up on A2C."

Check the front page of A2C on any given day of the year, and you'll see dozens of the same kinds of worried posts, albeit with different targets. Social media more generally amplifies the stress and accelerates limitless desires to consume information. More distractions also mean less time to get actual work done. Living by Epictetus's advice "to keep company only with people who uplift you, whose presence calls forth your best" is considerably more difficult in our disconnected and anonymous digital age. Following the wisdom of "surrounding yourself with a positive peer group" is less accessible nowadays than when your parents and grandparents were growing up.

Once all decisions are released, you might think April and May would provide some reprieve, but no. Anxious students worry that a C in AP Calculus AB will result in a university rescinding their offer. One student emailed me after already gaining admission to their first choice three months prior. They stressed whether the program would revoke their offer due to a typo on their resume's work section. Purgatories such as waitlists, deferrals, appeals, and "letters of continuing interest" drag out the process that exclusively serves university needs, which I discuss in chapter 8.2. According to NACAC's 2019 State of College Admissions, 80 percent of applicants nationwide won't gain admission via waitlists.[65]

College admissions is a factory for producing confusion and suffering, a predictably repeating cycle that not even a global pandemic can slow. It's an insidious system perfectly tailored to expose flaws and open wounds, especially for perfectionists, risk-averse life planners, and micromanagers terrified of uncertainty. The issues that affluent families confront seem less about college literacy and cultivating a college-going atmosphere, absent in many low-income and rural schools where I used to visit. Instead, their issues are almost entirely psychological, with a secondary concern about their child composing the highest stakes essays they may ever write.

Students and families know many best college application practices already because they've received coaching at school or have read one of the thousands of "come on, your applications won't be so bad" books and blog posts. They're well prepared for practical and logistical questions about taking the SAT or registering for campus visits, yet their emotional and anxiety centers overwhelm higher-order rational thinking.

When I share reasonable advice, they—or the worry centers in their brain—often promptly ignore it. They wonder: Do I have enough volunteering hours? Am I applying to the "right" major? What happens if every university rejects me? Will my essays ever be good enough? What can I do to add to my resume?

What students believe will alleviate their suffering—receiving an interview or even gaining admission to their dream school—produces another cycle of worry about something in the future. One of my most well-adjusted clients, who sees through the madness and has a genuine thirst for learning, wrote to me: "With the interview coming soon and Yale's decision coming back on December 15th, my anxiety has increased. I'm prepared for the absolutely probable denial of admission, but I am nonetheless hopeful and pray at least twice a day to get in."

Admitted students receive their lackluster financial aid packages and stress whether they'll be rescinded for making a B or two. They second-guess whether they should have applied to higher-tier schools that their classmates are bragging about on social media. Some report problems finding future roommates after interviewing many prospects. Students have a Fear of Missing Out (FOMO) for enrolling at one university rather than another, doubly so if they opt for community college. YouTube "admissions decision reaction" videos intensify envy from students who didn't gain admission. Epictetus may have lived almost two millennia ago, but his wisdom applies equally today.

> "Most of what passes for legitimate entertainment is inferior or foolish and only caters to or exploits people's weaknesses. Avoid being one of the mob who indulges in such pastimes. Your life is too short and you have important things to do. Be discriminating about what images and ideas you permit into your mind. If you yourself don't choose what thoughts and images you expose yourself to, someone else will, and their motives may not be the highest."

That "someone else" is YouTube and social media algorithms that seek to cause outrage and inflame insecurities to keep you watching more.

After enrolling, students' worries shift to making A's, changing their majors or university, getting their preferred classes, gaining leadership positions, securing internships, graduate school and fellowship applications, and job interviews. Harvard's most selective student organizations, such as Harvard College Consulting Group or the Crimson Key Society, admit fewer than one in eight of their applicants.[66]

The metrics and targets change after high school in part because the questions asked by your teachers, parents, and friends also change. "What's your top school?" turns into "where are you applying to intern?" Before you've finished your internship, an academic advisor asks about your graduate school or fellowship plans following graduation.

Our society always asks *what's next* rather than *what's right now*. Alan Watts writes in his 1951 book *The Wisdom of Insecurity: A Message for an Age of Anxiety*, "If happiness always depends on something expected in the future, we are chasing a will-o'-the-wisp that ever eludes our grasp."

Schools universally require Physical Education classes, while none from elementary through to medical school require or even offer Emotional Education classes that teach mindfulness or Cognitive Behavioral Therapy techniques. People of all ages lack the vocabularies and coping techniques to identify when suffering arises. The cycle continues *ad infinitum* until a midlife crisis, corporate burnout, or some other post-college catastrophe forces someone to take a step back and reconsider the world and their place in it. Many people go their entire lives without breaking the circle.

Living and traveling abroad introduces me to hundreds of people who chose to exit this system to cope with the crushing pressures of twenty-first-century living. I meet the investment bankers, management consultants, marketing executives, doctors, and lawyers in their thirties and forties wandering the planet looking for their life's purpose. They, presumably, had many of the same dreams when they were teenagers, only for them to be brushed aside. Or they realize their childhood dreams resemble nightmares in adulthood. Many wandering burnouts eventually return home because creating a sustainable, balanced alternative is even more challenging than thriving under the weight of our overworked, sleep-deprived status quo. I applaud people for trying to live even a little bit differently and never fault someone for packing their bags and returning home.

4.3 Life and death decisions

TW: Suicide. If you or anyone you know is considering suicide, The National Suicide Prevention Lifeline is a free, confidential 24-7 service that can provide people in suicidal crisis or emotional distress, or those around them, with support, information and local resources. 1-800-273-TALK (8255).

For some, the pressure for excellence is a matter of life and death. One Redditor shared about their suicide attempt following rejections to each of their universities on Ivy Day, April 1, the deadline for universities to release their decisions.[67] Defining yourself by your admissions outcomes signals a breakdown in what matters most. French sociologist Emile Durkheim coined the term _anomie_ to describe "a condition of instability resulting from a breakdown of standards and values or from a lack of purpose or ideals." Since 2010, more American teenagers have died each year from suicide than homicide. More teens have died by suicide since 2018 than at any period in American history.[68] Suicide is the second leading cause of death for people aged 15–19, behind traffic accidents.[69]

In late 2015, Hanna Rosin with the _Atlantic_ sounded the alarm that something is wrong at highly competitive high schools. In her article "Silicon Valley Suicides," she investigates, "Why are so many kids with bright prospects killing themselves in Palo Alto?"[70]

Her story follows Palo Alto's Henry M. Gunn High School, which sends around twenty seniors to Stanford each year. It went viral, leading to a documentary two years later, *The Edge of Success*. Reading her piece reminds me of the Fallout Boy song "The Kids Aren't Alright," released around the same time, which captures feelings of hopelessness and loneliness, what Durkheim calls anomie.

Rosin writes:

> "Today Gunn is like countless other high-achieving high schools in countless other affluent communities—New York; Washington, D.C.; Dallas; Greenwich, Connecticut; Seattle; Los Angeles—only more so. It is an extreme distillation of what parents in the meritocratic elite expect from a school. The opportunities are limitless and the competition is tough, and the pleasant chatter among the parents concerns chances for enrichment."

In addition to the extreme pressures at school, Rosin raises a paradox in an earlier *Atlantic* article, "The Overprotected Kid." She wonders how, despite parents working longer hours than the previous generation, they're spending *more* time with their kids and not less.[71] The quantity of time spent micromanaging their children as "projects" comes at the expense of quality bonding. "It seems as if children don't get the space to grow up at all; they just become adept at mimicking the habits of adulthood…. they can talk and think like them, but they never build up the confidence to be truly independent and self-reliant." Parents are shocked when their children who seem happy report suicide ideation or other pathologies due to intense pressures to perform without any obvious ways to alleviate their workloads or society's expectations.

Rosin follows two "suicide clusters" at Gunn High School in the late 2000s and early 2010s. Each year, the nation experiences around five suicide clusters defined as "multiple deaths in close succession and proximity." She writes: "Starting in the spring of 2009 and stretching over nine months, three Gunn students, one incoming freshman, and one recent graduate had put themselves in front of an oncoming Caltrain. Another recent graduate had hung himself." The suicide rate for Palo Alto's two high schools is four to five times the national average. She adds, "Twelve percent of Palo Alto high-school students surveyed in the 2013–14 school year reported having seriously contemplated suicide in the past 12 months."

Gunn administrators and guidance counselors considered that suicide could be contagious, a finding supported by subsequent research. Multiple suicides in a community normalize it as an option and decrease the stigma around taking one's life.

Five years after the initial cluster, five students committed suicide within close succession of one another, producing a crisis within the community between educators, students, and parents. Unspoken taboos about race, gender, and mental health came to the forefront. "As the year unfolded, people with intimate knowledge of suicide—unwanted, indelible—began to speak up more." Teenage suicide remains an intractable problem, especially in America's most affluent communities. Despite "marshall[ing] legions of experts…the link between teenage alienation and the decision to die never much clarified."

Three years later, Scott Jaschik writes in *Inside Higher Ed* about the suicide of a sixteen-year-old student at Orange Country's Newport Harbor High. A breakdown of ideals heightens feelings of anomie among thousands of teenagers who question the point of it all. The student wrote in one of his last notes:

> "One slipup makes a kid feel like the smallest person in the world. You are looked at as a loser if you don't go to college or if you get a certain GPA or test score. All anyone talks about is how great they are or how great their kid is…It's all about how great I am. It's never about the other kid. The kid who maybe does not play a sport, have a 4.0 GPA, but displays great character… So much pressure is placed on the students to do well that I couldn't do it anymore…"[72]

An epidemic of clinical depression and suicide ideation places an additional burden on students who wonder whether and how they should discuss their struggles. If universities want students to return for their sophomore year and graduate in four years, at-risk students ask themselves: "Would they want to accept someone like me who is at a higher risk for not finishing? What if I seem like a burden on my classmates or on their healthcare resources?" I don't have satisfactory answers other than for students to honestly share their feelings and experiences in their essays if they are struggling. It is better to err on the side of disclosure rather than omission.

If it were truly the case that achieving your admissions goals alleviates future suffering, why are rates of mental illness and suicide on college campuses increasing? Researchers in the 2007–2017 Healthy Minds Study surveyed more than 155,000 students from 196 universities. They report that, although stigmas around mental illness are decreasing and a higher proportion of students seek help, mental illness is an epidemic on college campuses. "The proportion of students with a diagnosed mental health condition increased from 21.9 percent in 2007 to 35.5

percent in 2016–2017.... We also found that suicidal ideation steadily increased over the past decade, from 5.8 percent in 2007 to 10.8 percent in 2016–2017."[73] Ivy League universities report similar trends. Unless someone provides robust evidence to the contrary, I'm confident concluding that the average Ivy League undergraduate isn't significantly more or less happy than their peers at public or less-selective private universities.

When students from high schools such as Gunn lament the hypercompetitive landscape while simultaneously viewing admission to their dream school as a panacea, I challenge them. What kinds of students do you think pass through the admissions gatekeepers and enroll at top-20 universities? I tell them to consider the most intense students from their high school. Elite universities are largely composed of classmates like them, except from a selection pool of competitive high schools worldwide. Highly selective admissions processes filter precisely for your most neurotic and nakedly ambitious classmates. It's guaranteed that, even if you're the smartest or most accomplished person anyone in your community knows in living memory, you'll be one of many brilliant students in your eventual college classes.

Stanford Duck Syndrome describes the pressures that elite university students feel to appear calm and effortless while struggling underneath the surface. Just as ducks seem tranquil on the water's surface, their feet churn ceaselessly below. Stanford undergraduate Tiger Sun raises concerns in a *Stanford Daily* article "Duck Syndrome and a Culture of Misery."[74] He cites a "workaholic" mentality with a "grind or die" culture that values excellence and effortlessness above all else.

> "Seeing people around you effortlessly glide through their lives, acing exams, landing internships and turning up at parties while you feebly trudge through your four p-sets

and three projects on your nightly four hours of sleep can be difficult.... Sometimes, I wonder if students here are genuinely happy. We put on a brave face and a wide smile when we go to our classes and see our friends, but on the inside, the pressure is slowly tearing us apart.... It's not like this is a conscious decision to be miserable, but sometimes it feels as if taking care of our own health is a guilty pleasure. I talked to someone who said that they felt almost sinful for sleeping in one day. We subliminally equate feeling burned out to being a good student."

The "Stanford University Places I've Cried" (SUPIC) closed Facebook group includes 2,500 members. Dark humor memes and serious posts help students cope and share self-care tips. Moreover, students attending elite colleges might be more inclined toward clinical pathologies, especially if they have a mental illness history.

My former partner Julia Lurie challenges the culture of silence around discussing mental health and stigmas about accessing resources while attending Yale in 2011. She wrote in the Huffington Post:[75]

"[Yalies'] perfectionism about our academic and professional lives has worked its way into our personal lives; we are not only supposed to have attractive resumes and transcripts, but we're also supposed to be social, happy, and relaxed. We are supposed to maintain an image of control, when in reality, none of us are always in control. We are human, and in the long run, we will all be much happier and healthier if we can let our guards down and transform our culture of silence into a culture of honesty."

Universities have gotten better over the years at decreasing stigmas and providing resources. Still, the core pressures within society remain and have accelerated in the decade since she penned that piece. A prestige-minded college applicant might argue that the point of college isn't to maximize happiness or even to be happy at all but to secure a lucrative job or have wider future opportunities. Everyone knows, they contend, that elite universities are pathways to success. An elite degree is worth whatever costs to their health because they're securing their future happiness at the expense of their present suffering. Thousands of students make this Faustian bargain each year when they enter elite university pressure cookers. Many enrolling students suspect deep-down that the environment may not be nourishing for their well-being.

I'm skeptical of these suffer-now-for-happiness-later claims for philosophical and practical reasons. Alan Watts writes, "So many people of wealth understand much more about making and saving money than about using and enjoying it. They fail to live because they are always preparing to live." Later, he summarizes the illusion of maximizing wealth equating to happiness: "A person who is trying to eat money is always hungry."

I'm troubled by the recent death of nine-figures-net-worth Zappos Founder Tony Hsieh. He was, by all accounts, an immigrant dream story and visionary entrepreneur. In 2010, Hsieh wrote the book *Delivering Happiness: A Path to Profits, Passion and Purpose*. In hindsight, the title is tragically ironic because his death came in part due to increasing isolation from genuine friends, unchecked drug and alcohol addictions, and extreme "body hacking" techniques popular in Silicon Valley. The immediate cause of his death was an accidental fire, but he died because of an utter lack of purpose and meaning in life.

I cried the day that one of my favorite authors Anthony Bourdain died by suicide following a lifetime struggle with substance addictions. I set aside some of my Balinese *masak padang* and poured out some Bintang beer. His is the only celebrity death that made me grieve or that still upsets me to think or write about.

Kitchen Confidential will always be one of my top-ten all-time favorite books because it makes me feel so inadequate that I can ever taste, smell, or write with his depth and precision. His willingness to write what other food industry professionals couldn't or wouldn't, and his unapologetic style, inspires me to write the book you're reading. He found such profound joy in the world, yet his easy-going persona disguised his demons.

I ordered his coffee table book capturing scenes from his popular television shows, *No Reservations* and *Parts Unknown*. I opened it once and completely broke down. If my hero, who seemed to have it all, succumbed to life's struggles, what hope do I, or any of us, have? I never opened it again and gave it away. Alan Watts, who writes so eloquently about meaning and finding purpose through grounded spiritual practices, divorced three times and died prematurely due to alcoholism.

Suicide is the second leading cause of death for American teenagers. My prescriptions for viewing life stoically might be brushed aside as unrealistic or yet another thing to add to the overgrowing list of to-dos. But what choice do we have other than to struggle to maintain our sanity against the madness of our late-stage, increasingly unequal global capitalist world? Take back your power and sense of control siphoned away by society's expectations and the college admissions madness.

The odds are stacked heavily against you to live with moderation and get a consistent peaceful night's sleep, but life is still worth the struggle. Epictetus warns, "No person is free who is not master of himself.... The more we value things outside of our control, the less control we have." Being creative, having curiosity about the world, and developing meaningful relationships give me reasons to wake each day. French existentialist Albert Camus sums up perfectly in the *Myth of Sisyphus* that "there is scarcely any passion without struggle."

If striving for admission to elite universities is almost guaranteed to cause suffering, and if you probably won't be much happier after you arrive at your dream school, what's the point of it all?

Epictetus instructs that meaning and happiness won't be found when you depend on the admiration of others. He cautions that "there is no strength in it. Personal merit cannot be derived from an external source."

But it's hard!

Epictetus agrees. "Everyone's life is a war, long and various." Life is a struggle, and it won't get any easier as you age. If anything, attaining success, wealth, and power may make you miserable or perhaps suicidal. The only choice is to make efforts to understand yourself, identify and improve upon your flaws, and step outside of yourself to see if your anxieties and worries have a reasonable basis.

Every day, I'm grateful I'm not a teenager applying to college or parents raising a child. I don't envy your positions. Although my formal high school education was mostly worthless in a community where few "get out," I'm grateful I had a relatively normal childhood free from the adulthood stresses that college admissions imposes. I'm sympathetic to Watts's pessimism about wondering whether society will ever break free from repeating cycles of history, or in this case, the college admissions system.

Remarkably, he wrote the following seventy years ago: "There are few grounds for hoping that, in any immediate future, there will be any recovery of social sanity. It would seem that the vicious circle must become yet more intolerable, more blatantly and desperately circular before any large numbers of human beings awaken to the tragic trick which they are playing on themselves." If a global pandemic isn't enough to shake the collective consciousness of American society or deter still-record numbers of college applications, I don't think anything will. In our broken education system, it takes heroic individual efforts to navigate the madness without stepping on any landmines.

I'm highly critical of online college admissions forums such as Reddit's Applying to College (A2C). However, I still subscribe to them because, occasionally, there are incredibly thought-provoking and self-aware posts worth broadcasting.

Redditor Injustice_510 published a thread in January 2021, "I'll be dying soon."[76] They introduced themselves as an academically perfect student "that most parents would be proud to have." They were diagnosed with terminal leukemia and given three months to live. The outpouring of support from hundreds of users renewed my faith somewhat in the power of online communities to rise to difficult occasions.

Injustice_510 wondered what the point of it all was. They wrote, "All everyone ever knew about me were my academic statistics. No one ever realized the pain, loneliness, and depression I went through to get to where I was. Day in and day out, I went through the same routine of waking up, going to school, doing my work, going to work, scrolling the internet, and going to bed."

They share the wisdom that we could all make better efforts to follow. I've reproduced their thoughts in full, with their permission.

> "I always wished I could turn back the clock and start my life over again, but with all the memories intact. But I never wanted to die. Never. I've known about it for a month or so, and all I could do in that time was cry. I cried that I would

lose my life at such a young age. I cried that I would have to say goodbye to my younger brother without ever seeing him grow up. I cried that I could never understand how it feels to fall in love with someone for the first time. I cried that I could never hear my child call me "father" for the first time. I cried and cried until I couldn't cry any longer…

…All you guys out there that are crying and stressing about life, college, and applications. Let me assure you that those are not the only aspects of life. I want you to understand that life is not a simulation that someone can do over and over until they get what they desire. Life is a static flow that gives you no second chances at all. Make the most out of it. Go love someone. Go hang out with friends. Go watch that movie you've wanted to watch. Go tell someone how much they mean to you. Live your life. Don't look down on others. Instead, join with them and prosper. Live your life to the fullest with no regrets, because one day you may not have the opportunity to do so. In retrospect, life and living is a beautiful thing. I feel like I should have given myself room to live and breathe. Maybe things could have ended differently."

Following this uncomfortable and emotionally demanding chapter, let's take a step back and ask: How did we arrive at our current state of college admissions madness? Do things have to be this way? How do countries around the world select their university students?

In the next chapter, I provide an overview of how holistic college admissions came to be and consider alternative admissions systems worldwide. Later, in chapter 7, we will return to this discussion of cognitive distortions, mistakes to avoid, and building a reasonable college list.

5. Historical Perspectives and Admissions Systems Abroad

Holistic college admissions is not a new phenomenon. It emerged as part of the broader civil rights movement to extend educational resources to more people. Examining newspaper and academic journal articles about college admissions from the 1950s and '60s mirrors our current college application landscape today. What's changed is less about *how* elite universities make their decisions and more about the college admissions madness's magnitude and scope.

Elite universities half a century ago had an impossible task, just like today. Consider the September 1968 essay by John R. Reitz in *The School Counselor*.[77] He wrote: "The standard criteria of class standing, board scores, significant activities, and recommendations are no longer sufficient to differentiate between the one, two, or three thousand or more applicants who look alike on paper." Add a zero or two to those numbers, and you arrive at today's competitive admissions landscape.

After admitting outstanding and rejecting poor academic students without further consideration, how do universities distribute a small number of spaces for the 50–75 percent or so of applicants in between who have roughly the same academics?

Reitz cites an example of a New England–area university that needed to review 3,500 applications for 500 spaces. Divvying up limited spaces among many highly qualified applicants is the same problem MIT encounters today when they know they must reject 90 percent of applicants with near-perfect SAT math scores.

Reitz describes an admissions review process that parallels contemporary holistic review. He cites a new "fifth dimension" introduced into the college application process. The subjective discretion of admissions reviewers plays a significant role in deciding who gets in or not. "Admissions reviewers, when asked what they were looking for in this group, will invariably pause, reflect, then say something to the effect that they would like to see some strength which will assure them of a class that is alive, ambitious, curious, and interesting."

When Reitz interviewed counselors to explain a given outcome, they boiled it down to a "hunch." Decisions result from "a combination of several nebulous factors." What Reitz calls this subjective and arbitrary "fifth dimension," we call holistic review. Admissions counselors then and now, unsurprisingly, feel they're **better-than-average** at discerning one's character and selecting for talented students. An essay written six years prior in the same journal by Rick F. Yacone raises the alarm that "the ever-increasing number of students applying to college reduces the time factor in judging adequately the candidates for admission."[78] Holistic review was largely hocus pocus in its inception, and it has remained mostly bullshit into the present, as I unpack in the next chapter.

The story of selective college admissions begins, unsurprisingly, with Harvard. John Harvard founded his namesake university in 1636 to train male pilgrims in the clergy. Into the 1800s, there were few, if any, academic requirements. Admission depended on birthright. Getting in through one's merit wasn't possible or even conceivable for a society where few were literate or high school educated. In an 1894 survey of early admissions practices, Franklin Dexter noted that, in addition to courses largely reserved for society's most privileged, students were selected based on their father's profession and standing in the fledgling Massachusetts colony.[79]

Class distinctions weren't cut and dried. "Considerations of ancestral distinction, of family estate, of paternal position, and the like, entered into each case in ever-varying combinations." After identifying several conflicting cases that defy any standard rules, Yale, he notes, had far fewer complicating factors or instances where some students inexplicably gained admission while others didn't.

After arriving on campus, Harvard and Yale students were sorted into a hierarchy that afforded those at the top higher standing and access to the most influential friends. Students sat in arranged places during chapel or "recitations in the Commons" so everyone knew each other's standing. Franklin observes that there was "a much more formal behavior of pupils towards teachers than later generations would have relished." Naturally, older students teased or bullied younger ones. Every student remained subordinate to the teachers and ministers running the university. By the 1760s, Harvard and Yale had mostly abandoned the ranking and sorting system, not coincidental with the rise of America's revolt against the British Crown and landed aristocracies.

Throughout the 1800s, there was little uniformity in admission standards among an increasingly large number of colleges and universities, except for one's ability to pay. Trinity College (CT) Professor Jack Dougherty suggests in "Accepted: The Evolution of College Admission Requirements" that rapid and dramatic changes in America following independence led to increased demands for more higher education options and degree offerings beyond divinity and medicine.

Universities followed Harvard's lead in requiring Greek and Latin. Admissions requirements began changing in the mid-nineteenth century with the inclusion of geometry, algebra, and history. After the required subjects expanded to eight at the end of the nineteenth century, even fewer students could pass through university gatekeepers. Dougherty writes,

"After 1870, colleges were updating and adding requirements, which can be assumed to be the foundation of requirements today. As the subject English became more prominent in admission requirements, Harvard decided to require a short essay based on a particular prompt each year which is likely the foundation of the various essay prompts the majority of colleges still use. The continuous development in admission requirements is directly correlated with the demand for higher education."[80]

Throughout the 1800s, almost any graduate attending a college-preparation academy could gain admission. New England elite preparatory schools were established in conjunction with colonial-era universities to serve as pipelines to universities. Compared with college prep educations, nineteenth-century public high schools provided a practical, rudimentary education for students who wouldn't continue their studies. Of course, significantly fewer students received any secondary education or could read and write, so the pool of potential college students was much smaller than in the twentieth century.

The beginning of the twentieth century saw a shift toward standardizations of, and more access to, college-preparatory curriculum. The Association of American Universities (AAU) was formed to promote academic research. A collection of twelve leading universities founded The College Board in 1900 to issue college entrance exams covering English, French, History, and Chemistry. Harvard dropped their requirement for Greek and Latin to attract public school students.

Admissions spaces were theoretically open to anyone who passed the College Examination Entrance Board exam (CEEB). Dougherty notes that colleges struggled to assess and weigh academic skills in math and writing versus soft skills such as charisma, leadership, and character—a dilemma that persists today. Women attended women's colleges, and white Protestant men attended private colleges. Catholics enrolled at Jesuit colleges, public school students went to state institutions, and African Americans attended Historically Black Colleges and Universities (HBCUs).

Many campuses tried to limit or exclude entirely Jewish students through the first half of the twentieth century. Harvard's President Lowell, concerned with the number of Jews arriving on campus in the 1920s, shifted admissions qualifications away from an exclusive focus on academics and toward an early form of "holistic review."

The *New York Times* reports comments by Lowell on January 16, 1924, that, given the absolute limit of 2,000 enrolling freshmen, which remains into the present, "In order to be quite fair, we give the individual applicant a personal conference" that does not depend exclusively on GPA.[81] Yale and Princeton developed Harvard's techniques and introduced essay and interview requirements.

The three universities argued in the courts and public that they can practice institutional discretion about who to admit and exclude applicants based on subjective criteria. Holistic review is rooted in a history of anti-Semitism and exclusion rather than today's promise of inclusion and diversity. Discrimination against Jewish students a century ago fuels suspicions today by Asian and Asian American applicants.

The early 1900s also sees the first marketing and brochure materials from universities such as U Penn and U Chicago advertising their offerings. In 1919, Columbia University invented the first modern college application. In addition to submitting the CEEB scores, applicants completed an eight-page form including information such as their mother's maiden name and religious affiliation. All applicants submitted a photograph.

The National Association of College Admissions Counseling (NACAC) was formed in 1937, ushering in the first college admissions counselors. College Board administered administrated the first SAT in 1926 as a supposedly objective measure of students' academic abilities. By 1939, all Ivy League schools required the SAT. The University of California was the first public university to implement the SAT in 1952.

World War II marked a departure from explicit admissions standards based on high school and social class and toward a more meritocratic system. Harvard President James B. Conant anticipated in the *Atlantic* in May 1943 that the return home of soldiers fighting overseas offered opportunities for transformation in higher education and society in general.[82] He called for a "radical" alternative to conservatism and liberalism that "will favor public education, truly universal educational opportunity at every level."

He argued that returning GIs should gain access to future studies based on their merit and grit rather than "accidents of geography or birth." Calls for equality of opportunity, which wouldn't raise an eyebrow today, were indeed revolutionary in the 1940s because they called into question the entire foundation of American society.

The 1945 GI Bill guaranteed to fund military veterans wishing to pursue a college education. Cold War pressures and the Soviet Union's *Sputnik* in the 1950s led to significant increases in funding for what we now call Science, Technology, Engineering, and Mathematics (STEM). Dougherty writes about enrollment priorities following World War II: "The once white Protestant population that dominated schools like Yale would decline because college presidents wanted to expand their student body to a group beyond this white protestant upper class."[83]

Even though college admissions through the 1950s appear to be more accessible for white applicants from the lower social classes, most admitted students to Harvard, Princeton, and Yale came from a dozen elite private college preparatory schools. Objective measures such as the CEEB and SAT offered a façade of a meritocracy based on talent. In reality, a student's college prospects largely depended on their birthright and whichever private school they attended, which isn't much different in practice from today's elite college admissions landscape.

Until the late 1950s, admissions requirements remained mostly uniform based on a high school diploma, recommendations, SAT/CEEB scores, and an interview. The 1960s marks the birth of the college admissions madness. It begins at a period in American history where substantially more people demanded a college education from increasingly diverse backgrounds.

The civil rights movement broke down educational barriers at all levels of society. Universities began enrolling their first black graduates. Legislation such as President Johnson's Higher Education Act and the Pell Grant expanded access to students from low- and middle-income backgrounds. Educators and critics began questioning racial bias in the SAT and whether a single exam can accurately forecast a student's future achievement. Former Director of New York's Millbrook school writes in a letter to the *New York Times* editor on May 24, 1960, that "A 17- or 18-year-old is a complex organism, capable of growth or stagnation, of creative or unimaginative thinking.... The boy or girl with the highest test score does not always follow the predicted path in life."[84]

Admissions changes away from solely considering grades and test scores opened the door for genuine considerations of environmental or nonacademic character traits. The critical difference from the 1960s to today is that there were enough spaces to go around, and although competitive, the admissions process wasn't exceptionally so. Harvard admitted 20 percent of their 6,700 applicants in 1965. They received 57,000 applications in 2021.

The early 1960s also marked the first time when Ivy League universities considered geography. Institutions wanted a broader representation of students beyond the Northeast. An expanding admissions landscape also coincides with the lowest income inequality levels and highest rates of social mobility in modern American history.

The American Jewish Committee praised the liberalization of admissions policies in the 1950s and '60s as a step toward a rejection of anti-Semitism.[85] Rhetoric about holistic admissions in the 1920s intended to exclude Jewish students reversed into sincere efforts at inclusion and access for students from diverse backgrounds. One of the college admissions story's ironies is the most exclusive and inaccessible historically elite universities became early champions for inclusion and education reform.

However, their good intentions to include students produced unintended consequences. With more students attending college than ever, especially from historically excluded populations or who received inadequate high school educations, spaces at elite universities became fiercely competitive in the 1960s when the first Baby Boomers began enrolling.

The *New York Times* reported on April 24, 1963, that the eight Ivy League and Seven Sisters campuses received 58,625 applications for a total of 10,658 admitted seniors. "Heartbreak and frustration are inevitable when so many young people compete for so few spaces."[86] Then as now, educators and teachers emphasize that where you go is not who you will become. The article notes that spaces at state universities are becoming increasingly competitive, with fewer universities practicing open enrollment with admission available to anyone who has finished high school, driven in part by increasing numbers of out-of-state applicants.

On April 24, 1965, the *New York Times* reported in the article "College Capacity Held Inadequate" on the American Association of College Registrars and Admissions Officers (AACRAO) National Conference. Admissions officers and registrars from across the country "met in an atmosphere of gloom."[87] Attendees acknowledged that more than 100,000 students who wanted to attend college would not have access. Wisconsin-Madison Dean Dr. Joseph Kaufmann leveled the same criticism in 1965 that I make in these pages. "Instead of ancient goals of university learning…teachers [are] scrambling for grants and fees and often hear inarticulate and irrelevant messages from spokesmen for higher education."[88]

The *New York Times* State universities began expanding their dormitories, teaching positions, and degree offerings to meet the increased demand. Elite campuses also observed record acceptances and enrollment of Jewish and African American students. "Most admissions experts would probably agree that through active recruiting in urban areas and from among disadvantaged and minority groups, the character of the elite student body is gradually changing from that of the archetypal white Anglo-Saxon Protestant to reflect more realistically the mainstream of the nation's culture."[89]

Unsurprisingly, fewer spaces available to society's upper crust produced a backlash. An April 30, 1967 article "Ivy's Admissions Irks Prep Schools" details how administrators at "fashionable

New England Preparatory Schools" complained that more inclusion leads to "a gradual erosion against us. [We] have become victims of the college's search for diversity."[90]

Harvard, Yale, and Princeton admitted nearly two-thirds of applicants for Fall 1967 from public schools, a reversal from previous generations. A teacher at elite Philips Exeter commented that their graduates could simply choose which university they wished to attend, "but those days are over." Families responded with horror when Exeter staff began recommending their children attend "colleges their fathers had never heard of" once spaces in the Ivy League dwindled.

An exclusive New Hampshire prep school, St. Paul's, had sent around 70 percent of their graduates to the Ivy League two decades prior. By the end of the 1960s, they were sending half that many. St. Paul's was part of a broader movement of two dozen other New England schools that formed the organization "A Better Chance." It provided scholarships to working- and middle-class and African American students. Outreach efforts by prep schools founded on exclusion and explicit discrimination seem insincere when headmasters complain that merely a third of their graduates were gaining admission to top schools rather than the majority.

The 1970s also marked the beginning of political discussions and media conversations about which groups of students deserve what admissions spaces. More historically male universities opened their door to female students. Debates over affirmative action coalesced in *Regents of the University of California v. Bakke* (1978) that struck down quotas for underrepresented minorities. Universities and society have ever since grappled with enrolling diverse classes of students without discriminating against individual students based on membership of a racial or ethnic category. I rethink diversity in college admissions in chapter 9.

The Common Application went live in 1976 with participation by 83 members. The original Common App was a duplicate paper form that students mailed or faxed to colleges. Common App adoption increased significantly in 1995 when Harvard joined, resulting in over 800 colleges and universities today. Common App stipulated "holistic review" as a criterion for joining in 2000, which helps explain the proliferation of essay requirements at less-selective universities.

Efforts at standardization and meeting their original intent as "a modest stand against redundancy" fragmented for reasons I discuss later in this chapter. Universities also made concerted efforts to send recruitment officers to high schools across the country. Outreach coincided with branding and marketing campaigns through college fair brochures and unsolicited postcards.

Although elite universities received record applicant numbers, 90 percent of universities' applications remained stagnant or decreased. In the March 31, 1974, *New York Times* article "Colleges Shift to Hard Sell In Recruiting of Students," reporter Evan Jenkins interviews NACAC Assistant Executive Director Charles A. Marshall about increasing competition among middling and lower profile universities for a shrinking pool of students. "The stakes are millions of dollars nationally and, for some schools, survival. Some will not make it…. It's becoming a dog-eat-dog situation."[91]

Regional state universities such as Southern Illinois and technical colleges such as Colorado School of Mines followed America's elite universities. Recruiters hit the road to woo applicants into attending their colleges, often far from home. School districts began hosting college fairs to create "college-going environments." Controversy surrounded the alleged practice of fledgling colleges enlisting independent counselors compensated by bounties for the number of students they recruited.

Less-popular universities waived application fees and hosted elaborate on-campus recruiting events. Universities that couldn't recruit enough students closed their doors, a process that continued through the twenty-first century that has accelerated during the COVID-19 pandemic. Then the same as now, if a student and their family are open minded about where they would like to enroll, many "Colleges That Change Lives" would love to admit and throw scholarship money at you. An obvious way to alleviate admissions anxieties is not to focus exclusively on top-50 universities, but that's easier said than done.

Anxieties among wealthy families about their privileged status atop American society clicked into a higher gear. *New York Times* coverage of "Bloody Monday" for the Fall 1979 admissions cycle in "College Admission: Confronting the Tensions Between Student and Parent" introduced the once-ubiquitous envelope thickness notification. "A fat envelope, which contains all the necessary information regarding registration, means acceptance. A thin one simply announces rejection."[92]

Nowadays, students receive a deluge of email notifications on the afternoon of April 1, Ivy Day. The late 1970s and into the 1980s were when some Ivy League campuses began accepting less than 20 percent of their applicants. Many universities reported 25 percent increases in application numbers year over year. "No longer, these parents know, is wealth or prestige necessarily passed along…. Hence the growing pressure to enter the competitive world through the privileged gateway of the Ivy League."[93]

Reporters in the same article interviewed a Yale child psychiatrist Herbert Sacks. He collaborated on one of the first books examining the college admissions madness, *Hurdles: The Admissions Dilemma in American Higher Education*. Dr. Sacks reports students crumbling under the weight of expectations that draws parallels today.

"They procrastinated over their college applications. They developed symptoms of sleeplessness, chronic weight loss or gain, depression, lassitude. They started staying out later than usual, using the family car without permission, experimenting with drugs or alcohol, often for the first time. Many became deeply involved in a sexual relationship."

Contrast the promiscuous outlets of anxiety and stress of the final batch of Baby Boomers with today's digital native generation that is having less sex, experimenting with fewer drugs and alcohol, and acting out at record low levels. Dr. Sacks reports that parents are significantly more involved with their child's prospects than a decade before. Decrying the obsession over the Ivy League and families closed-minded to other possibilities, it's no surprise to him that tensions erupted over dinner tables when students received their Bloody Monday letters. "As for what can be done to help the situation, Dr. Sacks said he was certain that if families can understand that this crisis is a normal rite of passage, then a major step will have been taken toward diffusing it." Sound familiar?

The college admissions madness accelerated in the 1980s with the arrival of Generation X high school graduates. Whereas in the 1960s and '70s, educators and families worried about too many applicants, administrators began panicking when the supply of high school graduates started declining. Marketing and recruitment efforts increased significantly, resembling today's current climate.

The *New York Times* Education Editor published the first college guidebook, *The Fiske Guide to College*, in 1982. It was more akin to restaurant reviews than the quantitative rankings systems that came afterward, such as the *US News and World Report* Best Colleges in 1983. Universities began scheming to meet metrics that boosted their rankings in a zero-sum race against their peer institutions.

Minority enrollment increased in record numbers, as did the number of students attending college more than a few hours' drive from their home. More public high school students than ever are receiving college degrees, even from elite private universities. Universities that practice legacy admission are questioning or abandoning policies that privilege affluent families. The most notable reform of the past twenty years is "need-blind" universities that admit students regardless of their ability to pay. They promise to cover their financial need with grants that don't require repayment.

Still, inequities persist and are growing—the vast majority of college students come from college-educated upper-class families. Holistic review began as a tool to reject Jewish students. It evolved alongside the civil rights movement to promote genuine inclusion and breaking down historical education barriers. Our contemporary broken meritocracy reverts to a tool of oppression that excludes almost everyone except the savviest and wealthiest applicants.

5.1 Admissions systems abroad

Exploring the history of America's genuinely unique holistic review admissions system makes me curious how other countries worldwide assess their college applicants and distribute spaces at their universities. There is no perfect or fair admissions system, but some are better than others. As far as I can tell, no country places as much or any emphasis on essays, the resume, and intangible qualities integral to American holistic review. Noble intentions to evaluate each student as unique and see them as more than their grades and test scores produce unintended negative consequences.

I'm writing this chapter in part because most of my friends are not American. One upside is that I rarely have to discuss the banalities of work since few non-Americans and even many Americans lack background knowledge of American college admissions. When I'm unable to avoid discussing how students apply to college, they greet my elevator speech about the college admissions madness with disbelief. Outsiders see American college admissions for what it is: absurd. Looking abroad helps put our American admissions madness into perspective and suggests room for improvement. It also offers reasons to be grateful that the situation could be much worse.

I examine South Korea, China, and India to consider what happens if a system weights almost exclusively the results of a single exam. Exploring Brazil's and Malaysia's strict racial and cultural quotas system will make you think differently about America's comparatively less-rigid affirmative action system. Germany, the Netherlands, and Belgium are excellent examples of centralized admissions systems that are open enrollment (and free tuition! Even for non-Europeans!) for most study areas. Finally, I conclude by examining corruption at Russian universities to suggest what America might look like if the Varsity Blues bribery scandal and pay-to-play were the only ways to succeed rather than exceptions to the rule.

Every year, South Korean students aspiring to attend the country's three premier universities—Seoul National University, Korea University, or Yonsei University—must sit for a single eight-hour exam offered once annually, the *suneung*. The exam includes calculus, statistics, English, and philosophy, among others. Because everyone takes the same core subjects, South Korea's education system is highly centralized, with each school using the same textbooks.

The *Atlantic's* Anna Diamond writes in "South Korea's Testing Fixation" that the entire nation essentially comes to a halt on testing day. Parents pray at temples and wait outside the school gates. "Businesses delayed opening to keep traffic off the streets, and planes paused takeoffs during the English-language listening section of the test. For students running late, local police offered taxi services."[94] Students prepare twelve years for the exam. Around 20 percent will retake the exam the following year.

South Korean high school students attend classes an average of 220 days each year, one of the world's highest rates. Starting sophomore year, many take three or four hours of daily after-school tutorials to prepare. Families spend more than three times above average on private tuition than other developed countries to supplement an underfunded public education system. Yale Professor Daniel Markovits cites data that 12 percent of total household expenditures go toward private tuition, "and millionaire after-school tutors have become national celebrities."[95]

South Korea is one of the most popular and well-paying English teaching countries for foreigners in the world. However, friends of mine complain that teaching English in Korea is like "being a human tape recorder." The curriculum offers zero flexibility or creative adaptation. When I meet Koreans abroad, their ability to communicate is usually limited, despite studying English in the classroom for hundreds of hours and acing their college entrance exams. Teaching to the test is one consequence of a high-stakes, if transparent, college examination system.

Education reform critics of over-testing in the United States usually deride the number of exams that American students are subjected to. But Americans have no equivalent of the Korean *suneung*. South Korean students believe with good reason that the results on their exam determine the course for the remainder of their lives. Although there are alternative pathways to lesser universities, their top three are equivalent to the Ivy League. They garner a disproportionate amount of attention.

Michael Seth in *Education Fever* comments that "the fever-pitch obsession with education has been a fixed feature of South Korean society."[96] He cites the "examination mania" (*sihŏm chiok*) and "the nearly universal drive for high-status degrees" as defining the adolescence of many South Koreans.

Prioritizing education and excellence above all else comes with the benefits of performing among the highest on global exams. Pundits often ask, "Why can't American teenagers dominate math and science like students in East Asian countries?" Academic excellence comes at the cost of student well-being and mental health. The National Statistics of Korea commissioned a survey in 2014 that concluded South Korean children are the least happy among 30 developed countries. "More than half of children aged between 15 and 19 who are suicidal give 'academic performance and college entrance' as a reason."[97] Whereas the admissions madness in the United States is mostly contained in affluent suburbs, in South Korea, it's a nationwide obsession that penetrates every household.

Like America's highest achieving students, researcher Liang Choon Wang notes a correlation between South Korea's top students and suicide ideation and attempts.[98] Students have less time for hobbies, extracurriculars, or spending time with friends. Although GPA, and to a much lesser extent extracurriculars, play a role in admissions, one benefit of the *suneung* system is the pathway to their prestigious universities is straightforward. It doesn't have the ambiguities of holistic review. Score better than most all other applicants, and you're in. You don't have the problem of MIT denying an overwhelming majority of perfect SATs. That's easier said than done because competitive applicants need to score in the top 0.5 percent on the *suneung*, *ten times* more selective than Stanford.

Similarly, in the People's Republic of China and India, high-stakes exams are the primary determinant of admission to their most elite universities. In their final year of high school, Chinese students sit for the National College Entrance Examination (NCEE), or *Gaokao*, administered once annually. All applicants wishing to enroll in any college must take the *Gaokao*.

One surprising difference with the Chinese system is the overall acceptance rate has been *increasing* despite a quadrupling of the number of examinations since 1995. The primary reason is the expansion of China's higher education system offering more universities. Eighty percent of applicants who wish to attend college will qualify. However, Peking and Tsinghua Universities are the country's most prestigious, with an admissions rate of less than 1 percent. Because China allots quotas that favor students from tier-one cities such as Shanghai and Beijing, the admissions rate for less geographically favorable regions is less than 0.1 percent.

There are possibilities to receive bonus points for academic Olympiads, sports achievements, and so on, but they're concrete amounts and not subjective considerations of leadership or extracurriculars by admissions reviewers. Still, the *Gaokao* largely determines a student's university options. Unsurprisingly, students' mental health suffers when they prepare fourteen or more hours per day for an exam that largely determines their future.

Indian students wishing to enroll at the most elite university system, the Indian Institutes of Technology (IIT), must take the Joint Entrance Examination—Advanced (JEE-Advanced). No other admissions factors are considered. There are fifteen IIT campuses with approximately 16,000 undergraduate spaces for a country containing more than 1.3 billion people, leaving approximately 4,000 spaces for incoming first-year students. Fifteen million students sit for the first exam, JEE Main. The top 225,000 JEE Main students qualify to sit for the JEE Advanced.

Consequently, less than 1 percent of JEE Main test takers have sufficient credentials to enroll at any IIT campus.

Within IIT, there is a hierarchy of school prestige. Delhi, Madras, and Bombay are the most in-demand. Like in South Korea or SAT prep in the US, India has a multibillion-dollar test prep industry. Because the exam is conducted only in English and Hindi, students speaking other mother tongues have a distinct disadvantage. Only 20 percent of IIT students are women, and that's after implementing a quota system to double female enrollment.

High-stakes exam systems in South Korea, China, and India have the advantage of clear and transparent admissions standards. Every student is acutely aware of which scores are required. However, nationwide exams create a rigid, nationalized curriculum that allows for little creativity or critical thinking, hallmarks of the American system. Ambitious students in high-stakes exam systems are even more miserable than their elite American counterparts. Although American college admissions is deeply flawed, having a decentralized application system that doesn't depend on a single exam helps a larger number of students receive college degrees.

Affirmative action in college admissions looks a lot different in multicultural Brazil and Malaysia. Considerations and constructions of race are culturally dependent, and it often looks dramatically different in non-Western countries.

NPR's *Rough Translation* first podcast episode, "Brazil in Black and White," follows Pedro Attila's story.[99] Pedro is a middle-aged man applying for a prestigious civil service position following a lifetime of underemployment. Thousands of people took an exam, with only a dozen qualifying for a final interview. Except Pedro's interview wasn't a conventional test of skills or seeing if he's a good fit for the position.

A 2014 law established 20 percent of government jobs for black Brazilians to correct inequalities, which isn't dissimilar from the history of race and discrimination in the United States. If an applicant checks the "black" ethnicity box on their application, a panel decides whether an applicant appears sufficiently black to receive one of the quota spaces.

Pedro compares himself to Usher and Cuban-born actor Andy Garcia. He presents his race credentials. "I have a black guy's nose, a black guy's lips but white guy's hair."

Hosts Gregory Warner and Brazilian-born Lulu Garcia-Navarro interviewed other applicants who consulted Wikipedia for skin tone definitions. Others worried if their hair appears too straight. Unlike America's emphasis on one's roots and heritage, in Brazil, "If you look black, you're black. If you look white, you're white."

A plurality of Brazilians are multiracial *pardos*, due to the history of Portuguese colonialism. Following the end of slavery, Brazilian policy tried to limit interracial marriage and "whiten" the population, to little effect. An unintended consequence of the new quota system is that black-appearing applicants didn't check the box. One applicant said, "I knew I was black. But I thought I wouldn't apply via quota because I had a white education."

Host Warner chimes in. "And you know who was checking this box marked black? White people." It was as if a subset of ambitious Brazilian whites suddenly became Rachel Dolezal. She is a white American woman who passed as black and even led a regional chapter of the NAACP before a local reporter interviewed her dad, who confirmed that both of her parents are white. Dolezal spawned a nationwide controversy over cultural appropriation.

Warner flies to Brasilia and meets Mario Theodoro, the architect of the quota policy and panels that determine one's race. They examined a photograph of 51 medical students who all appeared white despite at least 20 percent of them gaining admission by checking "black." A public uproar resulted in the expulsion of 24 students. The panels must adopt a conventional racist mindset that tries to decipher the width of one's nose or texture of their hair suggests their heritage. Pedro's panel decided he was sufficiently black to earn a coveted, life-changing government position.

A comprehensive analysis of race and colonialism in Brazil could fill bookshelves. I raise the example to establish that the same quota and panel system for admission to Brazilian government jobs and spaces at universities is dramatically different from anything in American college admissions history.

Malaysia is an extremely interesting case about what roles race and access to opportunities can play in society. I taught English at a failing public high school in a fishing village called Kampong Raja (the King Village) on the border of the east coast states of Kelantan and Terengganu. This region is known as the Malay/Muslim stronghold of the country. My school was 100 percent Malay/Muslim without a single Indian or Chinese student or teacher. Cities such as Penang, Malacca, and Kuala Lumpur are much more mixed, but in the hinterlands, life remains largely the same as in generations past.

Malaysian students are "streamed" starting in elementary school. High-stakes exams place the best students in the top classes. The second tier of students are grouped together and so on to create a caste hierarchy system. The highest stream in each school is allocated the best teachers. Schools are also rated with the best ones receiving the most resources.

The top elementary students funneled into a single magnet school in my rural district, so the top classes at my school were well below the district-wide magnet's lowest-performing students. Students entering high school in the lowest streams are highly unlikely to advance to the middle or top groups. Only the top two classes in each grade at my school were eligible for advanced math, chemistry, biology, and physics, unlike in the American system where all students take core math and science subjects.

Malaysian students in their final year take a series of high-stakes exams (SPM) required for admission to four-year universities, which is modeled on the British A-Level system. Students who fail SPM have the option to enroll in "Form 6" to receive a year of instruction and attempt the exam again. They also don't receive six-weeks or semester grades in the usual sense, so GPA doesn't play a role in their college admissions.

Malaysia practices a constitutional affirmative action policy, *bumiputra,* that provides extensive advantages for the Malay majority and a small number of indigenous *Orang Asli,* considered the "original peoples." Unlike in Brazil or the US, where affirmative action tries to provide opportunities for historically marginalized minorities, Malaysia's *bumiputra* system privileges the Muslim majority who hold almost all the country's political power.

Malays enjoy admission to universities with lower scores, earn domestic university and study abroad scholarships, and some students attend *bumiputra*-only college classes. Malays also receive discounts on property purchases, lower interest rates on loans and mortgages, and access to more favorable retirement mutual funds. Every Malaysian business must have at least one Malay partner or member on the Board of Directors. Affirmative action in the private sector aims to counteract the historical dominance of the economy by the Chinese, who have settled the peninsula for hundreds of years. Malay-run businesses receive priority for government contracts.

Although the constitution promises to practice religions freely in Malaysia, you can never renounce your faith if you're born a Muslim. Although Malays have access to many benefits, they're also subject to religious laws that punish alcohol consumption, homosexuality, and adultery. Religious police routinely raid clubs and bars in Kuala Lumpur to nab offenders against Islamic morality subject to punishment in *Sharia* courts.

During my time in Malaysia, my best friend was a gay Muslim guy from a Terengganu *kampung* who eventually left Malaysia to find lucrative work in Singapore and Hong Kong. When the police would approach us on a night out, he answered in perfect English that he's Filipino to avoid scrutiny. Understandably, the *bumiputra* policy is highly controversial with Chinese, Indians, progressive liberal Muslims, and non-religious Malays.

Could you imagine if the United States Constitution codified explicit benefits for whites and Native Americans to receive better home insurance rates? It's inconceivable. Most political systems seek to exclude minorities directly, like America's Three-Fifths Compromise, or implicitly by practices such as redlining and gerrymandering. Malaysia doesn't explicitly discriminate against minority populations. Instead, it props up a legal regime highly preferential to the Malay majority.

Brazil and Malaysia are excellent cases demonstrating how conceptions of diversity, fairness, and access to resources vary widely worldwide. An American-centered perspective doesn't begin to capture the complexities of cultural differences. As universities recruit international applicants in record numbers, there is ambiguity about what diversity means in a cross-cultural context. It's especially problematic when elite American universities require students to write about "diversity" or race when these concepts are highly dependent on one's culture, a problem I discuss in chapter 9.1.

Germany practices a federal system where much of the power is allocated to the states, including education. Still, college admissions depends on the nationwide *Abitur* exam that corresponds to the European Qualifications Framework (EQF) that aims to standardize credentials across the European Union. Similar systems are practiced in Belgium and the Netherlands, where bachelor's degrees are free or very inexpensive. Exams are graded on a 15-point scale, and around half of exam takers qualify for a four-year university.

Alternative assessments are available for students who receive inadequate *Abitur* scores. Most programs are open enrollment except for in-demand subjects such as psychology or medicine, which might require a personal statement essay or an interview. Although the grading is the same nationwide, each German state establishes slightly different variations of the exam. For states such as those in former East Germany that are comparatively less wealthy than those in the West, students are at a disadvantage when scored on a nationwide bell curve, not unlike disparities between the American North and South.

The system is more centralized than America's highly fragmented education landscape. However, "a total of 61 percent [of Germans] said they would prefer a centralized system, while 28 percent are in favour of the current system." An overwhelming majority of German students desire a standardized exam with the same questions distributed throughout the country.[100] Nevertheless, Germany has several world-renowned universities whereby students apply with a single application a few months before their fall college enrollment. They also have a robust apprenticeship program and trade schools that provide excellent alternatives to a bachelor's. Notably, there are few private universities. Legislation prevents excessively expensive daycares or elite secondary schools from operating, producing a more egalitarian society.

Western European countries, generally speaking, don't have the corresponding madness for limited university spaces as in the US, India, China, or South Korea. One downside of open enrollment and low or free tuition fees is that dropout rates are high. Degree completion rates often take longer than expected. Although it may be an inefficient use of taxpayer money, at least European students aren't absorbing the costs of not completing their degree. European millennials are highly unlikely to be saddled with crippling debt if they decide or are forced to drop out. Career alternatives that don't require a bachelor's degree are more viable and socially accepted in many European countries. I believe that partly explains why many European students take time off before beginning a bachelor's fixate less on prestige. If I were to raise a family anywhere globally, I would be willing to pay higher taxes to live in a more equitable and socially mobile Western Europe.

Finally, let's briefly examine higher education in Russia and, more generally, the former Soviet Union. One of my takeaways from reading Alexander Solzhenitsyn's *Gulag Archipelago* about the systems of mass imprisonment and arrest of Soviet citizens during Stalin's reign is that, for a theoretically classless society, your family's pedigree and social network conferred high degrees of favor. An unfavorable background, such as being Jewish or non-Russian speaking, accompanied a set of disadvantages in the Soviet Union's informal caste system. Nevertheless, the Soviet Union once had a premier higher education system theoretically open to anyone and free to its students, particularly in math and science.

Following the Soviet Union's collapse, runaway corruption during the 1990s and early 2000s during the tumultuous transition to market economies produced rent-seeking behaviors from government agencies and nominally private businesses. Completing simple tasks such as acquiring a driver's license or registering for school required bribes.

British researchers investigating graduates finding jobs in Ukraine suggest that, because many post-Soviet public agencies couldn't adequately provide for their citizens, entrepreneurs and business people have an incentive to maximize their wealth to decrease their dependency on the state. Corruption and bribes become a legitimized norm and a staple of daily life. There are fewer protections relative to other countries with a strong rule of law for unemployed workers, exploited students, or medical malpractice. The reviewers conducted interviews with many recent graduates looking for work. "Numerous women interviewees discussed how the initial meetings with employers were often extremely exploitative. Many women discuss feeling intimidated during interviews, and several noted how they have, after passing the first interview, been asked to meet potential employers at a restaurant or sauna where further 'discussions' are to take place."[101]

Having spent time in and visited most of the former Soviet Union and Eastern Bloc countries, it's difficult to ignore how hard it is to complete basic tasks. American students can take for granted that they can register for the SAT and receive their scores for a fee, have free access to their transcripts, and any number of routine behaviors.

College students in former Communist countries pay professors for grades. High schoolers might need to bribe their principal to release their diploma. Wealthy families push through their thoroughly unqualified students to earn lucrative positions in government or medicine. Many white-collar jobs require a probationary period where they're paid only after a few months on the job. Comparatively few employees are taken on full time.

A Macedonian friend who worked at a youth hostel shared that, although she has a master's in architecture, it's impossible to get a job. She lacks family connections to access the few open positions. Earning an education and doing what's expected of society, yet being unable to secure employment, generates high resentment and brain-drain degrees. Many millennials living in post-Communist countries move away to nations with more robust legal systems and higher-wage jobs or seek work in informal economies. Nepotism is the rule in much of the developing world and not the exception, as in America's Varsity Blues scandal. I feel sympathy for my friends who live in countries that do not reward hard work and where there are few if any possibilities for advancement or even earning a reasonable wage. Living abroad makes me even more thankful for having the utter luck to be born in the United States.

The European Union commissioned an anticorruption study in 2015 titled "Academic Dishonesty or Corrupt Values: The Case of Russia." The opening sentences read: "Academic corruption in Russia is extensively spread; it is not an isolated phenomenon. Rather, academic corruption is tightly embedded into the general corruption in society: in politics, business, and in everyday life."[102]

Russia's recently created *Edinyi Gosudarstvennyi Eksamen* (EGE) Unified State Exam simplified admissions by standardizing qualifications across the country. It didn't require prospective students to interview on campus, a prohibitive cost for many families. The EGE)expanded opportunities for students outside of major cities to access opportunities in Moscow or St. Petersburg. At first glance, an 80 percent college attendance rate with most students finishing their degrees makes Russia appear like a model for efficiency and access. However, the exam itself is ripe with corruption. Students buy answers in advance or bribe proctors to allow mobile phones during the examination. Some proctors provide the solutions directly.

The government funds universities based on the number of students who continue to enroll, so there are disincentives against expelling underperforming students. Universities depend on student fees more than students rely on their services. Because Russia has one of the world's lowest birth rates, universities compete amongst themselves to recruit and retain a decreasing population of teenagers. The study observes: "Often, university administrations pressure professors to water down their course requirements by adapting them to the students' actual level of knowledge and to be more tolerant with the students who pay high fees."

Professors often make $300 or less per month, an unsuitable living wage, while spending more than twenty hours per week in class in addition to extensive administrative duties. It's no surprise that there are temptations to "find 'easier' ways to work, such as by ignoring cheating and plagiarism." A report by Russian-born researchers in *International Higher Education* (IHE) summarizes the effect of corruption: "The lowering of standards creates a breeding ground for cynicism, professional disappointment, and resentment toward students as well as the government."[103]

Professors may solicit underachieving students for bribes. One professor reports that an administrator "[made] requests for over fifty people. Does this mean she has so many relatives? No way, she arranges the grades for them, either at a very cheap rate or just by crying, and some give the grades for free. And they pay her right away."

Downloading assignments from the internet or paying agencies to complete a thesis is also a common practice. College students offer gifts or money to professors who collude and rubberstamp assignments with high grades. Universities often hire their graduates to become professors, so the cycle continues. Corrupt behaviors normalize. Conscientious objectors who wish to teach with integrity are subject to lower living standards, ostracism from colleagues, and pressure from administrators if they fail too many students.

The IHE) authors conclude that "many professors and university administrators often support their friends, relatives, neighbors, who study at their schools" as a side benefit to compensate for low wages. Despite attempts for reform at the government level and at a handful of elite universities, corruption and pay-to-play persist at all levels of society. A flawed American meritocracy is preferable to systemic post-Soviet nepotism, but that's also a pretty low standard to set.

5.2 Decentralized application portals and requirements contribute to the madness

One of the most significant issues with American college admissions is a lack of uniformity in requirements or application portals. India, Germany, China, Russia, and almost every other country use a centralized admissions system. There is one test, a clear set of admissions standards, and a single portal to apply most everywhere.

America practices a decentralized college admissions landscape. Recall from the introduction that former Carnegie Mellon President Thomas Stockham Baker criticized 1907 America's decentralized application process. He wrote in an era where elite boarding schools served as pipelines for admission to the Ivy League and Seven Sisters schools. Membership at rarified institutions preserved the power of early American aristocrats. Universities routinely excluded students based on their gender, race, religion, and even physical appearance. Baker criticizes how "the dependence upon the dictates of higher educational institutions is almost absolute." He worries that "the distractions of a schoolboy's life are by no means decreasing," or what we would today call recess, unstructured play, or, simply, free time.

He contrasts our complicated system with the much more straightforward and centralized German admissions system that Germany practices today. Baker observes that "there are hardly half a dozen institutions whose demands for admission are precisely the same" and warns about "the difficulties entailed by the almost infinite variation in college requirements." Unique and inconsistent combinations of requirements, deadlines, essay topics, test scores, and recommendation letter expectations, and application portals for America's more than 4,000 colleges and universities make for an unfriendly college application experience for most families.

Universities nominally participate in shared portals such as the Common and Coalition Applications or Apply Texas. But these applications provide little relief or clarity for applicants when each campus has different deadlines, expectations for counselor and teacher recommendations, and varying testing and essay requirements. Requirements that change from year to year or even within a single admissions cycle place burdens on high school counselors, families with multiple children, and consultants like me who compensate by charging more.

I want you to consider that the American college application system isn't the only possibility. Considering alternatives helps applicants and families see the admissions madness more clearly. The British college application system has remained mostly the same since the early 1960s. Deadlines are nearly uniform among all universities and programs. Fred Crossland (1965) discusses the origins of the standardized British system.[104]

"The British universities are tackling the problem of cooperation through an ambitious undertaking called the Universities Central Council on Admissions. Now entering its second year of operation, the UCCA is the creation of all the major British institutions. Today virtually any young man or woman seeking admission to a British university submits only one application, listing six institutions according to their preference. All applications are directed only to the UCCA, which *serves as a communications clearinghouse and traffic control center for access to all British universities....* You will not be surprised to know that when the UCCA scheme was introduced, Oxford and Cambridge remained outside the fold. But now they are in!" (emphasis mine)

Usually, elite universities adopt a policy, like holistic review in the case of Harvard and Princeton, and the others follow. Widespread adoption of the UCCA system is notable because it started as a movement among less-prestigious universities before those like Oxford or Cambridge joined. Somewhat analogous, the Common Application began as a coordination effort between a handful of private universities in 1975. Around 130 other universities joined over the following two decades. Still, the Ivy League institutions were reluctant to join until Harvard was the first to adopt it in 1994. The other seven Ivy League universities soon followed, and today the Common App reports over 900 institutions.[105] MIT and Cal Tech are notable elite universities that haven't joined the Common App and only accept an application specific to their institutions.

Crossland criticizes America's "topsy-turvy Alice-in-Wonderland [process that] we call getting into college" as coming "dangerously close to administrative anarchy" unsuitable for 1965 and "unthinkable for 1980." If Crossland thought American college admissions was mad in 1965, imagine what he would think if he were alive now? The British admissions system continues to work well even today. Giving up some institutional control doesn't sacrifice British universities' quality control over who they admit or reject. I wouldn't be surprised if MIT and Cal Tech eventually join the Common Application within the next few years.

Americans may object that we're a collective of 50 states, each requiring 50 unique sets of experiments. However, the "Universities and Colleges Admissions Service" (UCAS) replaced the UCCA by bringing research-oriented universities and STEM/trade-focused polytechnic campuses across England, Wales, and Northern Ireland into a single fold. If a country composed of four distinct nations can coordinate their systems, failure to cooperate among American universities means applicants and their families suffer. "The day of rugged individualism and laissez-faire in the administration of American higher education has already ended, if only we would admit that fact to ourselves.... Education must live in the future tense." Yet here we are, rehashing the same arguments from three generations ago.

I credit the University of California system application for a genuine single portal with the same essay requirements and deadlines for each of its eight campuses. Students choose four 350-word responses out of eight options. The applications allow students to self-report grades and test scores, so they don't need to submit official documents until they're admitted and decide to enroll. Self-reporting academic credentials decreases the workloads of high school counselors and registrars. Even the UC's flagship Regents' and Chancellors' Scholars financial aid programs require nothing extra, unlike UT-Austin's cumbersome Forty Acres scholarship portal. Everyone who applies to a UC system school is considered.

The UC portal differs from UT-Austin, where some applicants are submitting upward of three Princetons' worth of essays to a single university. Each Texas university requires separate transcripts, test scores, and recommendation letters. Prospective California students submit 1,400 words in one set of documents covering eight schools and their scholarship programs. The if-it-ain't-broke-don't-fix-it California application has remained the same without surprises for as long as I can remember.

A related issue is the utter lack of standardization of academic records. Public, private, magnet, and charter schools deploy a vast array of methods to assess students' transcripts. Weighted or unweighted GPAs come on a four- or five- or six-point scale by assigning either grades or numbers. Some schools measure out of 100 whereas others from ten. Students in one district or school receive a class ranking, and others don't.

Experimental schools dispense with quantitative assessments entirely in favor of long-form written performance evaluations. Neighboring school districts often favor entirely different calculation systems. Courses that one district awards as bonus grade points for might be evaluated as on-level for another district. Incompatible systems pose a problem when students move districts or transition between public and private schools. Homeschooling becomes increasingly problematic after middle school. Likewise, universities practice a similar discontinuity, with some discarding freshman year grades, looking only at the weighted GPA, or exclusively favoring the class rank.

A December 1962 article by Rick F. Yacone in the *School Counselor* argues, "The crux of the problem is the independent way that schools and colleges go about their jobs with various methods [even though] they are working towards the same goals of identifying youngsters for admissions." I'm probably naïve in having the same thought as Yacone when he asks why can't "one permanent record card be established in all high schools?"

He concludes that there is a lack of coordination between the varied stakeholders in our highly fragmented education system. Most British college campuses make decisions based primarily on the results of a single battery of curriculum-based exams called A-levels. Examiners grade A-Levels on a "standard distribution" where the average grades are between a B and C, correcting for runaway grade inflation. Eight percent of applicants on a given exam receive the highest mark, an A* (A-Star). Scoring on a bell curve could solve grade inflation concerns at some American high schools where more than half of the senior class earns straight A-pluses. That would be an unacceptable reform to many American parents because it might imply that their child is average or worse. Unless all high schools adopt a bell curve approach, applicants with inflated grades will almost always have the edge over their peers.

British university applicants know upfront how many A's or A*'s or equivalent qualifications are likely to grant admission. Transparency with admissions expectations deters mediocre applicants scoring B's and C's from wasting one of their six applications or the universities' time by applying. Only select majors at the most prestigious universities, such as the University of College-London, Oxford, or Cambridge, require an additional exam called the Thinking Skills Assessment (TSA) that requires half the time as the SAT. Yacone concludes his assessment of Britain's centralized UCCA application system by stating, "The greatest beneficiary, of course, is the individual student."

To the critic who claims without evidence, "that sort of thing would never work in America. We're exceptional, remember?" let's contrast further the nearly infinite requirement configurations of American undergraduate college admissions with entry into American medical, law, and graduate schools.

Some of these programs, especially for PhD candidates, are even more selective, with lower acceptance rates than Ivy League undergraduate degrees. Yet, graduate applicants almost universally can expect to submit a single essay and one or two reference letters adequate for all their applications. The graduate/medical/law personal statement asks the applicant to discuss their background and why they're applying for their desired program. Simple! These essay topics are similar to mostly uniform "statement of purpose" requirements for students transferring from one university to another. So when I critique undergraduate college essays, I'm narrowing the scope even further to first-time freshman admissions rather than transfers.

Graduate admissions certainly attracts a much broader range of people, with applicants aging anywhere from their early twenties to post-retirement. One might think that graduate programs need more essays to find the gems whose academics they might otherwise overlook. However, elite graduate programs seem to have no problems attracting highly talented applicants and hitting enrollment management targets without forcing adults to jump through endless hoops that undergraduate admissions officials deem appropriate for teenagers.

As a society, why do we apply less-demanding application requirements to future human rights lawyers and physicians than USC does for Bachelor's of Science candidates to Lifespan Health or the Music Industry? Could you imagine Harvard law asking applicants to reflect on "followership" or how a prospective Yale MBA eats their potatoes? What sounds patently absurd in a job interview or a graduate school application remains unquestioned in another. Asking someone how they eat their potatoes or their theme song is better suited to speed dating on *The Bachelor*.

A decentralized education landscape is a significant issue, but the most ridiculous aspect of American college admissions is holistic review.

6. Holistic Review
is Bullshit

One of my favorite books and movies is Michael Lewis's *Moneyball*. Oakland A's General Manager Billy Beane, played by Brad Pitt, pioneered data-driven player assessments, upended the conventional wisdom of evaluating prospective Major League Baseball pitchers and hitters. Beane's Oakland A's back-to-back 100-win seasons in the early 2000s yielded the best results with the lowest payroll in baseball history.

Since baseball's inception as America's pastime, an old guard of scouts identified players who hit the ball with the most *pop*, pitchers who *zing* their fastballs, and future shortstops who turn double plays like the second coming of Ozzie Smith or Derek Jeter. Scouts argue that only former ballplayers and sandlot junkies have the "right stuff" to find hidden gems. Their gut feeling and first impressions tell them all they need to know.

A new generation of non-ballplaying statisticians portrayed by Jonah Hill as the Oakland A's Assistant General Manager Paul DePodesta crunched the numbers and determined the old guard were utterly full of crap. Traditional scouts were no better than average, and some worse than chance at forecasting which players would return the most value to their franchises. Why employ expensive, arrogant scouts when throwing darts at a roster yields similar results?

"Sabermetricians" like DePodesta introduced scientific rigor to counter the old guard's hocus-pocus. If we lived in a fair world that distributed resources with maximum efficiency, baseball talent scouts would have vanished overnight. Moreover, recent advances in player development diminish the emphasis on identifying natural talents. Nowadays, player development specialists matter more than traditional scouts. Yet two decades later, most Major League Baseball teams still deploy the old guard and their radar guns to wayward diamonds across the country and world.[106]

Baseball franchises supposedly motivated by the efficiencies mandated by capitalism still allocate their resources ineffectively. Likewise, for college admissions, reviewers are subject to the spectrum of human flaws and systematic error-making. Admissions reviewers are overconfident about their ability to select talented future college students. Universities have changed their review processes little in the past decades despite revolutionary advances in data analytics and machine learning. Baseball scouts who purport an uncanny ability to identify talent are equivalent to admissions reviewers who claim magical skills to detect the next Rhodes Scholar or Yale law school attendee. Consequently, like traditional baseball scouts who fail to identify talent reliably, admissions by holistic review is bullshit.

6.1 A note on definitions

Before exploring the mechanics and sorcery of admissions readers assessing applicants through holistic review, let us distinguish between terms. Admissions review is a process distinct from *recruitment* and *enrollment management*. Recruitment occurs throughout the year by enticing prospective applicants to submit and complete their applications. Recruitment efforts are the emails you receive, postcards in the mail, or college representatives who visit your school and stand behind college fair tables. In the spring of a student's senior year, universities host on-campus or virtual recruitment events, conduct outreach campaigns, and offer programs such as research opportunities to persuade admitted applicants to enroll.

Enrollment managers assess the number of available spaces in each program and the university overall. Every university, including Harvard, admits more students than they have spaces. Not every admitted student enrolls, especially in our present era of the typical applicant submitting eight or more applications. Enrollment managers have the challenging task of predicting the "yield," or how many admitted students will arrive on campus. From previous years, they examine how many admitted students enrolled and attempt to forecast for the present cycle how many students they need to accept to fill the available spaces. Enrolling too many students means insufficient spaces in residence halls or first-year courses; enroll too few, and a budget crisis and staff layoffs follow.

Enrollment managers are on the frontlines for assuring a university's solvency. They're also the puppeteers behind the scenes that pull the admissions strings and produce power disparities between universities and their applicants. Part of the powerlessness that families feel when confronting college applications is the hidden role of enrollment management offices. If you're looking for someone to blame, don't take your frustrations out on junior admissions counselors who answer the general admissions telephone. Instead, harangue the enrollment managers—if you can find them.

Enrollment managers also survey which other universities are poaching their admits. Even Harvard loses 20 percent of its admitted students to MIT, Cal Tech, Princeton, Yale, and Stanford. Middling universities lure outstanding students with generous financial aid while accepting less-qualified applicants who are likely to pay full tuition. Like the arms race among applicants to gain admission to the best universities, there is a parallel competition among universities to persuade desirable applicants to enroll at their campus relative to their other options. Enrollment managers are also looking for "hooked" students for sports, diversity, unique talents, and so on. Financial aid and scholarships are often the responsibility of enrollment managers who want to attract certain students.

Enrollment managers confront pressures from institutional budget offices to admit wealthy or international students more likely to enroll at the sticker tuition price. Big data gathering techniques help recruiters and enrollment managers target students more strategically and precisely than a generation ago. Admissions reviewers may wear recruitment or enrollment management hats, and although there is overlap between these terms, I discuss questionable enrollment and recruitment practices in chapter 8.

6.2 Reliably selecting talent is impossible

Admissions reviewers who use holistic review, regardless of the university, seek students who demonstrate a high level of "fit" for their academic pursuits or other needs of the university to craft their ideal freshman class. Reviewers argue that the multiplicity of essays, recommendation letters, and academic credentials are necessary to "get to know each applicant." They reward students who have maximized the resources in their environment.

Exactly what universities seek is open to interpretation. What they want changes based on how many admitted students have already enrolled or whether a university needs to fill more diversity or athletics spaces. Shifting needs that are hidden from public view is one reason you're unlikely to find clear answers on official admissions pages. Journalist Jeffrey Selingo writes, "While both applicants and colleges like to pretend that the decisions they each make are rational, the system as a whole is ambiguous because the main players are constantly defining and redefining their agenda."[107]

"Fit" is a moving target that depends mainly on the whims of your assigned admissions reviewers and the priorities that enrollment managers dictate. In the 1920s, not being the "right fit" served as an indirect way to exclude Jews from campus. Just as there are few standardized application portals (discussed in chapter 5.2), there are even fewer consistencies between universities regarding how they evaluate their applicants.

Universities deploy a wide variety of evaluation techniques, scoring systems, and review processes to determine which applicants are the most desirable. Some universities review applicants in stages to winnow down applicant funnels until arriving at the narrow list of admitted students. Others may score an applicant a single time. Reviewers are sometimes allowed or encouraged to make comments in the margins or write other observations. They might deploy numerical scores with pluses and minuses or assign each essay, resume, and recommendation separate scores and average them together. Files might be reviewed in pairs with senior counselors guiding junior readers or dividing up the labor among the components of a single application. Irrespective of the scheme or scoring system, each iteration falls under the umbrella term "holistic review."

And it's all bullshit.

Many students make the mistake of trying to decipher precisely how Michigan and UT-Austin or Stanford and MIT differ in their review mechanics. Points system or specific criteria about *how* you are evaluated doesn't matter very much. Swimming in minutiae misses larger points about *why* universities practice holistic review at all. After all, bureaucracies are almost entirely outside of your control or ability to access. So much of the admissions guidebook industry, including my UT-Austin–specific book *Your Ticket to the Forty Acres*, focuses on the nuts and bolts of college admissions. Readers wonder how the University of California might consider hardships or exactly how Harvard evaluates applicants based on their quirky "athleticism" criteria mandated by its seventeenth-century founders.

College admissions is essentially a human resources problem common to corporate or government hiring practices. There are a finite number of spaces for many qualified applicants. How might Google or Goldman Sachs hire the applicants most likely to contribute to company culture and produce excellent work? No institution or organization has figured out how to evaluate talent perfectly. It's one of society's most challenging questions. Whoever designs the algorithm or set of tests that reliably sort applicants from one another will instantly win a Nobel Prize in Economics or Physics and make redundant admissions reviewers, baseball scouts, and corporate human resource offices.

In the Atlantic article "Science of Smart Hiring," Derek Thompson writes that "it will always be difficult to predict fit and performance because humans are complex, and humans interacting in human systems are even more complex. The right lesson is more subtle: Hiring is hard, and nobody is very good at doing it alone, whether you're a Google boss, a high-school principal, or a sports general manager." Google has experimented with several strategies, including brainteasers, conducting a battery of twenty-five interviews, or having prospective employees submit a three-hundred-question interview. Most of their efforts proved inconclusive.

Michael Lewis in *The Undoing Project* investigates the relationship between, and careers of, pioneering behavioral economists Amos Tversky and Daniel Kahneman. Kahneman eventually won the Nobel Prize in Economics and published his widely read magnum opus *Thinking Fast and Slow*. In the mid-1950s, Kahneman served in the Israeli Defense Forces' psychology department, responsible for evaluating candidates for promotion to the military officer program.

Candidates in teams of eight needed to cooperate in traversing a six-foot wall. The Israeli military expressed great confidence that the test accurately selected the most promising leaders. In subsequent feedback sessions, Kahneman and his young researchers found that the test was negligibly better than blind guessing. Retaining officers was a key priority, but the test did nothing to identify which recruits might stay past their minimum enlistment commitments.

Moreover, the exam's failure comes from a one-hour test's inadequacy in an artificial setting that bears little resemblance to active combat. Even when confronted with the statistical evidence that the tools don't work, a **status quo bias** precluded discarding the exam or considering alternatives. Uncovering these inefficiencies convinced Kahneman that humans aren't always the rational actors that economic theories suggest.

Israeli military officials experienced what Kahneman later coined the **illusion of validity**. Overconfidence in one's tools or prediction abilities fools us into thinking we are better than average at forecasting outcomes. The Israeli officials convinced themselves the exam worked, found data that supported their narrative, and ignored findings that suggested otherwise. They reasoned that some assessments are better than none.

Likewise, America's most selective colleges haven't cracked the talent selection code since not every student returns for their sophomore year or graduates within six years. Admissions officers express confidence in their ability to select promising college students, similar to the Israeli talent assessors looking for their next group of squadron leaders. Reviewers' overreliance on college essays or identifying supposed character traits from a student's resume encounter the same artificial setting problem as the wall-traversing exercise.

Because most freshmen at prestigious universities eventually graduate on time, admissions officers credit themselves for maintaining the graduation rate. The tail wags the dog. In chapter 10.2, I advocate for a partial admissions lottery in part because the top quarter of any applicant pool at elite universities, by their own concession, are capable of doing the work and graduating, so it probably doesn't matter much which of them enroll.

Admissions by partial lottery would correct the **illusion of validity** just as random guesses were likely to select for reliable officers in the Israeli military. A lottery would also save hundreds of thousands of labor hours and tens of millions in admissions staff salaries. However, I'm under no illusion that bureaucracies will relinquish their holistic review tools anytime soon. Many tools are better than few, they reason, even if the tools are bullshit like MLB baseball scouts.

Holistic review is a questionable tool because high school performance isn't necessarily an accurate indicator of future success. All the admissions tools in the world are unlikely to identify the figurative Tom Brady, who was an overlooked late-round draft pick before becoming the greatest NFL quarterback of all time. Many students are late bloomers, or they simply haven't learned in a sufficiently nurturing environment.

I was a late bloomer with an unremarkable high school record who thrived in college after arriving at UT-Austin's Liberal Arts Honors program that allowed me to explore my interests freely and build friendships with curious and motivated classmates. I wouldn't have gained admission with my mediocre credentials if I were applying today. Many promising late bloomers are denied access to a quality college education.

In *Range: Why Generalists Triumph in a Specialized World*, David Epstein argues that late bloomers who delay specialization or overly committing to a narrow path early on tend to do better. His research supports the claim I make in the next chapter that community college students, despite on average coming from more disadvantaged backgrounds, tend to graduate at higher rates when enrolling at a four-year university compared with students who change from one four-year university to another. Delaying specialization supports my stance that a gap year between high school and college enrollment provides long-term benefits.

Holistic review preferences students who commit to activities early on, prioritize their academics above all else, and who possess overconfidence about their future major or career ambitions. They're biased toward specialists rather than generalists, even though research suggests that generalists tend to have more successful careers and respond better to adversity. It's no wonder that mental health is a crisis on all college campuses because college admissions sorts for students who are as likely to burn out as they are to contribute to research or occupy campus leadership positions. College admissions helps contribute to teenagers' collective *Fear of Failure* outlined in Jessica Leahy's insightful work. They're less open to unfamiliar ideas and alternative pathways, as noted in Greg Lukianoff and Jonathan Haidt's *The Coddling of the American Mind*.

6.3 Community college transfer applicants are especially screwed

Transfer students are often initially overlooked or are ill-equipped to navigate the first-time freshman admissions system. Some of UT-Austin's top graduates every year begin their studies at community college. Transfer admission allows universities to enroll first-generation and low-income students who might want to save money at community college. Many have family obligations requiring them to stay close to home following graduation. Transfers often come from nontraditional backgrounds, including mid-career professionals, military veterans, and parents.

They're my favorite students to work with because they have at least a year or two of post–high school experience. Compared to high school seniors, they often have more precise goals about what they want from their education. There are far fewer resources available for prospective transfer applicants than first-time freshmen, especially at four-year universities where there aren't designated offices to help students transition away from their campus.

Information for honors programs and research opportunities are geared toward first-time freshmen. An intrepid prospective transfer is often left guessing whether they're eligible for a particular program. Identifying prerequisites adds an additional challenge to whether a student might be eligible for enrolling in upper-division courses in their major because degree plans are suited for students already on campus. Incomplete information on their sites complicates applying to universities such as Michigan Ann-Arbor, making it difficult to write the "Why Michigan?" essay.

Erecting barriers for transfer students decreases diversity on college campuses because it deters nontraditional students from applying. Prospective transfers applying for the University of Washington's Paul G. Allen School of Computer Science and Engineering receive a surprise requirement weeks after completing their application. They have only two weeks to submit a separate application to the program on an almost identical topic required on the Coalition Application.

Recall from chapter 1.3 that an increasing number of less- and non-selective universities require essays and practice holistic review. Transfer admission for universities that admit more than 75 percent of their applicants is usually straightforward. Transfer applicants gain admission solely based on minimum GPA thresholds, usually a 2.5 or 3.0. Some less-selective universities, such as Arizona State (ASU), will admit transfers with as few as 12 hours and a 2.5 GPA. ASU admits any student who isn't on academic probation from their previous university if they have more than 60 college hours. Straightforward transfer admissions criteria increase access for transfer students.

UNC Asheville admits 94 percent of their applicants, yet they take an opposite approach to clear and transparent admissions requirements. They've mindlessly adopted holistic review procedures so that they can learn about "your successes, challenges, interests and goals—everything that makes you who you are."

Students are more than their grades. Few would debate that point. But admissions requirements aren't the appropriate place to communicate an institution's commitment to embracing the student as a whole. Their holistic review process accompanies a "Statement on Civic Engagement" whose intent is unclear.

"At UNC Asheville, our comprehensive admissions review process ensures each applicant is assessed on an individual basis with the safety of our campus as a primary consideration. We welcome peaceful action and purposeful civic engagement among UNC Asheville students, and also support those actions among our prospective students. Participation in non-violent civil protest and peaceful expression will not influence admissions decisions at UNC Asheville."

I can't make sense of what they're trying to accomplish besides virtue signaling the kind of counterproductive institutionalized diversity I criticize in chapter 9.3. I'm confident they don't have in mind peaceful if horribly misguided QAnon protestors who decried mask-wearing and social distancing at various state capitols.

Moreover, UNC Asheville has a downright bizarre require-ment for all transfer students to submit a "Transfer Student Academic & Disciplinary Form." Occasionally, if a student is on academic probation or has issues with their transcript, a univer-sity might request a form to be signed by their current registrar. I've never seen a university require such a form of all applicants, which assuredly erects more barriers to access to their campus.

Attempting to research the requirement also yields few clues. Clicking the "Transfer Policies and Resources" link produces a 404 Page Not Found error, and "Course Requirements for Major" triggers my browser's antivirus, flashing bright yellow *Warning: Potential Security Risk Ahead.* To recap, UNC Asheville, who admits basically every transfer student eligible to apply, practices holistic review with a promise that protesting won't hurt one's admissions chances (we're left to wonder what political activism they have in mind). One of my clients declined to apply because of the silly application requirements and unclear admissions stan-dards. UNC Asheville's transfer policies receive an F for Foolish.

At many highly selective universities, transfers regardless of socioeconomic status or ethnicity are an underrepresented cohort. The Jack Kent Cooke Foundation published a comprehensive report on transfer student success called *Persistence.* They deter-mined that transfers represent 11 percent of the undergraduate population at top public universities and only 3 percent at private schools. "35 selective public institutions enroll four times as many transfer students as the 140 selective private institutions." [108]

For example, Princeton, Harvard, Dartmouth, and Stanford admit around 1 percent of their transfer applicants compared with more than five times the admissions rate for first-time freshmen. MIT, Yale, Amherst, and Claremont McKenna accept fewer than two dozen transfers each year. Williams, America's top liberal arts college, admitted 11 transfers, whereas Cal Tech accepted only three transfer applicants in 2019. These disparities between freshman and transfer admissions rates represent a deliberate institutional preference for privileged students over historically marginalized populations. Given the scarcity of spaces and lack of information at elite universities, it's surprising that any prospective transfers apply at all. A lack of viable transfer pathways puts added stress on getting things right the first time as a high school applicant.

By contrast, Cornell, Brown, Pennsylvania, Columbia, and U Chicago admit transfers at similar rates to first-time freshmen. Still, transfers to elite universities are twice as likely to come from another four-year university than a community college. Their preferences reflect society's bias toward four-year degrees while shunning local colleges. The *Persistence* report found that community college transfers are slightly more likely to complete their degree relative to first-time freshman or transfers from four-year universities. Given the higher success rates of community college students, it's peculiar that transfer admissions at elite universities prefer students originating at four-year universities.

Closing the door to transfer students, especially from community colleges, sacrifices opportunities for enrolling a more diverse and capable student body. Transferring into Michigan's Engineering program requires a very specific math course sequence that includes linear algebra and differential equations. These two courses go above and beyond any other public university that usually just require engineering physics and a few calculus semesters.

One of my clients took these beyond-calculus courses at their community college under the impression that they met the prerequisites. However, the credits didn't transfer because they're classes that are ordinarily only offered at four-year universities. Michigan's transfer equivalency system didn't recognize them. Despite being a first-generation black student with a community college 4.0 GPA—the kind that Michigan purports to value highly—they were denied without further consideration (after wasting time with their required five essays and the application fee). He considered emailing and then decided he is better off enrolling at a university that would treat him better.

Any elite university that claims to value diversity and college access yet admits significantly fewer transfers relative to first-time freshmen is hypocritical. A sincere commitment to diversity and college access would decrease barriers for beginning at a community college and accept first-time freshmen and transfers at similar rates. They need to maintain some balance between incoming transfers from two-year colleges and four-year universities. The *Persistence* executive summary concludes:

> "Because lower-income students are three times more likely to begin their postsecondary pursuits at a community college than higher-income students, strengthening transfer pathways to selective institutions has the potential to increase bachelor's completion rates for our nation's brightest students. It also can assist selective higher education institutions increase the diversification of their student bodies along lines of socioeconomic status, first-generation status, or age."

6.4 Cheaters often win

The biggest myth that admissions offices present is that the review process is a science. Holistic review isn't a precise thermometer that measures temperature accurately. In reality, it's neither an art nor a science but a series of hunches and gut feelings. Even supposedly objective criteria such as grades and AP scores can be gamed by savvy students, further calling into question whether reviewers can decipher what is authentic or not.

By cheating, I don't have in mind falsifying resume credentials on an application or lying on an essay. I see posts from time to time about admissions counselors who claim they can tell fraud or not, but can they really when they read applications in less than ten minutes and hundreds if not thousands of applications each cycle? They're reading way too quickly to assess the claims you make at anything other than face value. Reviewers usually take the applicant's word for it.

Some portals, such as the University of California, have shifted to students self-reporting their grades and SAT scores. Because that information is easily verified with an official transcript required for enrollment, very few students cheat on that portion of the application. I imagine for every thousand students who misrepresent themselves on an application, perhaps one is actually caught and "blacklisted" with their name circulated among elite institutions. Reviewers can't detect fraud with any reliability, although they love to claim omnipotence on the subject to scare would-be deceivers.

Rather than lying on applications and resume misrepresentation, the extent of which is impossible to quantify and assess, by cheating, I have in mind the time-tested tradition of looking over your classmate's shoulder. Donald McCabe with the Center for Academic Integrity conducted a longitudinal survey of 70,000 high school students from 2002 to 2015. Two-thirds of students admitted to cheating on a test or plagiarizing a paper, with 95 percent of respondents admitting to some form of cheating.[109]

Because the penalties for academic dishonesty are so high, no student will ever publicly admit to fraud. On the contrary, people accused of cheating will deploy any means to denounce the charge and preserve their reputations, often committing themselves to further lying on top of the initial cheating. There are no incentives to come clean unless a plea bargain offers leniency if the offender snitches on the other cheaters.

I don't think human nature tends toward liars and cheaters but instead to cooperation and honest behavior. Even after completing my undergraduate genocide research and making visits to Bosnia and Rwanda, I believe that people commit evil because they think they're doing good or don't see any viable alternatives. Circumstances drive people toward dishonesty and violence. Even in wars, acts of heroism and selflessness equal or exceed the atrocities. Few among us, including most teenagers, are Machiavellian psychopaths who trample others without regard to their well-being or violate norms only for the fun of it. Students who behave honestly in most areas of their life confront intense pressures to act dishonestly in academic environments. Professor Daniel Markovits shares a similar sentiment: "People are more benign than the common view supposes, but circumstances are much more malignant."[110]

Rutger Bregman in *Humankind* undermines the conventional narrative that humans are innately selfish and prone to evil. He argues that people are generally decent and aren't intrinsically motivated to lie and cheat. We want to get along and feel included in our family and communities. Insufficient incentives within society nudge people toward unsavory behavior. Our modern society inverts pro-social virtues such as honesty and integrity in favor of winning, even if that means fraud, deceit, or manipulation.

"Blaming the system" doesn't excuse or absolve the cheater who deserves some form of punishment. "Everyone else is doing it" also isn't an acceptable defense. We're left with a situation where the unfortunate few who are caught pay steep penalties. Harsh punishment seeks to deter others from cheating in the future, except the admissions stakes remain so high that future students will wager that it's worth the risk to take shortcuts. As long as the admissions arms race persists, cheating will be a natural response, a problem most educators and admissions staff prefer to ignore. Consequently, cheating is a silent yet systemic social problem.

Many of my clients go on extensive rants about pervasive cheating in their classes (although, predictably, none ever admit to cheating themselves). Some even write college essays criticizing their underhanded classmates. A group of students once pulled me aside at a high school visit when I worked for UT-Austin, begging me to do something about their unscrupulous valedictorian. Honest students resent their classmates who show up to class unprepared and swipe scantrons from a teacher's desk or circulate answers among a group of cheaters. Traditional definitions of plagiarism are inadequate for the smartphone generation.

As a society, we're quick to demonize cheating yet applaud those who achieve at the highest levels. Tom Brady is celebrated for his seventh Super Bowl championship. We experience collective amnesia over his four-game suspension for pressuring staff to deflate footballs that gave his offense an edge over their opponent in Super Bowl LI. Had his career ended with the scandal, Deflate-Gate would figure more prominently in recalling his reputation. We lionize him as a hero rather than questioning the integrity of his otherwise greatest-of-all-time career. Winning cures all, just as gaining admission to elite universities validates an applicant. That even Tom Brady feels compelled to cheat signals a structural problem in how our society issues its accolades. He wagered that he would get away with it, and even if he were caught, a Super Bowl win outweighs the punishment.

Only after the fact and under substantial pressure and mounting evidence do we ask more questions about how Lance

Armstrong won seven straight Tour de France races after recovering from cancer. He justified doping because everyone else was doing it, and he has a point. Of the top ten finishers during his championship run, 87 percent were confirmed dopers or suspected of doping.[111]

Steroid-abusing baseball player Barry Bonds still maintains his name in the record books for most home runs hit in a season and for career home runs. He hasn't yet earned a place in the Hall of Fame, but in 2021, he received the most votes after his tenth year of eligibility. Earning more votes suggests that, although Major League Baseball has cleaned up its act, there isn't a severe enough stigma against dishonest behavior. Passing time brushes away previous sins. A Harvard education elicits oohs and ahs and never comes with an asterisk, even if the graduate pursued fraudulent means to achieving their degree.

There is no part of the college application that a determined family can't manipulate. One recommendation by Varsity Blues ringleader Rick Singer involved referring students to online schools where students could independently study AP classes. Earning high grades at less-rigorous high schools boosted the applicant's overall GPA and class rank.[112] Supplementing coursework isn't explicitly illegal. Few if any artificially inflated GPAs will get detected by admissions counselors. Many students opt to take summer school classes at their primary campus to earn more grade points and free up space for more GPA-boosting AP classes.

In the past few years, I noticed a substantial uptick in students earning 4s and 5s on more than 15 AP exams, many of who self-studied. I asked a few how they managed to balance what seemed like an impossible course load for even the most ambitious students. Never implicating themselves, they admitted that on obscure corners of the internet, you could illicitly access AP question test banks provided by College Board intended for use explicitly by teachers to help their students prepare. Memorize the test bank and skim official preparation resources, and there is a decent chance you will pass, especially during the COVID period's online exams reduced to less than an hour. Cheating is an efficient strategy for overworked and sleep-deprived students.

A Redditor laments in a mocking post, since deleted, about a cheating classmate who gained early admission to Harvard. "[Their cheating] coupled with all those posts about people faking passion and being admitted to schools that are like wE cAn TeLl WhEn yOu ArEn't PassiOnate, should remind you that AOs AREN'T ALL-KNOWING JUDGES OF YOUR WORTH." Because most students know at least one cheater who will inevitably gain admission, cheaters' successes undermine the entire higher education system's integrity. The college admissions madness incentivizes everyone to cut corners, with few unwilling to face social exclusion by being labeled a snitch.

Another user responded to the disgruntled post that "[the saying] 'cheaters never prosper' is absolute bullshit."[113] They're right. Admissions counselors aren't Saint Peter with an all-seeing God on their side that can pierce the hearts of any soul. They're more like a Judge Judy that squawks a lot but doesn't have any unique insights into human character. Cheaters often win, including electing to the presidency a man who cheats on his wives and lies about everything from recorded phone calls with world leaders down to his golf handicap.

Professor James Lang argues in *Cheating Lessons* that academically dishonest climates are pervasive at all levels of education.[114] He estimates at least two-thirds of all students will cheat at least once. A few become the habitual deceivers that appear in college essays or frustrated Reddit posts. Extrinsic rewards such as gaining admission to elite universities or earning a prestigious internship normalize dishonest behavior because the means justify the ends. Students are responding to incentives in their environment. Honesty requires more courage than surrendering to the pressures to take shortcuts.

Professor Mollie Galloway expands in a review of Lang's book that cheating isn't necessarily more pervasive than in previous generations. Still, dishonest behavior is less stigmatized and perceived as increasingly normal. "The [educational] culture encourages students, particularly those from upper-middle-class and affluent communities, to see cheating not as a compromising of their values but rather as a warranted and morally sound mechanism by which to attain the status they believe they are afforded."[115]

A few high schools cultivate a culture of cheating. Administrations feel pressure to maximize their AP exams passed or SAT scores earned to recruit future cohorts. Schools receive accolades when their graduates earn prestigious scholarships or university spaces. There are subtle pressures for teachers to turn a blind eye or administrators to cover up academically dishonest behavior. Teachers who are committed to honesty fight a never-ending battle like trying to stop alcohol consumption during Prohibition. Alcoholics will find a way to drink, and students will find a way to cheat.

Institutions punishing cheaters and plagiarizers is so rare that, when it happens, the incident often makes national news. Cheating at New York City's most prestigious magnet school, Stuyvesant, didn't end after they fired their principal, Stanley Teitel, for covering up a 66-student cheating ring in 2013. The *New York Post* reports five years later that "cheating is most common among students in their third year, the most academically challenging because the grades count heavily on college applications, the December survey found. A whopping 97 percent of juniors said they had engaged in academic dishonesty, while 56 percent of freshman said they had already cheated after just four months in the school."[116] Stuyvesant is the second-largest feeder high school in the country for MIT, Princeton, and Harvard.[117]

The most heartbreaking example of a culture of systematic cheating occurred at Louisiana's T.M. Landry. Named for the husband-and-wife-founders and principals Tracey and Mike Landry, it is an unaccredited college preparatory school housed in an abandoned factory. When Landry seniors started gaining admission to Cornell, Stanford, Princeton, and Harvard, among many other elite universities, between 2013 and 2018, it seemed like a tremendous success story.

Landry enrolls mostly black students from rural Louisiana, a state with one of the nation's lowest-performing education systems. Black families placed their trust in the Landrys, who promoted family and unity and an alternative education outside of white society's norms. The Landrys announced their 100 percent four-year college acceptance rate, made famous by viral YouTube "decision reveal" videos viewed millions of times. Wealthy families and organizations donated hundreds of thousands of dollars, and white and Asian students began enrolling.

Educators and school administrators nationwide wondered how Landry students could overcome such long odds. A *New York Times* investigation revealed a culture of violence, abuse, and outright fraud. "Visitors and cameras paraded through what had become a Potemkin village."[118] Because the school wasn't accredited, they do not receive any government funding and consequently fall outside of regulations and oversight. Class attendance was optional. It was, as one student described it, a "house built on water."

Mike Landry humiliated and demanded absolute obedience from his students, resulting in a 2013 conviction for battery. He required students to begin class by saying "I love you" in different languages, including an invented language, Mike-a-nese, to him directly. "Love" in Mike-a-nese is the word "kneel."

Students and families began speaking out following abuse allegations and substandard classroom instruction. Mr. Landry threatened to withhold transcripts if anyone left the school or blew the whistle. Students who chose to leave had their grades altered to ruin their future college prospects. He threatened students that elite university admissions officers had cameras in the school, so they better behave themselves.

T.M. Landry's Ivy League success comes down to outright fraud. Mike Landry doctored transcripts to show outstanding grades for loyal students, even for advanced courses that they never took or weren't offered at the school. The Landrys pressured students to report their family incomes as low as possible on the applications. Teachers recycled recommendation letters to laud students for extracurricular activities that didn't exist. In some instances, teachers recycled recommendations from previous years for future students without changing the names.

The Landrys counseled students to "go deep" on their essays, which pressured students to exaggerate or fabricate hardships that play into racial stereotypes and poverty tropes. They were the kinds of hardship stories that elite universities eat up. The only genuine instruction that students received revolved around the ACT. It was the only admissions factor that T.M. Landry staff couldn't easily manipulate. One graduate, Bryson Sassau, commented, "If it wasn't on the ACT, I didn't know it."

T.M. Landry's graduates had mixed results at their respective elite colleges. Despite entering college with writing and math skills that were many grade levels below their college classmates, some earned their degrees despite entering college with writing and math skills. Others, especially those who spent the most time at T.M. Landry, floundered and dropped out. Because their high school degrees weren't accredited, some alumni had to earn their GED to enroll at local colleges and begin their studies again. Landry college prep destroyed dozens of families whose elementary-age children didn't learn phonics. High school juniors tested in reading at a fourth-grade level.

Mike Landry defended himself by appealing to a culture that values credentials over character. "So what, we're not accredited… Three years in a row, Harvard took us. Stanford has taken us." Taking a page out of the corporate public relations playbook, the Landrys employed the law firm Couhig Partners to respond to the *Times's* allegations. Couhig based their 23-page report on five interviews that excluded the dozens of testimonies investigated by the *Times*. Predictably, their internal investigation minimizes the claims and amounts to "move along now, nothing to see here," while noting that there might be areas for minor improvement.[119]

In other words, the means justify the ends. Tom Brady keeps his seven Super Bowl rings, and Barry Bonds stays in the record books even though they cheated, too. T.M. Landry can brag to prospective families that their alumni hold Ivy League degrees. Although enrollment fell, T.M. Landry remains open.

The tragedy of T.M. Landry embodies the admissions madness taken to its logical conclusion. The Landrys are a symptom of the admissions madness, not a cause.

Elite universities seek diverse, academically stellar students. High schools everywhere will respond to these incentives, and families want to send their children to schools with a noted track record of success. In the worst-case scenarios, school cultures cater their entire curriculum and deploy any measures to meet those expectations at the expense of genuine learning or even a safe learning environment.

T.M. Landry and Varsity Blues are two sides of the same coin. The former exploited an admissions system that values diversity, whereas the latter defrauded universities by leveraging extreme wealth and privilege. As with the Varsity Blues scandal, university administrators responded in horror, wondering how such a thing could occur. Yet, they're the architects of a system that creates such perverse incentives that distort basic human decency. Look in the mirror!

It's also ironic that, on the one hand, admissions officers claim to know the context and resources of a given high school, while on the other, the Landrys hoodwinked dozens of elite colleges over a series of application cycles. If universities can't reliably catch a fraudulent high school, why would we believe they can consistently identify individual cheaters?

In *Talking to Strangers*, Malcolm Gladwell suggests that we're generally trusting and tend to **default to the truth**. In UT admissions, senior staff trained us to presume what a student writes or reports on their resume is true. Admissions processes aren't set up to identify fraud or look for subtle discrepancies in transcripts relative to a school's profile.

I don't believe the posturing of a former Stanford admissions counselor who posted a Reddit thread under the username "empowerly," insinuating that applicants will get caught if they cheat.[120] Given infinite time and resources, it's theoretically possible to catch most cheaters most of the time. However, there simply isn't enough time, sufficient information, or willpower to detect fraud in practice. Admissions gatekeepers are not the gods that they convey themselves to be publicly. Pretending to be all-powerful causes more harm than good and injects more anxiety into the system.

The immediate result of posts like that of the former Stanford counselor was to create a sense of paranoia among student Redditors. Dozens of comments wondered, "Will my ECs seem exaggerated? What if they contact my counselor?" The most honest response reads, "I presume you know that some students will take advantage of this information and lie better."

Sentiments like /u/empowerly's reinforce college admissions counselors' omniscience that provides the architecture for T.M. Landry to deceive their students that universities watched them. We are reluctant to acknowledge cheating unless there is overwhelming evidence suggesting fraud occurred. Educators are also averse to leveling claims of fraud against a student unless they're highly certain. Their reputations and careers are at stake if they wrongly accuse a student. It isn't surprising that the Landrys' deceit succeeded for many admissions cycles. To their credit, at least some of their unwitting alumni earned life-transforming elite college degrees that wouldn't have been possible otherwise. Cheaters, whether they are aware of their dishonesty or not, often win.

Even if we lived in a perfect world where every student reported their resume accomplishments honestly and earned their grades with integrity, three significant issues surround holistic review, regardless of a given university's particular review processes or student integrity. In the following sections, we explore issues around calibrating score criteria during file review training, maintaining consistency among all file reviewers throughout the admissions cycle, and drawing granular distinctions between borderline applicants during "re-reads" that "shape" an incoming class.

"Shaping the class," when committees move students from the admission to the waitlist and rejection piles and vice versa, is the most bullshit among all the admissions review witchcraft. Borderline students never know how close they are to admission because all rejection letters read the same.

Next, I share my experiences reviewing files for UT-Austin to expose their haphazard approach to college admissions before exploring college admissions literature that calls into question holistic review more generally.

6.5 Reviewing files as a UT-Austin Undergraduate Admissions Counselor

At UT-Austin, file reviewers received office-wide training in Austin in early August.[121] For a few days, an English Department professor who trained other university admissions review teams and consulted for College Board instructed all admissions staff to read sample files to "calibrate" our scores. We silently read files and then raised our hands whether we felt the file was a 1, 2, 3, and so on, out of a possible 6 points. The idea was that if we reviewed and discussed files collectively, we would have an idea of what 4s and 5s look like when we are reading at home or in the office.

I witnessed during training that no matter how hard they tried to standardize the review process, it was impossible for every reviewer to see a file in the same way. What some saw as a 5, others saw as a 4, and a few scored as a perfect 6. The professor had his own strong opinions on what each file should receive. There was always an argument and rarely a consensus. When you get right down to it, there are no exact definitions for each score. With over 60,000 applications, there will be many different kinds of 4s and 5s, yet the only tool available was to fit applicants into these imprecisely defined boxes.

For any given applicant, there are arguments to be made about which score they should receive. Moreover, a 6 late in the admissions cycle looks different than a 6 early on, because the strongest applicants tend to submit their applications first. When reviewing a sea of crummy applications near the end of the cycle, a mediocre 3 during training might look like an above-average 5. It isn't possible to maintain calibration throughout an admissions cycle.

Jeffrey Selingo noted the same phenomenon while observing Emory University's review system. "Adhering to consistent standards over many months of reading season is a Sisyphean task for admissions officers given the tensions inherent in their jobs."[122]

Starting in mid-September, admissions counselors and outside reviewers begin the review process. Not everyone who reviews UT-Austin applications is an admissions counselor. It is standard practice for UT and other universities such as the U California system with high application volumes to hire people with advanced degrees or previous admissions experience to help review. In one year, UT financial aid counselors and graduate students helped with admissions review.

File delivery is random, so I reviewed files from across Texas and around the world. I never knew the students I reviewed, but at smaller universities, they might only review applicants in their territory. I typically read my files at home or when I was bored at high school lunchroom visits. File review takes place on an online portal, and applications are uploaded twice each day once the application is complete.

I assigned a single score from 1 to 6 based on an applicant's fit for their major and overall desirability. Each reviewer's score is supposed to make a bell curve, with most applicants receiving a 3 or 4. In practice, however, very few counselors achieved an equal distribution. One staff member in our office assigned tons of 3s and 6s but few 4s and 5s, so his graph looked like a double-humped camel. He and others received reprimands from senior staff tasked with monitoring consistency, but they never revoked review privileges. It's impossible to maintain consistency and accuracy among potentially hundreds of file reviewers. Whichever reviewer you receive and their score distribution pattern—whether strict or lenient or random—determines potentially more than whatever you submit in your essays and resume.

Each UT-Austin application is scored twice by junior reviewers—a recent development to counter reviewers with uneven distributions. If there is a discrepancy between the two scores, a senior reviewer adjudicates the dispute. Junior reviewers do not see each other's scores. Suppose you're unlucky enough to receive two strict reviewers who are not sympathetic to your application. In that case, you may not gain admission despite possessing academics well above average for your desired program. That helps explain why applicants with stellar academics and strong resumes still occasionally get denied.

When I worked for UT, we were severely overburdened with the number of files assigned. There was a "collective action" problem where a few counselors read a disproportionate number of files. We had to compensate for those who didn't adequately do their job. One-third of our job description required file review. All of December and January was dedicated to file review, yet many counselors would fall far behind every year while others read their files each day.

By December, some counselors had more than two hundred files waiting to be reviewed, some of which had been completed by students as early as September. Learning your admissions decision earlier than others may come down to whether your early application has stagnated in someone's inbox for months. Senior staff then reassigned files from low-output readers to responsible ones.

I woke up one day in the middle of my busiest college fair week, driving hundreds of miles daily in Fort Worth and West Texas, to see over a hundred files deposited into my portal. There was intense pressure to read files, and undoubtedly, at times, precision was sacrificed for speed. That puts added stress on high-performing counselors to carry the burden of their incompetent colleagues. Internal office politics drive much of the admissions mechanics at all universities, which is unknowable and outside of an applicant's control. A few counselors doing most of the review work was a classic *Animal Farm* problem. In George Orwell's famous critique of Stalinist communism, some unappreciated animals like Boxer did most of the work on the farm while the lazy pigs refused to do the dirty work.

By the end of my last semester working for UT, I had read over 800 files. Other counselors read fewer than 300. Some reviewers were more accurate than others. They may have been reprimanded, but I never heard of anyone being fired or having their review duties relinquished. Sometimes, especially for files in the C group, which are applicants with very poor academics who would not gain admission even with a perfect review score, I spent fewer than five minutes reviewing. I once got reprimanded by senior admissions staff for reading too quickly—as if I had a choice, given the reassigned applications burden—but not for scoring inconsistently or inaccurately. On average, I read eight to ten files per hour.

The biggest takeaway is that—and this applies to all holistic review universities' admissions processes—your application is a "quick read." Reviewers are spending no more than eight to ten minutes on your application. That doesn't stop some programs from requiring five or more Princetons' worth of essay submissions, yet they dispense with them within minutes. Skimming also exposes the absurdity of nearly endless essay requirements even at nonselective universities that I highlight in the first chapter. The asymmetry between the dozens of hours students spend on their essays and the skimming of their application highlights the power disparity between universities and families.

6.6 Shaping the class and related hocus pocus

For certain UT-Austin majors, particularly for applicants on the border, senior staff conduct "re-reads" in January and February to allocate admissions spaces for borderline applicants. Committee re-reads help "shape" the incoming class at most holistic review universities. Shaping the class is arbitrary, inconsistent, and inaccessible to anyone except the admissions' high priests and university presidents who have the ultimate say in which students get in. Re-reads is also the time when the university decides whether to create a waitlist.

Junior counselors like me—the ones who actually visited high schools and interacted with the public—weren't allowed input in UT's shaping process. Most of us weren't even aware of how senior staff revised scores and drew the final lines on Excel spreadsheets that determined who gained admission. I rely instead on secondary sources.

While observing the committee review process for borderline applicants during Yale's re-read process, William Deresiewicz in *Excellent Sheep* writes, "In six hours of committee work, we disposed of somewhere between 100 and 125 cases or about three or four minutes per applicant." There simply isn't enough time in the day or staff to sift through record numbers of applications year after year. Disposing applications so quickly calls into question the admissions official line that they care about getting to know their future students.

Journalist Jacques Steinberg embedded himself for a year inside highly-selective Wesleyan's admissions and recruitment office. His 2003 book *The Gatekeepers* does an excellent job of humanizing applicants and their admissions reviewers. Wesleyan scored applicants on a scale of 1 to 9 on a half dozen categories. Steinberg details the arbitrary distinctions reviewers must make to determine why one student is more deserving of a space over another.

How might a reviewer evaluate an academically excellent student of color from a wealthy family relative to a slightly less credentialed peer from a first-generation, working-class Asian family? He concludes, "The daunting task of determining who makes the cut and who does not is anything but scientific.... The officers will often rely as much on their gut feelings as on numbers."

Wesleyan admissions counselors concede that the process isn't universally fair nor always consistent. Two decades ago, when Steinberg wrote, their staff lamented that their record number of applications made their jobs more difficult. Wesleyan has received double the number of applications and admitted less than half as many students since Steinberg's publication. The incoming freshmen class sizes have remained the same at around 750–800 students.

Review by committee is one mechanism to distribute the eventual decision to many staff members and give each student multiple looks. Fewer spaces allotted to higher applicant numbers means reviewers have the impossible task of making increasingly finer delineations between who receives a space or doesn't make the cut.

Jeffrey Selingo spent part of his research observing Davidson University's Early Decision admissions review process. Davidson may not have a Brown or Rice brand name, but they're highly selective, admitting less than 20 percent of their applicants. He observes that application review is like wading through "a sea of sameness."

Applicants and their personal statements begin to look very similar. For a Western society that emphasizes individuality and each person's uniqueness, little distinguishes one applicant from one another. During the final shaping process, Davidson admits, denies, or defers students on "a small element in a file that turns the group's opinion."

Selingo narrates a scene where the Davidson committee considers a borderline applicant who at first seemed unremarkable in the sea of sameness. Despite scoring a 32 on the ACT, the applicant was initially placed in the deferral/deny pile. "The admissions officer says he felt the student 'didn't check off all the boxes' on academics because she focused on other things." Further scrutiny of her essay reveals that her commitment to wildlife preservation went beyond a casual hobby. She's a mahout, which the assigned reviewer shares with the committee, is a person trained to take care of elephants. The applicant spent time in Thailand working at elephant sanctuaries. "'Did her privilege give her the chance to do that?' someone asks. The committee member wants to be sure his colleagues are not easily swayed by a glamorous tale."

After an exchange that lingers for more than the usual minute or two, the committee seems satisfied that she's sufficiently checked her privilege. Cleaning elephant feet in Thailand seemed to outweigh great but not outstanding academics. The committee moved from rejection to unanimous support for admission, an example of the **Von Restorff effect**. An item that sticks out is more likely to be remembered and given greater emphasis than other items. She distinguished herself among the sea of sameness. Applicants gaining admission through rare or exceptional achievements fuels anxiety for younger students seeking ever more obscure ways to differentiate themselves in crowded applicant pools.

Selingo observes that holistic review is not formulaic. Although he acknowledges that shaping processes are inherently unfair, he stops short of calling the process arbitrary or random. Admissions committees meet a final time before releasing their decisions to assess whether their upcoming class matches previous years' enrollment metrics. They evaluate geographic and racial diversity and even gender, especially as male students become rarer at liberal arts colleges or STEM-heavy colleges desire more females. Staff moves applicants between admit, waitlist, and deny piles to meet institutional needs based on major choice, legacy status, athletics, and so on.

Even need-blind schools may use nonfinancial cues such as zip code or high school to assess a student's ability to pay and admit a wealthy applicant over one that might require substantial need-based aid. Applicants will never know whether they gained admission outright or received an initial placement on the waitlist or reject pile before institutional forces dictate their admission.

Although admissions committees may use imperfect talent selection systems, the *perception* is that the process is arbitrary and random. Whether the process is arbitrary on the inside, to the students and families outside of the Ivory Towers who receive their decisions, it gives the impression of being random. Perceptions of randomness matter more than the reality of the mechanics of file review.

Suspicions of unfairness motivated recent lawsuits among Asian American communities that elite universities deploy holistic review as a tool for subtle exclusion. A recent unsuccessful lawsuit forced Harvard to reveal its admissions "trade secrets" that raised more questions than it answered about how they winnow down their applicant pool. Reading coverage like the *New York Times* article "'Lopping,' 'Tips' and the 'Z-List': Bias Lawsuit Explores Harvard's Admissions Secrets" dizzies families and high school educators trying to make sense of what *really* matters.[123]

6.7 Bias, errors, and privilege

Bias and errors are bound to enter the process in subtle ways, depending on the reviewer's background, mood, or whether they've had lunch or their morning coffee. COVID-19 undoubtedly places added stress on admissions committees and potentially clouds their judgment.

Steinberg in *The Gatekeepers* reports that Wesleyan admissions officers are trained to actively bring in their background and find students they relate with, contrary to a scientific approach that strives for objectivity. The *Chronicle of Higher Education* conducted a survey presented in an April 2016 article, "In Admissions Decisions, the Deciders' Background Plays a Big Role," that confirms a practice I witnessed. Admissions reviewers are more likely to view favorably those who come from similar backgrounds.

"Women gave applicants better admissions recommendations overall than men did. They showed a preference for the low-income applicant, who was described in the simulation as having lower standardized-test scores and having taken less-advanced courses than one other applicant. They showed no preference for the simulation's high-achieving applicant from an upper-middle-class high school. Admissions officers of color were much less likely than were white admissions officers to admit the simulation's high-achieving, upper-middle-class applicant."[124]

Regardless of an admissions officer's background or ethnicity, reviewing files is tiring, demanding, and thankless. All reviewers are susceptible to fatigue, amplified by record application numbers each year. Jeffrey Selingo provides further commentary: "[File readers] each bring their own bias to the table and they learn as the process unfolds, especially readers new to the job.

"They work with incomplete and imperfect information provided by applicants and high schools. They review an ever-increasing number of files under immense time pressures and sometimes with different colleagues. And they struggle with the same human frailties as any of us—they get distracted, tired, hungry, and sick. It's not that their choices are arbitrary, but their reasoning for those choices is sometimes unclear."[125]

Later on, he concludes, "It's nearly impossible for admissions officers to avoid viewing applicants through the prism of their own lives. Everyone has a soft spot for someone like themself. Professional training, paired reading, and committees are meant to root out bias, but that doesn't make the process necessarily fair, nor is it meant to."[126]

Simply put, you can never know why a given student gained admission or not, partly because no single reviewer is entirely responsible for an outcome, nor do you have access to their mind at the time of application review.

Compounding perceptions of unfairness are that many spaces aren't equally accessible to all applicants. I discuss the Early Decision racket in chapter 8.1, whereby up to a quarter of spaces are reserved for mostly privileged students with the know-how and financial assurances to submit an early application.

Universities claim that they want students from rural backgrounds or from states such as North Dakota or Montana that are less likely to send students to elite Northeast or West Coast schools. However, their budgets do not allow recruiting students from obscure high schools. When UT-Austin shuffled our bureaucracy in 2013, the first admissions counselors and regional recruiting centers to receive the ax were less densely populated West Texas regions in Lubbock, Abilene, Amarillo, and Midland, along with the East Texas outreach center located in Tyler. Universities want geographic diversity but are often unwilling to admit a slightly below-average SAT applicant to compromise their average test score, a factor in *US News* college rankings.

College admissions privileges students who attend high schools that send most of their graduates to four-year universities.

One belief I've modified after reading *Who Gets In and Why* is the oversized role one's high school plays in the review process. Before, I didn't think your high school mattered much or at all. However, Selingo writes, "During my time inside admissions offices I quickly discovered that the unit being evaluated was less often the *applicant* than the applicant's *high school.*" (emphasis his)[127] High schools with better reputations receive subtle advantages in review processes in addition to the benefits allotted to high schools that spend larger sums per student.

Universities develop close relationships with high school counselors who can refer their most interested students. A mediocre kid from an excellent high school may receive the benefit of the doubt from admissions reviewers. In contrast, a similar student from a rural high school seems like more of a four-year graduation risk or might be less likely to enroll. Universities are also more likely to take the top tier of high schools with dozens of applicants than students in the second tier whose academics may be stronger than the top tier of a similar high school with fewer applicants.

Students in college-going communities are more likely to "demonstrate interest" by having access to and attending college fairs, visiting campus, emailing their assigned admissions representatives, and attending online events. Savvy high school counselors at elite schools help their seniors demonstrate interest by liaising with admissions officers.

According to the 2019 NACAC survey, 16 percent of four-year universities report that "demonstrated interest" is a factor of considerable importance, while another 24 percent rate it moderately important. Demonstrating interest helps enrollment managers predict which students are more likely to enroll. Demonstrated interest matters more at selective universities than extracurriculars, class rank, teacher and counselor recommendations, and interviews.

By contrast, only 4 percent of universities prioritize work experience as of "considerable importance"—the same institutions who claim to want low-income students—disregarding that the students most likely to have jobs are those whose families need an extra source of income. Students with jobs also presumably have less time to dedicate to their college search and applications. Making it your job to demonstrate interest is a more optimal admissions strategy than working at an actual job.

Interacting with a university seems like a neutral way to gauge a student's propensity to enroll. However, it favors students with the savvy and admissions literacy to try harder than the students from underserved communities. Universities rarely publish precisely how they calculate demonstrated interest nor what role it plays, despite 40 percent saying it's at least moderately important. Advanced marketing and analytical tools deployed by university marketing departments that I unpack in chapter 8 are easily gamed by students who open every email or click-through to feign interest.

Demonstrated interest is yet another tool that increases a university's control at the expense of most applicants. The simplest way to bring more equity to college access is to outlaw demonstrated interest as a factor. Forgoing demonstrated interest will never happen on a broad scale because universities are unwilling to surrender their enrollment management powers. They also don't want to be the first mover for relinquishing the advantages conferred by considering demonstrated interest.

A more pronounced benefit for educated families comes from preferential treatment to "legacy" applicants whose parents or extended family received their degrees from a particular institution. Daniel Golden produced one of the most original books

Factor	N	Considerable Importance	Moderate Importance	Limited Importance	No Importance
Grades in All Courses	220	74.5	15.0	5.5	5.0
Grades in College Prep Courses	220	73.2	16.8	5.9	4.1
Strength of Curriculum	219	62.1	21.9	8.7	7.3
Admission Test Scores (SAT, ACT)	221	45.7	37.1	12.2	5.0
Essay or Writing Sample	220	23.2	33.2	24.1	19.5
Student's Demonstrated Interest	218	16.1	23.9	28.0	32.1
Counselor Recommendation	218	15.1	40.4	26.6	17.9
Teacher Recommendation	219	14.2	40.2	26.5	19.2
Class Rank	220	9.1	29.1	34.1	27.7
Extracurricular Activities	219	6.4	42.9	32.0	18.7
Portfolio	219	6.4	11.9	26.9	54.8
Subject Test Scores (AP, IB)	219	5.5	18.3	35.2	41.1
Interview	219	5.5	16.4	28.3	49.8
Work	217	4.1	28.6	36.9	30.4
State Graduation Exam Scores	218	2.3	8.7	18.8	70.2
SAT II Scores	216	1.9	5.6	14.8	77.8

SOURCE: NACAC Admission Trends Survey, 2018–19.

written on college admissions, *The Price of Admission* (2006). He cites that legacy students applying to universities such as Notre Dame, Stanford, Duke, and Harvard, among many others, routinely "make up 10 to 15 percent of the student body, often despite lesser credentials." In practice, some universities confer a legacy advantage equivalent to over 100 points on the SAT. Universities such as Johns Hopkins ended legacy admission with little impact on alumni donations or graduation rates, so there are few compelling reasons to continue a practice that overwhelmingly favors privileged students. Universities who still practice legacy admission cannot credibly claim that they're principally concerned about diversity and college access.

Golden's research suggests that as high as 25 percent of admissions spaces at elite universities are reserved for already well-off and well-connected "hooked" populations. In addition to legacies, many universities provide tremendous advantages for the children of wealthy donors and non-alumni "development cases" whose families may donate in the future. Donald Trump's son-in-law Jared Kushner gained admission to Harvard in 1998, despite a mediocre academic record, following a $2.5 million donation by his convicted felon father, Charles Kushner. Not only do cheaters often win, but advantages accumulated through dishonest means amplify the benefits gained from subsequent cheating. Regardless, universities compromise admissions standards and dilute their student body's quality when they court children of high-profile celebrities and athletes.

Affluent families are quick to criticize African American scholarship recipients for sports such as football and basketball. However, Golden's research suggests that academically under-qualified female athletes playing less popular sports that are guaranteed under Title IX, such as polo, squash, rowing, and equestrian, receive significant admissions advantages. He writes,

"[Title IX] has increased gender diversity in college sports while decreasing socioeconomic diversity on athletic teams and campuses as a whole."

Atlantic staff writers Derek Thompson and Linda Flanagan have spent years covering dropping youth sports participation rates among low-income families. Nowadays, only wealthy families can afford the high participation costs.[128] Selingo updates Golden's 2006 book, assessing that little has changed. If anything, the youth sports madness has taken on an outsized role. He writes, "Athletics can assist applicants in a different way, one likely to prove far more valuable than a meager scholarship: access to an elite school that otherwise might be off-limits academically."[129]

He references Division III small liberal arts college Amherst as a textbook example of how "rich kid sports" advantage society's most privileged. Division III schools do not offer athletics scholarships, so most of their teams are composed of student athletes who come from wealthy families.

Amherst's total enrollment is 1,900, with 676 athletes on campus during fall 2018. They enroll six more athletes than all of Division 1 powerhouse Alabama where athletes make up less than 2 percent of the student body. Amherst's admissions rate, when accounting for athletes, is in the mid-single digits compared with its published 13 percent rate. At Georgetown, 10 percent of incoming students are athletes earmarked with special advantages, and at Bucknell, the rate is nearly double. Selingo raises a compelling question of why one kind of extracurricular—sports and athletics—should receive such an overwhelming admissions preference. He hypothesizes, "The outsized role athletics plays in admission is a relic from a previous era in higher education when sports defined the character of a man." Recall that seventeenth-century John Harvard stipulated athletics as a primary admissions criteria relevant to applicants today.

Since three-quarters of Amherst's athletes are white, and nearly all are affluent, they must over-admit low-income and students of color to meet their diversity metrics. Overall admissions rates are deceptive because they don't account for "hooks" such as legacies, earmarked athletes, the sons and daughters of university faculty and government officials, or connections with wealthy donors. Well-connected and savvy families pressure presidents and admissions directors who routinely bend admissions standards to let in their unqualified offspring. The perception that elite college admissions disadvantage middle-class families has validity.

Informal quota systems and outright fraud come at the real or perceived expense of Asian Americans, middle-class Americans regardless of race, students attending public high schools, and those who will be the first in their families to attend college. Your parents' educational background, wealth, and zip code matter more to college admissions than your efforts. The recent Varsity Blues scandal reinforces suspicions that, with enough wealth and connections and a lack of scruples, mediocre students can gain admission anywhere. Therefore, holistic review means different things for different applicants contingent on the whims of your admissions reviewer and the unknowable and constantly shifting needs of the university.

6.8 Do recommendation letters make a difference?

Recommendation letters don't make much of a difference for most students most of the time.

My favorite finding from the college admissions commentary archives comes from January 7, 1979, with a refreshingly honest headline: "An Admissions Man Says It Isn't So Hard."[130] The

Admissions Man is Richard M. Moll, a former Harvard and Yale admissions reviewer and then Director of Admissions at Vassar. An accompanying cartoon graphic features a nervous Yale admissions administrator cutting a house in two with a knife and fork as the family looks on.

Moll's polemic on the application process reads the same then as today. He complains about non-standardized grading systems, "lifeless" essays, unhelpful interviews, and universities that possess all of the power at the expense of families. He cites the 1974 Buckley Amendment, more commonly known as FERPA, that struck down institutional confidentiality.

FERPA allowed students to view their reference letters, among other materials. In the years following the Buckley Amendment, Moll observes that teachers and principals are less inclined to write honestly about a candidate's character or ability. "Principals, counselors and teachers fear that they might be sued if they boldly—and honestly—write on a college admissions form: 'Martha's record is rather good, but Martha is rather dull.'"[131]

Today's Common Application strongly urges that applicants "waive" their FERPA rights so that they cannot see their recommendation letters. Reference letters remain mostly confidential, yet all recommendations are subject to the **courtesy bias**. Counselors and teachers are highly unlikely to write anything less than complimentary platitudes and superlatives. Referees may feel flattered when someone asks them for a reference and feel subtle pressure to highlight positive characteristics. Reference letter hyperbole is the norm, muddying up the terrain for genuinely exceptional candidates to distinguish themselves from every other "best of" applicant.

Moll contrasts the contemporary watered-down recommendation letter with its origins. Reference letters originally formed the "old boy" system where a well-placed reference from people in power could pass an applicant through Ivy gatekeepers without further consideration. Going further back in history, Margaret Ferguson in "The Letter of Recommendation as Strange Work" cites Roman statesman Cicero as an early example of "the asymmetries of power and knowledge endemic to the letter of recommendation in its long and multicultural history."[132] Cicero lived in a period of human history with rigid hierarchies between the aristocratic class and the masses.

Recommendation letters historically tied the sender's reputation to the recipient, making them a substantially higher-stakes affair than today's prosaic teacher's letter. Teachers today might write dozens of references in a single year, whereas historically, a person in power issued them very sparingly. Cicero's interesting technique to generate reference material was constructing a scenario or moral dilemma to showcase how their reference might respond, which distinguished their candidate from others. Even in Cicero's time, most reference letters read the same, so it took considerable effort and ingenuity for a referee to differentiate their submission.

Ferguson reports how letters throughout history have functioned as passports to cross borders, testimony to a craftsman's character or skills, a type of gift, membership to enter the clergy, and signal of social class, among many others. VIPs or highly connected individuals who give contemporary applicants a substantial advantage in the holistic review process is a throwback to less democratic, more aristocratic times. Nowadays, VIP letters are rare exceptions, relative to the hundreds of thousands of applicants that lack wheel-greasing connections.

Teacher and counselor recommendation letters are a fixture at elite universities. Their precise role in holistic review remains unclear and subject to the whims of each institution. Some universities provide a separate score in their internal file review process, but recommendation letters suffer from vagueness, like most essays. It's questionable how much utility a distinct recommendation letter score provides reviewers.

Ambiguities abound about which universities require, recommend, or allow letter submissions as an option. According to the federal Common Data sets, at least 1,000 universities consider reference letters as part of their admissions process. Like the proliferation of essay requirements at less-selective universities, campuses that could admit most of their applicants on academics alone still require recommendation letters. Some universities explicitly require a core subject teacher, whereas others don't. Many universities that require counselor letters—which provide context to a student's course rigor or discrepancies between grades and test scores—request their submission on templates specific to that university. With more students applying to an increasing number of universities, counselors recreate the wheel many times.

When I worked for UT, there was no limit on the number of letters a student could submit. The record I observed was eight. Moll writes, "Now we say, 'The thicker the folder, the thicker the kid,' surmising that a stack of unsolicited recommendations usually means an attempt to disguise a weak candidacy." Recommendation letters are the most "try-hard" aspect of college admissions because students incorrectly assume that the quantity of letters matters more than the quality. It's always preferable to submit a single strong letter where you've collaborated with your reference than four half-baked ones.

Except for interviews, letters are arguably the most time-consuming application item relative to the difference they make. For high schools with upward of 900 students per counselor, and with many *US News* top-100 private schools requiring counselor letters, references require tens of millions of work hours worldwide from already-overburdened high school staff. Fifteen percent of universities report that references are of "considerable importance" in the review process, less than the importance of essays but substantially more than extracurriculars and interviews.

Among the thousands of applications I reviewed for UT-Austin, I can recall less than ten times that an outstanding letter bumped up a student's review score. Like college essays, most teacher reference letters aren't especially well written or insightful. They're vague, not specific to the student, and a repetition of what's already on the transcript or resume. Students don't provide adequate documentation about the specific examples or events they desire their letter writer to discuss. "Brag sheets" often amount to regurgitation of what will have already been mentioned elsewhere in the application, so reference letters add little if any depth. They miss opportunities to discuss exceptional circumstances in favor of clichés. Consequently, references make claims like "Jared is the most promising student in my 20 years of teaching" without providing any evidence or examples to corroborate what makes Jared supposedly unique. When every letter claims a student is seemingly outstanding, that means nobody is.[133]

Rare are the teachers with reputations for writing excellent letters with a clear framework for students to request them. They have rigorous standards, decline more requests than they accept, and submit comparatively few letters. Other teachers are reference mills who churn out dozens each year. Most write superficial letters that could apply to most of their students most of the time.

High school teacher Andrew Simmons shares an educator's perspective in an *Atlantic* essay, "The Art of the College Recommendation Letter." Reference letters tending toward courtesy use loaded terms that "reduces students to bland shades of their real vibrant selves" or are blatantly misleading. "A 'respectful, quiet' student might sit in the back of class and never contribute to discussions. A 'gregarious, social' student may be a pain in the ass unless his talkativeness is harnessed for an academic purpose. A 'late bloomer' probably tanked his freshman year."[134]

As with college essays, it's challenging to decipher what, exactly, the writer intends to communicate. Simmons observes that he and his colleagues, despite their best intentions, contribute to "admissions officers see[ing] hundreds of letters and encounter the same clichéd phrases and trite euphemisms again and again." Teachers are busy enough sponsoring extracurriculars, attending staff development meetings, and other non-classroom commitments where they're not compensated.

Simmons provides concrete tips for writing better recommendation letters that portray a student beyond their resume or academic statistics. However, he admits that his suggestions require heroic efforts to investigate a student and communicate them in honest, non-hyperbolic ways. If there were ever a time to relax or discontinue reference letters, it's the pandemic, but the madness continues all the same. As far as I can tell, no university has discontinued teacher or counselor recommendation letter requirements despite a tidal wave of institutions opting out of the SAT. I suspect this admissions cycle will see a notable downtick in reference quality due to virtual learning.

Admissions veteran Jon Boeckenstedt, formerly the Director of Admissions at DePaul University, calls into question the utility and fairness of recommendation letters in a March 4, 2016, *Washington Post* article.[135] He observes that the recommendation letter system has changed little in the past century. He questions their supposed utility "to illuminate nuances of character, intellect, curiosity, and special talent that help an applicant rise above the masses of otherwise similar students." Like this book, he urges looking at recommendation letters from the students' rather than the institutions' perspective. Teenagers navigate the reference letter process blindly.

Attaining references privileges students who can sort out which teachers are the strongest writers and willing to dedicate adequate time to submit their best effort. Boeckenstedt writes, "The letter has virtually nothing to do with the *student's* performance, and a lot to do with the *teacher's ability* to turn a phrase, note interesting character traits, structure a cogent series of paragraphs that tell a story, and even throw in a few instances of *discordia concors* to show his or her own wit and charm. In short, it's as much about the teacher as the student."

He makes the obvious point that students attending small college preparatory schools will receive more thoughtful letters from staff who know them better than their public-school peers. Universities that require counselor letters confer an added advantage to prep school or high-resource public school students who often have a dedicated counselor or a small army of staff members exclusively responsible for helping their students navigate university gatekeepers. Counselors at most public schools cater not to their highest tier, college-going students. Instead, they focus on resolving family crises, discipline issues, accommodating special needs students, identifying signs of abuse, and more routine drudgery such as schedule changes.

Boeckenstedt cites an example of how phrasing common to one part of the country or world may not translate to admissions reviewers at elite universities.

"These Iowa teachers would frequently write about how the student is intellectually head and shoulders above his peers, then add something like, 'He is never afraid to ask a question when he doesn't understand a concept.' If you don't speak Iowan, you may not realize this teacher has sent a coded message, saying, 'This student is brilliant, but among his peers, he still exhibits that most-prized Midwestern value called 'humility.' Yet invariably, one member of the admissions committee, a hard charger from the east coast, would take this to mean, 'The kid is slow on the uptake.' How could the student or the teacher anticipate this?"

He acknowledges that letters can help promote an applicant's candidacy *when done well* but concludes that recommendation letters are yet another barrier to increasing college access, which calls into question the sincerity of the diversity zeitgeist.

Staff at the University of North Carolina Chapel Hill published a study around the same time as Boeckenstedt's op-ed. They identified "small but significant differences by gender and race in the average length of letters as well as the types of language used to describe students."[136] The researchers collected and coded over 5,000 undergraduate admissions recommendation letters. They found female recommenders wrote lengthier letters than their male counterparts, and humanities or social science teachers wrote longer letters (415 words, on average) than math and science instructors (374 words, on average). One obvious takeaway is it may be beneficial to ask your female social studies teachers for a reference.

Letters exceeding 600 words correlated with an applicant's acceptance rate relative to those submitting letters totaling 200 or fewer words. Longer letters support the claim that students attending high-resource schools gain subtle advantages from teachers who know them better and are willing and have the time to write longer letters.

Moreover, female recommenders wrote letters on average 25 words longer for males versus 14 words for female applicants. STEM teachers used slightly fewer "ability" words for females relative to academically similar male students. The researchers qualify their findings by stressing that the differences in race and gender are slight, with more similarities than differences. Still, they found other differences in the adjectives or types of language references used when discussing students of color.

Gaps in expectations about what kinds of students should receive bachelor's degrees influence a recommender's potential bias. An innovative longitudinal study evaluated two teacher's perceptions of more than 6,000 high school sophomores. White teachers were more enthusiastic about the prospects of white students compared with their black classmates. "When teachers of different races evaluated the same black student, white teachers were nine percentage points less likely than their black colleagues to expect that student to earn a college degree. This gap was more pronounced for black male students than for black female students."[137] Because black teachers are underrepresented in American schools, aspiring black college students have fewer opportunities to solicit reference letters from teachers who may be more supportive of their future goals.

Even though recommendation letters favor the privileged, are potentially prone to bias, and require a disproportionate amount of time relative to the difference they make for any given applicant, they're likely here to stay. Students attending resource-rich schools experience burdens and pressure to secure the best references. In contrast, students living in poverty are unlikely to understand their importance or have the wherewithal to secure high-quality letters at all. First-generation college students or children living in non-professional families may not have family members or friends to consult about navigating the reference process. Because many top universities require reference letters for admissions eligibility, reference letters erect barriers to college access even though they're rarely a deciding factor.

6.9 The truth about interviews

College interviews are a waste of time and resources. Most universities seem to agree.

Of the 16 admissions factors from the most recent NACAC survey, interviews rank fourth to the bottom. Interviews rank below AP/IB scores, extracurriculars, and recommendation letters and above only work experience, state graduation exam scores, and even SAT II Subject Tests. Half of responding universities say they're not important, and another quarter report that interviews are of little significance. Only 12 out of 219 universities (5.5 percent) rank it as considerably important compared with 24 universities in 2007.

The emphasis on interviews in the holistic admissions process seems to be declining over the past decade, yet more programs than ever require them. In fact, no other criterion has witnessed such a steep decline. Many institutions openly concede that interviews are rarely the decisive factor for a candidate, usually couched in the language of "don't worry so much about it, anxious applicant." Unsurprisingly, if you google "college interview," you're offered nothing but guides and tips, yet no popular blogs seem to question whether they should exist at all.

If interviews are less critical, then why in the hell do many students interview half a dozen or more times each year? Madness!

Determining how many universities recommend or require interviews is a challenge because, unsurprisingly, there isn't a comprehensive database of interview requirements.[138] They change from year to year. At least 70 universities offer the option, which isn't including honors programs or scholarships that often require an interview component. Some universities and programs allow students to upload a short video of themselves like they're auditioning for reality television.

Most Ivy League universities and *US News* top-50 private universities allow for interviews. Adding confusion to exactly how they factor into admissions are whether they're optional, recommended, strongly recommended, or required. In most applicants' minds, the nuances between the first three not-optional optional options are perceived as equivalent to being required by applicants seeking any way to gain an edge. NACAC's website features a guide titled "The Truth about Interviews," which leads with "the truth is, most college interviews are relaxed, informative, and *even fun* (emphasis mine)."[139]

The Truth about Interviews is that they're utter bullshit. Visit Reddit's A2C any time between November and January, and you can see the stark disconnect between how universities perceive the importance of interviews compared with the subjects they're interviewing. For most, it's neither relaxed, informative, nor fun.

Reassuring students that, if they're unable to interview, it in no way harms their chances seem suspect. Naturally, corporate-speak reassurances do nothing to dampen worry flames. Students may not be penalized, flagged, or assigned negative points for opting out of an interview. But the claim that interviews don't disadvantage applicants is also suspicious. Suppose some students are helping their candidacy by interviewing, and spaces at universities are a zero-sum game. Doesn't it follow students who opt out or are unable to interview incur a subtle penalty? At MIT, only 1 percent of students who opted out of interviews gained admission compared to ten times the number interviewed. If NACAC were being honest rather than serving as a shill for universities' interests, they would correct the record. Everything universities communicate about interviews is misleading and arbitrary. Students are correct to feel doubt.

Every university that conducts interviews weighs them differently, which adds another layer of opacity into an already foggy holistic review system. Students and families scour the internet to find "what the interview really means" at whichever universities they apply. Alumni volunteers or admissions representatives usually conduct them. Your interviewer may or may not be the first to read your admissions file or serve as the counselor assigned to your high school's recruitment territory. They might make written notes or assign you scores based on varied criteria such as curiosity, ambition, fit for major, etc.

Universities might request an interview of you, but for others, you're expected to reach out. Not every student who gets interviewed gains admission, and not all admitted students pursue an interview. Corporate or graduate school recruiting practices have an obvious and predictable funnel that begins with an application or HR screening. Next, an applicant receives a phone or group interview followed by an in-person or solo interview with senior staff before receiving an offer. Undergraduates have no idea what an interview signals for their admissions chances, if anything at all.

Some universities use interviews for evaluating your candidacy, and others for "informational purposes." It's naïve that Cornell, for example, communicates their interviews are for informational purposes while expecting a prospective applicant to act any less neurotic. Students often attempt to set up interviews for universities that don't provide them, such as UT-Austin or the University of California system schools.

The interview apparatus requires thousands of contact hours and tens of thousands of emails to coordinate and carry out for each highly selective university. Applicants conduct hundreds of thousands of interviews each year. It might be the single most time-intensive and wasteful aspect of the collective college admissions system, even though universities themselves admit it rarely makes a difference![140]

Some but not all Harvard applicants who receive an alumni interview are asked to complete a lengthy questionnaire duplicating what they already submitted on the Common Application. Their interview instructions read, "The alumni interviewer does not know you and has not seen or read any part of your Harvard application." A dozen questions and prompts follow about academic interests and achievements, notable extracurriculars, music or athletics pursuits, "describe what you did during the past two summers," and list any books you've read in the past year, among others.

Theories abounded on an admissions counselor Facebook group about whether the interviewer was "rogue" by making the student complete the questionnaire. Whether an interviewer is violating expected protocol is an irrelevant question to a nervous applicant who wants to do the right thing. They wouldn't fathom pushing back on the onerous questionnaire request or even wonder whether it's reasonable that they need to complete what amounts to an entire application. They're also unaware of what constitutes college interview standard operating procedures. An anxious student will undoubtedly spend hours dutifully completing their questionnaire late into the night, lest they potentially damage their dream school prospects. Like the application and holistic review process, more generally, interviews are not standardized or calibrated for consistency.

The college interview started around a century ago, first at Harvard. The other Ivy League schools followed, but the interview functioned less to determine their academic qualifications or "fit" and ensure they came from the "right" backgrounds. Adoption spread to other universities with the rise of modern holistic review in the second half of the twentieth century.

Programs that conduct interviews claim it allows them to "get to know the whole student" better, presuming incorrectly that a half-hour interview can adequately assess a candidate's interests and character. College interviewers occupy a position of power over the interviewee whether they're conscious of it or not. To an admissions reviewer, you're just another application, and the same analogy applies that you're just another interviewee among many. Whatever an interviewer's real or perceived capacity to influence a decision, applicants feel pressure to make their best first impressions because their lifetime goals hinge upon it.

Every implicit bias and systemic cognitive error relevant for admissions reviewers also applies to interviewers. Errors in reasoning are amplified by the power imbalances between interviewer and interviewee, insider and outsider, older and younger, gatekeeper and supplicant.

Malcolm Gladwell's recent book *Talking to Strangers* examines how making snap assumptions about others complicates interactions with people you don't know. We misinterpret one another and struggle with identifying when people are being deceptive or sincere. For example, personality traits exhibited by a policeman at a traffic stop are likely entirely different than at their child's birthday party. A cop can be aggressive in one context and loving in another.

The **fundamental attribution error** mistakes someone's personality or behavior as fixed rather than subject to changes in environment or context. A highly talented programmer who writes beautiful code might be less able or willing to verbalize their talents. Gifted poets might write eloquently yet are terrified by an open-mic night at their local coffee shop. Each one may be talkative, humorous, and playful with their siblings or best friends and silent to teachers and adults.

Interviews naturally privilege extroverts and conversationalists, providing ripe territory for bullshitting. America's obsession with "leadership" adds a further disadvantage to introverts who may be substantially more talented than a first impression or their resume indicates. Interviews are supposed to offer opportunities for students to "get off the resume" and discuss their interests and hobbies. However, students are coached so thoroughly to identify themselves through their accomplishments that they're less inclined to share about them even if they have noncurricular interests.

An interviewer may conduct dozens of calls or meetings, whereas, for the applicant, it may be their only face-to-face connection to the admissions committee. Before COVID, many interviews were limited to metropolitan areas, disadvantaging students living far from cities. It should be evident by now that students living in poverty or non-college-going communities are less equipped to navigate the etiquette of the nominally meritocratic interview. Nor do they have the resources to hire consultants to prepare them.

The *Atlantic* journalist Hayley Glatter interviews MIT Admissions Dean Stu Schmill in "The Futility of College Interviews." Dean Schmill makes the predictable argument that interviews supposedly level the playing field. "These interviews can be particularly important and helpful for students who come from under-resourced backgrounds."[141] MIT is one of the more forward-thinking and transparent admissions offices. Still, they succumb to the illusion that interviews help select talent *and* increase access for marginalized populations. Both claims are suspect. First-generation students who might benefit the most from interviews are the least likely to access them or even know they exist. The ubiquity of college interviews further calls into question the sincerity of elite universities' commitment to diversity.

Much of the social science research and cultural commentary surrounding interviews concerns jobs and corporations. Job interviews tend to be much more intensive and rigorous, deploying a battery of questionnaires, analytic puzzles, groupwork consultations, and so on. The corporate assumption is the same as college admissions: More information produces better forecasts. However, the best minds and most powerful computers at Google, McKinsey, and Goldman Sachs still haven't figured out how to reliably select for and sort their applicants.

Malcolm Gladwell, covering the corporate interview process in a 2000 *New Yorker* article "The New-Boy Network," concludes that conversations are less valuable and potentially more misleading than intuition suggests. Preempting *Talking to Strangers*, published two decades later, he writes, "That most basic of human rituals— the conversation with a stranger—turns out to be a minefield."[142]

Yale School of Management Professor Jason Dana makes the same point 17 years later after Gladwell's article.[143] Free-form, unstructured interviews offer the pretense of getting to know an applicant. The problem is "interviewers typically form strong but unwarranted impressions about interviewees, often revealing more about themselves than the candidates." His research suggests that interviews don't reliably provide information relevant to evaluating a candidate's fit. They may even be harmful, calling into question universities' absolute insistence that interviews can only help and never hurt applicants.[144]

Trained interviewers and admissions counselors, like MLB scouts, feel themselves **better than average** and demonstrate **illusory superiority** in their ability to assess talent. I assume interviewers from the corporate world or who assess talent for their occupation overrate their abilities even more relative to alumni interviewers who work in unrelated fields. Said another way, undergraduate students may be just as good at selecting future college students as career admissions professionals.

Dana concludes in his 2013 study that "interviewers probably over-value unstructured interviews. Our simple recommendation for those who make screening decisions is not to use them." He advises that people who interview or occupy talent selection roles recognize the limitations of their judgment and not overweight their conclusions.

College interviews are not an important part of the admissions process, yet they persist. They consume a considerable amount of institutional resources, time for the interviewers and their subjects, and are prone to bias and error. Among essays, standardized exams, recommendation letters, and other application materials, interviews seem to have the highest costs yielding the least benefits.

6.10 "Chance me" and the ludic fallacy

Holistic review isn't a tabulation of one's achievements, leadership positions, or volunteer hours. It also isn't a process that lines up applicants from one to 40,000 and draws an admissions line. Individual applicants are rarely, if ever, compared directly against one another. Although the perception of college admissions is that it's a zero-sum game, the reality is a lot more complicated.

Even if they desired to—and they don't—universities can't tell you why a given student gained admission, and another didn't. Admissions reviewers have the impossible task of reading between the lines about the broader context and character of an applicant and whether their "fit" for major and campus culture is sincere or not. They are making, at best, educated guesses and, at worst, are blinded by their own biases and errors in reasoning. Jeffrey Selingo observes, "Every year, top colleges turn away tens of thousands of students who could succeed on their campuses. It's never clear who is the more qualified, the better fit, the truly deserving—or what any of that would really mean."[145]

Much of the suffering caused by college admissions comes after admissions decisions are released. Seniors scour "college results" forums and YouTube videos to try and decipher why a given student gained admission at their perceived expense. An obvious folly of comparing yourself to an internet stranger is that you're unlikely to have access to their essays, resume, or recommendation letters and rely instead on their nonsensical self-assessments.

The Chance Me subreddit is a community mostly of unqualified college students assessing the chances of worried high school juniors and seniors who self-report their credentials and college list. Reddit's Chance Me and A2C is itself a highly distorted community. The average Redditor likely is in the top 1 percent of applicants worldwide, which gives the impression that every applicant posting their "stats" is phenomenal, discouraging merely excellent but not world-class students who come to the faulty conclusion that they're below average.

Survivorship bias means that you only see the most talented admissions students or those who got incredibly lucky. MIT admitted a single applicant with an ACT between 25 and 27 among 236 applications. Success stories from applicants with academics substantially below average give mediocre students the impression that they have a chance. By definition, you will never see college results posts and videos from the 235 MIT applicants scoring 25 to 27 who did not gain admission. Only the survivors boast of their successes.

Redditors love to attempt to call out supposed liars who post their anomalous admissions decisions, which is the **argument from incredulity**. Incredulous students assert that they cannot imagine how such a low academic student could get in; therefore, it must be false. However, there will always be some highly questionable outcomes in a large enough sample size that defy straightforward explanations. You're more likely to see anomalies publishing their results due to the survivorship bias than the hundreds of similar applicants who were rejected.

Nevertheless, MIT offered admission to zero applicants scoring less than 690 on the SAT Math, but that doesn't stop over 1,300 from trying each year. No amount of holistic review for a mediocre SAT math will tip the MIT admissions scales. Yet, students routinely mistake holistic review for meaning that if their resume and essays are Nobel worthy, they might have a chance. If your academics aren't perfect, you're not gaining admission to MIT.

I sometimes feel like Lauren Holly's character Mary Swanson in *Dumb and Dumber* when significantly below-average students ask me their admissions chances to universities way beyond their league.

My favorite scene occurs during an awkward moment in Mary's hotel. Jim Carey's character, Lloyd Christmas, makes an unwanted advance on Mary after traveling across the country to return her suitcase that she left at an airport. It should be obvious which character symbolizes MIT, and the other, a desperate applicant aiming out of their league.

After a few stutters and false starts, Lloyd begins. "I like you, Mary. I like you a lot!"

> Lloyd Christmas: I want to ask you a question, straight out, flat out, and I want you to give me the honest answer. What do you think the chances are of a guy like me and a girl like you ending up together?

> Mary Swanson: Well, Lloyd, that's difficult to say. We really don't...

> Lloyd Christmas: Hit me with it! Just give it to me straight! I came a long way just to see you Mary, just... The least you can do is level with me. What are my chances?

Distribution of SAT scores (Math)

SCORE	APPLICANTS	ADMITS	ADMIT RATE
750-800	11,342	1,081	10%
700-740	1,613	23	1%
650-690	758	0	0%
600-640	312	0	0%
<600	254	0	0%

Table 1 MIT SAT Math Subscores Class of 2024

Mary Swanson: Not good.

Lloyd Christmas: [he gulps, his mouth twitching] You mean, not good like one out of a hundred?

Mary Swanson: I'd say more like one out of a million.

Lloyd Christmas: [long pause while he processes what he's heard] *So you're telling me there's a chance.* YEAH!

Lloyd draws the absolutely incorrect conclusion. No, Lloyd, you don't have a chance, but Mary doesn't come out and flatly reject him either. It's also unclear whether Lloyd desires a sincere answer. Most applicants who have academics substantially below average sometimes act like Lloyd. Their chances of admission are between one hundred and one million at some universities, but not quite zero.

Occasionally, in a given year, a school like MIT might admit a 1220 SAT or a 2.2 GPA who invariably reports their outcomes on Reddit or makes a viral YouTube video. Even for applicants who are aware of the long odds, they remain undeterred. They **neglect probability**, assuming that really *really* wanting to gain admission somewhere is sufficient.

Because elite universities never apply academic eligibility minimums for first-time freshman admission, they inevitably receive thousands of utterly unqualified applicants who shouldn't have bothered wasting their time applying. In the centralized British application system referenced in chapter 5.2, applicants can only apply to six universities. Mediocre British students won't waste one of their applications on Oxford when they know their admission odds are low to nonexistent.

I appreciate that MIT offers a comprehensive breakdown of how many applications they receive, broken down by test score. It may discourage some Lloyds of the world from completing one of the country's most time-consuming college applications. Nevertheless, MIT doesn't have a policy that outright excludes applicants scoring less than a 600 on the SAT from applying, despite the zero percent success rate from over 1,300 applicant attempts. MIT in Fall 2020 earned almost $100,000 on application fees from students who will never gain admission.

Harvard's admissions FAQ asserts that "most admitted students rank in the top 10–15 percent of their graduating classes." The qualifier "most" leaves open the door to the second-quarter student who has a one in a million but not quite zero chance of gaining admission. The FAQ repeats throughout, "There is no single academic path we expect all students to follow."

I'm confident that, except for the Jared Kushners of the world whose daddy can evade taxes to fund a new campus building, no student earning straight C's in non-honors classes has gained admission to Harvard. Why doesn't the university establish applicant minimums? If they've never in living memory admitted a student from the bottom half of their high school class, why not save everyone's time and money and be transparent? I don't have an answer other than it gives the veneer that they're an accessible institution and lets them accumulate as many applications (and fees) as possible. We will revisit Lloyd's "so you're telling me there's a chance" fallacy when discussing building a reasonable college list in the next chapter.

I have a questionnaire that students can submit to receive a free UT-Austin admissions consultation. I practice the policy whereby if I assess a student is highly unlikely to gain admission, say a less than 5 percent chance, I say outright that they have zero chance. Responding with "not good" or "less than one in a hundred" makes them react like Lloyd.

Enough students, and especially parents, got angry with my directness that I added a banner at the top of my free UT-Austin admissions questionnaire. "If I don't think you are competitive for admission based on your academics and UT-Austin first-choice major, I will speak honestly and directly." Even still, some disgruntled people bluster when I suggest that their 920 SAT isn't going to cut it for UT-Austin's extremely competitive Computer Science program. The sorts of parents who I imagine cajole the baseball coach into playing their unathletic child send me hatemail when I suggest their child may not be as exceptional as they believe.

I'm occasionally inevitably wrong with some of my admissions forecasts. I hear from one or two gloating survivors each year who I told were "highly unlikely to gain admission" and managed to succeed. I never hear from the hundreds who I suggest correctly will get rejected and do. "You were right, Mr. Martin, I didn't make the cut" is a message I've never received. Forecasting which universities you're highly unlikely to gain admission to is much more straightforward than wondering whether you have what it takes to rise above the "sea of sameness." Still, I would rather be wrong in the direction of lowering expectations than artificially inflating a student's confidence, only to leave them disappointed when they're rejected.

One reason I love independent consulting is that I can assess an applicant's chances honestly. It frustrated me when I worked at UT-Austin when a family might talk to me for 20 minutes at a college fair, only for me to learn later that they ranked in the bottom 10 percent of their class. I wasn't permitted to suggest that they shouldn't waste their time because they don't have a chance.

It's an admissions officer's job, after all, to accumulate applications and their fees. Admissions counselors at universities who practice holistic review can't tell a student their chances are close to zero.

Students line up at university tables during college fairs expecting advice or admissions statistics when the representatives in attendance are there to make a sales pitch. I know with certainty that some high school counselors and college advisors send their underperforming students to my questionnaire because I will break the disappointing news to them. I don't mind being the hatchet man. That allows their college advisor to have conversations about more realistic options.

Most universities are not transparent with their data, reporting only the minimum information required of the Common Data Set. Incomplete data forces ambitious families and educators to find self-reported data or access Naviance scatterplots. Naviance is a tool at many high schools to help counselors and families navigate the college admissions process. Naviance "scatterplots" show the high school's recorded history of admitted and rejected applicants to a given university based on GPA and test score.

Students plot their academics compared with their school's previous applicants to estimate their chances. Scatterplots can be an excellent way to avoid the Lloyd fallacy if no student with your academics has been even close to gaining admission. However, most students will fall somewhere within the range of previously admitted applicants.

Looking for a signal in the Naviance noise will not help you make sense of the admissions madness or assess your chances. Because Naviance doesn't break down admissions outcomes by major, it provides an **inconsistent comparison**. At universities such as UT-Austin, UC-Berkeley, or Carnegie Mellon (CMU), admissions rates for in-demand majors such as Engineering and Computer Science differ drastically from non-STEM programs.

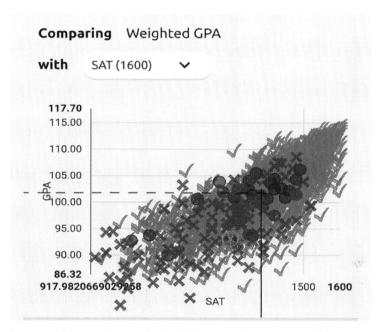

Figure 1 Naviance Scatterplot for UT-Austin from a Central Texas area high school. The blue stick figure is where a particular student interested in their admissions chances falls. Few students are guaranteed to fail or get in, so most applicants fall somewhere within a middle 80 percent of having a chance but no guarantees.

CMU admits only 7 percent of their computer science applicants compared with 31 percent to their music program.

A Naviance scatterplot might show a CMU music admit far down the bottom left quadrant, and a prospective Lloyd-like CS applicant might mistake that for them having a chance. CMU makes its admissions rates between majors transparent, but most universities don't. Elite private universities such as Rice might enroll everyone into undeclared. However, the institution still seeks a balance between majors to not over-enroll future computer scientists and under-enroll economists.

Even when universities are transparent with their overall admission statistics, if they don't provide information about admission to specific majors, especially for STEM, it's of little help to applicants. There is increasingly a bifurcation within most prominent universities between high-demand STEM and business with non-STEM programs. STEM or Business at some universities is substantially more competitive than Communications or Liberal Arts. Computer Science applicants to Stanford or Princeton confront a steeper hill to climb than someone applying for History.

Illinois Champaign-Urbana admits 59 percent of their applicants to the university overall, yet their prestigious CS program accepts less than 15 percent. Carnegie Mellon (CMU) is a leader in transparency because they break down their admissions rate and average GPA/test scores for each of their ten colleges and schools. An excellent but not exceptional prospective CMU student might apply for Engineering (20 percent admissions rate) over Computer Science (7 percent admissions rate) to improve their chances. Nevertheless, STEM applicants routinely overestimate their probabilities by focusing on the overall admissions rate.

Some websites, Niche, for example, offer an "admissions calculator" that even breaks down admission by major, but the data is self-reported, allowing for, at best, **incomplete comparisons**. Relatedly, many applicants, despite taking AP Statistics, are **insensitive to sample sizes**. Niche's self-reported data size for UCLA is around 30,000 applicants dating back a few years, but UCLA receives over 110,000 applications annually. Even the largest sample sizes will only ever capture a small percentage of total outcomes. Without a comprehensive data set, comparisons can never be accurate. Accessing complete data sets for most universities is impossible; therefore, dissecting scatterplots is an exercise in futility.

Examining scatterplots is like gamblers at the horse track who look for patterns in previous results to gain an edge. Acquiring and analyzing mountains of data gives the bettor an illusion of knowledge and control. Although a gambler might find some marginal advantages through sophisticated machine learning systems, few gamblers will reliably turn profits. Gamblers have access to many more known variables than college applicants. At least in horse racing, you can see the horses, jockeys, track conditions, and weather. In college admissions, you have access to almost nothing beyond your own application.

We've now arrived at the meat and Pomona Potatoes of identifying cognitive biases that cause families to trip on admissions landmines. Nassim Taleb, in his landmark 2007 book *The Black Swan*, coined the **ludic fallacy**. Ludic comes from the Latin *ludus* for game or sport. Even though something might feel like a game, applying probabilities more suitable for games of chance like Monopoly is less helpful in messy, real-world situations with a high degree of uncertainty with relevant variables unknown.

In casinos, roulette players have complete access to the odds of winning a given bet. The odds are consistent, published for all to see, and narrowly defined. Placing a bet on red yields a 2 to 1 payout because it occurs roughly half of the time on a given spin of the ball. Roulette is a game with *complete information*. Roulette players know what game they're playing, whereas college applicants don't. Still, a gambler or croupier cannot predict the outcome of any given role given the chaotic physical forces bouncing the ball around a spinning wheel. Although the game is unpredictable, it's possible to bet optimally to diminish but never overtake the house's advantage.

Other games, such as Texas Hold 'Em, are ones with *incomplete information*. Each player holds two cards face down. Everyone at the table can play from a set of five community cards dealt in three rounds. With 52 cards in a deck, each player assesses the probability that a favorable card will turn over on the next round while trying to predict which cards their opponents might have. Once the fifth and final community card is dealt, the remaining players turn over their cards.

It's possible to analyze after-the-fact which players were betting optimally, holding a foolish hand, or missed their desired card. "Assessing the counterfactual" means you can assess the exact probability of a given outcome and consequence of a jack of spades appearing on the final card rather than a two of clubs. Professional Texas Hold 'Em players study probability theory and their previous games to gain statistical edges over their opponents.

Studying admission statistics does not provide a comparable advantage to applicants. College admissions and games of chance are not analogous. The ludic fallacy entails misapplying probabilistic thinking to making complex decisions under uncertainty. The ludic fallacy is central to Taleb's thesis that humans are poor predictors of making decisions, or why political scientists and economists fail to detect unprecedented "Black Swan" events such as 9/11 in advance.

I've dedicated my entire career to college admissions. I consider myself an expert, yet I often get things wrong. Some students I'm sure will gain admission, don't. Others who I think stand very little chance, get in. I'm like a stockbroker who might do a little bit better than chance at picking stocks, but I'll never reliably predict with a high degree of accuracy who will or won't gain admission. The outcomes are too random to predict reliably.

Even though it can feel like a game with a known set of rules and odds, college admissions isn't roulette, Texas Hold 'Em, or betting at the horse track. The ludic fallacy fools someone into thinking we're playing by casino rules when the reality is substantially more complex.

I cannot assign probabilities such as 20 percent or 50/50 odds to one's admissions chances. Students want numbers because they're soothing. Instead, I offer unsatisfactory subjective assessments like "you're in the ballpark" or "I would be surprised if you didn't gain admission." Any admissions calculator that attempts to quantify one's chances will necessarily be imprecise, yet that doesn't stop proprietors from assigning exact probabilities to give a veneer of scientific precision.

Unlike casino games, where it's possible to arrive at statistical certainties and develop optimal playing strategies, most college admissions variables are unknown and inaccessible. Recall that a poker player can know precisely after the fact whether their decision to fold or raise was the optimal move. In college admissions, it isn't possible to assess how a given applicant might have fared had they, for example, completed a summer internship or not. Applicants cannot "assess the counterfactual" of what could have been.

A rejected applicant may be prone to **hindsight bias** where they claim they knew all along that they had zero chance of gaining admission. Part of them at some point in the past must have believed they could get in; otherwise, they wouldn't have applied. **Regression fallacy** ascribes a cause where none exists, like when an applicant points to a lack of volunteering hours as the cause for their admissions rejection. There may simply be no discernable reason why you didn't gain admission.

Students focus overwhelmingly on known, easily quantifiable variables such as their GPA, test scores, AP courses taken, or the number of previous students their high school has sent to a given university. They underweight subjective variables such as leadership, diversity, or academic curiosity because they're harder, if not impossible, to quantify. They look at small sample sizes, usually limited to their high school, failing to realize that hundreds of similar schools have thousands of similar students.

College students sharing admissions advice on YouTube are subject to the **self-serving bias**. They are quick to claim credit for success and point to this or that factor in their application that tipped the scales when, in reality, they're bullshitting. They may have gained admission for the reasons they suggest, they could have gotten very lucky, or some other configuration of unknown variables produced a favorable admissions decision.

So much of the admissions madness takes place in online parent forums or private student chat groups. A **shared information bias** entails that members of a family or study group focus on the information they already know (e.g., grades) and ignore information they're unaware of (e.g., whether their reviewer will be drinking wine when they score the application). They're prone to **apophenia**, which is the tendency to perceive meaningful connections between unrelated things, producing a further mismatch between weighting admissions factors appropriately. Parent community Facebook groups practice the **availability heuristic** where they report and debate admissions outcomes of below-average academic students who manage to gain admission.

Cherry picking is a logical fallacy that plucks a sour or sweet cherry from a bucket and asserts that the entire batch is fair or foul. Families and high school educators make **hasty generalizations** about the nature of college admissions based on a few hand-picked cases. Neuroscientist Joseph Levitin cautions that "the plural of *anecdote* is not *data*. An anecdote is simply an observation or a story that comes from uncontrolled conditions. True scientific data comes from a systematic attempt to isolate variables, document conditions, and observe trends over a long number of cases" (emphasis his). I can excuse parents who may be far removed from their high school and college courses for pretending to play science. Students who've aced their AP statistics and science exams should know better than to apply unrigorous, pseudoscientific methods and wishful thinking to make sense of college admissions.

Hasty generalizations contribute to affirmative action lawsuits when proving discrimination among tens of thousands of applicants is demonstrably more challenging than demonstrating whether a particular student did or didn't gain admission based on their ethnicity. **Confirmation bias** pressures students and parents to look for data that confirms their theory that black or Hispanic students have an admissions edge over their son or daughter.

Motivated reasoning is a phenomenon studied in cognitive science and social psychology that uses emotionally biased reasoning to produce justifications or make decisions that are most desired rather than accurately reflect the evidence. Students and families tend to find arguments in favor of conclusions they want to believe, which they weigh more strongly than the evidence for conclusions that they do not want to consider.

Known variables are the tip of the iceberg, with 90 percent of the picture out of view. Families are utterly unaware of variables such as a reviewer's mood, the institution's needs, the time of day their application was reviewed, how close or far they were from admission, spaces allotted for athletes or legacies, whether their interview or recommendation letters made a difference, the holistic review scores assigned, and the other unknowns I highlight throughout this book. We latch on to what's available and observable. After the fact, YouTubers or Redditors on the "College Results" community explaining their decisions are prone to **causal oversimplification**. They assume that there is a single and simple cause of an outcome, say an especially impressive extracurricular or a killer essay. In reality, their favorable outcome comes from several interrelated factors.

At least in a horse race, you can see which jockeys beat yours or that your horse lost due to catastrophic injuries. Poker players can assess how good their two-pair in Hold 'Em was relative to an opponent's missed inside straight draw. In short, applicants don't know what they don't know. Nor can they ever know it. Application inputs enter the college admissions black box that burps out a decision months later.

It isn't possible to reliably "chance" a student at highly selective universities other than to deter students whose academics are so far below average that it isn't worth applying. My book is an attempt at examining the arbitrary admissions superstructure lurking beneath the surface. The following section details application mistakes you should avoid.

7. Avoiding Application Mistakes

I closed the previous chapter with the futility of trying to forecast concretely one's admissions chances at highly selective universities. "Chance me" is a waste of time. Obsessing over stats causes more psychological harm that outweighs potential admissions benefits.

I acknowledged in chapter 4 that I'm no better than anyone else at forecasting what will make me happy. However, I am better than most about knowing in advance what will *not* make me happy. That tendency motivates my alternative lifestyle, mostly free from the conventional world.

Avoiding false paths and walking away from activities or studies that don't serve you is a more productive mindset than striving toward an unattainable happiness end-point. Anticipating errors and buffering mistakes will get you further ahead on your journey than trying to do the right things perfectly. Striving for certainty in a highly unpredictable world is a recipe guaranteed to disappoint.

From the essays and resume to recommendation letters and interviews and even the transcript, college admissions is ripe with manipulation opportunities. The popular perception by families and high school educators is that holistic review is random and inconsistent. I call it what it is: pseudoscientific bullshit that benefits universities at the expense of most applicants. Short of radical admissions reforms allocating spaces by partial lottery, which I consider in this book's conclusion, you as an applicant still need to step through the application minefield without exploding.

College admissions is more about avoiding errors and potential pitfalls than following a template of "how-to's" or a recipe of easy steps. The easiest mistake to avoid is simply to forgo applying for highly selective universities. Instead, consider opting for universities that genuinely want you and might even pay you to study on their campus. You don't have to play this absurd holistic review game. Your regional public university that admits based on GPA is probably a fine place to go to school, even if your friends tell you otherwise.

However, telling families to ignore the prestige and rankings and reinforcing that their student can get an excellent education almost everywhere hardly ever works. Tens of thousands of families have read Frank Bruni's phenomenal *Where You Go Is Not Who You Will Be*, and shrug. They believe their college is directly tied to their self-worth and future opportunities, which is true to a degree. Although I'm less sympathetic to Bruni's arguments than previously, prestige isn't everything. The second biggest mistake families who buy into the prestige madness make is taking on crippling debt to attend their "dream school."

I categorize application mistakes into two broad yet related categories: counterproductive behaviors and their psychological consequences. Many of the admissions problems stem from building unreasonable college lists. Burdensome student debt is one possible outcome of an unreasonable college list. Before moving on to the next section, see how many of these obvious, but by no means exhaustive, list of self-sabotaging behaviors may include you:

- Waiting until the last moment to begin your college essays
- Submitting unedited applications
- Fixating on a single dream school at the expense of alternatives
- Overconsumption of social media and online message boards
- Lack of clear communication within the family
- Reading too much into marketing materials that are intended to drive applications and not to signal favorable admissions chances
- Believing academics alone are sufficient to gain admission to top-20 universities
- Fixating on post-bachelor medical or legal studies and viewing the four years following high school as a mere stepping-stone
- Valuing rank and prestige as an end in itself
- Overly comparing yourself to your classmates
- Perfectionism when writing essays
- Overloading on AP courses and ECs to the detriment of your sleep and well-being
- Blaming factors outside of your control, e.g., state or federal laws
- Tailoring your applications to what you think universities want to hear rather than sharing what's interesting and important to you
- Tying self-worth to college admissions outcomes
- Stressing over already submitted applications
- Refreshing your admissions portals dozens of times in anticipation of a decision release
- Taking the SAT/ACT more than four times
- Fearing failure

7.1 Minimizing debt

Saving money and graduating with minimal debt is critically important, even if you come from an affluent family. The biggest mistake students make is taking on substantial debt. Student borrowers hold over $1.6 trillion with an average load of around $35,000.[146] Approximately 15 percent of American adults carry student loans, with two in ten borrowers late on payments. Over 50 percent of current college students take out loans to afford their education. According to the Brookings Institute, approximately 14 percent of all borrowers hold more than $60,000 and account for 52 percent of the total debt.[147] Although undergraduate students estimate it will take six years to pay off their loans, "the Department of Education reports that the typical repayment period for borrowers with between $20,000 and $40,000 in federal student loans is 20 years."[148]

Nobody ever anticipates failing to finish their bachelor's, but only about half of all Texas college students, for example, finish their degree in six years.[149] The national average six-year graduation rate is around 62 percent.[150] Students who take out college loans but don't graduate are three times more likely to default than borrowers who complete their degrees.[151] Only one-third of all Americans hold a bachelor's degree. Not all loans are created equally, with private student loans offering exceptionally high interest rates or fewer repayment/consolidation options. Most borrowers will need to take out at least some private loans to cover costs.

Given the high degrees of economic uncertainty due to COVID-19, it's tougher to forecast employment prospects and macroeconomic strength five years into the future. You may not have a job in your field when you graduate, or your skills may be less applicable or irrelevant. Most bachelor's degrees at in-state public universities will set students and families back at least $100,000 before any aid or scholarship considerations. Attending an out-of-state or private university can exceed $250,000 for a four-year degree.

A recent study suggests that "young adults from middle-income families have a higher risk for debt than do those from low- and high-income families."[152] Middle-income families often make too much money to qualify for need-based aid yet don't have the savings to afford a six-figure college education, especially for parents with more than one child.

Rice University is the most common example that comes to mind because, unless your family makes less than $130,000 a year, you should expect to pay the full cost of attendance.[153] Even though Rice provides an excellent education—one of the best in the world—unless your family net worth is in the multiple millions of dollars, there are few universes where paying upward of $280,000 for a four-year bachelor's, including Rice, provides a sound return on investment. Do not apply to Rice or anywhere for Early Decision if you cannot afford it.

Unlike credit cards, student loan debt *cannot* be discharged except in very rare circumstances. Your opportunities will be significantly limited following graduation and years to come if you choose a university that will saddle you with debt far exceeding your expected starting salary. Especially in the COVID-19 climate, frugality should play a heavier weight in building your college list.

Potential opportunity costs of taking on significant student debt[154]

+ Forgoing or delaying graduate/medical/law school
+ Forced to live at home following graduation
+ Fewer opportunities for younger siblings if parents are supporting a pricey education

- Inability to afford or qualify for a home mortgage or car loan
- Working a less-than-ideal job to pay the bills sometimes at the expense of pursuing work in your field
- A lower net worth and fewer resources to invest in retirement funds or save for rainy days
- Exacerbation of mental illness, pathological stress, general anxiety, and even suicide[155]
- Delaying or deferring dream jobs
- Not visiting doctors' offices or seeking healthcare resources from fear of accumulating more debt
- Sacrificing hobbies and interests
- Delaying marriage and raising a family/kids
- Monthly loan repayments that exceed your rent or even food costs
- Working multiple jobs and/or 60+ hour weeks to afford repayments
- Lower credit score/failing to pay credit card or medical bills
- Disqualification from jobs if failing background checks that show delinquency on loans
- Federal government garnishing your wages
- Parents being on the hook for loans if students take out Federal Parent PLUS Loans or private loans that require an adult to co-sign
- Reluctance to pursue higher-risk occupations or professional opportunities such as joining a startup or launching your own business[156]

The above realities increasingly call into question the value of a college degree at all, let alone paying for most or all of the costs of an out-of-state or private university. Now more than ever are discussions necessary about possibly delaying college enrollment by taking a **gap year**, working, or beginning studies at inexpensive **community colleges** that guarantee credit transfer, options I consider in the conclusion.

One parent raised the compelling point that MIT and elite institutions have offered most or all of their courses and curricula online for free. Yet few people take advantage of these resources. Corporations and public agencies are reluctant to certify them as equivalent to a bachelor's degree.

An October 2020 *Atlantic* article asks, "Why Did Colleges Reopen During the Pandemic?" Georgia Tech Media Studies professor Ian Bogost gets to the heart of the matter that universities are much more than the classroom knowledge they transmit.

> "That shocking stability [of the demand for college degrees] is exposing a long-standing disconnect: Without the college experience, a college education alone seems insufficient. Quietly, higher education was always an excuse to justify the college lifestyle. But the pandemic has revealed that university life is far more embedded in the American idea than anyone thought. America is deeply committed to the dream of attending college. It's far less interested in the education for which students supposedly attend."[157]

High costs and the intractability of "the college experience" further calls into question applying to universities where you're either highly unlikely to gain admission or have few opportunities to afford it. There may be a tendency to apply *just to see if you get in*. Committing the Lloyd fallacy costs application time and money. If you're stressing over application fees, you probably shouldn't apply to selective out-of-state universities. By even applying, either consciously or subtly, you create unrealistic sets of expectations. Either you don't get in and feel disappointed, or you gain admission and receive an unaffordable financial aid package.

Affording universities also require a family to project their income stability years into the future. Families who earn income in volatile markets that depend on commodities such as oil and gas or real estate prices should reconsider enrolling at a costly university. It's increasingly harder to justify paying full price for a regional private university when the return on investment from a similar in-state public university will likely yield better returns.

The counterargument to filtering your colleges by cost is applying to your universities regardless of the sticker price. You may receive unexpected merit scholarships that bring the expected cost of attendance closer to or even lower than comparable public options. It's sometimes preferable to apply, see what your options look like during senior year spring, and then say no rather than regret not trying at all. Still, it would help if you have maybe two or a maximum of three reach schools based on selectivity or ability to pay.

7.2 Building a reasonable college list

Building a college list that's manageable and realistic is critical to decreasing the stress of submitting your college applications. Every year, students drastically underestimate how much time their essays and applications will require: the **planning fallacy**. Students, and especially parents, possess the **optimism bias** and practice **wishful thinking** with unrealistic expectations about high-reach schools where it's highly improbable that they will gain admission.

Everyone knows someone whose parents pressure them into applying to Harvard even when their local state school is a reach. The most challenging part of building a college list is imagining what your future self needs or prefers—the failure of **affective forecasting**—which I discussed in chapter 4. The **projection bias** tends to overestimate how much our future selves share one's current preferences, thoughts, and values, leading to suboptimal choices.

Failing to forecast your future needs leads to **hyperbolic discounting** observed when students enroll at four-year universities and transfer or drop out. The serotonin high of "getting in" fades into the prosaic realities of life at your dream school. Discounting is the tendency for people to prefer more immediate payoffs relative to delaying gratification. Hyperbolic discounting leads to choices that are inconsistent over time. People make choices today that their future selves would prefer not to have made, like when I drank too much at the Bobina/Sergey Zhukov concert and paid for it on the overnight train the next day. Another way to frame hyperbolic discounting is "if I knew then what I know now, I might have chosen differently."

Students have buyer's remorse because people tend to focus on items that are more prominent or emotionally striking. We ignore data or choices that are unremarkable, even though this difference is often irrelevant by objective standards. Students and families are terrible at weighting and measuring the benefits and downsides of a given college, often failing to price in the cost of attendance relative to others.

Conventional college admissions wisdom suggests that students need to visit their schools before applying—the proverbial summer after junior year college tour. Although I recommend visiting your top one or two choices before enrolling in the spring of your senior year, exploring campuses early on often cements a school as your top choice based on factors you may or may not be aware of. Falling in love with a campus's wide selection of cafeteria foods may emotionally outweigh more practical considerations such as cost, location, course rigor, and so on.

Students **anchor** their mindset based on the first colleges that reach out to them or campuses that they visit, distorting their subsequent assessments and research. They're more likely to fixate on colleges they hear of the most—the **availability heuristic**—from watching college sports, consuming university marketing materials, or obsessing over student blogs and videos.

Students are prone to the **Nirvana fallacy**, where they reject solutions because they're not perfect. It's frustrating when students grumble and groan at attending their second choice, while their backup is another's dream school. Another manifestation is finding faults with everything and failing to see a given school as "good enough" rather than flawless. It's like a perpetual bachelor who finds flaws in all his partners because of unrealistic expectations.

"Maximizers" try and find the perfect solution. In contrast, "satisficers" are satisfied with a sufficiently adequate option. Nobel Laureate economist Herbert Simon coined satisficing to help provide rules of thumb for making decisions when information is less available or the outcomes are uncertain. Unchecked high standards and expectations, a common trait among ambitious students and families, produce "analysis paralysis." Unsurprisingly, maximizers are especially prone to indecision. They tend to apply to too many schools. Asking yourself whether you're a maximizer or a satisficer will help identify underlying tendencies that lead to unmanageable college lists or overediting essays in pursuit of an unattainable "perfect."

A common theme for students applying to out-of-state or private universities far away results from the **mere exposure effect**. Also known as the "I gotta get out of my home state!" mindset, mere exposure is the tendency to express undue liking for things merely because of familiarity with them. **Information bias**, where more data leads to less clarity, is problematic when students apply to more than a dozen schools, making the eventual enrollment decision even more complicated.

People acquire information to fulfill their insatiable worries. Alan Watts warns that "there is a contradiction in wanting to be perfectly secure in a universe whose very nature is momentariness and fluidity." College admissions is highly uncertain, and no quantity of information will offer you peace of mind sufficient to cast aside your doubts.

A related concept is **mission creep.** Students tend to apply to too many universities to "keep their options open" or because "it doesn't hurt to apply." Subtle changes happen between applying for a high-reach school in September, mistakenly believing, "I know there's no way that I'll get in, and I'm okay with that." Within a few weeks of the decision release, the anxiety ramps up, and students cross an expectation tipping point, setting themselves up for heartbreak. Your August self cannot forecast what your December self will feel about their Early Decision application notification. You wouldn't be applying to Princeton or Stanford at all if some tiny part of you didn't hope to gain admission. False hope blossoms into a thorny rose. Forecasting your future states of mind is nearly impossible, and that's the hidden cost of applying somewhere because "it doesn't hurt to try."

A reasonable list in the summer of six to eight universities balloons to fifteen or twenty reach schools by December where the student is highly unlikely to gain admission or enroll. Although some eventually transfer, almost every college student adjusts to their environment and makes the most of their opportunities. One positive cognitive bias mentioned in chapter 3 is the **choice-supportive bias,** where we tend to remember chosen options as having been better than rejected options. The disappointment students feel when a university rejects them inevitably passes. Staying angry forever is impossible, even if it means begrudgingly accepting your less-preferred alternative. **Fading affect bias** is when the emotion associated with unpleasant memories fades more quickly than the emotion associated with positive events.

Many students feel deterred from attending community college because it isn't the cool thing to do in their community. Society's "four-year college for all" expectations produce an **availability cascade**, a self-reinforcing process whereby a collective belief gains more and more plausibility through its increasing repetition in public discourse.

Similarly, fixation on top-50 universities comes from teachers, parents, and the media. Our zeitgeist claims that the only way to secure your future happiness and financial success is by attending an elite school. Students fail to consider a broader range of options, including gap years or alternative certifications, because of the **false dilemma effect**. Two alternative statements are given as the only possible options when, in reality, there are more. Another way to phrase it is how some students declare, "I'm only attending my dream school and won't consider anything else."

I raise this battery of cognitive biases because building the college list is arguably the largest minefield of the entire application process. Especially if your state has a robust public education system with a flagship campus that provides wonderful opportunities, I question applicants who apply all over the place when, most of the time, they will end up at an in-state public university.

An overview of common college list missteps

+ Submitting many applications to selective private or out-of-state public universities that offer little to no merit scholarships or are far out of reach, the **"just to see if you get in" fallacy**.
+ Desiring both a prestigious university and one that offers generous merit scholarships. Prestigious universities

rarely offer merit scholarships. You can choose one or two but not three among prestige, price, and ease of admission.

- A safety isn't a safety school unless you'd be content enrolling. Reddit user seaelixir shares, "One of the safeties I applied to was a school I wouldn't even consider attending, yet applied for the sake of having an "acceptance," which was not the right mindset, and I wish I hadn't applied to it."

- Failing to apply to any university or program where they are 100 percent guaranteed admission based on their rank/grades and ACT/SAT scores, a "security school." Every reasonable list needs a security school.

- Applying to only one or two "dream schools" where you're not guaranteed, potentially leaving you with few options during your senior year spring semester.

- Applying to too many schools that require unique applications and supplements.

- Only applying to out-of-state or private universities if the cost is in any way a factor to affording your studies. Barring exceptional circumstances, leaving your state just for the sake of it is usually not a good reason, the **"I can't stand it here!" fallacy**.

- Having unrealistic expectations for exceptionally selective schools that admit less than 8 percent of their applicants: Harvard, Princeton, Stanford, MIT, Cal Tech, Columbia, UPenn, Yale, and others. These are reaches and high reaches for everyone. The **"It doesn't hurt to try!"** fallacy relates to *Dumb and Dumber's* **Lloyd's "so you're saying there's a chance" fallacy**.

- Listing many of the same kinds of universities that offer little substantive difference, especially with Computer

Science and Business applicants submitting applications to most *US News* top-20 universities without compelling reasons for each school on their list.

- Over-weighting pre-med or pre-law as a deciding factor of where to apply. Medical and law school plans are almost totally irrelevant for choosing a university, and there is a high probability your plans will change by the time you graduate.

- Continuing to add schools rather than substituting or subtracting them, especially if your senior year has already started. Your list should shrink over time, not grow, unless you've finished all your applications and feel motivated to continue submitting apps.

- Placing too much emphasis on *US News* rankings at the expense of other college search rankings and resources.

- Falling in love with a dream school and tying your self-worth to that particular admissions outcome. Reddit user mungbeanmimi shares, "I applied to fourteen schools, all the UCs, and a few Cal States, but my dream school was UC San Diego. I dreamt of UCSD ever since I was little, and I collected merch from that school. Rejection hit really hard and I was really depressed for days. I'm still bitter about it."

- Applying to more than 20 universities, a strategy known as "shotgunning." Reddit user Qlzto suggests, "18 schools is too many schools. I didn't need that many target/safety schools. (Also, I applied to schools I knew I couldn't afford. Why did I do that?) I'd probably have been better off cutting out some of the target schools on my list to put more time/effort into the reach apps."

- Adding schools to your list because people pressure you and it isn't somewhere you'd ever see yourself enrolling under any reasonable circumstances.

College list best practices

+ Having a healthy balance between high reaches, reaches, targets, safeties, and at least one school where you're 100 percent guaranteed admission based on your grades or rank and ACT/SAT scores

+ Very rough classification boundaries: High reaches are those where you have a less than 5 percent chance of gaining admission; reaches are a less than 25 percent chance, targets are a wider range of a 25 percent to a 70 percent chance of success, safeties are 70 percent to 99 percent probability, and assured/security schools are those where you will 100 percent gain admission. There can be slight reaches and safer targets.

+ Keeping the list to fewer than 12 schools and no more than 15 total. Reddit user spoon_potato provides an excellent summary: "I applied to 9 schools total. 1 safety (state school), 2 targets, and 6 reaches. Honestly, I'm satisfied with what I applied to. My parents had little say where I applied. I only considered schools I could afford and I only applied to 9 because application fees are high."

+ Your academics are within or higher than the middle 50 percent of applicants on GPA/Rank and test scores range for most or all of your universities. If you scored a 28 on the ACT and make a mix of A's and B's with a moderately challenging course load, top-20 universities may not be realistic.

+ I recommend *keeping your high reaches*—schools where you fall below the middle 50 percent academic ranges and/or schools that admit less than 10 percent of their applicants—*to a maximum of three*. These are Hail Mary universities like the Ivies and their equivalents where you might decide it worth paying in full to attend. *Lists that include six or more high reaches need to be trimmed significantly.*

+ Substitute reach schools for target or safety schools where you have a greater than 90 percent chance of admission and a decent shot at scholarships, honors programs, or viable out-of-state tuition waivers

+ A maximum of three out-of-state public flagship universities, e.g., Michigan, Georgia, UCLA/B, etc. Most flagships aren't substantially different from one another.

+ Texas residents, for example, ask yourself: Would you ever full-pay for a Berkeley degree relative to UT-Austin, or Indiana/Purdue relative to Texas A&M? Current college student and Reddit user justheretohelpyou_ advises:

> "Focus on target schools. Focus on target schools. Focus on target schools. So many kids on Reddit shotgun/apply to more than 20 schools and either get denied by all of the reaches or they get in a T20 and are stuck with a $75k/year bill. Meanwhile, other kids are weighing a full ride to a target school against the $75k bill. You'd much rather be the second kid in that example....$40K-$50K in debt total wouldn't be terrible. More than that can snowball quickly."

+ If you're going to apply to UC-Berkeley and/or Los Angeles, you may as well apply to four or five UC campuses since they're all on the same application. If you don't want or can't afford to pay the additional application fees, you probably shouldn't be applying to the UCs anyways. The UC application is time-consuming, so my rule of thumb is to apply to none or to four or five, not one or two. Redditor Justheretohelpyou_ agrees: "The UC system should be treated like a T20 school without the aid for an OOS student. They are insanely expensive."

+ Limiting the number of applications to universities that offer few merit scholarships or out-of-state tuition waivers if enrollment would strain family finances or place you in significant debt

+ Pay careful attention to universities that require little to no time to apply and limiting the number of "unique" applications or supplements. Applying to UC-Berkeley is not the same as applying to Illinois because the former requires substantially more work than the latter. Applications to Stanford, Columbia, MIT, and Princeton, and others require considerably more time and effort to apply than Harvard, Dartmouth, Penn, Johns Hopkins, and those with fewer supplemental essays. Prestige isn't always an indicator of how much time an application will require.

+ Keeping an open mind about possibly attending a handful of universities rather than fixating primarily on one "dream school"

+ If you have multiple interests, selecting different majors or unique programs at your universities rather than putting all your eggs in the same academics basket

+ Consulting various rankings lists beyond *US News*, e.g., the *Times Higher Education* World University Rankings, *Super Money* Best Return on Investment, *Forbes* Best Value Colleges, *Colleges That Change Lives*, and *Niche*'s various rankings lists

+ Paying careful attention to how their prospective majors/ program rank against similar programs. Major rankings and overall university standings often differ, particularly for STEM.

> *Example:* Even though U Penn, for example, ranks number 11 in the world overall by *Times Higher Education*, they rank number 37 for Engineering, two spots lower than less-selective or expensive Purdue. Similarly, Illinois ranks 23 for Engineering despite being just within the top 50 globally. Oklahoma State has an especially strong Aerospace Engineering program comparable to Michigan, Notre Dame, Virginia, and Cal State Poly despite being less rigorous for other engineering majors or overall. Wichita State ranks number 5, higher than UT-Austin. Princeton ranked high in a top-20 law school survey despite lacking a law school. Be wary of prestige and name brands for your preferred major.

+ Creating at least one realistic scenario for enrolling at every college on your list
+ Using Net Price/Cost calculators if available that estimates potential merit/need aid
+ **Building a spreadsheet** with some or all of the following fields: ranking based on interest; high reach/reach/target/safety/security; major; whether unique supplements are required; the Princeton quotient of approximate words required; honors program options; expected cost of attendance; EA/ED/Priority deadlines; which application to use; acceptance rate to your major if available; application fee; allow for superscoring; assigned admissions counselor email; whether they require or recommend reference/counselor letters, SAT subject tests, a paper resume, interview

+ Researching particular resources, courses, research labs, study abroad programs, student organizations, professors, and other opportunities unique to each university on your list. This also helps answer the "why this university?" prompt because you should already have particular reasons for applying.

+ Being mindful of climate, location, school culture, Greek life, religion, size, political orientation, diversity, etc. Don't want to attend a smaller university in a cold climate? Dartmouth may not be your best fit regardless of anything else, for example. Reddit user thinker111111 agrees:

"I wish I had thought more about what I actually wanted out of my college experience early in the process. It's so easy to get caught up in rankings/prestige, size, study abroad programs, research opportunities, weather, food, dorms, or whatever quirky clubs they're advertising on the college tour without truly considering what you want your college experience as a whole to look like. You can probably do without the fancy dorms or Squirrel Watchers Club. What do you want four years from now, other than a piece of paper with your name on it? How do you want to grow as an individual during this time and what environments would best support that growth? I came to this realization on January 1st, when writing my CMU supplement on "What do you want out of your college experience?" I really wish I had written that one first, rather than last since it would have helped me to frame my college search so much better."[158]

Chapter 4 provided an overview of how the college admissions process is uniquely suited to exploit our psychological vulnerabilities. I highlighted various cognitive biases and distortions within the broader context of Stoic philosophy and our physiology. One of the most promising developments in psychotherapy is Cognitive Behavioral Therapy (CBT). CBT provides a vocabulary for identifying unhealthy thought patterns with practical tools for breaking anxiety feedback loops.

7.3 More cognitive distortions to avoid

Throughout this book, I've emphasized that the college admissions madness isn't your fault, students and families. I'm sorry that you must pass through arbitrary gatekeepers responsible for piloting a dehumanizing college admissions machine. College admissions is highly uncertain and arbitrary. It isn't fair. Much of it, you cannot control. Outcomes from year to year are inconsistent and unpredictable and are often unhelpful for forecasting the future. Your college applications will consume you emotionally and psychologically only if you allow it.

As I discussed in chapter 6.10, admissions isn't like poker or soccer, where you know the rules in advance and what it takes to succeed. You can do everything right and to the best of your ability and still not meet your goal of gaining admission to your first-choice program. Unlike in poker, where you can see your opponent's cards and identify flaws in your betting strategy and adapt for similar future situations, college admissions gives you either a yes or no. You have no idea what, if anything, you could have done differently. Unless you transfer, there is no second undergraduate admissions chance, unlike a poker player who will play in many tournaments.

Another source of anxiety is that people misplace and forecast incorrectly that if only they acquire a little more data and information, they will answer their questions and lower their stress. The solution isn't to be less informed but, instead, to digest and assess whether the information you receive is accurate and constructive.

Ask yourself: How does what I'm reading affect what I can control as an applicant? If it is something outside of my control, is it worth worrying over?

Although undergraduate college admissions might be the first process you encounter like this, it won't be the last time you must navigate a non-transparent gate that you need to pass. Learning to identify and manage counterproductive thought patterns now will help you confront similar situations later: honors college course sections; undergraduate research opportunities; summer internships; your first big breakup; scholarships and grants; medical, graduate, and law school admissions.

Stress, worry, and jealousy can be powerful signals about that which isn't serving you. Our fight-or-flight nervous system is configured to address immediate threats in our environment, but the admissions process hijacks our neurology and throws those systems into persistent overdrive. Resisting the temptation to let it define you is a challenge for humans everywhere across time and location. College admissions presents an opportunity to learn from setbacks. Winning or losing with grace is incredibly challenging. You cannot dictate factors outside of your control, only your response to them.

You might find yourself asking these often-unhelpful questions or worrying unnecessarily about the following. I provide straightforward answers in italics.

- Are my SAT/ACT scores good enough to get in, or should I take the exam a fourth/fifth/sixth time even though they haven't improved at all in previous attempts? *You should probably not take the exam again.*

- Are my essays good enough? How can I make them better even though I've reviewed and revised feedback four or five times already? *They're probably fine and ready to submit.*

+ Should I submit an extra essay to show I'm really committed? *No*

+ Will that one B sophomore year sink my admissions chances? *No*

+ Which majors are more competitive than others? What if I choose the wrong one? *Pick whichever you feel you would be most happy spending four or five years studying.*

+ Will I be penalized if I drop an AP course or not take a fourth year of foreign languages? *No*

+ What if I don't spend my summer volunteering as much as I can or attending multiple camps? Will others have an advantage over me? *No, you're doing fine.*

+ What if my resume isn't as strong as others? *Submit **your** best application and stop worrying about "others."*

+ What if I leave blank some of the resume boxes on Apply Texas or the Common App? *That's fine. You don't need to check every box.*

+ Why haven't I received my admissions decision yet when some of my friends already gained acceptance? *Give it some time, be happy for your friends, and remain optimistic while preparing for potential disappointment.*

+ Would my admissions chances be different if I came from a different race? *This is outside of your control and something you cannot change. It is a counterfactual you cannot assess.*

+ Can my dream university rescind my admissions offer if I make a few B's or even a C? *Highly, highly unlikely. You're fine, don't fail multiple classes, and enjoy senior year.*

It's expected that, even if you haven't experienced anxiety or depression before, college admissions brings out unfamiliar and confusing negative emotions that psychologists identify as **cognitive distortions**. Dr. John M. Grohol writes, "Cognitive distortions are simply ways that *our mind convinces us of something that isn't really true*. These inaccurate thoughts are usually used to reinforce negative thinking or emotions—telling ourselves things that sound rational and accurate, but really only serve to keep us feeling bad about ourselves (emphasis mine)."[159]

Drawing on previous cognitive behavior therapists, Dr. Grohol identifies 14 common cognitive distortions, many of which are relevant to college admissions. Consider if any of these resonate with you.

1. **Filtering:** "A person engaging in filter (or 'mental filtering') takes the negative details and magnifies those details while filtering out all positive aspects of a situation."

   Example: Students lament attending a competitive high school while neglecting that they're receiving a far better education and have access to substantially more resources than low-income high schools that send few students to college.

2. **Polarized Thinking:** "Things are either 'black-or-white'— all or nothing. We have to be perfect or we're a complete and abject failure—there is no middle ground. A person with polarized thinking places people or situations in 'either/or' categories, with no shades of gray or allowing for the complexity of most people and most situations."

   Example: "Either I earn an A+ / gain admission to my dream school / score perfectly on the SAT | or I'm a failure."

3. **Overgeneralization:** "In this cognitive distortion, a person comes to a general conclusion based on a single incident or a single piece of evidence. If something bad happens just once,

they expect it to happen over and over again. A person may see a single, unpleasant event as part of a never-ending pattern of defeat."

Example: I see overgeneralizing, especially in the spring when admissions decisions unfold. One university rejects a student, and they worry they won't gain admission anywhere. Even favorable admissions decisions fall flat because disappointed students "filter" positive outcomes by dwelling on the setbacks.

4. **Jumping to conclusions:** "Without individuals saying so, a person who jumps to conclusions knows what another person is feeling and thinking.... Jumping to conclusions can also manifest itself as fortune-telling, where a person believes their entire future is pre-ordained (whether it be in school, work, or romantic relationships)."
Example: Jumping to conclusions most frequently occurs in the period after submitting your application and awaiting your decision. Since some universities roll out their decisions in "waves" rather than all at once, the many thousands of students who don't hear back in late November conclude they won't get in.

A client wrote me in January: "I am sad after tonight's wave and not hearing back from them—I feel like after each wave my chances go down... I seriously don't get why they do it like this, it just prolongs all the worst parts of the process. Literally a couple nights ago I woke up at 12:30 am and couldn't go back to sleep at all because my anxiety was so high."

5. **Catastrophizing:** "When a person engages in catastrophizing, they expect disaster to strike, no matter what. This is also referred to as magnifying, and can also come out in

its opposite behavior, minimizing. In this distortion, a person hears about a problem and uses what if questions (e.g., 'What if tragedy strikes?' 'What if it happens to me?') to imagine the absolute worst occurring."

Example: College admissions is rife with opportunities for hyperbole and worst-case scenario thinking. "What if I don't get into my dream school? I will never get a job / my friends will all be happy at their universities, and I'm left behind / my parents will disown me / medical schools won't admit me / I will be depressed and miserable at my safety school."

6. **Personalization:** "Personalization is a distortion where a person believes that everything others do or say is some kind of direct, personal reaction to them. They literally take virtually everything personally, even when something is not meant in that way. A person who experiences this kind of thinking will also compare themselves to others, trying to determine who is smarter, better looking, etc."

Example: The most obvious instance of personalization is that universities rejected *you* personally. You tie your self-worth to your admissions outcome in both directions: "I am a great student *because* UT admitted me" or "UT doesn't think I'm worthy, so I'm not."

A parent once messaged: "Not good news from UT. My son is pretty bummed out.... Seems UT has a different criteria for who they pick.... So much for the well rounded holistic reviews.... Sorry to sound bitter. Just sad to see these super bright kids get rejected.

I responded: "The reality isn't that UT wants to deny bunches of talented kids. There truly aren't enough spaces....

It still sucks, I know. UT is missing out on a great student."
Admissions officials are not out to get you.

7. **Fallacy of Fairness:** "A person feels resentful because they think that they know what is fair, but other people won't agree with them. As our parents tell us when we're growing up and something doesn't go our way, 'Life isn't always fair.' People who go through life applying a measuring ruler against every situation judging its 'fairness' will often feel resentful, angry, and even hopeless because of it. Because life isn't fair—things will not always work out in a person's favor, even when they should."

Example: College applications and admissions outcomes are the quintessentially unfair system. Great students get denied from schools where they have a high probability of gaining admission, and cheaters sometimes win and take spaces away from honest applicants.

8. **Blaming:** "When a person engages in blaming, they hold other people responsible for their emotional pain. They may also take the opposite track and instead blame themselves for every problem—even those clearly outside their own control. Nobody can 'make' us feel any particular way—only we have control over our own emotions and emotional reactions."

Example: Admissions decision release provides ripe territory for placing blame on external factors and rationalizations to frame your disappointment, which can often turn quite ugly: the competitiveness of one's high school, Asian Americans earning the highest grades and crowding out the top, perceived discrimination and bias against whites or Asian American people.

I dedicate a significant portion of *Your Ticket to the Forty Acres* to identifying and clarifying myths and misconceptions to decrease blaming factors either outside of your control or that don't play an actual role in how decisions are made. It's exceedingly rare for me to hear students admit: "I tried my best, and maybe that wasn't enough, but that's okay" or "I see areas where I could have applied myself better. I'll try and make up for it in college."

9. **Emotional Reasoning:** "The distortion of emotional reasoning can be summed up by the statement, 'If I feel that way, it must be true.' Whatever a person is feeling is believed to be true automatically and unconditionally. If a person feels stupid and boring, then they must be stupid and boring. Emotions are extremely strong in people, and can overrule our rational thoughts and reasoning. Emotional reasoning is when a person's emotions takes over our thinking entirely, blotting out all rationality and logic. The person who engages in emotional reasoning assumes that their unhealthy emotions reflect the way things really are—'I feel it, therefore it must be true.'"

Example: One reason my data-driven counterarguments regarding diversity and race in admissions in *Your Ticket to the Forty Acres* often fall flat is that students and families overweight their personal feelings about who should and shouldn't gain admission. They *feel* the state's top 6 percent law that guarantees admission to highly-ranked students is unfair while ignoring that UT balances obligations to half a million Texas high school graduates; therefore, it must be unfair. Emotional reasoning also occurs when students confront the Appeals Process and try to bargain in their letters that they deserve a space because they really *really* want to go to UT, ignoring the reality that tens of thousands of other disappointed applicants also really, really want to enroll at UT, too.

10.   **Global Labeling:** "A person generalizes one or two qualities into a negative global judgment about themselves or another person. This is an extreme form of overgeneralizing. Instead of describing an error in context of a specific situation, a person will attach an unhealthy universal label to themselves or others."

Example: It's common for me to receive dozens of emails after receiving UT's Coordinated Admissions Program (CAP) pathway program and rejection decisions. Parents and students make sweeping generalizations:
  "I hate UT."
  "I always knew Texas A&M was a better university."
  "I will never enroll at CAP because it's a waste of time, and I don't want to go to UT anymore anyways."

11.   **Always Being Right:** "When a person engages in this distortion, they are continually putting other people on trial to prove that their own opinions and actions are the absolute correct ones. To a person engaging in 'always being right,' being wrong is unthinkable—they will go to any length to demonstrate their rightness."

Example: I most commonly observe this cognitive distortion in online communities like Reddit and College Confidential.

Students and parents feeling tremendous pressure and anxiety lash out at anyone who attempts to question their perspectives. Nobody can talk them out of their cognitive distortions with constructive advice like "everything will be okay in the long run. Where you attend university isn't who you will be. Try your best, and if it doesn't work out, that university maybe wasn't your right fit anyways." They are **"unable to disconfirm"** their beliefs.

Unsurprisingly, teenagers and undergraduates, my younger self included, are most prone to feeling they are always right because they lack the perspectives and experiences that you can only develop with age. Related advice: Stay off Reddit and College Confidential. They're both cesspools of misinformation and a hurricane of anxiety and stress.

12. **Heaven's Reward Fallacy:** "The false belief that a person's sacrifice and self-denial will eventually pay off, as if some global force is keeping score. This is a riff on the fallacy of fairness because in a fair world, the people who work the hardest will get the largest reward. A person who sacrifices and works hard but doesn't experience the expected payoff will usually feel bitter when the reward doesn't come."

This distortion strikes at the heart of the college admissions dilemma. It may sincerely be the case that you've tried and worked your hardest. Your parents rightly gave you advice growing up that hard work pays off. Maybe your classmate that you know cheats or is ranked lower than you in school gained admission, and you didn't. Or a very high-achieving classmate that admittedly works harder than you got denied while you gained admission. College admissions outcomes are erratic and unpredictable, but we live in a world where bad things happen to good people.

13. **Judgment Focus:** "You view yourself, others, and events in terms of evaluations as good-bad or superior-inferior, rather than simply describing, accepting, or understanding. You are continually measuring yourself and others according to arbitrary standards, and finding that you and others fall short. You are focused on the judgments of others as well as your own judgments of yourself. 'If I didn't get into my dream college,' or 'If I take up tennis, I won't do well,' or 'Look how successful she is. I'm not successful.'"[160]

14. **Bargaining:** Not typically considered a cognitive distortion but worth including here as the "third stage of grief," the others being denial, anger, depression, and acceptance. "The normal reaction to the helplessness and vulnerability that comes through loss is an attempt to regain control.... Bargaining takes place within the mind by trying to explain the things that could have done differently or better... The bargain struck is not one that could actually be kept, but it assists in bringing more control by identifying what could have—or should have—been done to handle the circumstance more effectively."[161]

Bargaining usually occurs after decisions are released. Many students and parents often navigate denial. "Could I really have gotten rejected? There must be a mistake" before moving quickly to anger "that university sucks anyways! They're losing a great student!" Usually, the grieving process ends there, but sometimes weeks and months later, I receive distressing messages, almost always from parents rather than students.

Families stuck in the bargaining phase begin their messages by listing all their accomplishments before moving on to questions of what could have or should have been done differently. Where could we have showcased his leadership positions more effectively? Would a higher ACT/SAT score have tipped the scales in their favor? Should they have applied to a different major? How can we be sure an error wasn't made evaluating the transcript? Who could we call to reverse their certainly mistaken decision? And on and on, endlessly. Remaining in bargaining limbo doesn't allow the family to move on and acknowledge the favorable admissions decisions received. Severe cases might lead to depression.

Bargaining is an understandable reaction not just because of college admissions' inherent randomness and unfairness but as a byproduct of universities' aggressive recruitment and questionable enrollment practices.

8. Questionable Enrollment and Recruitment Practices

The college admissions arms race between families is largely due to the competition among universities to enroll the highest quality and the most diverse applicant pool while still balancing the budget. As discussed in chapter 5, with universities branding and marketing themselves since the 1970s, our digital era ushers in another degree of madness. Jeffrey Selingo comments, "The name-buying and resulting direct mail are both a cause and symptom of our national obsession with selective schools."[162]

Regional public universities or lesser-known private universities must recruit and market aggressively or risk closing, especially during the pandemic. Around half of all colleges and universities do not meet their enrollment targets.[163] But even and especially at *US News* top-100 universities, elite universities are deploying niche branding techniques increasingly. Brown University's pitch is their "open curriculum," while Columbia prides itself on its "core curriculum." Even after taking into account for-profit colleges' substantial marketing efforts, public and private universities spend hundreds of millions of dollars on marketing and public relations each year, not including exposure generated from NCAA college sports.

Before the internet, households received dozens if not hundreds of postcards, viewbooks, or other swag left on the proverbial kitchen table or discarded in the bedroom junk drawer. Decades ago and today, universities hire outside agencies and marketing firms specializing in creating student desire and practicing "consumer-driven marketing."

A 1979 article in the *Atlantic* reports a practice that rings true today, pre-pandemic anyway. "Many colleges also invite students to come to the campus and take another look before making the Big Decision, and these weekends can become quite elaborate. Vassar, for example, regularly draws 600 potential freshmen to its weekend and treats them to festivities ranging from barbershop quartet singing to Ultimate Frisbee contests."[164] Here's an entertaining if alarmingly patronizing excerpt:

> "One result of the new professionalism in college advertising is that promotional brochures are beginning to look like cigarette ads. A College of St. Elizabeth brochure, for example, shows a girl with long blond hair lying in a field of flowers and holding one gently in her hand while staring wistfully into the camera's eye. 'Especially for women,' reads the italic caption underneath, 'because women are creative, intelligent and beautiful, resourceful and sweet and generally different from men.'"

The article mentions an especially ingenious technique to collect prospective student names. "Dakota Wesleyan solved this problem once by raffling off bicycles at state fairs to get names and addresses of high school students, but fortunately, a better way is now available." Nowadays, universities buy lists of PSAT scores to receive a student's address and other biographical information. Students are likely to check the opt-in box on their exam to receive marketing materials because they frequently misunderstand that opting out signals a lack of college-going interest. When brochures begin appearing in your email or physical mailbox from universities you've never heard of, the College Board selling your data is one reason why.

The *Wall Street Journal* reported in 2019 that "1,900 schools and scholarship programs buy combinations from among 2 million to 2.5 million names" from the College Board for as little as 50 cents each.[165] Tulane alone bought almost 300,000 names. Their efforts yielded a 55 percent increase in applications for Fall 2021 compared with the COVID-free previous year.

Jeffrey Selingo reports that a student's name is sold, on average, 18 times over their high school career, with some names purchased upward of 70 times. These figures don't include targeted advertisements on Google or Facebook. During a ten-week period in 2020, universities spent $55 million on Facebook ads.[166] Unsurprisingly, universities spend a substantial portion of their recruitment budgets targeting wealthy communities with students more likely to pay full tuition.

The College Board earns over a billion dollars annually, doubling its revenue since 2010. It's deplorable that a supposed nonprofit that charges students $12 to send their SAT scores electronically or $16 for their financial aid CSS profile earns additional revenue off student data. The College Board's in-house research on marketing effectiveness calls into question the tens of millions of emails sent and brochure pages printed. "Students whose data it sells are only 0.1 percentage point more likely to apply to the college than identical students who didn't receive outreach, the paper concludes, and the probability of enrolling in the college increased by 0.02 percentage point."[167] Buying names to increase application numbers adds fuel to the admissions madness fire.

Why do Ivy League colleges and their equivalents feel compelled to advertise and market themselves? Most elite universities have four-year graduation rates of around 90 percent, so there isn't a limited pool of students capable of doing the work and earning their degrees.[168] There is more than enough talent to fill the spaces at America's most selective campuses.

Universities argue that they need to recruit aggressively because qualified students are scarce, and they only want the best. They indeed compete with other elite institutions for the most rarified tier of exceptional students. Even attempts at coordinating decision releases on the April 1 "Ivy Day" doesn't stop elite universities from sending "likely letters" in February and March to their most desirable applicants. Likely letters imply an eventual acceptance, but less than 20 percent of students who eventually gain admission will receive them. The tens of thousands of applicants who inevitably don't receive likely letters fuels the anxiety of the admissions decision waiting game. Likely letters are used as a recruiting technique to assist yield managers in predicting which of their admits is expected to enroll.

Aggressive application recruitment from elite universities and offering likely letters to their most sought-after applicants is part of a broader public relations and marketing campaign. Their primary objective is to generate as many applications as possible, even if that means soliciting thousands of students who have an infinitesimal chance of gaining admission.

Every summer, I have to deflate students' expectations who feel important when they receive a Dartmouth or Yale brochure in the mail. They interpret these solicitations as "so you're saying there's a chance" rather than what they are: generic marketing schemes to feed a university's prestige metrics that maintain their US News rank. I reassure talented applicants that not failing to receive a likely letter doesn't mean they're denied.

Every campus sends out a deluge of emails, invitations, social media pings, and even direct SMS messages to lure a student's application. Students nowadays create dedicated college emails to absorb the onslaught. One Redditor reported a university whiting out their unsubscribe button to complicate opting out. Another changed their phone number entirely because they grew tired of receiving endless SMS messages. Like a corporation buying highly specific ads on Facebook and Google, advanced analytics allow universities to target potential nontraditional students, transfers, midcareer professionals, veterans, and others who may not have taken the PSAT or applied in high school. Universities will claim their personalized ads increase access by targeting these historically underserved groups. However, their public intentions mask a much more pervasive campaign to attract their bread-and-butter demographic: wealthy students attending top high schools.

Despite sophisticated data gathering and marketing tools, universities still routinely make rookie mistakes. All-female Barnard College sent repeated emails to male students even after they attempted to unsubscribe, possibly due to duplicated records within their recruiting software or a mistaken query on Barnard's PSAT list name purchases. Providence College sent out an email blast to all their applicants in early March 2021 with the headline "Re: Your College Acceptance" that wasn't a notification of admission. Instead, it was yet another promotional email with a clickbait title that drives up the marketer's open rate. One Redditor remarked in a since-deleted post, "This is super trashy, especially in a time when so many students are nervous about admissions decisions."[169] Johns Hopkins sent out similar fluff email sequences that provided zero new information and only served to heighten anxieties.

Competing for attention means that universities must deploy clever strategies to encourage students to click through.

Swarthmore recently sent a mirror graphic written in reverse that required a separate tool to rotate it so the student can read the message. One Redditor wondered, "Who at Swarthmore is smoking crack??" A similar message sent a cryptographic series of letters and numbers requiring students to decode the meaning.

The University of Chicago (remember their downright wacky essay topics?) appears to be a leader in cutting-edge physical mail marketing by sending full-size posters and glossy magazines. They're desperate to maintain that 7 percent admissions rate by attracting thousands of applicants (and their application fees) who never have a shot.

The marketing outreach ramps up after a student gains admission. Admissions offices hammer their admitted students to enroll at their university over a competitor. In March 2021, admitted students with scholarships to USC's Marshall School of Business received a pair of AirPods to entice enrollment. The custom-made gold box came with a USC Marshall carrying case, a USC branded state of California pin, and an acceptance letter rolled into a scroll and bounded with a gold cord. The $85 application fees from four rejected students could likely subsidize the gift's cost. It also had the unintended consequence of alienating non-business scholarship recipients who felt left out. In a previous admissions cycle, Marshall scholarship recipients received an Amazon Fire tablet. USC undergraduate Grace Shan in the *Daily Trojan* wrote a critical opinion piece.

> "In their mission statement, USC claims to prioritize students' education and seek to '[develop] human beings and society as a whole through the cultivation and enrichment of the human mind and spirit.' AirPods do not contribute to the enrichment of the human mind, but perhaps this is yet another thing so complicated that administration must

leave students in the dark about. After all, making current students feel welcomed or providing adequate financial aid is nothing compared to a higher yield, right?"[170]

Around the same time, USC settled a $1.1 billion lawsuit for sexual abuse against more than 500 female students by health center gynecologist George Tyndall during his three-decade career. USC knew about the allegations for years, yet they only terminated his employment in 2017 when the allegations started becoming public.[171] They also recently increased their tuition rate by 3.5 percent; customized AirPods don't come cheap.[172] Had USC not continued to employ a rapist that shattered the lives of hundreds of families, the cost of the class-action lawsuit settlements could have covered four years' worth of tuition for over 4,500 USC undergraduate students. They could have also purchased AirPods for every person living in central Los Angeles.

Often, universities confuse their mailing list funnels. They send redundant messages or communications that are inapplicable to certain applicants. Many of my UT-Austin clients were confused by a blast "encouraging them to apply for honors" even though many already had. They asked me if attending the virtual event would help their admissions chances. Officially, UT and many other universities do not consider demonstrated interest because it favors wealthy students who have the time and money to tour colleges. Sometimes, universities invite rejected applicants to admitted student events.

A deferred Redditor to Case Western received an email encouraging them to apply and "join our community of bright, creative scholars." Universities' automated mailing list sequences wish happy birthday to students they had recently rejected. Transgender students are noting an alarming trend of universities sending mail to their homes under their "preferred name" for students not yet out to their parents who know them only by their name assigned at birth. A simple solution suggested to me by an affected student is to include a yes/no question on the application whether to use their preferred name for official communications. Outing students to their parents results from rolling out woke application reforms without considering potential unintended consequences.

If elite universities don't care about their applicants, less-selective colleges with low yield rates care a little bit too much. Redditor applying2021 shared about Hofstra's endless email sequences.[173] They sent out over a hundred emails with titles like "[Name], will I see you on Sunday?" and "Re: Your personality e-quiz" and "[Name], this will put you ahead of the pack!"

Even after applying, Hofstra sent out dozens of emails to students like Redditor Agitated-Big7618 with pending, but not yet submitted, applications with cringe headlines "January 4 notice, just for you" and "The next step to claim your awards." Only 9 percent of Hofstra's admitted students choose to enroll, so they truly are like the last kid at the prom looking for someone, anyone to dance with.

Another Redditor said they applied to Hofstra with the hopes of not receiving any more emails, but that backfired. "And oh god, did they send 100000 more." One student reported receiving 73 emails in a single day among their varied universities. Aggressive marketing from less-popular schools is the desperation equivalent when dating: "Hey, you up? Hey, what are you doing? Did you get my text? How's your day? U there?"

With increasingly precise Customer Relationship Management (CRM) tools, it's hard to imagine university enrollment managers won't defer to these tools and a student's engagement with the university to forecast enrollment projections. Students mistake these "invitations" as indications of their favorable honors or scholarship chances. Corporate marketing techniques raise students' hopes and expectations when it signals nothing meaningful beyond a university wanting to meet their varied recruitment, application, and enrollment metrics.

Facing pressure from the federal government for cartel-like behavior, the admissions governing body NACAC recently scrapped a recruitment stipulation in its ethics code. Before 2019, NACAC barred its 1,700 member universities from recruiting students who have already submitted their enrollment deposits. Following policy changes that favor universities, they can offer scholarships and other incentives after the May 1 National Decision Day to entice students to abandon their enrollment deposits. Poaching soon-to-enroll students from each other amplifies recruitment aggression, intensifying confusion for families who have already made up their minds during the senior year spring semester.

Ratcheting up application numbers makes it even harder for universities to provide adequate customer service. Prospective applicants and even admitted students often fail to receive responses from admissions and financial aid staff. Chatbots are poor substitutes for knowledgeable counselors. Staff overburdened by aggressive recruitment practices means accidents are bound to occur.

Admissions offices often bungle at their core responsibility: admitting the students they intend to admit and rejecting those they don't want. In 2019, the University of South Florida distributed 430 acceptance notifications. "Once again congratulations on your admission to USFSP!" before an hour later sending a correction they blamed on human error. "There was an error in the system. Please disregard the previous email."[174]

Johns Hopkins in 2014 sent the email headline "Embrace the YES!" to 294 Early Decision applicants they had rejected a few days prior. "The decision posted on the decision site reflects the accurate result of your Early Decision application. We regret this technical mistake and any confusion it may have caused." MIT the same year sent "You are on this list because you are admitted to MIT!" to thousands of students, more than their entire freshman class.[175] The University of California at San Diego accepted all 46,000 Fall 2009 applicants when they intended to admit only 18,000.[176]

Some universities honor their mistake by allowing students admission, but Vassar in 2012 made the peculiar decision to *refund their $65 application fee.* It seems you can put a price on grief and devastation, and Vassar values that approximately at a dinner for four at Applebee's.

Many private universities practice "need-blind" admission where they admit students regardless of their ability to pay. Need-blind admissions policies aim to increase opportunities for low-income and first-generation students. Some meet all need-based financial aid requirements to families making under certain income thresholds.

Harvard, MIT, Princeton, Yale, and Amherst are the only major American universities that are both need-blind and wealthy enough to meet the total demonstrated financial aid for all admitted students, whether they're domestic US residents or foreign. Over three dozen universities meet the financial need for all enrolling domestic students. However, except for a handful of universities with the largest endowments, enrollment managers face budgetary pressures to admit a sufficient number of "full tuition–paying" students to compensate for financial aid and scholarship schemes in addition to covering university operating costs. When doing your college search, find the percentage of students who receive financial aid and subtract from 100 to determine how many full fee–paying students are on campus.

Public universities have an incentive to recruit out-of-state students who often pay more than double the tuition compared with in-state residents. In 2016, many University of California campuses facing budgetary pressures were caught over-admitting underqualified out-of-state students because they pay higher tuition than California residents. More than 4,300 California residents were rejected over ten years. An investigation concluded that the rejected California residents had "academic scores that met or exceeded all of the median scores for nonresidents whom the university admitted to the campus of their choice."

Out-of-state enrollment nearly doubled from 2011–2012 and 2014–2015 relative to in-state students, while only 11 percent came from underrepresented minority groups.[177] When in conflict, meeting financial bottom lines seems to outweigh commitments to diversity, even for the country's most politically liberal public university system. Increasing competition among California residents calls into question the commitment of public universities to their tax-paying residents.

International college recruitment is big business, especially as state legislatures continue cutting public education budgets.[178] Foreign student fees at public universities can sometimes amount to more than three times the price for in-state students. Ohio State's Global Gateways outreach and recruitment centers in China, Brazil, and India increase their campus's visibility and reputation. Recently, they've aggressively recruited full fee–paying Chinese nationals who now constitute more than two-thirds of their total international student enrollment, doubling from a decade ago.[179] The China outreach office budget has tripled to nearly half a million dollars since 2017. Taiwanese, Indian, and Korean student enrollment declined significantly in the same period. Some Ohio State international students report feeling like a number to check on a diversity spreadsheet.

Many universities love to promote the precise number of nationalities represented on their campuses without mentioning that their international students come almost exclusively from the wealthiest and most elite echelons of their home countries. Financial pressures to recruit a higher proportion of full fee–paying students call into question precisely what universities mean when they embrace diversity as an institutional value. Ambiguities around which universities are sincerely need-blind cause middle- and working-class families to pause and wonder if wealthy applicants are securing yet another advantage in the college admissions arms race.

I make these preliminary observations to preface the following three sections. As discussed in the introduction of chapter 6, enrollment managers attempt to predict the "yield" of how many admitted students will decide to enroll. You're at the mercy of a university's admissions and enrollment management officers and accountants. I open with a brief history and current practices of Early Decision and other deadlines. After, I criticize what I call a special kind of purgatory for students neither admitted nor denied to their preferred universities. Finally, I share a troubling story as a UT-Austin admissions counselor when a Big Data algorithm system unintentionally denied hundreds of low-income admitted students their financial aid.

8.1 The Early Decision racket

Many elite universities offer binding Early Decision deadlines that oblige students to enroll if offered admission. Early Decision (ED) differs from Early Action (EA) or Priority deadlines because students may only apply to a single ED school. In contrast, most universities permit students to apply to as many EA options as they wish. The first early admissions deadlines arose in the 1950s.

The 2003 book *The Early Admissions Game: Joining the Elite* found that applying ED confers a 100 point SAT advantage, which subsequent 2012 research by Antecol & Kiholm supports.[180] ED deadlines usually fall one or two months before the school's Regular Decision (RD) deadlines. As a result, prospective ED applicants must begin their college search and application process much sooner than their RD-only peers, usually starting no later than the end of their junior year.

Students applying ED have a significant admissions advantage because universities admit ED students at two or three times the rate of applicants applying at the final deadline. Still, many ED applicants are deferred to the regular decision pool and receive their decision later on. If a student receives their ED admissions offer, usually sometime in late November through December, they're supposed to withdraw all their other applications.

A common question I receive is whether ED is *really* binding. What happens if an admitted ED student chooses to break their agreement, especially if the family's financial situation changes? Others may simply change their minds. The answer is a grey area and depends on the universities.

Legally, there is no recourse available to universities to coerce you into enrolling or paying any penalty. However, a university might "blacklist" a student or threaten to contact the student's high school guidance counselor to prevent them from sending transcripts to other universities, although I have no idea whether or how many times this has happened in practice. Blacklisting seems like a vague threat necessary to maintain the myth of admissions omnipotence. Threats also reinforce cartel-like behavior that maximizes a university's position at the expense of student well-being.

ED deadlines are the most obvious example in the application process of the asymmetry of power between universities and families. Universities leverage binding ED deadlines to entice students into putting all their eggs into a single basket. Initially, they were created to reduce stress for students who would find out their decision in the fall and could close their application process. Instead, it's the most powerful tool in a university's enrollment management arsenal because ED students guaranteed to arrive on campus help them forecast how many students they need to admit through regular deadlines.

Some universities who consider legacy may use the ED pool to inject that preference into their process, giving legacy ED applicants an added boost. For universities that practice ED, many of them admit half their total student body early. That helps them admit a more precise number of RD applicants to forecast how many students are likely to accept their offers and arrive on campus.

Even at the highest echelon of the university hierarchy, *only* 75 percent of admitted Harvard students enroll. The Ivy League, Stanford, Cal Tech, MIT, U Chicago, and their equivalents compete for the same students. ED poaches students who might otherwise gain admissions and enroll at prestigious peer institutions. ED practices obscure a university's overall admissions rate with the effect that many campuses are closed off to many regular decision applicants most of the time. That's one reason I strongly caution against a "shotgun" approach of top-50 universities because many of them practice Early Decision. But ED practices encourage shotgun approaches because students know their chances at any given RD university are slim, so they're incentivized to apply to many more universities.

ED limits families, particularly when it comes to scholarships and financial aid, because ED binds students to enroll before seeing the total cost of attendance. Students need to think very carefully about whether to apply ED at all. Few of my Texas clients

Freshman Year	ED Apps (a)	ED Admits (b)	ED Admit Rate (b/a)	Total Enrollment (c)	Enrollment filled by ED Admits (b/c)	Total Apps (d)	Total Admits (e)	Overall Admit Rate (e/d)	RD Apps (d-a)	RD Admits (e-b)	RD Admit Rate (e-b)/(d-a)
2012-13	38,840	11,471	29.5%	32,349	35.5%	441,414	91,034	20.6%	402,574	79,563	19.8%
2013-14	41,668	11,965	28.7%	32,245	37.1%	460,125	89,200	19.4%	418,457	77,235	18.5%
2014-15	44,535	12,887	28.9%	33,325	38.7%	489,518	90,153	18.4%	444,983	77,266	17.4%
2015-16	48,104	13,281	27.6%	33,150	40.1%	507,082	89,644	17.7%	458,978	76,363	16.6%
2016-17	51,466	14,003	27.2%	33,546	41.7%	527,956	88,376	16.7%	476,490	74,373	15.6%
2017-18	55,128	14,800	26.8%	33,702	43.9%	545,985	84,271	15.4%	490,857	69,471	14.2%
2018-19	62,598	16,328	26.1%	33,843	48.2%	596,080	77,615	13.0%	533,482	61,287	11.5%
2019-20 (est.)	71,882	16,940	23.6%	32,792	51.7%	623,294	71,818	11.5%	551,412	54,878	10.0%

Figure 2 Admission Statistics for Early Decision. Schools with an overall admit rate < 25 percent. 16 Universities - Columbia.[11] Brown, Penn, Dartmouth, Cornell, Duke, Northwestern, Vanderbilt, Johns Hopkins, Rice, WUSTL, Tufts, Carnegie Mellon, Emory, NYU, Boston University (data from Common Data Set or school publications). Accessed on Wikipedia "Early Decision (ED)" page on December 3, 2020

apply ED because their top choice is UT-Austin, which only offers a non-binding priority deadline. Applying ED means that the school is far and away your top choice, and you would enroll under any circumstance regardless of whether you receive your desired major or adequate funding to cover tuition costs.

ED application numbers nearly doubled in the past decade. Students feel pressure to apply ED because it's yet another college arms race incentive that aids universities at the expense of a student's flexibility. ED requires a substantial degree of maturity and foresight about what their future selves want, problematic for reasons detailed in chapter 4. Most know they won't stand a chance at a given university unless they attempt an ED application, so they cave in to the temptation and hope for the best. Jeffrey Selingo argues that "few things have contributed as much to the insanity of the admissions process" as Early Decision.[181]

Applying ED produces a hidden opportunity cost where students applying for long-shot universities wait until they hear whether they gained admission or not, leaving many scrambling in late December after receiving bad news. If we had a centralized college application and admissions system like the UK's ranked preferences, or residency matching for American medical students, the system could more efficiently distribute spaces to applicants.

An all-or-nothing ED option for a single school incentivizes students to game the system by finding a school that admits at ED rates substantially higher than their RD rate. Cornell admitted almost 23 percent of their ED applicants compared with 9 percent for regular decisions. It's questionable whether applying ED signals to universities that they're a student's genuine first choice. Dispensing with the pretense of their stated goal to match students with their top choice, some universities, such as U Chicago and Emory, offer Early Decision II with January deadlines. ED

II allows rejected ED I students a second ED opportunity else-where. Universities likely don't care whether a student opts for ED I or II as long as they arrive on campus, finish their degree, and pay their tuition.

James Fallows of the *Atlantic* wrote a damning 2001 article, "The Early-Decision Racket." His observations ring as true today as two decades ago.[182] He interviewed more than 30 public and private high school college counselors who all felt the negative outweighed the positive. "They had three basic complaints: that it distorts the experience of being in high school; that it worsens the professional-class neurosis about college admission; and that in terms of social class it is nakedly unfair." One student shared that "for the great majority, no. It makes things more stressful, more painful." And this was 20 years ago when college admissions wasn't quite so insane!

Fallows establishes a correlation in the 1990s between the increasing prominence of rankings systems like *US News & World Report* and a rise in ED practices. Perverse ranking incentives and society's disproportionate focus on prestige produce unintended consequences where students pay the price. If a university admits half of their total enrollment through ED, it allows them to push down their overall admissions rate by rejecting a far larger portion of RD applicants. Since acceptance rates are a heavily weighted criteria in rankings such as *US News*, enrolling a higher propor-tion of students through Early Decision propels a university up the charts or maintains its position. "Today's professional-class madness...that being accepted or rejected from a 'good' college is the most consequential fact about one's education. Viewed from afar—or from close up, by people working in high schools—every part of this outlook is twisted."

Less-selective universities have an incentive to give the impression of higher selectivity. Highly selective universities are not incentivized to ditch ED schemes for fear of appearing less prestigious and therefore ranked lower. Every campus has an added incentive to drive application numbers higher to select the highest-scoring SAT students further to bolster their *US News* standing, easier with ED when universities know the highest-scoring students must enroll.

Fallows references Penn and Swarthmore that depended on ED schemes in the '90s to boost and eventually secure their prominence at the top of the *US News* leaderboard. A puzzling implication of higher student yields is that bond rating agencies such as Moodys and S&P rated a university's risk level better, determining their interest rates. Universities then as now are most concerned about their bottom line and the business of education and research.

> "The long-term financial viability of a college can be influenced simply by its reported yield. 'I was flabbergasted when we were having our college bonds evaluated by Moodys and S&P,' Bruce Poch, of Pomona, told me. 'These bond raters were obsessing about our yield! They were chastising me because Pomona's yield was not as high as Williams's and Amherst's, because they took more of their class early. We explained that our regular-decision yield was quite high, and finally got a triple-A bond rating. Obviously there were other considerations, but this saved the college millions in interest.'"

The most controversial debate surrounding Early Decision involves a common theme: who gains access to spaces at elite American universities. Universities have debated whether to have binding ED options. A collective action problem means that if a critical mass of elite universities fails to dispense with ED practices, institutions that opt out will be punished in the rankings and their relative prestige. Harvard's long-time admissions director William Fitzsimmons laments the ED arms race among elite universities: "In an ideal world, we would do away with all early programs."

Fallows responds, referring to Harvard's influence on admissions practices nationwide, that "his 'ideal world' is significant news. What holds him back is the need to know that other schools will lower their guns if he lowers his." Fallows notes early reform efforts to cap an overall enrolling class admitted through ED at 25 percent. Still, the ED to RD ratio has been increasing ever since at more than 50 percent of enrolling students on some campuses.

The primary difference of Fallow's article comparing then and now is that families and high school staff are acutely aware of ED and how it differs from nonbinding EA and RD choices. Navigating ED practices and options still heavily favors wealthy families in the know.

A winter 2006/2007 article in the *Journal of Blacks in Higher Education* discussed the evolving ED landscape since Fallows's 2001 article.[183] Yale announced in late 2001 that if Harvard and Princeton discontinued their early deadlines, they would follow suit. Harvard discontinued their Early Action deadline for Fall 2008 applicants. They practiced nonbinding Early Action deadlines rather than binding ED deadlines because their yield hovered around 80 percent, the highest in the nation.

They lost few students to their peer institutions, so they were in a unique position to be the first mover to discard their early deadline. Harvard's Interim President Derek Bok commented that "Students from more sophisticated backgrounds and affluent high schools often apply early to increase their chances of admission, while minority students and students from rural areas, other countries, and high schools with fewer resources miss out."

Princeton and the University of Virginia followed suit and abandoned ED before adopting it again a few years later. It's too tempting an enrollment management tool, so its practice outweighs the benefits of enrolling a diverse student body. The article notes that few universities followed Princeton and Harvard's lead. As more low-income and minority communities became aware of ED practices and new financial aid guarantees for families making below a certain income, elite universities such as Harvard and Princeton attracted the most talented students nationwide. Universities on lower prestige rungs have an incentive to continue practicing ED to attract the highest-achieving students possible. There is a finite pool of academically exceptional students from non-college-going communities.

To add another layer of confusion, Harvard and Yale recently implemented a Single-Choice Early Action (SCEA) that doesn't restrict applicants to EA schools but does for other universities (e.g., Stanford), who practice Restrictive Early Action (REA). Nearly five times as many nonbinding early applicants to Harvard, Princeton, and Yale gain admission relative to their RD counterparts. REA policies supposedly don't permit students to apply to ED/EA/SCEA at other universities, although I have no idea how this is enforced.

The primary difference between REA and ED is that students are not bound to enroll at the university and may notify their preferred college by the May 1 National Candidates Reply Date. REA offers slightly more enrollment flexibility to the student at the expense of applying EA elsewhere. In our continually shifting and confusing admissions environment, enrollment managers cook up SCEA and REA policies to give the impression of student flexibility without the stigma of ED.

Are you having trouble keeping up with the acronyms? Don't worry. I have a hard time keeping track of the ever-evolving alphabet soup of the early application ecosystem, too. And if I struggle to keep up, let's consider what role ED policies play in recruiting students from marginalized communities.

A 2012 study by researchers at Claremont McKenna in the *Journal of Law & Economics* tested the hypothesis of whether ED promotes or deters enrolling diverse classes of students.[184] They surveyed 189 national universities and small liberal arts colleges from 2004–2007 and found that "ED has a negative impact on cohort diversity." ED practices, unsurprisingly, yield significantly more white and out-of-state applicants. "The most pronounced negative effects are for Asian American and Hispanic students.... Their representation decreases more as schools increase their reliance on ED and/or EA programs."

Even for universities that publicly commit to need-blind admissions, researchers suggest that universities have an incentive to admit slightly below-average students through ED. The latter are more likely to pay full tuition. The researchers hypothesize that increasing tuition prices are driven in part by ED practices that bind some portion of their enrolling class to pay full price. Universities can charge more for their services.

It's theoretically possible that ED could promote diversity and a more heterogeneous student body. One hypothesis they considered is whether more fees secured from wealthy ED applicants could be allocated for financial aid to low-income students. The researchers found that universities have incentives to reallocate that money elsewhere to luxury amenities such as rock-climbing walls and lazy rivers. Administrators are incentivized to provide flashy student resources to attract full-pay students.

Moreover, because ED enrollees occupy increasingly higher proportions of spaces, fewer spaces remain for the significantly more competitive RD applicants. If universities admitted a lower proportion of ED students, the researchers' economic models suggest that would leave more spaces for academically strong yet still below average underrepresented students. Pressures to maximize control over enrollment management, however, outweigh administrative priorities for maximizing diversity recruitment. Subsequent recent findings by Inside Higher Ed and the left-leaning Center for American Progress report the same conclusions as the Claremont McKenna 2004–2007 ED survey.[185] Consequently, most universities, most of the time, will admit more students through ED at the expense of underrepresented populations.

The two key takeaways from this discussion of Early Decision practices is that universities use them to exercise more control over enrollment management. Prioritizing enrollment management reduces every applicant's flexibility, and it compromises liberal universities with public goals of enrolling the most diverse classes possible. Only the most highly exceptional students are likely to benefit from ED practices, perhaps 5,000 or fewer worldwide, whereas it's detrimental to tens of thousands of other applicants.

The next section discusses a situation most applicants find themselves in: the third and fourth choices to the Senior Prom.

8.2 Admissions purgatory: deferrals, waitlist, appeals, and letters of continued interest

The majority of students applying for Early Decision or Early Action will neither be admitted nor denied outright. They're usually deferred until the regular admissions deadline when their application is considered among all other applicants.

Deferred applicants often scramble to complete a battery of RD applications before the January 1 deadlines. Mathematically savvy students will sometimes filter their single ED application, not by the overall admissions rate but according to the proportion of students admitted after being deferred.

A 2020 data assessment by Ivy Coach crunched the numbers to determine which Ivy League universities admit ED applicants deferred to the regular admissions pool.[186] They estimate that, on average, 90 percent of deferred students are eventually denied. Brown admitted only 7 percent of deferred students, for example. Occasionally, deferred students are offered a spot on the waitlist, a kind of double-limbo. Deferral is the enrollment management equivalent of texting "hey, you up?" after going home from the party alone.

Another tool in the enrollment manager's kit is the elusive waitlist. No applicant knows why they're "invited to join" the waitlist rather than outright denied. They might assume they're a borderline applicant, but that isn't always the case. Perhaps the enrollment manager is worried about putting enough butts in the seats for a given major.

Waitlists are like contestants on *The Bachelor* "invited to join" the rose ceremony when everybody knows in advance Arie will choose either Hannah or Becca. But hey, better than an outright rejection, right? I'm doubtful.

Waitlists are a special kind of hell for applicants because universities provide no guarantees to notify applicants of admission or rejection after the National Decision Day on May 1. Carnegie Mellon contributed an added layer of confusion with a tiered "priority waitlist," whereby some students received their decision by May 10, with the remainder hearing back by June 1. Almost everyone is fiercely resistant to admissions by lottery, but in practice, waitlists are precisely that.

Universities want to see how many students submit enrollment deposits and admit students from the waitlist depending on the number of spaces available at the university or specific programs. Applying to highly in-demand programs decreases the likelihood of gaining admission off the waitlist or after an appeal for reconsideration. Waitlists and appeals are similar, except if the former are contestants on *The Bachelor*; the latter are the thousands of rejected contestant applications begging for their 60-second video submission to get a second look by the reality TV producers.

The first and worst waitlist case I ever encountered was in 2012 when I worked for UT-Austin. UT that year offered a few hundred students an invitation to join the waitlist. Some years, everyone gains admission off the waitlist. In other cycles, maybe only a handful get in. Few students were offered admission off the waitlist in 2012. A student who had been communicating with me throughout the cycle sent a handwritten note on the back of a Google Maps printout showing the route from Plano to Austin. She brought our office cookies in April after I insisted that we had no power over waitlists. But who were we to refuse fresh-baked snickerdoodles? Admissions counselors aren't monsters or dentists, after all.

Enrollment managers, on the other hand, subjected this student to an insidious purgatory. She received the notification in early May that she was not offered admission off the waitlist. She called me, crying. Because so many enrollment deadlines had already passed for her backup universities, she began the groveling process at her backup schools (that she had declined) for them to allow an exception. She put down an enrollment deposit elsewhere only to receive a phone call a few days later from senior UT staff that they had made a mistake. They actually intended to admit her from the waitlist, but someone had hit the wrong button. *Congratulations, you're a Longhorn!*

It's analogous to being dumped at the prom only for your date to have a change of heart, except they sent their rejection text to the wrong phone number when they really meant to send you the heart emoji because they *totally* don't like Aaron, so baby do you still want to dance with me???

Most universities are relatively stable in how many students they invite to join the waitlist and subsequently admit, but it isn't easy data to find. Universities are rarely forthcoming with their waitlist statistics. NACAC reports around 20 percent of waitlisted students will eventually gain admission, but the range varies widely depending on the university. Cal Tech and Drexel admitted 1 percent of their waitlisted students for Fall 2018. Boston University recorded 3,446 students who joined the waitlist in the same admissions cycle, with only a single student gaining admission. Case Western Reserve admitted zero among 9,908, like a lottery ticket where everyone is a loser.

Indiana University admitted 427 out of 467 (91 percent), while UC-Berkeley admitted one-third of their waitlistees.[187] Some universities rank their waitlisted students, whereas others don't, so you can never be sure why a decision went one way or another. A lack of waitlist transparency casts doubts on students who do succeed because they wonder if they're a genuinely desirable applicant or a number to meet an enrollment metric, particularly if they're an underrepresented minority. Maybe it was due to the university's needs, or perhaps you just didn't make the cut. Waitlists contribute to imposter syndrome after arriving on campus because students admitted off the waitlist wonder if they're good enough. Of course, an individual student may receive many waitlist places, so they get the special pleasure of receiving a series of rejections over the summer as they increasingly surrender to their twelfth-choice university.

UT-Austin is notorious for sometimes having a waitlist of thousands of applicants and other years with hundreds or none at all. In Fall 2019, for example, UT didn't offer a waitlist, yet they admitted an unprecedented number of students from the Appeals pool. A few hundred students from specific majors received surprise acceptance notifications late into the summer that they gained admission without further explanation. In Fall 2021, UT didn't offer a waitlist upfront. Instead, a handful of students who appealed were "invited to join" a new waitlist, leaving them in further limbo.

UT deployed a bizarre technique for Fall 2020 when they randomly admitted students they'd rejected earlier in the year. In some cases, they denied a student's appeal request for reconsideration before accepting them a few weeks before the fall semester began.

Congratulations, you're a Longhorn, and nobody can tell you why!

An analogy might be your crush saying no once and no a second time before texting six months later out of the blue, "Can we meet for coffee?" Practices like these reinforce my belief that universities are increasingly out of touch and unaccountable to the public they purport to serve. They suffer no consequences for their actions because they know the demand for their services is "inelastic." They know they will always have butts in the seats, and all else be damned.

A practice related to waitlists that exclusively serves enrollment managements' needs is trickling out acceptance decisions in "waves." I don't have in mind less-selective universities that practice assured admissions and notify acceptances within a week or two of applying. UT-Austin begins releasing batches of decisions of varying sizes randomly starting in late November until late January or early February.

As soon as the first trickle of acceptances is released, social media and high schools around the state enter pandemonium. I receive hundreds of inquiries about when students can expect to receive their decision. A "decision timeline" blog post is my most trafficked in December and January. Anxious students browse

Reddit and College Confidential, where charlatans claim "insider access" and are inevitably incorrect when trying to read the admissions tea leaves.

UT has never released its criteria for why some students receive news earlier than others. They don't publish in advance when to expect the decision releases. During January, their Twitter feed is nothing but promotional pieces that aim to persuade families to enroll who are desperate even to gain admission. I can't detect any correlation, as some of my strongest clients are some of the last to hear, whereas my strong but not exceptional students sometimes receive good news early.

Many students mistakenly believe that the most challenging part is drafting and submitting their applications. Trickling decisions adds more anxiety to the waiting game. Waiting is often the most unexpectedly challenging part of the process, especially when some of their friends hear back while they're left waiting in limbo.

An additional layer of hell is the "letter of continued interest" along with other "invitations" to improve your candidacy, an especially fun time for Fall 2020 enrolling students coping with the pandemic during the spring and summer. Prep Scholar provides several helpful tips for the devastated student stuck in limbo.[188] They suggest writing an unsolicited letter of interest, sending resume updates, midyear grade reports, staying in touch with your assigned admissions counselor, and even retaking the SAT/ACT.

Students experience waitlist fatigue, a kind of **non-adaptive choice switching** whereby even after gaining admission off the waitlist to their dream school, they decide to enroll elsewhere. Others suffer from **plan continuation bias** where they cannot accept that the admissions door has almost undoubtedly closed, so they exhaust every avenue to overturn a decision. What the waitlist means for most applicants is yet another battery of essays.

How many tens of thousands of additional essays are written at the end of the admissions process only for the vast majority of students to still not gain admission? Many Redditors report simply copy and pasting their continued interest essay for their varied waitlisted universities. I can't say I blame them.

Many universities have made a sport out of a student's desperation into a kind of Groveling Olympics. They generously "allow" students to submit recommendation letters, placing additional burdens on already overextended high school staff. Because others have less-clear policies about updating the application, there's always an ambiguity around which universities do or don't want additional materials. UT-Austin is emphatic that they don't want new information for waitlists, but students who are appealing are "invited" to submit new information. Most universities are relatively transparent that the waitlist or appeals process depends almost entirely on the institution's needs, making the entire infrastructure of purgatory application materials a theater production.

Applicants are fooled into thinking they exercise some level of control over their outcomes. Implicit in appeals or continued interest letters are a kind of **special pleading** where the applicant is attempting to establish themselves "as an exemption to a generally accepted rule without justifying the exemption." Really, really, really badly wanting to enroll doesn't distinguish you from the thousands of other hopefuls. That didn't stop an extended family coming into our office wearing burnt orange with a three-ring binder filled with football game ticket stubs, multigenerational Longhorn gatherings, and a bedroom decked out in all things UT.

Naturally, families assume that an unfavorable decision *must certainly be a mistake* of the decision-makers—the **furtive fallacy.** Except as I discussed in the opening to this section, universities routinely make mistakes. Holding out that a mistake was made gives credence to the belief that a miracle may well happen. Errors on the university decision release side add another layer of cognitive distortions on top of the madness. If elite universities cared about their applicants, they would limit or eliminate practices like waitlists, appeals, deferrals, and letters of continued interest.

The next section covers a nefarious set of unintended consequences following UT-Austin's integration of Big Data algorithms into the financial aid process.

8.3 Dashboard and the darkside of big data

On August 20, 2018, UT-Austin announced the Texas Advance Commitment Award that guaranteed need-based financial aid for families making below $100,000 annually. The following year, UT raised their guarantee to provide partial tuition coverage for families making under $125,000 while covering the total tuition costs for families making below $65,000. Texas's median household income is around $60,000, so the Texas Advance Commitment is the most notable financial assistance program in the university's history. It covers one-third of all undergraduate students, including full tuition for 8,600 out of UT's approximately 40,000 undergraduate students.[189] UT-Austin's tuition commitment joins Rice, Michigan, Colorado, and many highly selective private schools nationwide. Making college more affordable for all is an ideal worth implementing.

However, UT's generosity wasn't always the case. On the contrary, in the early 2010s, when I worked as a counselor, they systematically denied need-based financial aid to low-income students forecasted as less likely to graduate in four years.

Universities almost always give a student's total financial aid package well in advance of the May 1 National Candidates Reply Date. That way, families can make informed decisions about which education is affordable and adds the most value. UT financial aid practices in 2013 violated NACAC's ethical guidelines to provide transparent information to students about their expected total cost of attendance.

Until now, I've kept the following story secret for fear of backlash or retribution. I would have kept it private if not for their recent tuition guarantees. If UT ever revokes their tuition guarantee for low-income families, the public needs to hold them accountable for how they disperse and allocate need-based financial aid in the future. The following story is one example of a broader university trend of not disclosing their financial aid offers and total cost of attendance before enrolling.

After visiting a low-income urban West Dallas high school for an admitted student financial aid consultation in early April 2013, I walked directly into my boss's office and slammed two papers on his desk.

"Tell me how in the hell we're supposed to compete with this?"

I raged while he tried to make sense of the financial aid notification one of our admitted students received from Texas A&M College Station. He compared A&M's offer with ours.

> "Look at their offers. Texas A&M gave them eighteen thousand dollars in gift aid grants that don't need to be repaid while we gave the same amount in ****ing Parent Plus Loans. The kid's counselor cried when they saw it! How in the **** are we supposed to expect kids who may or may not have two or any parents and almost certainly have low or no credit score, supposed to co-sign on eighty thousand dollars in loans over four years? Would you pay a hundred thousand dollars for a UT-Austin education with a family income of less than twenty thousand? This is ****ing ********, and you know it."

Except my boss didn't know what was happening. These loan-heavy packages were news to him.

UT had routinely granted the maximum amount of university and state grants regardless of a student's academics. In 2013, many students only received the federally guaranteed Pell Grant, around $5,500 per year. Before then, we assumed that these other grants were guaranteed by law, but it seems like it had just been the norm. I had just received my Fulbright grant notification, so with nothing to lose, I nearly resigned on the spot. It's the one and only time working for UT-Austin that I felt disgusted beyond words. In that moment, I knew I was complicit in a system that was screwing over Texas's most vulnerable families.

My boss and our in-house financial aid counselor started making calls. Across the regional admissions centers and at the university, front-line counselors like me reported the same experiences. In one case, the older brother of a recruited student the previous year received the gift aid he was entitled to. Typical highest-need packages back then reduced the total cost of UT for room and board to around $5,000 in federally subsidized loans, a reasonable load assuming the student graduates.

We gave that student's younger brother nearly $20,000 in Parent Plus Loans. Parent Plus Loans require a parent to co-sign the loan, so they are on the hook for repayments if the student fails to pay. Some parents don't qualify because they have low or no credit scores, leaving private loans with high-interest rates the only option to attend.

We used to designate many low-income schools as part of the Longhorn Opportunity Scholars (LOS) program with generous merit component scholarships and guaranteed a student's first choice major regardless of their academics. High school counselors could always count on reliable and predictable UT aid packages when helping their students apply in the fall. Pissed-off counselors emailed and called for weeks asking me how they're supposed to tell their students they can't afford their dream school. In an email to a colleague, I wrote:

> "When I visited his school in April for financial aid conversations, my top recruit was denied aid. His tuition was covered for the first year under a state law that exempts the valedictorians' tuition for their freshman year if they attend a public university. Still, the prospects of his attendance dwindled drastically after receiving this news. I watched him cry in front of me, his counselor, his counselor's boss, and my financial aid colleague. It is beyond me how a student could qualify for a competitive major like Engineering yet denied aid. This is a student UT wants, but for some reason, Dashboard doesn't. There is a disconnect between the admissions algorithm and the dashboard algorithm...

> ... Another 'falling through the cracks' student has high test scores, black male, low socioeconomic status, admitted to first-choice major of Engineering, perfect in the holistic review of 6, even awarded a departmental merit scholarship. He received zero discretionary aid (institutional and state). This is a student UT should want and that we actively recruit, but that Dashboard doesn't like...

> The denying of aid wouldn't even have been so bad if we hadn't physically visited all of these schools, met with counselors, met with parents. Devastating. Morale was extremely low in April 2013. A few people quit, choosing to not be a part of a system they viewed as unjust."

LOS schools were our highest recruitment priority because they were largely composed of Hispanic and black students. During the same year, the university was litigating Fisher vs. UT-Austin at the Supreme Court, arguing in favor of considerations of race in college admissions. Why would a university that publicly values and spends millions of dollars fighting for diversity in the courts for eight years actively exclude the very populations they purport to prefer?

My disastrous visits to inner-city high schools were just the beginning of learning about the consequences of a new Big Data analytics system, Dashboard. Dashboard is a story about the misapplication of technology and how the road to admissions Hell is paved with good intentions.

A few years prior, UT-Austin commissioned a massive task force to identify areas of reform. They aimed to increase four-year graduation rates from 51 percent to 70 percent by 2016.[190] One area for improvement involved matching students to their first-choice major. Matching students to their majors corresponded with the university making it more difficult to internal transfer after arriving on campus.

Although UT-Austin guarantees admission to students ranking in the top 6 percent of their class (top 7 or 8 percent back then), no student is guaranteed their first-choice major, especially for high-demand programs such as Engineering, Business, and Computer Science. Before I saw the loan-heavy aid packages, I realized something was amiss. In previous cycles, LOS students almost always received their first-choice major and no longer received their preference most of the time. Every student with awful packages also did not receive their major—some of whom had managed to obtain admission to majors with higher academic standards, such as Engineering and Business. Only a handful of students received both their first-choice major and an affordable grant-heavy financial aid package.

An obvious way to increase graduation rates is to deter less-capable students from enrolling even though state law guarantees them a space. In late April, upper management started panicking when their diversity enrollment numbers declined steeply from previous years. Their first move was to blame frontline counselors like me, claiming we weren't working hard enough. They quickly backed down when we showed them the generous aid offers from our peer universities. I suggested they fly up and visit schools together, see for yourselves the disaster you've wrought. They declined. Additionally, the low enrollment of minority students would make for an uncomfortable meeting with urban state legislators.

Students have until May 1 to notify their desired university that they wish to enroll. On Friday afternoon, April 26, 2013, I received a call to come into the office first thing Saturday morning.

An email from a senior admissions official instructed me to make phone calls to students denied financial aid. That's when I saw Dashboard for the first time, an endless spreadsheet that quantified a student's chances of graduating in four years based on millions of data points. It contained the phone numbers for my assigned students.

Conveniently, the university "discovered" additional scholarship money in the budget to distribute to students last minute as enticements to enroll. I received a motivational text message from a senior staff member that I was "doing great work," while I personally called over a hundred students to notify them of recurring scholarship offers between $5,000 and $20,000. Doing great work requires getting things right the first time and not covering up mistakes without admitting fault. Frontline counselors like me were forced to absorb senior management's utter lack of accountability. The conversations were really awkward for the students who answered their phones, like being asked to the prom by the boy who had rejected you once already.

Next, I wondered, why were students receiving arbitrary amounts of money? How come some got $5,000 and others $20,000? I found the cell column predicting the four-year graduation rate. I noticed that any student projected to graduate in four years with less than a 40 percent likelihood were the ones denied aid, but not all. Some students with a 50 or 60 percent chance also didn't receive aid. These last-minute phone calls resulted from adjusting the parameters to permit more aid to damage control minority recruitment and avert a public relations disaster. Still, many students were left without gift-aid packages sufficient to cover a UT education.

What happened to the money ordinarily reserved for our highest-need populations? The institutional and state aid was redistributed to middle-income, typically suburban, students who crossed a certain unknown threshold in Dashboard's four-year graduation prediction algorithm.

Students otherwise excluded from need-based aid started receiving it in 2013. Administrators redistributed the merit-based with a need component Presidential Achievement Scholarship (PAS) away from working-class families to middle-class ones by raising the threshold for what constitutes need. But then I received phone calls from suburban families complaining that the amount was too low!

I couldn't say to them that in any other year, they would have received nothing. In the interim years between Dashboard's birth and the Texas Advance Commitment guarantee, officials reconfigured PAS to help low-income students. However, many of our former-LOS schools were neglected. It made me feel like the rapport and goodwill I developed during my six to eight annual visits to each of my seven LOS schools was for nothing.

Unknown to me at the time, UT-Austin was part of a broader, emerging data analytics trend for universities to assign scholarships in specific amounts, but not too high, to increase the probability of a given student enrolling. The most interesting and original chapter in Jeffrey Selingo's *Who Gets In and Why* comes toward the end, "Paying for College: the Best Class Money Can Buy." He details an emerging industry of data analysis consultants with quantitative and computer science backgrounds hired by colleges to optimize their scholarship budget.

He interviews Human Capital Research "who answer questions like this: Would that teenager from the Boston suburbs choose a particular college if the financial aid offer were sweetened by another $1,000? Would $500 be enough?"[191]

Adjusting the parameters for their enrollment management forecast models means that neither an applicant's merit nor financial need solely determine their award. Budget officers may split up a single scholarship historically given to a low-income student into many smaller ones to entice their middle-income peers to enroll and pay partial tuition.

Scholarship awards seem even more random and arbitrary than admissions offers. That's because they are. Selingo writes, "Colleges don't reveal [these] financial aid strategies in the glossy brochures they send to prospective students."[192]

While UT's questionable scholarship distributions unfolded, I went against policy. I secretly suggested to my high school counselors to email the head director and organize with the media and their elected representatives. Financial aid counselors found ways to reassign discretionary funds to the Dashboarded students. I wrote a 2014 email about the high-achieving black male engineer denied financial aid.

"A financial aid counselor tried to assign him additional aid through TEXAS grant, but the May 1 deadline passed once they received permission to do so, and the student failed to meet the enrollment deposit deadline. There are good people working on the inside, and in some ways risking their jobs, to assign aid on the back-end on a case-by-case basis for the 'came anyways' kids who were denied aid on the front end."

UT-Austin's haphazard rollout of their analytics-inspired scholarship distributions forced them to scramble after the May 1, 2013 enrollment deadline passed. Around 500 students the administration tried to deter by denying them their first-choice major and financial aid chose to enroll anyway. In a stroke of public relations damage control genius, the university hastily rolled out a new "college access" program called University Leadership Network (ULN). Press releases promoted it as an effort to increase student success in vulnerable populations by offering free summer school on campus, financial aid, mentorship opportunities, etc.

UT-Austin invited enrolling students to join ULN *after* May 1, yet in public, they promoted their initiative as a recruitment effort for students before the enrollment deadline. They also invited "select students" to apply for a prestigious-sounding program called the Texas Interdisciplinary Plan (TIP).

ULN and TIP scrambled to accommodate hundreds of students who would have otherwise experienced severe financial hardship and have a high risk of not returning for their sophomore year or graduate in four years. ULN and TIP coincided with the quiet phasing out of UT's flagship low-income recruitment program, Longhorn Opportunity Scholars, which was initiated following the passing of House Bill 588, Top 10 percent law in the mid-1990s.[193]

At an admissions-wide meeting in August 2013 at an auditorium conference room in the Student Activities Center, we received a presentation from the Senior Vice Provost of Enrollment and Graduation Management—a position created the year before to oversee the four-year graduation rate push. Beloved chemistry professor and interim College of Natural Sciences Dean Dr. David Laude—a man I had admired for his unconventional views on higher education—offered the university's official stance on the enrollment management madness to the 150+ admissions staff.[194]

Before that meeting, I was dimly aware of the existence of the bureaucratic shuffling that promoted a new marionette responsible for pulling the admissions strings. Among other techniques enabled by Dashboard's data analytics, we learned that administration officials experimented with offering different scholarship values to different students. Enrollment managers intended to see which amount would entice a student to enroll but not spend too much when a lower figure would suffice. Scholarship distributions are a genuinely random process that I could never decipher even when I worked for the university.

In a May 2014 *New York Times* article titled "Who Gets to Graduate?" by Paul Tough, Dr. Laude lays out the public case for Dashboard.[195]

"Laude wanted something that would help him predict, for any given incoming freshman, how likely he or she would be to graduate in four years. The Institutional Research team analyzed the performance of tens of thousands of recent U.T. students. From that analysis, they produced a tool they called the Dashboard—an algorithm, in spreadsheet form, that would consider 14 variables, from an incoming student's family income to his SAT score to his class rank to his parents' educational background, and then immediately spit out a probability, to the second decimal place, of how likely he was to graduate in four years."

Identifying high-risk students to target for retention programs and financial aid is a worthy idea and one I support. However, data used haphazardly or without virtuous intentions can lead to unintended consequences.

A few softball questions from middle management to Dr. Laude failed to acknowledge the financial aid elephant in the room, so I stood up. I thanked him for his time, and as warmly as I could manage, I challenged him less on Dashboard's ethics. I confronted him on the sequence of events that placed unprepared admissions and financial aid counselors on the chopping block at the schools we deemed our highest priorities. I asked Dr. Laude, why not offer ULN and TIP to students *prior to May 1* rather than after they decide to enroll against their best financial interests?

Tough's article lays out the public relations surrounding these programs and Dr. Laude's answer given at that August 2013 conference. "Laude's most intensive and innovative intervention, though, is the University Leadership Network.... To be selected for U.L.N., incoming freshmen must not only fall below the 40-percent cutoff on the Dashboard; *they must also have what the financial-aid office calls unmet financial need.*"

Recall that these genuinely excellent programs targeted students who received invitations *after* May 1 and not before to entice them to enroll. Low-income students less likely to graduate in four years had "unmet financial need" because they were explicitly denied funding that they would ordinarily receive in previous admissions cycles, not because of a relatively small gap occupied by federally subsidized loans.[196]

I sat down as my junior member colleagues and regional directors gave me smiles and thumbs up. Dr. Laude is the kind of person who has an answer for everything, but at that moment, he shuffled his papers and turned to his assistant. When he finally spoke, his answer shocked me. He apologized! And promised to communicate better next time. I'm grateful he didn't continue spinning misinformation.

He wouldn't discuss the architecture of Dashboard itself or even acknowledge its existence—that came later in Tough's article. Still, frontline counselors and I saw his admission of error as a minor victory. When he exited the auditorium, senior staff followed him outside to assuage his ego. Our Director of Admissions, whom I hadn't spoken with since my final interview two years before, reprimanded me. Later, a colleague said, "I wouldn't have had the balls to do that," while another thanked me for sharing what was on all of our minds.

During my remaining four months before moving to Malaysia, before senior management even knew I was leaving, I became something of a pariah in the bureaucracy. Undermining authority came at a price. Despite exceeding expectations on my annual performance review before the August meeting, I received increased scrutiny, making it more challenging to do my job. Management tripled my admissions file assignments without compensation. *Pettiness* isn't a value I've found on any university's Vision Statement, but I imagine it's a quality universal in medium-to-large bureaucracies.

In retrospect, I don't think UT-Austin was purposefully excluding the students they claimed to value. They implemented budget-conscious reforms too hastily and failed at covering up their errors. At the time, it seemed like a few nefarious actors were plotting to achieve a four-year graduation rate, even if it meant compromising university values and human decency. The push for four-year graduation rates led to unintended consequences that I'm sure no individual would have endorsed if they knew ahead of time that hundreds of families would experience heartache and hardship. Rolling out so many reforms so quickly produced sloppy policy. Maybe senior university officials thought the marginalized populations wouldn't notice; I don't know.

I found it ironic that our African American female Director of Admissions scolded me for speaking truth to power while I defended minority student recruitment as a white person. She advised my gay African American boss "to keep me in line," echoing segregationist language that white people deployed against black people during Jim Crow.

I was simply doing what my UT-Austin liberal arts education taught me: stand up for what is right. I still respect her as a person because she was just occupying the professional position expected of her, even if Dashboard may have conflicted with her personal value system or position on the *Fisher* Supreme Court case. She needed to keep junior counselors like me consistent with the university's message, even if that message was unfair and unjust.

Nevertheless, I'm grateful that I leveraged my relative independence as a lame-duck employee without concern for future advancement, a luxury none of my colleagues had. Dashboard also demonstrates the tension between a university's role of enrolling the highest-achieving students while enrolling students from diverse backgrounds who often underperform their more privileged peers.

My personal takeaway from this saga is that fighting for reform within a system is less valuable than chipping away at the walls from the outside. Pushing back against inefficient policies during my Fulbright grant to US and Malaysian government officials landed with similar futility. These experiences contributed to me exiting the conventional world for good in 2015.

There was minimal upside to me taking the Dashboard story public and all of the downsides that accompany whistleblowing. Edward Snowden and the NSA leaks occurred around the same time, and I didn't want to experience professional exile or potential litigation. I didn't want to throw my former colleagues under the bus who were feeding me information.

Dashboard is an instance where connecting the dots of a few seemingly unrelated events yielded a legitimate conspiracy with far-reaching consequences. I'm thankful that my alma mater eventually did the right thing and enacted a transparent, consistent policy for distributing financial aid untethered to an incoming student's high school academics or other criteria.

I have no idea how or whether UT uses this system currently or to what admissions purpose, but it doesn't matter because it's entirely outside of an applicant's control. Within the bureaucracy, the Office of Enrollment Management remains above the Office of Admissions, a crucial distinction because Enrollment Management determines how many students the university wants to enroll. That affects the number of available admissions spaces.

A final takeaway is that, just like any bureaucracy with internal politics, what happens behind the scenes at any given university is almost impossible to decipher. Office politics are a factor entirely outside of your control and, as the Stoics would suggest, not something worth worrying about. Data analytics that assigns "desirability" ratings will continue influencing enrollment and recruitment practices behind the scenes in unknowable ways. Enrollment management offices independent of the public-facing college applications system obscure exactly why some students gain admission or scholarships, and others don't. The predictive technology is too tempting for universities not to implement.

Put another way: you can never know how many cellists or Science Olympiads Harvard wants in a given year.

9. Rethinking Diversity

Affirmative action remains an ongoing debate since the civil rights movement of the 1960s. Four years before the landmark *Brown v Board of Education* that required desegregation of American schools, the Supreme Court ruled in *Sweatt v Painter* (1950) that UT-Austin's School of Law did not provide equal resources to white and black students. Black students could only attend the Texas State University for Negroes in Houston, known today as Texas Southern University.

The *Painter* decision spawned a series of contentious court cases over the ensuing decades regarding the constitutionality of racial quotas, bonus points, and how, if at all, race can be considered an admissions factor. Currently, universities do not reserve spaces using a quota system or assign bonus points for minority applicants. Instead, the Supreme Court ruled in *Grutter v. Bollinger* (2003) that race can be one factor among dozens that reviewers can consider when determining a student's score through holistic review. That ruling was upheld in the second adjudication of *Fisher v. UT-Austin* in 2016.

Providing a comprehensive overview of college campuses serving as battlegrounds for discussions of race and educational opportunity is outside this book's scope. I stand behind reviewers knowing the race/ethnicity of applicants and its consideration in their admissions score. Some states, e.g., Michigan and California, have outlawed considerations of race as an admissions factor, which the courts have upheld as the constitutional prerogative for each state to decide.

One central area of contention in *Grutter* (2003) and *Fisher* (2016) is whether enrolling a diverse student body provides educational benefits. Research suggests that enrolling a heterogeneous student body from varied cultures, ethnicities, and social classes facilitates an exchange of ideas that enriches the learning environment.[197] I benefitted personally from attending a diverse UT-Austin, and I support universities that value diversity as an educational goal worth striving for.

I staked my reputation by publicly defending UT-Austin's top 6 percent law that guarantees admission based on one's class rank and considerations of race in admissions policies in *Your Ticket to the Forty Acres*. My readers primarily come from affluent and privileged backgrounds. My book helped stimulate conversations among people who often haven't deeply considered what roles race and class play in contemporary society.

One belief that I've changed since writing *Your Ticket* four years ago is that I support halving UT's automatic cutoff admissions rate to top 3 percent, a proposal the former UT President Powers advocated when the law changed in 2009. Most top 6 percent spaces go to students attending high-resource public schools, and too few applications come from low-income schools, so halving the admissions cutoff may promote more inclusion rather than less.

One highly controversial change unpopular on both the political left and right, but I was sympathetic, was the SAT's Adversity Score experiment. I believed it would help correct implicit bias and inequalities in society by contextualizing a student's neighborhood environment regarding poverty, crime, and a dozen other factors. Quantifying adversity offers a more precise alternative to wishy-washy holistic review considerations. The SAT and ACT are deeply flawed exams, but I also think there is a need for some nation- and worldwide metric to compare college readiness. Time will tell whether throwing out the exams entirely and moving toward test-optional helps increase college access while maintaining graduation rates. I suspect there won't be much of a trade-off in the quality of the student body.

I prefer not to unpack the debates regarding the SAT or test-optional here. I raise the debate to suggest that it symbolizes the challenges of reforming higher education. I also do not comment on recent litigation on alleged Asian American discrimination at Harvard and other elite universities. The cases, although fascinating given the history of holistic review methods used to discriminate against Jewish students in the 1920s and '30s, as discussed in chapter 4, so far have not successfully yielded anything incriminating. However, I discuss later on how diversity-themed essay topics disadvantage Asian American and Asian diaspora students.

Underrepresented minorities and students living in poverty are also considerably less likely to score in the top 10 percent of ACT/SAT takers. On the other hand, 50 percent of low-income black students enrolled at elite private colleges were scholarship students at prestigious private high schools that are dominated by their affluent white classmates. Caitlin Flanagan from the *Atlantic* writes, "This means that these schools, which collectively educate a tiny proportion of Black teenagers, have a huge influence on which of these kids get to attend the best colleges."[198]

Race and class aren't either/ors, and where one attends high school is an important consideration for diversity and inclusion. It's possible to consider both alongside many other potentially adverse factors, which is one reason why I'm not in favor of discarding race as an admissions factor. It's nonsensical to consider the totality of a student's portfolio *except* for race and ethnicity. I'm encouraged by the more prominent roles that first-generation college status and socioeconomics play in the holistic review process.

Still, on average, African Americans and Hispanics are much more likely to live in poverty or attend low-resource schools than white and Asian students. Before the pandemic, the average white family's net worth was more than ten times that of African American or Hispanic families.[199] A year into the pandemic, the employment rates for people earning more than $60,000 have largely returned to pre-pandemic levels.

As of January 25, 2021, the unemployment rate for workers earning less than $27,000 is 22 percent.[200] Americans in the top 20 percent by wealth, who are largely white and Asian, own almost all US stocks and securities.[201] While eight million American families descend into poverty, with African Americans disproportionately represented, 46 millionaires became billionaires. During the pandemic, America's 660 billionaires have increased their net worth by over $1 trillion.[202]

The rich are growing richer, and the poor even poorer at higher rates than anyone living today can remember. The middle classes continue to shrink. College admissions is a demonstrably unequal playing field. The defining characteristic of a student's future opportunities is whether they grow up in poverty or not. Considerations of poverty expand the circle of empathy to encompass more people regardless of their ethnicity.

Segregation in America's wealthiest public-school systems is higher today than during Jim Crow. Consequently, there are lower rates of mixing between middle- and low-income students and their more affluent peers.[203] Wealthy families have the luxury of moving neighborhoods and selectively choosing their school districts, whereas more impoverished families remain stuck. School choice, lottery systems, and forced integration are policy steps in the right direction, but inequality along racial lines remains intractable.

However, class seems to correlate more strongly with educational opportunities and adverse life events than race, and class captures a broader range of society. For example, wealthy black students attending a private school have different opportunities than white students living in rural poverty, so holistic review aims, imperfectly, to consider these differences. A black student with two parents who hold advanced degrees will usually have better educational outcomes than a white or Asian student raised by a non-college-educated single parent. The problem is, there are few African American families wealthy enough to afford annual tuition, sometimes exceeding $30,000 for a private primary or secondary education.

Just because it is a challenge to untangle class and race doesn't mean holistic review, even in its deeply flawed current state, shouldn't make attempts to tease them apart. Edge cases that I reviewed when I worked for UT—for example, a white student attending a predominantly black high school or a Hispanic student who attends a Korean church and speaks the language— leave a different impression on the reviewer when they know their ethnicity. Class and race both have essential roles to play in evaluating applicants holistically. Still, conversations about equity and access should focus more on class to capture an increasingly larger segment of society, both urban and rural, that is excluded from accessing a quality education.

Rural white students living in poverty confront similar educational barriers as urban African Americans and Hispanics. In fact, the original 1997 top 10 percent legislation guaranteeing automatic admission at Texas public universities passed because of an odd bedfellow bipartisan coalition of rural Republicans and urban Democrats. Then-Governor George W. Bush signed it into law.

So far, three years after publishing, I've not received a compelling challenge to my defense of race in admissions, or any Twitter mobs. I've made section III, "Dispelling Myths: Race, Privilege, and Affirmative Action," from my book *Your Ticket to the Forty Acres*, available free to download in this endnote.[204] I also continue the discussion of economic inequality in this book's conclusion regarding our Meritocracy Madness.

The most vocal critics of diverse learning environments come from families who don't want their children exposed to new ideas or people from diverse backgrounds. Sixty percent of Trump's Republican party believe that colleges and universities are bad for America.[205] They imagine "liberal universities" will corrupt their children. I witnessed this suspicion firsthand when I attended college fairs on behalf of UT in more rural school districts.

Better to feel secure in their ideological bubble, they reason, than risk their children growing into independently-minded adults who question their parents' beliefs. Liberal universities should want to recruit these applicants rather than push them away. I argue that diversity-themed essay topics and antiracism in college admissions amplifies and hardens our partisan echo chambers.

An open-minded Christian client remarked about not applying to Liberty University, like many of his classmates, following a visit to their campus: "I don't want to attend a milk-toast college where everyone looks and thinks and acts in the same ways." It's an irony of America's evangelical right that the man Jesus Christ questioned authority, dared to ask big questions, and whose unconventional beliefs reshaped human history.

Jesus's gospel stresses that people ought to be treated with compassion, regardless of their background, with careful attention paid to society's most marginalized members. What would Jesus do? I have to imagine He would favor students attending diverse schools so that people can challenge one another and grow in their faith. Jesus would advocate that societies should provide educational opportunities for the least fortunate. My Christian client prefers UT-Austin because he believes it will strengthen his Christianity and encourage him to expand his worldview to accommodate different perspectives outside his narrow denomination.

It's a shame His life has been weaponized and distorted by politics. Deeply flawed men—and it's almost always men—warp His teachings to expand their personal wealth and power. Most followers absorb the dogma without questioning their religious diet. I make this observation as an agnostic free thinker who grew up in a community hostile to anyone who didn't toe the Southern Baptist party line. High school is hell for black sheep. If anything, I have strong biases tempting me to reject Christianity and all things monotheism because of its many hypocrisies. Still, a reasonable person should find reasons to admire Jesus' biography, uncontaminated from the exclusionary and callous politics surrounding mainstream evangelical Christianity.

I'm attempting to thread the eye of a highly controversial needle. If I've presented my arguments well enough, I think they will be persuasive to audiences across the political spectrum, but for different reasons.

Nevertheless, I anticipate that my nuance will miss readers with politics motivated to the far right who think my views will serve their backward-looking agenda. I'm antagonistic to both the far right and the liberal left. Questioning Patriotically Correct evangelical Christian doctrine or what African American NYU Linguistics Professor and critic John McWhorter dubs "the New Religion of Anti-Racism" of progressive liberals is bound to inflame.

I do not doubt that some progressive ideologues will dismiss anything I say for no other reason than my skin color. I can never hope to reach those detractors, nor do I care to communicate with someone for whom race is the singular criterion for whether one is or isn't allowed to participate in a conversation. Only through inclusion and dialogue can we hope to build bridges, heal wounds past and present, and advocate for a more equitable society.

Since I'm far from politically conservative, I anticipate the most significant pushback from the progressive left. They fear my uncomfortable arguments might just be onto something because my perspectives come principally *from a liberal point of view.*

Distressing truths often produce the most stinging triggers. I'm touching this third rail because I believe holistic review and essay requirements, especially those dealing with diversity, are tools that unintentionally oppress marginalized populations. Erecting barriers to applying to college undermines access for the underserved populations that most universities claim to value highest. Elite universities fool themselves into thinking they're doing great work. In reality, they're exacerbating racial and socio-economic inequalities. I am exposing this hypocrisy.

Standing up for society's most marginalized students by speaking truth to power in the previous section, "Dashboard and the Darkside of Big Data," should buffer against accusations that I'm a white supremacist or alt-right ideologue. I'm emphatically against alt-right rhetoric intent on inflaming prejudices. Black Lives Matter. "All" or "Blue" lives matter are disingenuous positions that completely miss the point about persistent structural oppression. Hate speech is neither free nor decent. I stand behind peaceful protestors speaking out against police brutality and our unfair justice system. I don't think riots or the destruction of property is an effective means of activism. Still, I understand on some level why a small number of peaceful protests sometimes turn violent.

For the first time in my life, I voted for a Democrat for president and donated to down-ballot campaigns nationwide. I abstained from voting in 2016 in part because I didn't have a fixed address, nor did I stay anywhere that autumn for longer than a week at a time. Regardless of my difficult-to-categorize personal political identity, my overall point remains the same apolitical message: College admissions is madness. It screws over almost everyone. Its madness includes a proliferation of essays that increasingly ask for applicants to respond to topics concerning diversity. Good intentions around inclusion and equity produce unintended consequences. Universities do not care about their applicants in part because they're blind to their own errors. My purpose is to seek the truth regardless of who it makes uncomfortable.

9.1 Diversity-themed essay topics are problematic

Unlike many themes whose origins date many generations ago, the "diversity" college essay is a recent invention of the past two decades.

University of Michigan Women and Gender Studies Professor Anna Kirkland and Statistics Professor Ben B. Hansen trace the first instance of the diversity college essay at a major university to the University of Michigan following the 2003 landmark decision *Grutter v. Bollinger*. *Grutter*, adjudicated alongside *Gratz v. Bollinger*, struck down assigning points for racial categories and allowed for considerations of race when evaluating applicants.[206]

Their study was the first of its kind. They examined 176 diversity essays submitted in the 2003–2004 admissions cycle where applicants chose their response to one of the following:

1. "At the University of Michigan, we are committed to building an academically superb and widely diverse educational community. What would you as an individual bring to our campus community?"
2. "Describe an experience you have had where cultural diversity—or lack thereof—has made a difference to you."

They cite previous research that diversity-themed essays emerged from a broader diversity movement in corporate settings dating back to a 1987 publication, *Workforce 2000*. The researchers address the ambiguity surrounding how to define diversity and what diversity means subjectively to each college applicant. To an urban Hispanic applicant attending a mostly black high school, diversity means something different from an affluent white applicant attending an elite private boarding school. What each university means when they say diversity, inclusion, cosmopolitanism, and so on remains open to continued interpretation. There is no consensus on what diversity is or entails, either for applicants or their reviewers.

Kirkland and Hansen focus only on what the students wrote and not how reviewers read and scored the essays. They could not gain access to Michigan's admissions office because of "the publicity and ongoing litigation." They stress how difficult it is to conduct admissions research because many universities do not open their records or allow outsiders to observe their processes. Jacques Steinberg notes a similar access problem in *The Gatekeepers*, where he asked many universities for permission to monitor their review process, before Wesleyan University opened its doors.

It took Kirkland and Hansen two years to obtain their 176 essay samples. I raise these preliminary issues to highlight just how difficult it is to lift the hood and inspect the admissions engine. A lack of transparency obscures what universities mean and expect when requiring essays on any topic, let alone those as charged as race and diversity.

On a related theme about whether the Michigan applicants in question received outside help or their applications were written by someone else, the researchers support my claim that most applications are not very good. They go out of their way to write, "Many essays did not read as though anyone had even helped the applicants hone what they were trying to say, let alone reveal evidence of coaching. Pitfalls like vagueness, cliches, recaps of the resume, claims of 'passion' and lack of a clear point were extremely common." It's safe to conclude that Michigan was receiving tons of poor responses around vague notions of diversity, a trend that undoubtedly continues at universities nationwide today. If most college essays aren't very good, diversity essays are especially poorly written.

Kirkland and Hansen also noted their surprise how, after searching Amazon and dozens of universities, "it looks like the diversity question is not particularly common." Nowadays, it's nearly impossible for an applicant applying nationwide to avoid the topic. There are two main kinds of diversity-themed essays: those that explicitly ask about race, gender, religion, etc., and others that reference diversity indirectly. Michigan's 2003–4 prompts indirectly ask about diversity. The implicit assumption in all diversity-themed essays is that diversity benefits classroom discussions and learning environments.

The diversity-themed essay is a natural if problematic extension of diversity as an institutional value. Many universities have followed Michigan's open-ended essay prompts that leave open to interpretation what diversity does or doesn't mean to each applicant. Applicants must read between the lines and decipher each university's expectations.

Unsurprisingly, applicants from homogenous communities wrote what the researchers label "war movie" essays. "The classic World War II movie brings together discrete racial, ethnic, and geographic subgroups from American life in fairly predictable fashion." War movie essays are a variation on sentiments like "we can all get along if we look past the surface." Many applicants wrote essays where they acted the role assigned by society. The white student wrote dutifully about learning from non-white friends. Students of color provided the lessons. White applicants, for example, wrote about playing basketball with people from different backgrounds.

Contrasted with war movies, minority applicants who chose to reveal themselves wrote about "bringing diversity" to campus, but not necessarily in the ways intended from the prompt. Some wrote about discrimination, such as being the only Hispanic family at a Christmas tree lighting ceremony. Other students of color took pains to downplay the significance of race in their school or community.

Kirkland and Hansen note an immediate problem with diversity-themed essays whose requirement has the opposite of their intended effect. "Both 'bringing diversity' and 'war movie' diversity rely heavily on easily recognizable group stereotypes in which a person's contribution to the group is re-enacting those shared scripts about group identities (being black and knowing about hip-hop, being Jewish and supporting Israel)." The researchers noted that each applicant struggled with presenting varied aspects of their race and religion and to what degree, particularly multiracial and multiethnic students.

Thirty-nine essays neglected to address diversity explicitly. Instead, they preferred an "everyone is unique, and I am, too" approach, including a few underrepresented minorities who opted to discuss hobbies, interests, or life experiences unrelated to race.

A few areas that didn't arise in their essay samples from 2003 were discussions of gender, sexual orientation, or disability as diversity, themes that are much more discussed by today's generation.

Diversity essays are a legal gray area because it is unconstitutional to discriminate against or favor individuals based on membership in group categories. For example, in California and Michigan, it's forbidden to consider race as a factor at all. Essays can be a side-door for admissions reviewers and enrollment managers to enroll a "critical mass" of underrepresented minorities to achieve their goal of attaining a diverse learning environment.

In practice, however, diversity-themed essays have the opposite effect of enrolling diverse student populations. The article dismisses conservative critics' concerns that Michigan's diversity essay is a back door to meet affirmative action quotas. Applicants who seem to benefit the most are those familiar with what a diversity-oriented liberal university expects them to write. The authors suggest that the applicants disadvantaged the most from the essay topic are low-income students of color.

"Those who have only the tedious tension of lower-income segregated American life to write about will fall further outside the corporate/educational diversity loop. Then the question becomes how to confront the possibility that the essay itself has reinforced a great deal of crude racial representation...[that] may leave some lower-income minority students feeling like they somehow missed the point...[the diversity essay] creates a hierarchy of stories and experiences that are more accessible to some young people than others."

Their conclusion is counterintuitive because the conventional wisdom suggests that students from minority backgrounds can leverage their status to gain an edge by "playing the race card." Students attending low-resource schools who are below-level academically confront the added burden of writing an essay for a person they will never meet. At least when writing a school paper, they can ask their English teacher what they expect. Anonymous reviewers read college essays with unknowable and shifting expectations.

What happens when low-income students receive essay coaching that helps close the gap between the "hierarchy of stories and experiences" and gain an edge in the admissions arms race? English Professor James Warren examines what happens when 42 seniors receive essay coaching in his 2013 article "The Rhetoric of College Application Essays: Removing Obstacles for Low Income and Minority Students."[207]

He argues that college essays are the most problematic for the diverse students that holistic review purports to help. "The lack of transparency surrounding the college essay complicates the admissions process for all applicants, but what is particularly troubling is that it widens the achievement gap between low-income, ethnic minority students and middle-income White students."

The college applicants studied supplied essays on the topic I used to review when I worked for UT-Austin: Apply Texas Essay A. Essay A asked applicants to discuss an influential person and their impact on them. During a two-week intensive in the students' English classes, Warren and his UT-Arlington English Department undergraduates provided concrete tips and essay feedback and revision. Applicants submitted their essays, and unlike in Kirkland and Hansen's investigations at Michigan, Warren was able to speak personally with the two UT-Austin admissions reviewers who assigned the scores.

Unsurprisingly, one reviewer complained that the applicant talked too much about the person of influence rather than their impact on the student. Others criticized some essays for writing too much about the impact and not enough about the person who influenced them. This disconnect is a variation on the "calibration" problem I discussed in chapter 6, whereby each admissions reviewer has varied interpretations on the essay questions.

There is no consensus on the meaning of essay topics. Students who responded to the topic at face value received lower marks even though "there is nothing in the essay prompt itself that suggests some influences are more valuable than others."

Poorly worded questions produce vague responses and arbitrary admissions scores, depending on the whims of an applicant's assigned reviewer. Carnegie Mellon University (CMU) asked Fall 2021 applicants to respond to an open-ended question. "Many students pursue college for a specific degree, career opportunity or personal goal. Whichever it may be, learning will be critical to achieve your ultimate goal. As you think ahead to the process of learning during your college years, how will you define a successful college experience?"

CMU's vague expectations are the perfect example of Warren's skepticism regarding a lack of essay transparency. Students are left wondering whether CMU wants a general discussion of their proposed college experience or an implicit assumption that they need to frame their college experience specifically. Every blog post online says CMU is *really* looking for the latter—a Why CMU essay in disguise—which privileges savvy students. It's necessary to read between the lines and insert specific CMU resources and courses that interest them.

A similar question from Syracuse University conflates diversity themes with another common topic requesting students write about why they've chosen that university. The topic asks, in 250 words, "Why are you interested in Syracuse University and how do you see yourself contributing to a diverse, inclusive and respectful campus community?" Combining two topics that are almost always separate questions pressures students to discuss Why Syracuse, and separately about diversity, inclusion, and respect in a relatively small allotment of words.

Warren suggests that open-ended prompts may, at first glance, provide more freedom. However, they penalize students from disadvantaged backgrounds because they cannot read between the lines and decode what universities like CMU and Syracuse expect. Compared with the control group, the students who received the intensive training scored considerably better, unsurprisingly.

Warren concludes with a word of caution that the college essay risks becoming yet another element in their educational journey that students need to be taught how to game. Calling for more transparency on how essays are scored, Warren warns that the college essay "may unintentionally favor applicants who are more familiar with academic culture."

Princeton, a leading voice in the university diversity movement, requires an essay response that at first seems open ended. "At Princeton, we value diverse perspectives and the ability to have respectful dialogue about difficult issues. Share a time when you had a conversation with a person or a group of people about a difficult topic. What insight did you gain, and how would you incorporate that knowledge into your thinking in the future?"

Students could conceivably discuss when they've changed a belief, resolved a conflict, or collaborated on any issue or problem. An added complication arises because the 250-word prompt expects a student to a) describe a conflict or dilemma, b) highlight the dialogue, c) identity how their belief changed and why, and d) what it means for them moving forward, presumably as a student on Princeton's campus.

Savvy applicants reading between the lines who understand Princeton's commitment to diversity will understand reviewers expect a very specific answer involving politics or social justice. Presumably, Republicans or Trump supporters won't be doing themselves favors by discussing a time they tried to persuade a stubborn liberal that a Tough on China foreign policy approach is optimal, even if the Republican's perspectives were thoughtful and grounded in sound data.

Prompts like Princeton's are the equivalent to writing an English or History paper for a teacher with strong political leanings. If your teacher shares pro-immigration content on Instagram, it would be academic suicide to submit a defense of Trump's border wall. You're better off writing what you know they want to hear, even if it's an insincere belief.

Princeton's biased prompt adds fuel to conservative talking points that Republicans aren't welcome on elite liberal campuses, which calls into question universities that commit to "a diversity of ideas and perspectives." It's hypocritical and shortsighted to espouse a commitment to diverse perspectives if some ideas are excluded from the conversation. A rise in popularity of conservative political organizations, e.g., Turning Points USA, reflects some students who feel alienated on college campuses.

Any applicant would be foolish not to pander to progressive liberal values. At least in a high school or college course, your instructors often hint at their biases. At the same time, diversity essay prompts reward students who know how to play the admissions game and are "familiar with academic culture."

University of Virginia Professor Jeanita White Robinson's Fall 2008 article in the *Journal of Negro Education* raises similar concerns to Warren.[208] She cites a lack of awareness for "strategies that maximize one's matriculation choices" whose preparation requires "a continuum of strategic choices that span the high school years" beyond the senior year application and essays. She lays out a comprehensive plan of attack to equip underrepresented minorities with the knowledge and skills to anticipate their eventual college enrollment. Robinson's and Warren's conclusions support my hypothesis that the college essay functions as a barrier to maximizing application numbers and reaching a broader society's expanse.

Diversity-themed essays are also problematic for white and Asian students from affluent families who may be reluctant to discuss their identity or feel guilt based on their background. Asian Americans and Asian diaspora students are excluded from institutional commitments to diversity. I routinely have conversations with Asian students who want to discuss their culture. Yet, they are reluctant to share their background, family history, mother tongue (or lack thereof), art forms, favorite foods, religious practices, etc.

The assumption motivating their insecurity is simple. *Is it okay to be Asian?*

I encourage worried Asian applicants that every story is unique. Please don't feel ashamed, and it's okay to be *you*. They fear judgment from anonymous admissions reviewers for being "yet another high-achieving Asian" stereotype. A vibrant variety of people and diverse backgrounds fall under the imperfect and overly broad Asian American classification invented by the US Census Bureau.

There is an added pressure to excel academically to fit the model-minority mold. When 35 percent of Asian SAT takers score over a 700 on the math section, scoring slightly lower but still objectively very good places good-but-not-great Asian applicants at a disadvantage relative to students from other ethnicities. Asian communities suspect that universities impose higher academic expectations relative to different races. Moreover, seeming "too Asian" is perceived as a detriment. Popular blog posts encourage them to seem "less Asian." Many Asians adopt traditionally white interests, such as football or cheerleading, to appear "well rounded."

Because Asians are overrepresented on many college campuses, diversity-themed essays aren't written principally with their backgrounds in mind. They don't "bring diversity" to campus, like Hispanic or black students encouraged to embrace and express their heritage. Many Asian applicants write essays demonstrating how they've "adapted" to and assimilated with the dominant white culture. If culture or heritage plays little if any role in one's life, then no problem. The issue is for the students who practice Indian Classical dancing or celebrate Lunar New Year rather than Christmas who feel reluctant to share their experiences.

Although nothing conclusive came from lawsuits on behalf of Asian families against Harvard, the perception of an Asian disadvantage is real. That affects what students write in their essays and the activities they pursue for their resumes. If universities don't care about most of their applicants, I'm inclined to conclude that they probably care about Asians the least.

It's strange to be a straight, white, and not particularly politically correct cis male who encourages Asians, transgender people, and otherwise marginalized students that they can and should feel empowered to share about their identities. A university potentially judging you for being "too Asian" or some other nonsense may not be a campus worth attending anyway. There are plenty of universities that would love to have you, which goes for students everywhere, regardless of their background or political beliefs.

9.2 Professional ethics revisited

Let's pause for a moment and consider professional ethics. I often reflect on my role in helping students already "familiar with academic culture" continue gaining an edge over marginalized students. Put another way, why do I help mostly rich white and Asian kids instead of students living in poverty?

After serving urban schools as a UT counselor, I knew I was not cut out for working full time in dysfunctional educational environments. The odds are stacked so heavily against the students ever leaving their communities in the most distressed high schools, let alone earning college degrees. I was raised in a community where "getting out" is something that few achieve. Only the most remarkable and lucky students leave my hometown. Going to college is the exception in many communities rather than the default.

Teaching in Malaysia's most impoverished corner in a severely failing public school for $7,000 that year taught me that I'm not a martyr. I sometimes had more than 50 students in my classes. Teacher absenteeism was a massive problem, so at any given moment, half of the classrooms wouldn't have teachers at all. I never felt so unproductive and underused than living in a community where I didn't belong and working at a school that didn't want me there.

Wages for working in the most challenging environments simply aren't worth it to me. More power to the educators, social workers, and development professionals who dedicate their lives to the less fortunate in exchange for subsistence wages and a lifetime of financial insecurity. I wish we had a society that esteemed and compensated adequately our workers who, it turns out during a pandemic, are essential, but it doesn't. I respond to economic incentives like anyone else. If I ever went back to a traditional education setting, I would enjoy teaching writing or English abroad to ambitious graduate students rather than schools that the system has already failed. My ability to help even the most ambitious and promising high school seniors is limited if the education system has them reading at a fifth-grade level.

Many independent counselors take on one or two "charity cases" each year, but I choose not to. I don't offer essay feedback and revision for free. I learned early on that I need to draw a clear line somewhere between answering inquiries for free and providing more substantive assistance. Offering services for free to a handful who will inevitably share their experiences would mean that I need to decline hundreds of other requests arbitrarily. Answering a few questions inevitably creeps into students who come to expect full-blown essay revisions. Placing a monetary value on my time means people are more likely to respect and appreciate my efforts. I would rather spend my time answering hundreds of short emails rather than helping a few students over a long period. I have no staff or employees, so I'm limited by the number of hours in a day.

I respect the efforts of nonprofits such as California-based Scholar Match, founded by best-selling author Dave Eggers. His organization and others like them provide intensive mentorship to at-risk youth, not just those applying to college but throughout their academic career and beyond. Government-funded college pathway efforts such as The Dallas County Promise are steps in the right direction for increasing college access.[209] The Promise pays the tuition at select four-year universities to qualifying graduates from 57 Dallas-area at-risk low-income high schools.

I reevaluate this question each year: Who do I serve and why?

I could volunteer with Scholar Match. But the honest truth is I just don't want to. I prefer to optimize my leisure time and work only as much as I need to sustain my life and well-being. I offer my skills to the highest bidder. No corporation, institution, or profession in the world could compensate me better.

I have many other interests besides education and college admissions that charging high fees enables. Becoming financially independent makes it easier to potentially pivot to something else, for instance, teaching yoga or embodied movement, which I suspect may be my long-term purpose. Teaching yoga without financial pressures is a dream few in the movement and wellness industry will ever achieve. I imagine a scenario in future years where I take on a handful of admissions clients that sustain my lifestyle and other interests. Regardless, financial security born from my Tex Admissions consulting allows me to fund *Admissions Madness* without loans or sponsors. This project costs much more (in the mid-five figures) than I could ever hope to recoup from a lifetime of book royalties.

I justify that my online presence, which reaches tens of thousands of people each year—the vast majority of whom I will never hear from or talk with—outweighs the feel-goods that come from mentoring one or two students that the system has already failed.

One parent that wasn't a client reached out to me when decisions were released. I receive dozens of unsolicited messages like this.

> "Thank you, Kevin. I think your videos are awesome, and I know you have helped so many kids get through a really difficult time over the past week or so. Between your blog, your videos, your contributions on Reddit, I wonder if you really know how far your reach is or how many students and parents you have helped. I doubt it! Please accept my thanks on behalf of probably thousands and thousands of anxious and worried parents."

She's right. I sometimes lose sight of the relative influence that I wield. I've lived an interesting and, at times, crazy life, but I still see myself as just another person sitting behind a laptop trying to do their best each day.

She wrote later in the message: "Your perspective and valida-tion helps so many kids work through the first real disappoint-ment that many of them have ever experienced."

I couldn't be honest if not for my independence and freedom from any institutions or sponsors. I find that people working in purposeless careers fill that void with volunteering or philan-thropy, whereas my business provides me with nearly limitless fulfillment. I have the impression that noted philanthropists are atoning for past or present sins in their professional lives. I have an incredibly fulfilling professional life that connects me with fas-cinating young people, so I don't feel any unmet desires to "give back."

Another open question I've considered is joining the Effec-tive Altruism movement to contribute 10 percent of my post-tax income to the highest-impact charities and NGOs. I've already made over 2,000 microloans to entrepreneurs worldwide on Kiva over the past decade.[210] I would rather exchange my money than my time. My tentative goal is to join the Effective Altruism move-ment by the end of 2022 to redistribute the money I earn from wealthy families to worthy causes that serve the less fortunate.

9.3 Antiracism in college admissions backfires

Is the college essay the ideal or even a suitable tool for increasing access to higher education resources for underrepresented popu-lations and ushering in post-racial harmony? I'm skeptical.

The most obvious potential beneficiary of diversity essays are black males, who are the demographically least likely to attend college or complete their degrees. They are also many universi-ties' highest recruitment priorities. For some institutions, "diver-sity recruitment" is a coded language for enrolling more black students. When I worked for UT, we were explicitly instructed to conduct outreach and recruitment to black-majority schools because they're the least represented ethnicity on campus. However, diversity-themed essay requirements have the opposite effect. They deter black students from applying or submitting their best efforts.

A Spring 2002 article in the *Journal of Blacks in Higher Education* notes with alarm the rising emphasis on the college essay for admission to selective universities. Journal editors cite three barriers for college-bound African Americans. They're more likely to come from families without a college degree, attend poor-quality schools, and have less access to assistance outside of their family, especially compared with their affluent peers living in college-going communities.[211]

They cite research by education consultant Sarah McGinty that 40 percent of black students didn't apply to universities because they had essay requirements. The editors suggest, "The requirement of writing an essay may discourage some black students from applying to good colleges." Anticipating the deluge of diversity-themed essays, the editors caution that underrepresented minorities must tread very carefully when discussing race.

In the almost 20 years since that publication, essay requirements have proliferated, as I discussed in chapter 1.2. Universities should make a concerted effort to examine the unintended consequences of essay requirements in general and diversity essays specifically. Antiracism and diversity training on college campuses have good intentions that produce counterproductive effects when universities require applicants to discuss diversity.

Consider Kentucky's 500-word honors and scholarship essay prompt: "Who are three people that you feel have made a significant impact on the world in the last 100 years? Who are they, and why did you select them? How would you want them to be recognized or *memorialized?* (emphasis mine)" They could have framed this question in other ways. Common essay variations include who would be your three ideal dinner party guests or discuss a person living or dead who has helped shape your beliefs.

Recall the findings of Warren (2013) and Kirkland & Hansen (2011). They argued that there is a disconnect between the language of the essay questions and what admissions reviewers expect. For essays like Kentucky's scholarship prompt and Michigan's former topics that don't explicitly mention race, Kirkland and Hansen report, "[The students] all acknowledged thinking and being told that the essay was meant to ferret out racial diversity in order for the university to practice affirmative action."[212]

The applicant is left wondering, what exactly does Kentucky want?

It isn't coincidental that this topic arises alongside the nationwide discussion and protests regarding Confederate statues. Many students may be forgiven for not realizing the question's timely context. In short, essay questions are not created in a vacuum. They respond to current events. Understanding the background context of essay questions is essential for writing strategically, which privileges the savviest students.

I assume sympathizing with and memorializing Confederate leaders and their ideological descendants is a losing admissions strategy. I also assume at least some Kentucky applicants, living in a heavily conservative state, support Confederate statues even if they're unwilling or afraid to admit it. The University of Kentucky is located in left-leaning Lexington, so it's safe to assume they're against Confederate statues. Taking the extreme case, I'm certain that not a single student responded in favor of memorializing former KKK Grandwizard David Duke even though a non-zero number of applicants and eventual enrollees come from white supremacist families.

I'm also confident few in-state applicants suggested a statue for the man David Duke endorsed in 2016 and 2020, former President Donald Trump, despite two-thirds of Kentucky punching their ticket for him. Applicants may be better off avoiding a statue of Senate Minority Leader from Kentucky Mitch McConnell. Nevertheless, when in doubt who to propose for a statue, KFC's Colonel Sanders holding a Double Down is undoubtedly a politically safe if questionable gastrointestinal bet.

Historically conservative, semirural, and mostly white, Texas A&M has taken the opposite approach of Kentucky by explicitly referencing diversity in their new essay topic. Every applicant must submit an answer to the following: "Texas A&M University believes that diversity is an important part of academic excellence and that it is essential to living our core values (loyalty, integrity, excellence, leadership, respect, and selfless service). Describe the benefits of diversity and inclusion for you personally and for the Texas A&M campus community."

Students are also directed to a hyperlink that pronounces A&M's accountability, equity, and campus climate reports. The expectation is that every applicant dutifully writes about the importance of multiculturalism and inclusion.

I received an unsolicited email from a concerned parent against A&M's requirement. "Student-applicants are compelled to agree with the University's official position on diversity and inclusion at the risk of being denied admission to the university... They should not be compelled to violate their conscience as the cost of admission." Although I'm in favor of providing more access and resources to first-generation students, rural families, and historically marginalized populations, I'm sympathetic to the diversity-essay skeptic because the college essay isn't an effective vehicle to promote genuine inclusion. It has the opposite effect of deterring applicants on ideological grounds or for the college literacy disparities I've already discussed.

The secondary problem is that public-facing admissions counselors don't decide or offer input for essay topics. Requirements are decided by senior leadership who have little if any contact with anyone beyond their senior staff inner chambers. I posed questions about A&M's diversity topic on an admissions professionals Facebook page. The consensus is you won't get an answer on a Facebook group populated primarily by junior staff.

It's impossible to find out why essays proliferate. The admissions high priests refuse to disclose their anointment of some topics rather than others. Why does Pomona ask about potatoes rather than some other topic that isn't completely ridiculous? Who knows.

To reiterate my thesis, more onerous essay requirements means fewer applicants. A sincere commitment to diversity and inclusion would provide for fewer requirements, not more.

Some applicants to universities that require diversity or identity prompts may not share progressive value systems, particularly to more politically conservative universities or religious institutions. If liberal universities want to spread their antiracism gospels, shouldn't they want to attract *more* conservative students onto their campuses rather than *fewer*? How do they expect to reach out to the 60 percent of Republican families—that's tens of millions of Americans—who already distrust not just a university education but also the roles universities occupy in society?

I expect at least some prospective applicants to Kentucky or Texas A&M forewent their application for politically motivated reasons rather than pander to a biased essay topic. Regardless, applicants unsympathetic to progressive identity politics will likely be persuaded to pander to what they know readers wants to hear—the **courtesy bias**.

Students must pander and write polite essays to pass an ideological purity test that often shields their true beliefs. Then Deans of Student Services wear their best Shocked Pikachu faces when a group of students party wearing blackface or host affirmative action bake sales next to the multicultural student center. I would love to read the essays of the ten students rescinded from Harvard's Class of 2020 for sharing racist and sexist memes to see if any discussed the importance of tolerance and multiculturalism.[213]

A staff member at a STEM-focused West Coast university lectured my Brazilian mixed European-Indigenous-African *pardo* client, who presents as light-skinned, about how their participation in Capoeira martial arts is cultural appropriation, among other perceived offenses against the woke dogma. I already highlighted in chapter 5.1 how conceptions of race and culture operate by entirely different norms in Brazil. Let's also set aside considerations of why an exclusively STEM school values political correctness so highly.

My client has myriad sincere diverse experiences based on class, language, culture, and background, yet it would never occur to him to call it as such. Despite coming from an affluent family, he spends a lot of time with friends living in a nearby favela because it has the best surf spots. He makes friends with favela kids and spends time in their neighborhoods because they also surf. His behavior isn't motivated by a commitment to antiracism, nor does he even have any awareness of what this very American-specific ideology entails. He doesn't seek out relationships with diverse populations so that his Instagram feed receives approval. He's not seeking diverse experiences for material that could be used for an eventual college essay. He just wants to hang out with other surfers who just so happen to be darker-skinned and poor.

Following a phone call with the West Coast STEM admissions representative, he wondered, "I don't know what to answer in these Common App questionnaires. Why do they ask these questions? In Brasil, nobody asks these questions. We are just a mixed fruit salad of various phenotypes, and who cares? This is all very foreign to me… Is it okay to be Roman Catholic?"

You can question or push back on his assumption that nobody asks questions about race in Brazil. It is a lively topic of conversation, especially since their society is, in some ways, more racially and socioeconomically segregated than ours. Not everything needs to be about politics and social justice; he just wants to surf. But the point remains that conceptions of race and culture are dramatically different there than in the United States.

After dismissing the West Coast university official as a well-meaning if confused fool, I reminded my client that we're playing a game. If you want to win, I advised, you need to pander. I responded, "This is the first time I've ever encountered a process like this where someone gets feedback from university staff. So if they suggest concrete changes, we should follow them…. These questions are also 'moving targets,' meaning what might be okay to say or do in one time or environment may not be cool in another time or space… At the end of the day, it's pretty difficult to tell exactly what they're looking for."

Part of my lengthy response included encouragements not to worry so much. I challenged him instead to think hard about which American state or university he eventually chooses to move to. He considered excluding schools in Washington or California. I responded, "That's something you will navigate when you arrive and live there. You're obviously very difficult to categorize and put into neat boxes. Americans love to box people when it comes to identity under the flag of diversity." He sold out, pandered, and wrote what they expected. Then he got denied admission anyway.

Checking the privilege of a non-American student who had never heard of identity politics before applying to West Coast schools backfired. He wrote, "At least in Texas, I don't need to expect to be so diverse and exotic like a Brazilian macaw. ☺ I can be white, European, and Christian." Rather than playing the role expected of him as an international student who universities can tote in their diversity marketing materials, my client greets me with howdy and jokes California doesn't like him. He's excited to apply for Texas A&M and hopefully live in Texas, although he subsequently second-guessed that consideration when he saw the A&M diversity topic. "There's the stupid diversity question... Every time I complete a question about race or background, I feel like I am a sperm donor."

Students like him don't need to hyperbolize their diversity credentials because they live genuinely inclusive, multidimensional lives. I credit UT-Austin for taking an expansive view of diversity in their required short answer prompt about how the student will "enrich the learning environment" rather than narrowing the topic to culture or ethnicity. Their prompt reads: "Please share how you believe your experiences, perspectives, and/or talents have shaped your ability to contribute to and enrich the learning environment at UT Austin, both in and out of the classroom."

I'm sympathetic to broad questions that invite students to discuss their perspectives, interests, and talents beyond or perhaps because of their race, class, or gender. That way, students aren't pigeonholed into discussing identity or race if it's less relevant to their background. Broadly worded questions allow minority students to avoid the tokenism of "bringing racial diversity" to campus, like with Michigan's initial clumsy diversity prompts.

Language around multiculturalism depends on the context. Americans apply their conceptions of race and diversity as if their constructs have universal meaning and application. The thrust behind postmodern conceptions of reality is that meaning is subject-dependent. We filter and make sense of experience, the postmodernists claim, through our varied identities and experiences in the world. Each person, they argue, is entitled to their truths.

It's ironic when American progressives apply—to use their language—an *ethnocentric* conception of diversity onto people from different cultures and nations. Diversity means what progressive, mostly privileged liberal Americans who tend to be white say it means. The antiracism gospel isn't open to interpretation or pushback, especially if you're white, straight, and male. Or, in my client's case, who is decidedly mixed-race except their phenotype happens to present as light skinned.

These confused positions fail to recognize that diversity means something different (or perhaps nothing at all) in Malaysia, Morocco, Russia, South Africa, Indonesia, etc. White South Africans who emigrated to America checking the African American box is the classic example of the imprecision around context-dependent interpretations of diversity.

An admissions counselor would respond: *But that's not what we really mean when we say African American!*

I'm sympathetic to this response given the history of apartheid and extreme societal divisions that I've witnessed firsthand, spending half a year in Southern African countries. Though technically born on the African continent, white South Africans should, in good faith, check white. White is a legal classification in South Africa, so they're also distinct from black people within that context.

We're left wondering about the three million or so Asians native to Africa who have experienced discrimination in their homelands. Would they qualify as African American if they emigrated to the US?[214] American ethnic categories start to fall apart when considered from a global perspective. Still, the rebuttal misses the point that there are implicit, American-specific assumptions that provide context to categories such as African American.

In an unintended way, impositions of diversity-themed essays on international applicants, especially from non-Western countries, are nonsensical at best and stifling at worst. American universities have an implicit bias in diversity-themed prompts because the progressive conception of diversity is a *very* American and quintessentially Western way to view the world. I know this in part because I've spent a quarter of my life outside of the United States.

Observing lofty American values about inclusion and diversity seems like madness when viewed through the lens of non-Americans like my Brazilian client. Donald Trump in 2020 received the most votes from people of color for a Republican presidential candidate since Ronald Reagan. His surprise showing among black and Hispanic demographics surprised Democrats. They incorrectly took minority voters for granted. A poor turnout for Democratic candidates might suggest the very populations that institutionalized diversity reports to benefit—an agenda that is driven largely by privileged, highly educated white people—may not see things the same way. Minorities who vote Republican are branded as "race traitors" for having a diversity of political perspectives.

Another unintended consequence of diversity-themed essays is that students who come from varied backgrounds are incentivized to exaggerate their identity or environment. Society uses the language of "playing the card" when an individual tries to gain a real or perceived advantage based on their gender, sexuality, religion, skin color, and so on. The most compelling dissenting argument against considerations of race in admissions in *Fisher v. UT* comes from Justice Clarence Thomas. He criticizes how race in college admissions incentivizes some students to "play the race card," to their detriment. I disagree with most of his decision, but he rightly asserts that their peers may perceive minority students as getting in due to their race rather than qualifications, which has the potential for alienation and resentment.

One of the more illuminating exchanges I've ever had on diversity comes from conversations with a middle-class student of Native American descent. They wrestled first with affirmative action generally and later as a transfer applicant how and whether to discuss their identity. "Being Native American, nonbinary, transgender and intersex sounds like a straight flush for the whole application deal, but to be honest with you, I am a little scared about bringing this side of me into an essay." They elaborated in a subsequent email that "650 words is really not enough to go into the depths and complexities of being Native American and how that is connected to being Two-Spirit." They struggled with weighing their middle-class upbringing in a large city to someone born and raised in poverty on a reservation. Socioeconomic status within racial categories complicates antiracism perspectives.

Despite UT being a vanguard member of the institution-alized diversity movement, the student held understandable worries about their admissions reviewer exhibiting transphobia. Their concern stemmed from potentially being judged by an anonymous admissions reviewer. They also worried about hyper-bolizing their background when "despite my identity, I never run into conflicts in real life.... I don't want to 'steal the valor' of queer people-of-color who have had it much worse."

Still, pressure remains to bolster one's intersectionality bonafides. Antiracism in college admissions produces an inter-sectionality race to the bottom. Institutionalized diversity is intended to recruit students like them, yet it produces unintended consequences that may deter them from disclosing their lived experiences.

We untangled a lot of their reluctance to write about their background and reconciled their misplaced guilt for not perceiv-ing themselves as sufficiently oppressed. Thankfully, they visited with a licensed therapist and felt more at peace with themselves, including a recent name change that fits their preferred gender. Regardless, much of their awareness came *only after* pursuing therapy and submitting their college applications. Deeply rooted trauma may not manifest or be accessible until much later in someone's life, which complicates the advice to "simply write about it" for applicants who experience adverse childhood experiences or continue to struggle with their identities.

The student in question wanted to avoid **misleading vividness** where applicants select the most extreme instance of discrimination or hardship even if it's a one-off occurrence to convince their reader that it's important. They **appeal to the emotions** of the admissions reviewer, which causes a backlash among students of not wanting to be "another sob story."

There is conflicting advice about whether and how a student should write a "sob story" at all. Questions that ask applicants to share about overcoming an obstacle or about what role identity plays in their lives invites submissions concerning trauma. Some admissions professionals encourage and invite students to discuss their hardships. However, the Native American student mentioned earlier was advised by their high school counselor, who polled many university representatives, to write nothing heavier than "I felt sad."

A current admissions officer posted on Reddit, discouraging students from discussing sexual assault or abuse because it may be triggering for the reader. My response: Don't ask questions about identity or "special circumstances" if the answers discomfort you. It isn't an applicant's obligation to lead with a "trigger warning" when answering a question that your university requires. Just as a nurse needs to be comfortable with blood, consider leaving the profession if you can't handle troubling realities.

Another user, a former Stanford admissions counselor and Reddit user "Empowerly-Admissions," posted a popular thread titled "STOP pushing 'sob stories.'" After calling sob stories non-sense, they write, "Nobody cares about how hard you had it if you didn't develop some valuable skills because of your experiences."[215] The message here is that losing a parent or experiencing a sexual assault is irrelevant unless there a direct college admissions implication. Advice like this deters affected students from speaking up at all. As I mentioned in the introduction, no aspect of your identity or interests is free from the pressures of the admissions gods. Everything must become a resume bullet point.

One of the worst essay topics of all time—coincidentally the one I submitted with my UT-Austin application in 2007—was Apply Texas Essay B. It read:

> "Many students expand their view of the world during their time in college. Such growth often results from encounters between students who have lived different cultural, economic, or academic experiences. With your future growth in mind, describe a potential classmate that you believe you could learn from, either within or outside a formal classroom environment."[216]

This American Life episode 625, "Essay B," mocked UT-Austin's and Apply Texas's discontinued topic. Host Ira Glass responds with initial disbelief to his guest Mariya (Mari) Karimjee—a Muslim immigrant from Pakistan attending a mostly white Christian school—when she shares the Essay B topic question. Mari clarifies that, yes, Texas universities expected students to conjure a hypothetical person.

Because she was also the editor of the school newspaper, many classmates approached her for help. Mari shared, "So I was sitting in this class, and I was reading all of these essays about a hypothetical future person that helps them grow. And they didn't actually write about a hypothetical future person. *They all wrote about me* (emphasis mine)." I remember writing when I applied in 2007 about our school's Russian exchange student as if he were a mythical creature rather than an actual friend who we hung out with most weekends."[217]

When her best friend and future bridesmaid Jenna shares her essay, it begins: "As-salamu alaykum. Hello. It's a customary Islamic greeting and so much fun to pronounce. Almost every evening when my cell phone rings, I'll see Mari's name on the caller ID, flip open the phone, and hastily cry, as-salamu alaykum."

Obviously, Jenna never greets Mari by Islamic custom. Mari never wearing a traditional sari doesn't stop Jenna from writing, "My eye caught the gorgeous, intricate beading of a handmade sari. At the time, I hadn't the faintest idea what a sari was. I was merely awestruck by someone who would willingly wear such a bold outfit."

The stereotypes and follies continue before Mari shares with Ira how she started asking for milk at dinner and mimicking Hilary Duff's accent to appear whiter and more American. Her anecdote ties into concerns many Asians feel that the dominant culture expects them to assimilate rather than embrace their diverse backgrounds. She continues, "It was not fun. And it was not pleasant. And I was in this classroom setting, and my friends were willingly giving me their essays to read, and everyone around me was acting as though it was this giant compliment... like how great that I was immortalized in all of these college applications."

Ira asks her to recall a cringe-worthy moment while studying for a genetics test. In their textbook, Jenna pointed out a section to Mari that human DNA differs only 0.2 percent and that we all share 99.8 percent of our genes in common. The following captures the problem with parents who raise their kids "not to see race" or be color-blind. Jenna writes:

> "I read the stats aloud to Mari, then I excitedly spilled the thoughts running through my head. 'That makes so much sense. So much sense. You know, I've heard we all smile in the same language, but it goes so far beyond that, and I never realized it was possible until I met you, Mari. I had no idea I could connect with someone so completely opposite of me on such a deep level. We can read each other's looks. And no wonder. There's only a 0.2 percent difference between us."

Mari responds:

> "And this like killed me, reading this. It kills me now because it's like, I didn't need science to tell us that we were the same, and she did. And she was supposed to be my best friend. And it wasn't until she read a quote in a social psych chapter that she realized that the genetic differences between us was so slim that it made sense that we could be friends."

The episode is worth listening to in its entirety because misguided prompts like the retired Essay B still arise. Antiracism in college admissions seems more like a discharge of white guilt than an appropriate mechanism to increase college access.

Questionable diversity-themed topics may not even be explicitly or implicitly about race and culture. USC requires applicants to Engineering and Computer Science to address: "Engineering and Computer Science students are sometimes assumed to have personalities with shared traits or characteristics. What is a trait or characteristic you believe you share with other engineering and computer science students and another where you differ? Please tell us about these two traits and why you chose them" (250 words).

Here, applicants need to posit stereotypes and well-worn nerd tropes and then compare and contrast themselves. Exactly none of my clients know how to respond or can decipher what USC is *really* asking. I don't have any meaningful advice to give other than to remind them the problem is USC admissions, not you. Consider looking at other universities instead.

Diversity-themed essay topics seem intended for white students like Jenna, who need to demonstrate their woke credentials. Students like Mari are the ones who "bring diversity" to their primarily white high schools. In addition to students "playing the race card," **misleading vividness** also occurs when white students hyperbolize their mission trips and one-week summer leadership camps. White students go out of their way to pursue extracurricular activities to bolster their diversity credentials.

A related scourge is students chasing 501c3 nonprofit status—no doubt with assistance from lawyer family friends—to inflate their community engagement and volunteering. Tutoring twice a week at a neighborhood community center suddenly becomes a registered nonprofit with a name like "Empowered Students Empowering Students."

Applicants adopt a **white savior complex** to purport how painting half of a schoolhouse in Guatemala opened their eyes to all sorts of amazing and worldly things that are then presented as selfless magnanimity in the name of "helping the less fortunate." In reality, many students knowingly undertake community service with the explicit purpose of bolstering their resume and wokeness credentials.

I'm not discounting the transformative potential of experiences abroad. I advocate for gap years abroad in my conclusion.

Conducting human rights work with youth genocide survivors in Bosnia and Rwanda for a month each during my undergraduate studies inspired my current life of permanent travel abroad. They remain the most meaningful experiences of my life.

The critical difference is I pursued those specific opportunities because I couldn't imagine studying anything other than genocide and its related issues. I wanted to explore the countries that intrigued me, however morbid. I loathed my high-achieving UT classmates who pursued research not because it fascinated them but because it was expedient to their graduate school prospects.

The issue becomes pursuing volunteering or serving abroad *primarily because it may help in admissions*. Admissions reviewers complain that they're tired of reading about mission trips. They're unaware or unwilling to acknowledge the incentives to inflate credentials or pad their resumes. Hence, the responsibility is on them to reform their requirements and communicate their expectations more transparently.

Linking diversity to the college essay comes at the expense of students with sincere volunteer commitments or unique backgrounds. I find some of the most interesting students are the least forthcoming with their experiences. College admissions rewards the bullshitters who mislead and hyperbolize. Applicants may be hesitant to discuss an intensive mission trip gap year or an actual NGO where they've contributed thousands of hours, fearing that they might be mistaken as immodest or phony.

Teenagers living with severe attention-deficit hyperactive disorder (ADHD) or crippling obsessive-compulsive (OCD) disorder may be tentative to share their condition at the risk of their reviewers having an implicit bias about "yet another student receiving a suspect diagnosis to gain an admissions edge." One client of mine living with severe OCD wrote at length in their UT-Austin "tell us your story" essay that their tics and involuntary movements are neither choices nor a preference for having the cereal boxes shelved in a particular way.

An admissions reviewer might answer: *We can tell the phonies from who's authentic!*

Really? When you skim your 28th file of the day and have 17 to go? I call bullshit. You're no better at detecting integrity than a Catholic bishop identifying pedophiles.

I can picture the lively debates and utter lack of consensus around committee tables deciding which borderline students make the cut. Admissions reviewers and experts more generally aren't any better at judging character or assessing probabilities than anyone else. We're all subject to **illusory superiority**, as discussed in chapter 6.

Redditors justifiably love to call out universities claiming to value authenticity when the perverse incentive structure obscures which applicants are genuine from those who inflate their credentials. Assessing candidates for grit, resiliency, zest, curiosity, selflessness, and so on becomes significantly more challenging when students are all playing the same game. Navigating unspoken sets of rules and expectations privileges applicants who understand these incentives.

Students who live in rural, low-income, or otherwise non-college communities—the same groups of students that universities claim to prioritize highest—fall further behind. Diversity essays also generate resentment from tens of millions of Americans who are less sympathetic to progressive values. The only people who seem to be winning in this system are the self-congratulatory egos of university bureaucrats. They feel desperate to assuage their complicity in the exploitation of hundreds of thousands of teenagers each year. Teenagers shouldn't have an obligation to answer for the racist sins of their country, especially in the form of a college essay.

Most books won't lay out how to argue against them. I welcome reasonable pushback that seeks common ground, especially for such an emotionally heated and historically fraught topic. Allow me to present the formal structure of my argument:

1. College essays increase barriers to accessing four-year universities for most students most of the time.
2. Diversity-themed essays are a subset of the broader category "college essay."

Therefore, diversity-themed essays increase barriers to accessing four-year universities for most students most of the time.

Proponents of diversity-themed essays occupy an uncomfortable position. It's a contradiction to accept my first premise that "college essays increase barriers" while also believing that diversity-themed essays are a net positive. Suppose you reject the first premise, entailing that you believe college essays are not inherently problematic and actually increase access. In that case, you have to contend with the body of research that suggests the students least likely to attend college are also the least suited for or willing to write college essays.

Questioning my core assertion throughout this book about the many ways essays are problematic is a conversation worth having. Even if you have evidence to suggest that college essays are generally a net positive, it may still be the case that diversity-themed essays are problematic in ways different from more neutral "discuss your major" or "why X university?" prompts.

To counter my argument, you must prove that *both* college essays generally *and* diversity-themed essays specifically are net positives that increase access for most students most of the time. You can argue that my conclusion suggesting that diversity-themed essays increase barriers to accessing four-year universities is problematic because I'm missing a key assumption. The conclusion doesn't follow even if both premises are true. Otherwise, my argument is "valid" in a formal logic sense.

If you accept that fewer essays and diversity topics are net positives, the other option available to you is to propose limiting requirements to a single required essay focusing on diversity. But that defeats the entire purpose of a college essay for students to discuss their previous experiences with reference to their academic and professional ambitions. I contend that the costs of requiring diversity-themed prompts and most essay requirements, in general, outweigh the benefits to nearly every applicant demographic.

9.4 Poverty matters more than race

Before rushing to Twitter to virtue signal the woke police and issue citations for racism or one-star brigade my Amazon reviews, let me remind the reader again that I support considerations of race in admission in *Your Ticket to the Forty Acres*. I'm highly critical of elite universities that pay lip service to inclusion yet fail to service the marginalized, low-income populations they claim to value. Progressive liberals, we're on the same team for the most part, even if I question the new religion of antiracism in institutional settings.

College admissions is largely a reflection of wealth and privilege where race and ethnicity play a secondary role. In the extreme case, Malia and Sasha Obama, graduates of the elite Sidwell Friends School, command the highest possible college admissions privileges imaginable despite being African American. Even if Barack Obama had never become a US Senator or the President, he and Michelle have advanced degrees from Ivy League universities with high salary employment. Malia benefitted in Harvard admissions because both of her parents are legacies.

Daniel Markovits cites research that "the academic gap between rich and poor students now exceeds the gap between white and black students in 1954" when the Supreme Court ruled against segregated schools in *Brown v. Board*.[218] Black students from wealthy, college-educated families attending great high schools will, all things equal, have privileges exceeding students of any race growing up in urban or rural poverty and first-generation households.

To take the argument to its logical conclusion, I don't think it is controversial to assert that a white student with deceased parents raised as a ward of the state in a rural community has fewer privileges than Malia and Sasha Obama. In both the case of a white orphan living in poverty and the attendant privileges of being the daughters of a two-term American president, race is a secondary concern to class. If someone wants to argue that the Obama children's skin color matters more than the totality of adverse life experiences of a white orphan, and that the white child has more privilege than the Obamas, I can't find common ground with that perspective.

The demographic that benefits most from race in admissions are high-achieving black students, especially males, who are the most sought-after demographic by elite universities. Only 1 percent of black students, regardless of gender, score a 700 or higher on the SAT Math compared with 9 percent of white and 35 percent of Asian test-takers.[219] Three in five white students and 80 percent of Asians meet "college readiness" mathematics benchmarks, whereas one in five black students do. Academically excellent black students are rare compared with the general population. They check two enrollment management boxes of "diversity" and "likelihood to graduate on time."

African Americans, regardless of wealth, will inevitably confront systematic racism in the workplace or other contexts.

Donald Trump's rise to power initially depended on the racist birther assertion that our first black president was born in Kenya. If President Obama isn't immune from racism, then no black person is. However, it's unlikely that students from elite families attending Ivy League feeder schools such as Sidwell Friends won't receive college degrees. Unless something goes catastrophically wrong, Sidwell Friends alumni have lucrative options following graduation, irrespective of race or ethnicity. Growing up in poverty, a rural white student, all things being equal, has fewer opportunities than Sidwell Friends alumni.

A key argument in this book is that decreasing essay burdens will increase application numbers, especially from underserved communities. Questions about how universities measure race in their holistic review processes are mostly separate from essay topics concerning diversity. The hypocrisy of universities offloading their and previous generations' white guilt onto teenagers in the form of diversity-themed college essays is difficult to ignore. Social justice–minded liberals wonder why conservatives make fun of them or why they're suspicious of universities more generally. These types of disconnects are one reason among many.

Liberal hypocrisy amplifies resentment in our highly polarized society. Many readers of the *Atlantic* or the *New York Times*, myself included, responded in disbelief at how Donald Trump could earn *10 million more votes* than the previous election. The pre-election polls were, once again, systematically off. I was raised in a staunchly conservative Republican family. Consequently, Trump's support and the Democrats losing seats in the House didn't come as much of a surprise to me despite my mostly liberal media diet.

In a tiny way, diversity-themed essay requirements contribute to our utter inability to find common ground with one another. Questioning the dogma of antiracism is bound to get you "canceled." The essays are a symptom of society's deep divisions and an imposition of coastal elite values onto tens of millions of a "basket of deplorables" living in "flyover country."

Markovits writes, "Populism is not a spontaneous eruption of malevolent resentment but rather a natural and even apt reaction to extreme meritocratic inequality."[220] Conservatives tend to reject the idols of antiracism in favor of false prophets such as Donald Trump. Better to "own the libs" and be worse off four years later than to capitulate. Institutionalized diversity in college admissions is a cause of our growing inequality rather than a remedy.

I support efforts to account for a student's background, parents' education level, and high school quality in addition to their class and race. Identifying adverse childhood experiences or indicators of structural poverty tells the reviewer more than a student's race. These holistic review considerations don't require diversity-themed essay responses.

One benefit of holistic review is that it attempts to untangle complicated biographies that don't fit into easy categories or defy generalizations, like a recent Asian immigrant from a single-parent, non-English speaking family living in rural poverty, or a high-income suburban Hispanic male attending an elite private high school. Conversations about relative privilege are worthwhile, but they need to extend much further beyond race, gender, and sexual orientation. My primary criticism about holistic review is it's inconsistent and arbitrary. There is no objective way to tease apart how much structural poverty or adverse childhood experiences a student might live with.

Even if universities implemented "grit questionnaires" or created models to quantify a student's adversity, affluent families would inevitably find ways to game the system to maintain their advantages. I'm also unsure who is benefitting from this system and whether diversity-themed essays are essential for universities to meet their diversity enrollment targets—ideals for equity and access, which, to reiterate, I'm in favor. It's the methods to attain equity that I call into question and one reason I'm in favor of UT's race-neutral top 6 percent policy.

I presume that universities gradually implemented diversity-themed topics to reflect institutionalized diversity-as-a-value born out of 1990s political correctness and the contemporary antiracism movement. College essays aren't the answer to promote inclusion or diversity on college campuses. The backlash within society in general likely outweighs the questionable claims that diversity-themed essays increase access.

Until the bottom 99 percent, whether liberal or conservative, can acknowledge their collective struggles and how the system is rigged against them, including college admissions, polarization between tribes and in-fighting will continue. Elites will become wealthier and more powerful as the middle and lower classes, regardless of race or ethnicity, are left further and further behind.

10. Meritocracy Madness

My thesis throughout this book is that a complex ecosystem of bad incentives unintentionally produces our collective college admissions madness. No single university or organization is the culprit, but each institution contributes to our broken system. I've argued that students, parents, high schools, tutors, and coaches respond to the admissions standards set by elite universities. They're symptoms of the madness rather than the causes. Aggressive recruitment and questionable enrollment practices accompanied by a bullshit holistic review system serve the needs of elite universities at the expense of student well-being. When in conflict, institutions mainly prioritize revenue-seeking over a genuine commitment to diversity and inclusion.

The admissions madness isn't a new phenomenon, nor is anyone alive today who constructed its original architecture. Little has changed since the 1970s. What differs today is the substantial number of families applying for roughly the same scarce enrollment spaces. Social media amplify anxieties. Harvard, for example, projects to admit only 3.5 percent of their 57,000 applicants for the Class of 2025, down from 20 percent in the early 1980s. That's a decrease from 9 percent in 2010 when they received around 23,000 applications.

Elite colleges don't exist in a vacuum. Instead, they're a direct reflection of our supposedly meritocratic society and value system. A common saying goes that a country's leaders and political system reflect its culture and values. Holistic review emerged from the 1960s civil rights movement to create a more equitable society. Women, Jews, African Americans, and Latinxs were admitted for the first time on many campuses and in record numbers. The multibillion-dollar college consulting industry didn't exist 50 years ago because there were enough spaces to go around. Education is the cornerstone for earning more than one's parents and moving up in society or away from one's hometown. More people from more diverse backgrounds than ever hold college degrees.

Progress in the '70s and '80s has paved the way for our contemporary road to an admissions hell. Because the number of enrollment spaces hasn't kept pace with the growing population of college entry seekers, scarcity has transformed holistic review into a tool of oppression, not inclusion.

Early promises of a more diverse and socially mobile society gave way to capitalism's tendency to accumulate resources and maximize advantages for a select few without considering the societal consequences. Universities placing profits over students is reflective of broader societal trends. Capitalism doesn't care about your feelings, and neither do universities. Holistic review and admission by merit depend on the myth of the American Dream, presupposing that anyone can succeed with enough elbow grease and hard work.

Whichever college you earned your degree from—or if you earned a college degree at all—mattered less two generations ago. Nowadays, where you go makes a substantive difference to your future opportunities and potential lifetime earnings. Yale Law School professor David Markovits provides a scathing critique of our contemporary wealthy-take-most society in his groundbreaking work *The Meritocracy Trap*. He observes that America's top 50 or so elite colleges provide qualitatively better educations and future opportunities than the thousands of other options. He writes, "When elites buy extravagant education, they directly diminish the education that everyone else has." Paying college coaches like me, securing private testing or music tutors, and paying test prep agencies for elite high school admissions exams necessarily excludes everyone else's chances of college admissions success. I acknowledge my role in this unequal landscape.

Wealthy families invest generously in their school's PTAs, community resources, and alma maters. Multibillion-dollar university endowments attract world-class faculty offering unparalleled resources, widening the gap between the rich and poor after arriving on campus. Most selective colleges spend more than seven times per student compared to less-selective ones.[221] STEM programs, which have exploded in popularity over the past decade, require intensive resource investments and attracting top professor talent.

America's ten wealthiest private universities' combined endowment is $197 billion, similar to New Zealand or Greece's GDPs.[222] Studying at Stanford with a $27.7 billion endowment is a fundamentally different experience than Cal State Polytechnic with a $100 million endowment—a 270 times difference. Consider that the Cal State system graduates more than eight times as many students compared with the entire Ivy League, at a fraction of the cost.[223] If any university could credibly claim to promote college access and reduce inequality, it is the less-prestigious public university systems in states such as California, New York, and Texas that enroll and graduate more students from the lower socioeconomic classes.

Elite graduate schools and corporations recruit students exclusively from the highest tiers of American universities.

Gaining admission to a top-50 school may produce earning differences averaging millions of dollars over a lifetime. Getting into a top-five school offers even starker advantages. Markovits observes that top financial firms often hire exclusively from Harvard, Princeton, Stanford, Yale, and perhaps MIT and Williams.

As elite jobs become increasingly scarce due to automation and multiple roles falling under single titles, the admissions madness intensifies. He cites research that suggests "fewer than one in one hundred jobs pays even close to elite wages."[224] Affluent families are acutely aware of these stakes and will do almost anything to pass through the gatekeepers. For less-affluent families, earning elite wages is necessary to pay off their often-considerable student debt.

Holistic review college admissions is a direct reflection of America's distorted meritocracy. On the surface, the system appears fair. No student is in theory excluded from consideration if they meet the prerequisites for applying. That's why even Harvard or MIT allows everyone to apply, including those who never had a chance of getting in. Establishing academic minimums would devalue the tenants of holistic review. In practice, structural barriers and increasing economic inequality create a system where a small minority of affluent students enrolled at elite high schools take most of the elite admissions prizes.

Admissions scarcity isn't because black or Hispanic or low-income students take spaces from wealthy whites and Asians through affirmative action or reverse discrimination. Affluent students at top high schools, regardless of race or ethnicity, essentially compete for slots against one another. Markovits argues that the gap between the rich and the middle class is growing faster than between the middle and working classes. In short, the rich few are leaving the remainder in their dust.

Many elite colleges aren't forthcoming with their student bodies' income distribution and parent education levels because that would conflict with their messages of diversity and inclusion. On your college visits, browse the parking garage to get a feel for a campus's wealth. One only needs to look at the Audis and Tahoes parked at Dallas's Southern Methodist University (SMU)—average total cost $79,000 per year—to take the pulse of their student body's wealth. Markovits calculates that students in the top income quarter outnumber those in the bottom quarter by 14 to one at America's 150 most competitive colleges and schools.

When adjusting the parameters for the most elite colleges that society obsesses over, that divide widens from 72 percent for top quarter students versus 3 percent for the bottom quarter. Less than 3 percent of students from Yale Law, where Markovits teaches, grew up in or near poverty. Exceptions like *Hillbilly Elegy* author J.D. Vance publish acclaimed memoirs because his experience of overcoming Appalachian poverty and graduating from Yale Law is so uncommon. If achieving the American Dream were the rule and not the exception, authors like J.D. Vance or Sarah Smarsh's *Heartland: A Memoir of Working Hard and Being Broke in the Richest Country on Earth* wouldn't be a subgenre or crossovers into Netflix specials.

We love to watch feel-good movies like *Stand and Deliver* about how an outstanding math teacher portrayed by Edward James Olmos can transform the lives of students who grow up in poverty. *October Sky* follows a student played by Jake Gyllenhaal growing up in West Virginia coal-mining country at the height of the Space Race who receives a full-ride scholarship and becomes a rocket scientist. Each film is based on a true story, yet Hollywood myths valorizing anomalies rising above their circumstances and succeeding covers up the crushing realities of poverty. Pundits cherry pick teachers like Jaime Escalante or students like Homer

Hickham Jr. to suggest that everyone can pull themselves up by their bootstraps.

Look at them. They did it, and so can you. All that success requires is a little elbow grease and ingenuity.

But they're exceptions and anomalies. That's why we make movies about them. Glorifying the American Dream makes policymakers less inclined to enact substantive reform or for wealthy communities to acknowledge glaring inequalities. Only the most exceptionally skilled and lucky people living in poverty will rise above their circumstances.

Markovits cites one study where overrepresentation of the rich at elite universities has increased by 50 percent from the 1980s to the early 2000s. That gap has widened in recent decades despite universities practicing need-blind admissions and offering tuition guarantees for middle- and lower-class families. He writes, "More distressingly still, across the Ivy League, the University of Chicago, Stanford, MIT, and Duke, more students come from families in the top 1 percent of the income distribution than the entire bottom half."[225] Coming from wealth is a necessary condition for most incoming elite college students. However, given the increasing competition, affluence isn't sufficient for getting in. Insecurities about getting in amplify affluent family anxieties.

Our supposedly meritocratic society that nominally allows everyone to compete on an equal playing field isn't much more fair or equal than pre-twentieth-century aristocracies. Aristocrats were historically characterized by their expansive leisure time and eccentricities. In contrast, today's meritocrats valorize excessive working hours and a lack of hobbies for their own sake. Overworked parents pass their distorted virtues on to their children at increasingly younger ages.

Affluent families maintain and improve upon their economic and social standings, not through inheritances or birthright, but an all-consuming, lifelong campaign of educational training and professional networking. With today's meritocratic professional elite, just like in college admissions, they're mainly competing against one another rather than the sidelined masses. The highest-paid corporate, technology, and finance executives accrue their wealth mainly in exchange for their long working hours and sacrifices to the firm rather than passive income from an inheritance. Ten million more Americans voting for Donald Trump in 2020 is a symptom of an acute awareness that vast swaths of "flyover country" are excluded from the elite lifestyle afforded to "coastal elites."

Criticizing meritocracy is a tricky task because pursuing elite educations is extremely demanding. Our society rewards people based on effort. Affluent students risk falling behind their ambitious peers, and they have to earn their spaces. Unless you're Jared Kushner, nobody is entitled to space at Harvard. Today's elite college students aren't the lazy sons and daughters of royal families. They aren't the American students from a century ago who gained admission to Harvard or Yale based exclusively on their family pedigree or which boarding school they attend.

Dispensing with admission by family association or "coming from the right stock" and favoring holistic review offers the veneer of admission by one's efforts. In reality, our society is more divided than ever. Rather than passing on the family business or large plots of land, affluent parents invest tremendous resources into preparing their child for college enrollment and lucrative professional or advanced degree opportunities following graduation. Students must work tirelessly to maintain their social status, and their effort provides a moral justification for our contemporary meritocracy.

Markovits observes that homeownership rates and unemployment based on social class have grown to resemble racial differences at midcentury. Class stratification, rather than race, is a more salient indicator of one's life prospects. America is bifurcating between two castes that are drifting further apart, precluding finding common ground or even having shared conceptions of what is true about reality. Scott Galloway remarks that "higher education in the US has morphed from the lubricant of upward mobility to the *enforcer* of our caste system" (emphasis his).[226]

Wealthy families cluster together in communities and high schools that amplify their advantages. A Harvard, Princeton, and Yale alumni survey found three-quarters live in zip codes that rank in the top 20 percent by income and education. Half live in the top 5 percent of zip codes.[227] People want to mix with and marry those from similar educational backgrounds and who hold common interests. One benefit among many is that family networks connect students with prestigious seeming "internships" that aren't accessible to less-privileged families. PTA donations and fundraisers support niche arts or sports activities. Admissions is less a reflection of a level playing field; instead, it tilts heavily in favor of wealth concentrated in a handful of zip codes.

Families earning more than $250,000 annually with parents holding graduate degrees are vastly overrepresented at elite universities. Forbes's top-20 private high schools send 30 percent of their graduates to the Ivy League, Stanford, and MIT, which Markovits estimates as a tenth of the total available spaces. He calculates that "the excess investments in human capital made in a typical rich household...today are equivalent to a traditional inheritance in the neighborhood of *ten million dollars per child*" (emphasis his).[228] Markovits concludes that "meritocrats may be made rather than born, but they're not self-made."[229]

Michael Sandel sums up perfectly the disconnect between wealthy students attributing their admission to elite universities solely due to their talents. They see the playing field as largely a competition between their affluent peers where it requires genuine effort to rise above a crowded pool.

"Although the new elite has now taken on a hereditary aspect, the transmission of meritocratic privilege is not guaranteed. It depends on 'getting in.' This gives meritocratic success a paradoxical moral psychology. Collectively and retrospectively, its results are almost pre-ordained, given the overwhelming predominance on elite campuses of affluent kids. But to those in the midst of the hyper-competitive struggle for admission, it is impossible to view success as anything other than the result of individual effort and achievement. This is the standpoint that generates the conviction among the winners that they have earned their success, that they have made it on their own. This belief can be criticized as a form of meritocratic hubris; it attributes more than it should to individual striving and forgets the advantages that convert effort into success. But there is also poignance in this belief, for it is forged in pain—in the soul-destroying demands that meritocratic striving inflicts upon the young."[230]

From a society-wide perspective, who earns a college degree is a matter of life and death. Poor, uneducated Americans die much earlier than their wealthy, college-educated counterparts. Although the average life expectancy for Americans regardless of gender has increased from 74 to 78 since 1980, those gains are not evenly distributed. The American Inequality Substack visualizes that Americans residing in the wealthiest counties live on average 86 years. In contrast, dozens of the poorest counties, mostly rural and in the South, have a life expectancy between 68 and 72.[231] It isn't coincidental that poor life expectancy areas also correlate with the lowest rates of people holding college degrees. The average life expectancy for Americans living in 1950 was 68, meaning some parts of the country today are literally stuck in the past while others are the wealthiest and healthiest in human history. This data from 2019 doesn't yet account for deaths from COVID, which disproportionately affects low-income families and people of color.

Consider that the residents of the mostly rural and white Union County, Florida, live for 67 years with an average family income of $41,000. They live shorter lives than the average person living in Rwanda (69 years), Syria (73 years), and Bosnia (77 years), according to 2019 data from the World Health Organization. The per capita GDP of the most impoverished state from former East Germany, Saxony-Anhalt, is $34,000. Despite having $7,000 per person less than Union County, Saxony-Anhalt residents live on average 76 years, nine years longer than Union County and only two years less than the US median.

The difference in life expectancy between East and West Germany was only 2.5 years at the time of unification in 1990, a tenth of the divide between America's most affluent and most impoverished counties today. The average East German in 1990 lived for 73 years, despite an adjusted per capita GDP one-quarter that of Union County, Florida. Inequality since German unification has shrunk, while divisions between the former states of the Union and Confederacy have widened. Life expectancy in a totalitarian communist regime decades ago was higher than in many American communities today.[232]

Princeton University economists Anne Case and Angus Deaton published the landmark book *Deaths of Despair and the Future of Capitalism*. They argue that the loss of good jobs and stagnating wages have left behind working- and middle-class families. In 2017, 158,000 Americans died from suicide, alcoholism, and drugs. Since the 1990s, African Americans' mortality rates have declined while uneducated whites have risen since 2010.

A subsequent study by Case and Deaton found that the strongest correlation for life expectancy comes not from race or even wealth, but whether one has a bachelor's degree.[233] They write, "Black men and women with a bachelor's degree, who used to have a lower adult life expectancy than whites without a degree, now had more expected years to live." Education attainment matters more than race for living longer. Only 9 percent of Union County, Florida residents hold a bachelor's degree, whereas, in Marin County, California, 59 percent of adults have a bachelor's degree or higher.[234] Marin County is mostly white, and its residents live on average 17 years longer than in Union County.

The United States is more unequal and less socially mobile than India, Morocco, Indonesia, Iran, Ukraine, and Vietnam. The American Dream of upward mobility and pulling yourself up by your bootstraps is more alive in "socialist" nations such as Denmark, Sweden, the Netherlands, and Canada.[235] Donald Trump, who campaigned heavily on portraying Joe Biden as a socialist, received 82 percent of Union County votes in 2020, suggesting that the populations most left behind in today's meritocracy vote overwhelmingly for populist politicians.[236] Interestingly, and perhaps not coincidentally, the countries with the lowest social inequality levels and highest upward mobility rates have some of the least complicated and most straightforward college admissions systems.

Markovits contrasts our present inequality with a robust middle class of the 1950s to the '70s that looked similar to Canada, Japan, and Norway. American adults two generations ago experienced lifetime employment with a single corporation that heavily trained its employees and promoted them from within. Employment practices following World War II that provided retirement pensions have given way to a cutthroat professional landscape that depends on elite education and self-funded training. High school and college provide the training ground for ambitious students to prepare for graduate studies or demanding corporate careers.

He summarizes the origins of meritocracy that resembles and supplants historical aristocracy. We live in a new caste system that "partitions the rich and the rest into separate and alien life-worlds…

…American meritocracy has become precisely what it was invented to combat: a mechanism for the concentration and dynastic transmission of wealth, privilege, and caste across generations. A social and economic hierarchy with these comprehensive, dynastic, and self-referential qualities has a name: an aristocracy. And meritocracy does not dismantle but rather renovates aristocracy, fashioning a new caste order, contrived for a world in which wealth consists not in land or factories but rather in human capital, the free labor of skilled workers…. But merit's allure is an illusion. Because the meritocrat's skills are valuable only against a backdrop of prior economic inequality…. It is an artificial construction, built to valorize the exploitation of human capital."[237]

In other words, almost everyone in our meritocracy is screwed, even the winners.

One solution Markovits proposes to increasing education access is to tie an elite university's tax-exempt status to the percentage of enrollment from middle- and low-income students. He cites that the top 20 university endowments derive a third of their revenue from tax-free endowments and tax-deductible alumni donations. Princeton University's tax exemptions amount to a $105,000 subsidy per student, more than ten or 20 times the subsidies provided for nearby public New Jersey colleges and universities.

He calls for reforms that "break up the club, insisting that schools and universities should be taxed as charities only if they actually function as charities—that is, openly and inclusively to educate the broad public."[238] Elite universities won't increase access under the current incentive structures. Their diversity essay requirements and inclusive campus press releases are Band-Aids patching a bloodbath. Strong regulations are a necessary carrot for nudging universities into expanding the scope of who they serve.

Expanding enrollment and removing artificial scarcity is another obvious reform that will dramatically increase the 115,000 or so elite university spaces that families currently obsess over. He estimates that Ivy League universities could double their enrollment and spend as much per student as in 2000. Ivy League administrations argue that more students on campus will dilute educational quality. These arguments aren't convincing when elite universities provided high-quality educations with far fewer resources than decades ago. They want to maintain their enrollment scarcity to preserve their luxury brand prestige. We need a more inclusive educational environment to spread resources throughout society rather than concentrated within the top 1 percent.

Both the rich and poor will benefit from a more equal society. More university spaces would decrease the anxieties for everyone, but especially in the learning environments and communities of affluent families. Relaxed competition will help reestablish academic honesty norms and reduce incentives to pad one's resume with soulless commitments. It's a self-deception to think that compromising yourself to gain admission to elite universities that lead to a grinding professional life won't come at the expense of developing your inner life. As I mentioned in chapter 4, "Stoicism and the Gap Theory of Happiness," the only hope you have for surviving the admissions madness is to understand the roots of suffering and reframe how you perceive the system that you've been born into.

Undoubtedly, elite private universities will cling to their exclusivity and argue for the necessity of their tax-exempt status. I'm confident that if we let them get away with it, universities will always prioritize their revenue over their students' well-being and their obligations to society beyond their vaunted Ivy-ringed walls. As their existence depends indirectly on American taxpayers, we as the public need to hold them accountable to the society they serve rather than our tax dollars bloating their endowment portfolios.

These are the questions I would ask elite universities that claim to value diversity yet enroll a predominantly wealthy student body. If you have the courage, give some of them a try on your next college tour or Zoom information session. Some may be more applicable than others, depending on the context:

- Why does your institution enroll so few transfer students, and the ones you do admit, why do they come primarily from four-year universities?
- How can you claim to have sincere concerns for decreasing the wealth gap when you admit students through legacy, early decision, development cases, and professors' children, among others?
- Do you think deferrals and waitlists are in the best interests of the mental health of your applicants?
- Why do you maintain the same number of enrollment spaces despite great strides in technology aiding the delivery of educational services? I've heard the enrolling class

has been the same for over a hundred years. Can't you expand enrollment some without diluting the quality of your university?

+ Do you publish the demographics of your student populations in full and make it easy for me to find your admissions statistics, or is this something I'm going to have to hunt down?

+ Do you require any essays beyond the Common Application? If so, what role do they play in your process? Are those additional essay requirements part of your commitment to college access?

+ Did you offer refunds or waivers for students whose semesters were disrupted due to COVID and therefore couldn't continue living on campus or pursuing their courses?

+ What percentage of your applicants are admitted or denied during the "shaping" process?

+ Does your marketing and recruitment CRM systems factor into how many scholarships I may or may not receive? Does my opening your emails or attending official events in any way impact how I'm evaluated, beyond a rigid definition of "demonstrated interest?"

+ How does offering multiple applications such as the Common and Coalition applications and one unique to your institution make this process clearer and more transparent? It just seems more confusing.

+ I read your institution's commitment to diversity. I agree that an exchange of ideas and having beliefs challenged is a net benefit. Do students across the political or religious spectrum feel welcome on your campus?

+ Since we agree that Black Lives Matter, why don't I see any black people on your admissions staff or as student tour guides?

- How can I know your holistic review process is fair?
- I notice that the application has essay requirements that aren't published anywhere on your website. What accounts for this discrepancy?
- When you offer first-year scholarships, presumably to convince us to enroll, do you provide reasonable pathways to renew that aid in subsequent years?
- Do you think recommendation letters and interviews increase access to your institution or reinforce perceptions that it's an exclusive club where only students with the best resources have a chance of getting in?
- If you could wave a magic wand and change anything about the admissions process as practiced, what would you reform?
- I've been deferred. Do you think it serves the interests of my mental health to require a letter of continued interest? What can you possibly hope to gain by yet another essay and piece of information? Would it be compelling to write about the lack of equity and access that such a requirement entails? I see that your university has a commitment to social justice, after all.
- I understand college applications are reviewed quickly and rapidly. How does holistic review allow you to "get to know me?" Aren't most applications largely the same, anyway?
- I see that your admissions rate is 10 percent. How many applicants are admitted for "hooks" such as athletes and legacies, and how many are "unhooked?" Even an approximate ratio would be helpful.
- I see that you brag about how many nationalities are represented on your campus. Does your university primarily

recruit international students because they pay full tuition or because they bring diversity?

+ Everyone wants to go to your university. Why did we just listen to a sales pitch?

Asking questions that demonstrate critical thinking, if articulated thoughtfully and tactfully, may provide an added admissions advantage by leaving a memorable impression on the admissions counselor.

I've sufficiently laid out the case the many ways that the college admissions system is so thoroughly broken as to constitute a public emergency. Some teenagers commit suicide each year due to the pressures borne from holistic review admissions. Most elite university counselors and administrations shrug their shoulders and carry on with business as usual.

Blood is on your hands, bureaucrats, even if single drops are distributed among thousands of palms.

Critics who push back on these suggestions and the reforms I propose and questions that I ask have the burden of justifying how our current admissions madness status quo is both more reasonable and better than any alternatives.

10.1 On moral luck

I raise these observations about our broken meritocracy not to "check your privilege" or make you feel guilty. But I want to point out just how heavily the deck is stacked in favor of families living in affluent suburbs. Acknowledging system-wide ethical concerns is not an academic exercise. Understanding your position within the bigger picture directly impacts living with decency and compassion in your daily life.

Only through utter luck is one child born into wealth and another into poverty. Although I grew up in a working-class community and attended a below-average public high school, I was lucky to have two parents who remained married. Most of my friends weren't that lucky. Neither of my parents are college educated. I lived in a stable household and applied for college when the landscape wasn't as competitive. UT-Austin admitted two-thirds of their applicants in 2007 and less than one-quarter today.

Many of my childhood friends and classmates were raised by their grandparents or aunts. They grew up in abusive environments and often lacked money for lunch or gasoline. My best friend and across-the-street neighbor growing up died of a heroin overdose. We went to the same schools and lived on the same street with home lives that weren't radically dissimilar. The difference between his bad luck and my good-enough fortunes is razor-thin. There's no compelling reason why our lives couldn't be switched.

My grandma paid for the college educations for we grandkids, giving me innumerable advantages as a student and after graduation. I did nothing to earn graduating from college debt free. Through some combination of lucky breaks, avoiding metaphorical landmines, and my talents, I've constructed an extraordinary life. I am one of the few millennials born in the working class that is likely to die wealthier than my parents. My life is, statistically speaking, anomalous, yet I don't masquerade that I'm 100 percent self-made or without the benefits of my relative privilege.

If you're born into an affluent community with two college-educated parents, you're one of the lucky few on the planet relative to the less-privileged many. Your life begins on a higher rung of the ladder, with subsequent rungs easier to reach.

Michael Sandel is a Harvard professor who teaches one of the most popular courses in the country: Justice. His recent book *The Tyranny of Meritocracy* builds on Markovits's investigation of the economic sources of meritocratic inequality. Sandel explores the moral and cultural dimensions of how society determines who deserves what. In a meritocracy, most of the benefits are enjoyed by a narrow segment of elite society. Our shrinking middle class feels an acute sense that there is a parallel society that they can never enter or participate, stoking populist resentments.

There is a felt sense, especially among recent college graduates and millennials, that no matter how hard they work, the cards are stacked against them ever paying off student loans, securing a mortgage, or having the financial stability needed to raise a family. They're a car accident or a COVID diagnosis away from financial catastrophe.

People in lower-income brackets justifiably sense that they can never achieve the American Dream, whereas wealthy families are desperate to maintain their position and esteem. Sandel writes, "The explosion of inequality in recent decades has not quickened upward mobility but, to the contrary, has enabled those on top to consolidate their advantages and pass them on to their children."[239] The pandemic has accelerated the gains achieved by wealthy families and large corporations.

Moral luck calls for acknowledging the role that good or bad fortune plays in one's life. Proponents of moral luck encourage us to extend sympathy and give the benefit of the doubt, especially when someone falls short of a goal. Context, upbringing, and life circumstances play as much, if not more, of a role as genetics. Hard work and effort alone aren't sufficient to earn an Olympic Gold medal or receive a multimillion-dollar compensation package. Success at the highest levels requires a combination of substantial training, inherent skills or aptitudes, a support network, and good fortune. Sandel writes, "The meritocratic ideal is flawed because it ignores the moral arbitrariness of talent and inflates the moral significance of effort."[240]

As a society, especially in criminal justice, we operate under the assumption that people behave with complete free will. We're quick to demonize criminals who commit armed robbery or child abuse without reflecting on how they came to be. Murderers are often made and not born. Our retributive justice system isn't equipped to consider the background structural circumstances that contribute to criminal behavior. New Zealand and Scandinavian countries account for poverty or a history of abuse in their sentencing schemes that focus on rehabilitation and restoration rather than criminalization. American meritocracy demands that people who fail are entirely responsible for their life situation, although the reality is more nuanced and complicated.

In college admissions, teachers and parents are quick to praise students who get in. They offer congratulations like "you deserve it!" Language around entitlement and just desserts have become so ubiquitous in modern America that Sandel notes the phrase "you deserve" tripled in books from 1970 to 2008.[241] We do and should offer praise to people when they find success or achieve their goals. It would be peculiar not to celebrate talent and effort, but one's success should come with an asterisk. Success in elite college admissions depends on a village that includes parent investment, teacher support, high school resources, access to sports and arts programs, test preparation and college consulting, etc., in addition to one's work ethic and natural ability.

The hardest-working student in the worst-performing schools will almost always come up short compared with mediocre children of affluent families. I observed this firsthand when I visited Dallas County's lowest-performing and most-elite high schools as a UT-Austin admissions counselor. Students living in poverty also have many more possible landmines to trigger, whereas wealthy parents can bail out their occasionally delinquent children with powerful attorneys or weighty donations.

Ethan Couch, the "Affluenza Teen," killed four and injured nine people when he was sixteen while driving under the influence. He received probation and only two years in jail after skipping bail with his mom to a beach resort in Mexico. Ethan walks while more than 2,300 juveniles tried as adults, most of whom grew up in poverty, live behind bars without the possibility of parole.[242]

Unless you've visited some of the nation's worst-performing schools, it's hard to wrap your mind around the scope of the challenges they face. Affluent parents or even teachers at great schools sometimes asked me, "So if the top students at poor-performing public schools aren't going to UT-Austin where they are guaranteed admission by state law, which colleges are they attending?" I answered that most don't attend any colleges at all, and even fewer receive degrees. The thought had never occurred to them because it's unthinkable to forgo enrollment in their college-going communities. Few students from elite families fail to complete their degrees. Many affluent families fail to realize that most Americans don't have a fair shot at going as far as their merit or talents can take them. They can't pull themselves up by their bootstraps when their shoes are frayed and torn.

Who society rewards is contingent upon its values and needs. Life circumstances go beyond race, gender, and sexual orientation. Although these indisputably play some role in our lots drawn in life, they're not everything. Identity is so much more complicated than surface characteristics.

Michael Sandel critiques meritocracy because receiving rewards and esteem from one's talents depend on the context and time in which one lives. I'm thankful to live at a time and context in history that rewards my communications skillset and liberal arts aptitudes. My training and background are perfectly suited to my particular and niche consulting career. If I had been born a decade later, I would be hopeless learning coding or computer science like high schoolers in today's STEM-obsessed environment. Had I lived in sixteenth-century Renaissance Italy that treated musicians and artists like today's Hollywood superstars, I wouldn't have had a chance. I received "unsatisfactory" kindergarten marks for cutting straight or coloring within the lines. I can't sing, and I failed recorder lessons in elementary school. No amount of effort or trying hard will ever make me anything more than a mediocre musician.

I have a terrible sense of smell and an undeveloped taste palate, so I could never rise to the top in societies that reward culinary aptitudes in gastronomies such as France and Japan. If I were born in the 1950s Soviet Union that highly prized advanced math and physics skills or chess prowess, I would have been relegated to the sidelines. My LEGO structures never looked quite right, no matter how closely I followed the instructions. Had I been born in a culture that values, or an environment that nurtures, table tennis or downhill snow skiing, the only sports that I have an innate gift for, I may have risen to become one of the great ones. Instead, I was a mediocre baseball, basketball, and indoor soccer player.

To extend the analogy beyond my personal life, Tom Brady reaches the pinnacle of professional success and esteem in part because he was born into a society that rewards athletic talents, especially football. If he were born in Argentina, perhaps he would have become a soccer star. Had Brady or I lived in an ancient agricultural society, we would be mostly useless, assuming Brady doesn't have a secret green thumb or skills that translate for bending over sixteen hours a day. Not known for his speed, he certainly couldn't chase down gazelles in the Serengeti with the same agility that makes for football's top wide receivers. His physique wouldn't be suited for winning the shotput in Ancient Greece's inaugural Olympic Games.

We live at a peculiar time in history when bankers, lawyers, physicians, corporate executives, some athletes (but not others), technology entrepreneurs, programmers, and media celebrities command the highest salaries and attendant societal esteem. Few of these careers would be valued so highly in different historical periods. A consequence of our meritocracy is that wages for esteemed jobs skyrocket while middle-skill professions such as manufacturing, secretarial, and transportation, among many others, stagnate, decline, or may disappear entirely due to automation or outsourcing.

In other cultures, educators are some of the highest-paid and most well-regarded members of society, while ours are underpaid, overworked, and less valued. Some people get lucky for the careers they choose or happen into. In contrast, others may, for example, be a master at repairing wristwatches, a skill prized in an analog society until it moves into the digital world. Regardless, our culture valorizes academic credentials and economic growth at the expense of the solidarity and community that middle-class expansion from the 1950s to '70s depended upon.

My unconventional, borderless lifestyle is possible only because Europe broke away from feudalism four centuries ago, untethering masses of people from their feudal lords and spurring migrations to urban centers. Before then, leaving your community was a great taboo or a harsh punishment. Perhaps I could have become an adventurer-scholar like Marco Polo or Ibn Battuta, but in all likelihood, I would have toiled land that I didn't own for my entire short life. Or the Inquisition would have sniffed out my heretical behaviors and burned me alive.

Nowadays, it's socially acceptable and common to attend college or work far from your birthplace. Ubiquitous internet connectivity allows me to start and run a business even from less-developed countries, an impossibility two decades ago. I'm lucky that I graduated just after the Great Recession rather than during, that allowed funding for additional admissions counselors, my only conventional job. American culture has deep flaws, but I'm fortunate it values entrepreneurs and risk-takers like me.

These reflections are not explicit considerations of my "privilege" in an identity politics sense. They are interesting hypotheticals to consider "what could have been." Thought experiments like these frame my lived experiences to help me make sense of who I am within the broader arc of human history. It might be a compelling meditation for you to conduct, too. I'm content and grateful knowing that I was born at precisely the right time and place. If I had been born in 2008 rather than 1988, I'm not confident my skillset or disposition would match what's required of ambitious students today. In innumerable ways, I've lived a lucky and privileged life relative to all the possible lives and places I could have lived. We don't choose when, where, or how we're born, or to which parents.

Non-events like narrowly missing a car crash, or departing Kyrgyzstan safely during violent elections, are as substantial as actual occurrences like gaining admission to your dream school. We're often blind to the non-events and overly aware of what actually occurred. That any of us are alive today is due to an unfathomable constellation of colliding physical forces and accidents of history. A nearly infinite set of cosmic and earthly variables are responsible for our births.

Some of us are born luckier than others, not because of Buddhist bad karma or Hindu reincarnations. I also don't buy into the New Age confused belief that you can "manifest" success or that good or bad things happen solely because of negative thoughts. Misfortune or an admissions rejection isn't a punishment for angering a vengeful God or not wanting something badly enough. If there is an omniscient God, I'm confident it doesn't care about our petty human affairs nor play any role in inconsequential admissions outcomes, cosmically speaking. Privilege and good fortune aren't gifts bestowed by providential higher powers. Nor are our fates predestined and fixed; we have some measure of voluntary control over our behaviors. Regardless, life, like college admissions, is chaotic, messy, and often utterly random and inexplicable.

Those fortunate few, who through circumstance and their efforts, flourish in a society that rewards their efforts, count yourselves fortunate. Sandel warns, "Meritocratic hubris reflects the tendency of winners to inhale too deeply of their success, to forget the luck and good fortune that helped them on their way. It is the smug conviction of those who land on top that they deserve their fate and that those on the bottom deserve theirs, too."[243]

We live in a society that's growing so far apart from one another that the suffering incurred by the elite's successes falls out of sympathy with the rest. Elites are so out of touch with middle- and lower-class families that it's hard to imagine those divisions softening. Union County, excluded from elites' opportunities, will continue voting for reactionary, populist politicians even if it means dying earlier. For those less fortunate or prosperous, their failures may be a product of structural factors outside of their control rather than character failings or a lack of talent.

A complete examination of the meritocracy madness is outside the scope of this book. Daniel Markovits's *The Meritocracy Trap* and Michael Sandel's *The Tyranny of Meritocracy* are two of the most illuminating books I've read on any subject. I recommend that anyone interested in the study of social inequality read them in full. I hope you take away from this section that we live far from a fair or equitable society.

Understand that your successes and failures come down as much to luck or fortune as talent and effort. Extend gratitude to the people who make your success possible. You need not even feel self-guilt or pity for the less fortunate. Instead, acknowledge that your potential life pathways could be radically different given different circumstances at birth. Through an alternative set of variables, you could be the kid at an inner-city school receiving tutoring rather than being the tutor.

I also raise the concept of moral luck as a preface to the next section, where I call for admissions by partial lottery. I believe it is a step in the right direction for decreasing barriers to spaces at elite universities. It captures the reality of moral luck more than our present arbitrary admissions system, especially when it comes to "shaping the class" that I discussed in chapter 6.6.

10.2 Admissions by partial lottery?

Among Princeton's Fall 2017 approximately 31,000 applicants, there were 1,890 admissions spaces. Twelve thousand applicants had a 4.0 GPA, and nearly 14,000 scored higher than 1400 on the SAT, placing them in the top 5 percent of test-takers worldwide. Dean of Princeton Admissions Janet Rapelye commented that "we could have admitted five or six classes to Princeton from [this year's] pool."[244]

Princeton and other elite institutions reject many more qualified applicants than they admit, creating the widespread perception that admissions decisions seem like a lottery. For borderline applicants at elite universities everywhere, their outcomes effectively are random in practice. UT-Austin call center employees have told some of my transfer clients that admissions outcomes are literally random.

We already have admissions by partial lottery, except we call them waitlists, deferrals, and admission by appeal. These processes are much less transparent or fair than what I propose here.

As winners and losers on the margins receive their decisions arbitrarily, why not convert a seeming lottery into an actual, partial one?

My modest proposal for a partial admissions lottery is simple. It appeals to pragmatics and fairness. It retains most elements of the holistic review status quo. A partial lottery brings more balance and decreases the power disparities between universities and their applicants.

A university can portion its potential admits into two pools: *discretion* and *lottery*.

Discretionary spaces are reserved for early decision (ED), legacy, recruited athletes and artists, honors college, development cases, diversity, exceptional talent, full-tuition international students, etc. Discretionary spaces go to the "hooked" applicants who are sons of professors or recruited athletes. They can also go to the "unhooked" applicants, who are the rare kinds of exceptional students that top universities clamor over. The most exceptional applicants currently receive "likely letters" from universities that recruit their top-tier prospects before distributing formal admissions offers. They're one of the top thousand prospects or so worldwide that I referenced in the opening pages who will gain admission to most or all of the universities they apply to.

The other academically qualified applicants are subject to a *lottery*. Who receives a lottery space and the proportion of discretionary versus lottery spaces are up to each university. Half of the spaces could be at the university's discretion and the other half by lottery or some other ratio.

Daniel Golden in *The Price of Admission* referenced in chapter 6.7 demonstrates that most universities already have unofficial quotas for students with "hooks." They admit a plurality or perhaps a majority of their applicants through a system that isn't based purely on merit but on connections or something that the university needs, such as athletes or donations. Internal, unpublished quotas leave unhooked regular decision applicants at the mercy of much steeper competition and longer odds. A lack of clarity of how many spaces go to legacies, athletes, and so on distorts a university's published admissions statistics. One can never know actual admissions rates at any given university because not all spaces are allocated purely on merit or holistic review.

Separating categories into discretionary and lottery would make an opaque process of admissions-by-access more visible. A lottery could bring clarity to exactly how many applicants gained admission without a hook. Students without hooks admitted through the discretionary process benefit from knowing they sincerely were the top applicants in the pool. They're one of the exceptionally rare applicants whose accomplishments could be acknowledged by a discretionary space. With admissions as currently practiced, nobody knows how close or far they were from a favorable or unfavorable decision. Exceptional applicants remain insecure, while borderline admitted students don't have any context for their incredible luck.

Recall the process of "shaping" the class in chapter 6.6, whereby admissions reviewers assign thousands of borderline applicants in the "sea of sameness" to admit, deny, and waitlist piles during the final weeks of admissions review. A partial lottery would remedy the most inconsistent phase of the admissions review process.

Many rejection letters stress that there are substantially more qualified applicants than spaces available. There isn't enough room on campus to accommodate every qualified student. Some universities place as many as a quarter of their borderline applicants on the waitlist, yet few and sometimes no applicants will gain admission through the waitlist. A partial lottery remedies this ambiguity by diminishing the stakes of the shaping process. It would alleviate tension among admissions committees to make arbitrary decisions about who gains admission or not, saving not only stress but also a lot of time and labor.

Most lottery ideas I've seen couple the proposal with a "matching" system among many universities. A matching system is where an applicant picks and applies at, say, their top five schools. Those schools pool their data and create a similar preferencing system. It's like sorority recruitment, where each chapter ranks their prospects, and the prospects rank their top sororities. Medical school residency currently practices a similar matching system.

Matching adds efficiency and limits the enrollment manager's guesswork, but it adds an unnecessary complication and would likely violate antitrust laws. Critics take advantage of lottery/matching bundles to construct straw man arguments and raise objections that may not be part of the proposal. I haven't found a lottery idea like the one I outline below, so I hope to renew this conversation and find weaknesses to improve it. Regardless, there is so much reflexive resistance to any mention of a lottery—without realizing our system already has a lottery in waitlists and appeals—that I doubt few will take the time to engage with the substance of my proposal.

Let's assume a hypothetical university receives 40,000 total applications for 3,000 admissions offers to enroll 2,500 students. For simplicity's sake, let's assume that they do not have a binding ED option, although there's nothing intrinsic to ED that excludes a partial lottery. Rather than deferral to the regular decision pool or placement on a waitlist, applicants could be deferred to the lottery. Of the spaces, 1,500 are "discretionary," and the rest receive admissions through a lottery.

Nothing changes with holistic review, only the categories where students are placed. Every application receives a holistic review rating as currently practiced. Whatever formulas or scoring systems a university uses need not change. In addition to approximate tags for definite admits, low admits, probable denials, and definite denials, we can add a new category: borderline, assign to lottery. Therefore, universities have full control over who they place in the discretionary, lottery, and outright rejection piles.

Most "low admits" could qualify for the lottery, with probable denials receiving a promotion to the lottery or definite admits demotion to the lottery, as institutional needs require. I envision lotteries replacing waitlists, which essentially are lotteries from the students' point-of-view that hardly anyone wins anyway, outlined in chapter 8.2. A lottery could reduce the workload and stress involved in letters of continued interest, appeals for reconsideration, and updating applications. Like a waitlist, students could accept an invitation to join a lottery pool.

Rather than having academic minimums or cutoffs, the universities could retain control over who receives lottery spaces while maintaining secrecy about their admissions procedures. Publishing the holistic review parameters of who received the lottery isn't necessary, just as no applicants today know why they're assigned to the waitlist or deferred piles.

Universities that admit a higher proportion of their students by lottery could use their reformed admissions policies to attract applicants who otherwise might not have applied. There would be an incentive for universities to offer the perception of fairness. Allotting a higher proportion of lottery spaces might drive application numbers higher, benefitting a university's bottom line and increasing its prestige in college rankings. Currently, rising application numbers result from a winner-take-most system where the top few thousand applicants occupy most of the admissions spaces because they gain admission to many schools. A lottery adopted by many elite universities would more evenly distribute the spaces and decrease an applicant's incentive to "shotgun" 20 or 30 applications.

We can assume that very few students with academics placing them in the bottom half of the applicant pool will gain admission. Our hypothetical university would reject around 20,000 of their applicants as definite denials, at risk of not returning for their sophomore year or graduating in four years, whether there is a lottery or not. They represent a higher risk to a university that wants to graduate its students on time. These definite rejections are not the borderline students who are denied during "shaping" rounds.

Early holistic review rounds could find those hidden gems in rural or urban areas and students who come from first-generation low-income families and show promise in other ways despite unremarkable grades and SAT scores. A rigid GPA and test score minimum would inevitably exclude students with exceptional skills and stories but who hold mediocre academics, so preserving holistic review is still preferable.

Of the 30,000 remaining applicants who are definite admits, low admits, and probable denials, approximately 3,000 will either gain admission through discretionary spaces or lottery. Let us assume that the top 1,200 "unhooked" applicants defined by their academics and holistic review scores will gain admission directly, leaving 300 "hooked" spaces for recruited athletes, legacies, artists, and so on. That leaves 18,500 applicants competing for lottery tickets.

Let us assume that 10,000 of these applicants are decent but unremarkable who would neither be admitted nor waitlisted in a non-lottery scenario. They represent low-admits moved to deny piles in subsequent committee review rounds or probable and definite rejections who wouldn't gain admission anyway. They are not borderline applicants who arrive at committee tables during the final "shaping" rounds.

That leaves 8,500 remaining highly qualified applicants for 1,500 lottery spaces, or an admissions rate of 17.6 percent, assuming every invited applicant joins the lottery. These are applicants who are roughly in the top quarter of the overall pool and are highly likely to succeed and graduate in four years. They're the ones who would gain admission or be rejected arbitrarily during shaping rounds, or the ones the Princeton dean could fill five or six classes with. Here is a breakdown of each category of applicants.

Total completed applications received	40,000
Total admissions spaces available	3,000
Unqualified applicants in the "definite denial" group	20,000
Applicants after further review who remain in the "definite" and "probable" denials group and are not offered a discretionary or a lottery space	10,000
Discretionary admissions spaces for "unhooked" students who gain admission based purely on merit and are close to "perfect" for what the university seeks	1,200
Spaces assigned to "hooks" (athletes, legacies, etc.) who gain admission partly by merit	300
Admissions rate for all discretionary spaces	3.75 percent
Applicants who are "good enough" to qualify for the lottery	8,500
Percentage of total applicants earning a lottery space	21.25 percent
Spaces available in the lottery admissions pool	1,500
Admissions rate among the lottery pool	17.6 percent
Overall admissions rate	7.5 percent

In a typical admissions scenario, the admissions rate for legacy applicants might be four or five times higher than the overall admissions rate, say 20 to 30 percent. The strongest argument supporting a partial lottery scenario is that the odds invert in favor of unhooked yet highly qualified applicants. They may not have the portfolio and good fortune of the 1,200 spaces allocated by holistic review merit, but they still stand a more than twice as good chance of getting in than the overall admissions rate of 7.5 percent suggests. The lottery admissions rate reflects better an ambitious applicant's chances because it necessarily excludes the 30,000 other applicants who are less desirable in any admissions scenario.

To reiterate, reviewers choose each of the applicants assigned to the lottery pile. They practice holistic review as they see fit. However, there can't be X number of winning lottery tickets for black students or Y spaces reserved for applicants living in the Great Plains. Reserving lottery spaces through quotas would be unconstitutional under the equal protection clause of the Fourteenth Amendment. Ethnicity, class, geography, or any other biographical factor need not enter into the process any more than in the current status quo defined by various affirmative action Supreme Court rulings in *Grutter* (2003) and *Fisher* (2016).

The only lottery subcategories that might be necessary are for allotting spaces in given majors. Suppose 25 percent of the freshman class are Computer Science majors at a STEM-heavy university. In that case, the lottery spaces could be tweaked proportionally dependent upon the number of computer scientists admitted outright through the discretionary process. There will inevitably be some imbalances with which majors receive spaces, but that's already the case with enrollment managers trying to forecast yield. Plus, since the average student changes their major twice before graduating, which department a student begins in is less critical in the long term. Lottery spaces are not assigned randomly, allotted to some groups of students over others, or through rigid cutoffs.

An algorithm managed by an independent department outside of the admissions office but within the university could distribute the final 1,500 spaces among the lottery pool. All lottery decisions could still go out by the April 1 National Decision Day. It isn't necessary to share student information with third-party vendors or other universities, preserving student privacy.

Lotteries already determine who is eligible for the United States' Diversity Visa Program, admission to public magnet or charter high schools, and jury duty, so "drawing lots" isn't an unprecedented selection process. The primary difference between these examples and a partial college admissions lottery is that holistic review depends on the assumption of distributing spaces by merit. Nobody presumably deserves jury duty, whereas some applicants can make valid claims at deserving admissions spaces based on their academic and extracurricular credentials.

Admissions by lottery occurs in limited instances abroad. Political science professor Peter Stone from Ireland's Trinity College considers proposals for lottery admissions to Irish and UK universities.[245] He references Queen Mary College, which chooses applicants who meet their minimum requirements by lottery. Other English universities admit by lottery applicants to in-demand majors such as Physiotherapy. The Netherlands chooses by lottery academically excellent candidates to limited-space programs such as Medicine and Veterinary.

Lotteries for specific programs are problematic because there isn't an alternative course of study for unlucky applicants. A friend of my Dutch girlfriend didn't receive a lottery space in dental school after trying three times, meaning they needed to move on with a different career. On the aggregate, internal investigations of each system affirmed their utility and fairness, and the practice continues. Irish universities assign points for admissions and break ties with a limited lottery, which is a proposal similar to mine. However, a partial lottery need not assign points and compare students head to head but rather place applicants into a general lottery pile.

Admissions by lottery has occurred in some narrow instances in the US. The earliest mention of college admissions by a lottery that I found is in a September 1968 *New York Times* article "Students Selected By a Lottery Begin College in Capital." Washington DC's Federal City College's (since consolidated into the University of the District of Columbia) mostly African American inaugural class of 2,400 "chosen by lot" among 6,000 applications. Tuition was $25 per semester.[246] Other open-enrollment universities admitted students by lottery in the civil rights era because the only criterion for admission was a high school diploma.

Since the partial lottery experiment has never been attempted at an elite American university, I can only propose theories and anticipate potential logistical concerns rather than evaluating data. I hope that some university experiments with a lottery to gather data and assess outcomes. I have no illusions that my proposal will receive serious consideration from higher education authorities. I'm writing primarily for students and families to consider that there are hypothetical alternatives to our admissions madness.

The fundamental issue with an admissions lottery is that the proponents try and solve too many problems simultaneously. Lottery advocates hope to centralize application portals, coordinate admissions processes between universities, increase diversity, promote transparency, and disempower universities with a single reform. This silver bullet approach is a mistake. A partial lottery must be one tool among many to increase access and demystify the admissions process.

Another error that lottery proponents make is that they want to dispense with holistic review entirely, which is a battle they will never win. Universities will not relinquish their control. I've never seen a lottery proponent break things down by the numbers of what it might look like in practice. Skeptics reject their lottery proposals without further consideration because it's perceived as excessively disruptive or impractical.

In addition to universities and admissions critics, the core complaint comes, most surprisingly, from the students themselves. They argue that admission through any lottery system is inherently unfair (again, failing to realize that waitlists and deferrals are even more unfair than drawing lots). When buying a Powerball millionaire sweepstakes lottery ticket, you know how many people hold tickets, the number of winners, and your odds of winning. With waitlists and appeals, those variables are often unknown. It's bizarre how a policy that would, on the whole, help more students than it harms is so fiercely resisted.

Reddit threads from time to time consider the proposal, with most subscribers decrying such a change. A lottery just doesn't "feel right." Applicants "deserve" to gain admission (while reassuring denied applicants that they didn't "deserve" rejection, a contradiction). Their **system justification bias** precludes them from imagining an alternative possibility even though there are myriad ways to admit students into universities, as described in chapter 5.1 regarding admissions systems abroad. Similarly, admissions professionals lack the imagination to consider there might be another way.

Their suspicion rests on meritocratic assumptions that applicants gain admission through their merit, hard work, and achievements, virtues that a lottery, they claim, would diminish. Luck, in their minds, plays little if any role in who gets in and why. There is an intuitive appeal to allotting spaces by perceived merit; however, admissions is a crapshoot. Yet, most live with the delusion that it isn't. An admitted applicant may have gotten extremely lucky, but they are under the false belief they deserved their position.

Conversely, a rejected borderline applicant may have gotten a grumpy reviewer, and a different person in a happier mood may have placed them in the admit pile. The vagaries of the shaping process mean luck plays arguably a more significant role in holistic review as practiced than a lottery would. Does the borderline applicant's rejection reflect on their merits and abilities? No, they simply got very unlucky, and they don't even know they were a borderline applicant because everyone receives the same boilerplate rejection template.

Throughout this book, I've demonstrated how admission depends largely on privilege, access to educational resources, and falling on the right side of luck and reviewer bias. Admissions is less merit than luck.

Perceptions of fairness don't line up with holistic review and enrollment management in practice. There is little equitable or meritocratic about the status quo, especially when applicants do not have access to why they are denied. When pressed, admissions reviewers themselves cannot justify admitting some students over others beyond hunches and gut feelings subject to change. Nevertheless, a partial rather than a total lottery still captures some of the intuitions that aim to preserve our problematic meritocratic system. A lottery brings luck and merit into closer alignment and provides more transparency regarding who gets admitted or denied and why.

Lottery skeptics contend that randomly assigning some spaces is either impractical or unfair without considering whether a lottery would be more or less practical and fair than the current system. Most critics fail to measure the benefits against the potential downsides. For example, Jeffrey Selingo asserts, without further elaboration, that it's a logistical impossibility that would add unnecessary complication to an already complex process. He builds a strawman lottery system that might conflict with federal antitrust laws and dismisses the possibility entirely. "Depending on how it was administered, it likely would require colleges to share information about applicants with each other."[247] He imagines a general lottery pool among many universities, but that would indeed be impractical and possibly illegal. A failure of imagination isn't a compelling reason not to experiment.

My core contention is that universities have an incentive to maximize control over their admissions process at the expense of transparency and applicant welfare. Unsurprisingly, universities view lotteries unfavorably because it infringes on their monopoly of power. To my knowledge, no major American university has ever allotted any spaces by a literal lottery.

Their **bias for the status quo** precludes original thinking or departing from how things have always been done. College admissions has a **first-mover problem** where universities are reluctant to adopt significant reforms unless they have reason to believe others will follow. Ironically, antitrust laws prevent universities from cooperating. Legislation creates a **prisoner dilemma** where universities cannot easily act in their collective interest and instead tend to act in their narrow self-interests. Moving first may jeopardize their ability to manage their enrollment.

As I outlined in chapter 5, it often takes prominent universities such as Yale, Princeton, or Harvard enacting a policy to legitimize the practice among other institutions nationwide. Being the first institution to admit women, Jewish, and African American students required leaps of faith and courage before others would follow. Obscure universities admitting by lottery will have less effect than if an Ivy League institution or its equivalent does the same. For example, Bowdoin College was the first to go test-optional in 1969. Still, it's only recently, after a critical threshold of prominent universities dispensed with the requirement, that most others have followed, especially after the COVID-19 pandemic.

One barrier to widespread adoption of admission by partial lottery is that Harvard and equivalents are the institutions least willing to forgo their control or bring transparency to their admissions process. They're unlikely to be first movers.

Moreover, enrollment managers depend on data analytics to forecast how many students are likely to enroll. A lottery substantially hinders their "yield forecasts" by clouding the data. In particular, waitlists help universities fill their final spaces so that first movers would lose at least two tools in their kit.

There would be significant growing pains in the years following a partial lottery adoption. Still, after their data analytics algorithms acquire enough information, their enrollment management and recruitment forecasts will be more accurate. Likewise, with time, the ratio of admissions by discretion versus lottery and how many lottery students eventually enroll would become more accurate.

One possibility is Lottery 1 and Lottery 2 decision releases whereby an institution publishes in advance when they will release some of the winners. They could release an initial Lottery 1 batch on March 1 to see who enrolls and how many spaces remain. Then they could tweak the number of remaining prizes offered for an April 1 final release. That would preserve some enrollment management tools.

Although it would require NACAC reforms, universities could put an expiration date on a lottery offer for a month after the offer is released, rather than the May 1 decision day deadline, similar to ED offers. A partial lottery's objective is not to drag out recruitment, waitlists, and students backing out of enrollment deposits over the summer. Regardless of a lottery, admissions and recruitment need to conclude by May 1 so both families and universities can move on.

University administrators are likely reluctant to incur short-term costs for implementing long-term reforms. Forgoing some enrollment management precision could be outweighed by perceptions of fairness. If adopted by many universities, admissions by lottery could lessen temptations to "shotgun" more than 20 applications because applicants are more likely to gain admission into at least one of their reach schools. It isn't practical or potentially legal to limit the number of universities a student applies to for various reasons. For reform to happen, it's necessary to nudge behavior through new incentives built into the system that deter shotgunners rather than explicit regulations.

Getting into at least one elite university is more likely if a student joins four or five lotteries with a 15 to 20 percent success. Currently, strong but not exceptional applicants often receive many waitlists where they have little if any chance of gaining admission. One client of mine was waitlisted to ten universities and admitted to none of them. Deemphasizing waitlists will bring more transparency because lottery spaces would be more consistent from year to year. In contrast, in some years, a university might admit a few or thousands from their waitlists. Waitlists are totally random, and they harm applicants for the benefit of a university's enrollment managers.

Widespread lottery adoption could distribute spaces among elite universities more efficiently so that more students can enroll rather than a few thousand of the most exceptional applicants who gobble up most of the spaces. Our current system allocates most of the spoils to a handful of winners. A much higher threshold for admission by discretionary spaces means the most exceptional applicants won't monopolize most of the spaces, as currently practiced. Exceptional applicants gain admission outright to many elite universities leaving scraps for the second yet still highly qualified tier of applicants.

An applicant who applies to and gains admission at all eight Ivy League campuses takes spaces away from seven others. A lottery system with far fewer discretionary spaces means a smaller pool of exceptional applicants will occupy so many admissions offers. At least a few of those eight Ivy League offers would be lottery spaces.

Swarthmore Psychology professor Barry Schwartz wrote a proposal for admissions by lottery in 2005.[248] He argues that widespread adoption of admissions by partial lottery would relieve the pressure students feel to maintain unsustainable excellence levels if there were greater odds of gaining admission to at least one elite university. Elite high schools may become less ferocious and de-incentivize cheating and resume padding if "good enough" becomes the standard rather than perfection. Students could afford to earn a few more A-minuses and opt out of one or two extracurricular leadership positions.

After cutting the applicant pool by two-thirds, Schwartz proposes that "the names of all of the 'good enough' applicants could be placed in a metaphorical hat, and the 'winners' drawn at random." Ten years later, he remains a proponent, writing in a 2015 *New York Times* article that a lottery "would enable colleges to be straight with the public about what they are currently doing.

> Any honest admissions dean will tell you that the current system already is a lottery. Only now, it's disguised as a meritocracy. By easing the pressure, a lottery may get teenagers to see the college admissions letter as the starting line, not the finish line, which in turn will make them more engaged and enthusiastic—better students—when college begins."[249]

Following the Varsity Blues scandal in 2019, Schwartz renewed his call for a lottery. He carves out far fewer discretionary admissions exceptions, limited to scholarship athletes. He proposes a near-total lottery, whereas my proposal calls for admitting half of an incoming class through a partial lottery.[250]

I'm sympathetic to his recent argument that a lottery may help correct some of the meritocracy madness and produce a more equitable society. As application numbers continue to skyrocket, with Harvard leading the way with 57,000 Class of 2025 applications, a 70 percent increase from the previous year, the system requires immediate reform. The status quo is unsustainable. He summarizes the benefits of admission by lottery:

> "Is it unjust that so many qualified students fail to get what they deserve? You bet. But what is a school to do? What ends up happening is that standards for admission keep ratcheting up, in an effort to be fair to applicants and at the same time keep these institutions from exploding in size. Under these conditions, what it means to 'deserve' admission is no longer that you are an excellent student but that you are a more excellent student than the competition. And this escalation of admissions standards is what induces students, or their parents, to try to game the system, a process that has been trickling down, so that now, parents subject their toddlers to coaching for private-school interviews, and their nine-year-olds to test-preparation classes designed to get them into the best middle schools.... Justice is an important value when it comes to college admissions, but it isn't the *only* important value. Other values that an admissions process might serve are the nurturing of empathy, community solidarity, care, compassion, and service to those whose dice came out snake eyes. Acknowledging the role of luck may

actually help nurture those values in students and in their parents. And admitting to the role of luck may encourage the institutions themselves to be more explicit about the importance of those values. It may get them to care a little bit less about where they rank in the *U.S. News* guide to colleges, and a little bit more about where they rank when it comes to nurturing good citizens."

Students without winning tickets walk away with the perception that they received a fair hearing, while successful applicants are eager to gain admission by any means necessary. Not receiving a lottery ticket means your application fell outside the top quarter of the applicant pool: You weren't even close to getting in.

My partial lottery proposal retains most of the status quo to seem more palatable to universities and fairer for applicants. It's an incremental suggestion that will nevertheless appear too radical for universities invested in justifying our current system. Still, I expect fierce resistance to my "radical" proposals.

A critic might raise the concern that there may be two divisions within a university setting, those who gained admission through discretionary spaces versus lottery. Many campuses already have freshman honors colleges or programs that carve out an elite cohort within the larger university. Considerations of race in admissions already make some students of color feel like they gained admission for reasons beyond purely academic and extracurricular merit, yet university life goes on.

Rather than an us-versus-them mentality, my experience as a UT honors student was that most students mixed irrespective of honors status. Any stigma of admission by lottery isn't unique because students already gain admission through waitlist and appeals, although a lottery would have a larger incoming cohort relative to direct admission discretionary spaces. Usually, students feel Imposter Syndrome if they knowingly pulled strings with VIP connections or if daddy donated $10 million for a new building, rather than feelings of inferiority by borderline applicants admitted by appeal. I suspect most students won't talk about or care whether they were admitted by discretion or lottery after the first month or two on campus. Everyone will simply be Yale Bulldogs and Princeton Tigers.

I counter to lottery skeptics, especially those who work at universities, that if they're resistant to change and experimentation, they have the burden of proof to justify our presently deeply flawed admissions madness. They have to contend with the previous 400 pages calling into question their core assumptions and their parasitic role in society. Proponents of the status quo, I am offering you a way out of the admissions madness you collectively created and sustained with my modest partial lottery proposal.

Think twice before dismissing it without further consideration. If there is widespread adoption of partial lotteries over the next decade or two, you don't want to be on the wrong side of history, like the shrinking few who still claim the SAT measures knowledge and not wealth. Consider that it was unthinkable even a decade ago that every major university would adopt test-optional policies.

The admissions madness is so out of control that if reform attempts don't happen now, especially during a moment of global upheaval during the COVID-19 pandemic, there might not be another opportunity. In the final section, I consider whether one should go to college at all or at least defer their enrollment until a year or two after graduating from high school.

10.3 Nietzsche's gap year

Should you earn a college degree at all? It's a serious question worth considering, even if you eventually dismiss the option.

Harvard Business School professor Arthur Brooks discusses his child who opted out of college in a July 2020 article in the *Atlantic* titled "A College Degree Is No Guarantee of a Good Life."[251] He proposes a typical scenario where students may be academically excellent yet not feel compelled to pursue a traditional four-year degree. He shares about the personal conflicts of being a college professor and raising an older child who was valedictorian while having a younger child with different goals and interests. An unquestioned assumption of a college education is that it provides a good if not the best return on your investment relative to the alternatives.

Arthur Brooks forewent immediate college enrollment to his parents' outrage to tour in a classical band. His wife Ester dropped out of high school to sing in a rock band. Safety-conscious parents often forget what it's like to be a teenager. A new generation of younger parents may have themselves been raised by the first wave of helicopter parents in the 1980s, so they don't know any different. Their son resolved not to attend college and pursue his passion—organic farming—before enlisting in the Marines. They agreed with his decision so as not to be hypocrites and because they trust his judgment.

Unlike in Europe or Australia, where students regularly take time off between college and high school, Americans fixate on immediate college enrollment. Brooks writes, "Some kids think they know what they want to do after college, but others don't, so for them college is like buying an expensive insurance policy."

He references research that correlates college degrees only mildly with happiness. Other studies call into question whether a college education *causes* happiness or is the result of other variables such as religious affiliation or income. "Some [researchers] actually believe that education is negatively linked to happiness, and hypothesize that some college attendees trade ambition for life satisfaction.... The evidence on the economic and happiness benefits of college is mixed."

Like Brooks, I also believe "in the power of higher education to change lives and create opportunity." It transformed my life and the lives of countless others. But is it the right fit for everyone? I'm skeptical. However, there are few viable alternatives to earning a living wage without a college degree.

Graduates like me during the Great Recession, and college students who are finishing degrees during the COVID-19 pandemic, struggle mightily to find gainful employment in their fields that pay living wages. Brooks writes, "Past performance is no guarantee of future returns. Many analysts see wage growth stagnating for college graduates, with average starting salaries increasing just 1.4 percent from 2015 to 2018—a period when the economy was roaring." Earnings among recent graduates have stagnated in the past decade while wealth among the Baby Boomer generation increases steadily.

However, times have changed since Arthur Brooks and his wife came of age. They grew up in an era with a robust middle class where people could access jobs that paid living wages without requiring a college degree. Healthcare, housing, childcare, and education were substantially less expensive in the 1970s and '80s relative to today.

My dad could make a living driving bread trucks for 40 years. My mom has worked in elementary education retail, neither of which required any college study. Those days are mostly over. The economy has shifted in remarkable ways even since the Great Recession. Overwhelmingly today, a bachelor's degree of any kind is required to get most types of jobs that pay living wages, let alone career advancement, or as prerequisites to continued graduate studies.

A bachelor's degree has become the new high school degree despite only one in three American adults holding a bachelor's.

Increasingly, master's or PhDs are becoming the new norm in corporate hiring practices, especially at prestigious firms. You can find Pollyannish YouTube videos from "stock advisors" or "entrepreneurs" who rail against a traditional college education and the "9 to 5 scam." They attempt to persuade high school students not to attend. I'm sympathetic and agree with much of what they have to say, but speaking from experience, opting out of conventional society is so much easier with a college degree. If my unconventional lifestyle failed, I could more easily get a job in the US than if I only had a high school degree.

For most high school graduates most of the time, a bachelor's degree is a necessary and unavoidable evil. Daniel Markovits estimates that the bachelor's degree premium on lifetime earnings was double that of the 1980s. Moreover, he writes, "Only about one worker in fifty from the bottom half of the educational distribution makes more than the median worker from the top tenth."[252]

I used to subscribe to Frank Bruni's insistence that whichever college you attend does not define who you will be. I even mailed his book to a few of my clients. But his data and anecdotes from pre-2010 seem outdated.

Our economy is increasingly bifurcating between the kinds of office jobs that allow for remote work during a pandemic and lower-paid yet essential jobs that must be done in person. Daniel Markovits calls this division "glossy" versus "gloomy" jobs. It's less likely today than a decade ago that jobs requiring bachelor's degrees work alongside those who do not. People with college degrees marry each other in record numbers, a departure from trends half a century ago when there wasn't much correlation between the education level of partners.

Failure to earn a college degree is an almost guaranteed consignment to a tenuous existence. Traditionally middle-skill white-collar jobs such as secretarial and paralegal are becoming automated or obsolete. Plumbers, electricians, and others who work in trades aren't compensated at rates that keep pace with living costs, especially when starting their careers. They also have much less professional freedom than generations past due to a few large firms crowding out many smaller ones or freelancers, a tendency toward monopoly experienced in almost every industry.

Receiving a degree from a regional or lesser-known university lowers one's ceiling for future career prospects. Some prominent investment banks and consulting firms told a transfer client of mine attending a public flagship university in the Southeastern Conference (SEC) point-blank that they will never get a job based on the name on their future diploma. Credential discrimination is the antithesis of a meritocracy that is supposed to reward people who "pull themselves up by their bootstraps." Human resources that filter not just by whether one has a degree or not but also the institution attended exacerbates the admissions madness.

Whereas corporate executives in the middle of the twentieth century were more likely to have only a high school degree compared with a college education, more than half of our current financial, political, and corporate leaders hold degrees from just 12 of the country's most elite universities.

Survivorship bias entails that we only hear about the handful of successful people without college degrees and not the thousands of others who failed. For example, even prominent technology executives such as Michael Dell, Bill Gates, and Mark Zuckerberg, attended college for a time rather than forgoing it entirely. Mark Zuckerberg met some of his early business partners in his Harvard classes and residence halls. Another famous college dropout, Steve Jobs, credits his time at Reed College for inspiring the iconic font on Apple's first Macintosh. Among US tech startups, at least 70 percent have one executive-level officer who holds an advanced degree. Almost every successful startup founder holds at least a bachelor's.[253] Many eventual cofounders meet and connect in college, even if they don't complete their studies.

College degrees often fail to reflect the skills they supposedly transfer. Competency-based certificates could be an alternative. One impressive institution and a first mover in the online education space is the nonprofit, private, and regionally accredited Western Governors University (WGU). Their self-paced curricula allow students to earn credit for skills they already have while developing new ones at an affordable cost. That limits repeating classes that a traditional degree often requires. WGU accommodates transfers of credit from most traditional brick-and-mortar schools. It may not provide the "college experience," but what does that even mean anymore in our pandemic era?

Transitioning away from degree credentials and toward a system that favors demonstrated skills and competencies, e.g., programming or web design, would provide stronger signals to prospective employers. A distributed certificate system would help nontraditional students, military veterans, or midcareer professionals who need additional training but aren't well served by traditional four-year degrees. Unlike their elite counterparts, which almost entirely exclude nontraditional transfer applicants, WGU enrolls nearly 140,000 undergraduate and graduate students, average age 36, two-thirds of whom are female.[254] Around 12 percent of their student body is African American, compared with 13 percent of the overall population. WGU is quietly democratizing education and providing the skills that multinational corporations, schools, and government agencies seek. They promote genuine inclusion and access without a brick-and-mortar campus—all with an $800 million annual budget.

NYU Stern Business School professor and education critic Scott Galloway considers what role the COVID-19 pandemic will have on higher education in *Post Corona: From Crisis to Opportunity*. Education is an industry that's changed little over the decades and is ripe for disruption. He observes that early promises of MOOCs, open courseware offered by universities such as MIT and Harvard, or celebrity teachers on the platform Master Class are unlikely to displace elite brick-and-mortar institutions. He agrees that elite universities are here to stay. Middling private institutions and underfunded state universities are at a high risk of failure. Time will tell how many go bankrupt in the next few years for failing to enroll a sufficient number of students.

One alternative he proposes is partnerships between universities and corporations. For example, MIT and Google could provide two-year degrees online, available to many more students, that offer the concrete skills employers need. Since employment practices still overwhelmingly favor a bachelor's degree or higher, they could play a role in crafting curricula and course content. That would secure the benefits of a competencies-based institution like WGU while also providing the gravitas conferred by elite institutions and leading technology brands. Another possibility is that corporations like Apple or Amazon create their own quasi-universities that confer degrees or have a cooperative vocational model that combines work and study.

In a self-serving way, whatever comes of technological disruptions or credential reforms, I'm not worried about losing my job or a decreased demand for my services for the foreseeable future. Our projected decline in high school graduates won't be enough to unseat the demand for spaces at top-50 universities. The gatekeepers are more likely to have their jobs made redundant by advances in artificial intelligence, informatics, and machine learning, or what philosopher of science Nick Bostrom dubs the emergence of "superintelligence." I have no doubt there will be human resource technologies and algorithms that holistic review better than humans, if those capabilities aren't already available today. As long as elite universities have scarce spaces, there will always be a need for services that help families navigate the gatekeepers, even if they become our automated Big Data overlords, rather than today's Diet Coke–guzzling bureaucrats.

As it stands, self-taught programmers often need the validation of a credentialed degree to gain employment. The traditional education system hasn't caught up to the demands of the twenty-first-century knowledge economy. American universities have an almost total monopoly on one's future prospects, just as prospective NFL football players have no other choice but to play collegiate football under the auspices of the NCAA. At least MLB prospects have the option to play college baseball or join, and receive a salary from, the minor league farm system in the US, Mexico, or Japan following high school graduation. Just because a bachelor's degree is unavoidable doesn't mean one needs to pursue it immediately after high school.

A **false dilemma** is a logical error where someone presents two choices—enroll immediately in college or not at all—as the only two options. In fact, there are many questions worth asking to at least consider possible alternatives, including gap years.

I wish more families, especially those from elite backgrounds, had honest conversations with their children about whether a traditional four-year degree, especially at an elite university, is in their best interests. Does their child's temperament fit well in conventional education settings? Are they mature enough and academically prepared to move away from home? Are there alternatives, such as vocational or technical school, to develop their skills and interests? Might there be possibilities for independent or nontraditional studies? If there are hesitations or deep doubts, why not take a year or two off to figure things out without paying a $75,000 tuition and housing premium for "finding yourself?"

I suspect most families fail to ask these questions either because they're unaware of the possibilities or they might be afraid of the answers. Perhaps they fear the shame of being the only family in their social circle to have a non-university-attending child.

Related, I wish community colleges where credits are guaranteed to transfer were a more appealing option, especially to middle-class families who would be burdened by outrageous tuition prices. My brother began his studies at our local college before moving away to earn his bachelor's. He's now a model educator of over 15 years at our former high school and will soon complete his second master's degree.

Affluent parents may pay lip service to the need for trade schools and apprenticeships, but always for "other" families, not their own children. It's certain that in most families, the parents largely dictate their child's academic and career trajectories. They want to mold their children in their own image. That image doesn't involve crawling into attics to repair ventilation systems. For some parents, their child as an engineer or a lawyer isn't good enough. They need to be a doctor, but not just any kind. General practitioners are unacceptable; *we're a family of specialists*, they remind their downtrodden children.

It used to break my heart in UT admissions when parents stepped away for a bathroom break during information sessions, and their children would pull me aside and whisper, "I know my mom is going on and on about medical school and pre-med, but I hate biology. Chemistry sucks. I like writing, and what I really love and want to study and make is film." Or pursue art, become an elementary school teacher, study history, become a social worker, or any number of perfectly fine if not financially lucrative options that in some elite social circles are unacceptable pathways.

Sometimes, my clients are reluctant to share the things they love the most, like baking or writing poetry, because they're not explicitly admissions-related. One girl loved to bake Key lime pies, which only came out at the very end of our call. Her dad said, "I have to tell her to stop making them or give them away! They're too delicious." Some of the best essays I've ever assisted with come from unassuming, non-resume hobbies pursued for their own sake, like the Key lime pies.

One major downside of growing up with affluence and privilege is the attendant sky-high expectations for a narrow range of life possibilities. The educational investments parents make in their children rarely come without strings attached. I meet people on my travels who escaped from the US in part because their parents required them to earn their PhD or enroll in medical school. Some Redditors report that their parents threaten to, or even do, withhold midway through their studies, paying for college if they pursue an "unacceptable"—meaning non-STEM or business—major.

I regularly work with transfer students whose parents coaxed them to attend a particular university and study a specific major, both of which they suspected in advance they wouldn't enjoy, who now need to transfer universities and change majors. I compliment the parent who might have forced their child to study accounting before switching gears, pivoting, and supporting their child's sincere interests unconditionally rather than pigeonholing them down a false path. I wish more parents were as heroically open-minded as Arthur and Ester Brooks.

Although I didn't grow up with much material or educational privileges relative to the kinds of students I work with nowadays, I was free to do or not do just about anything I wanted from elementary school through to university. My parents hoped I would go to college after high school, but it was by no means a foregone conclusion.

When I was at home from college during winter break, my dad once said to me, "I don't know what it is you study at the university, but I see it makes you very happy. You make A's, so you must be good at it, which isn't a surprise to me at all." My mom was thrilled to receive the car insurance discount that comes with earning good grades. If I were going to succeed or fail in my studies, it would be mainly on my own terms with minimal input from my parents. Without their intervention, and likely because of their relative lack of involvement, I thrived.

I raise these preliminary observations to highlight the most significant upside of a gap year. When students hint at a gap year and parents fiercely resist, which are conversations I regularly have, my response is: Why not? What's the worst that can happen? You save some money, and your child is one year more mature and independent than before. Ninety percent of students who take a gap year eventually enroll in college.[255]

Even offering the option of a gap year early on in a student's academic career can alleviate some of the pressures to excel. Offering alternative possibilities will undoubtedly help students establish a sense of control over their lives. When they commit to a course of study or a career, they have greater confidence in their choice.

Once you question the admissions madness and see through society's illusions and the many lies that universities tell, it's hard to see the downsides of taking a year off.

Prospective MBA students are expected to have a few years of professional experience before applying. Most elite law schools prefer applicants who have taken at least some time off following their bachelor's degree. Except for accidents of history and a society maniacal about prestigious undergraduate degrees, there are few if any compelling reasons for jumping straight into one's studies. In most developed countries, the standard is reversed. Immediate college enrollment is somewhat outside of the norm.

Gap years can allow a teenager to explore their interests and have a better idea of what they might want to do, or more importantly, eliminate less appealing academic or career possibilities. One benefit of pursuing a gap year abroad is it doesn't have the stigma of remaining in one's hometown or moving elsewhere in the United States that condescends to teenagers who don't immediately enroll in college. Going abroad, before the COVID-19 pandemic, anyway, guarantees that you're going to meet people from different backgrounds, even if it's an English-speaking tourist or in a volunteer program bubble. Still, you would have to try very hard not to have new experiences while abroad.

Some of the most interesting people I meet on my travels are the teenagers who had the courage (and their parents the willingness to allow them) to take a year off between their studies. I met one of my best friends, Jan from Germany, when he was 19 and I was 26 while he was on his gap year in Central America and Mexico. He filmed my first UT Admissions Guy YouTube videos when I visited him in the Netherlands after he began his business university studies. I've spent time with his family and met his younger brother Luka while he took his gap year in Southeast Asia. Once on a subsequent visit to their family home, I helped him on his high school Chernobyl project after I had recently visited that place.

A typical year abroad may cost anywhere from a little bit more than a year at community college to less than the cost of attending your local public university. One memorable American gap year teenage girl from rural New Hampshire deferred her Harvard enrollment to study indigenous languages in Mexico. Another was taking a mental health leave of absence from Brown University. We all met in 2015 in Quetzaltenango (Xela) in Western Guatemala at the Spanish school *Proyecto Linguistico Quetzalteco* (PLQE).[256]

PLQE provided one of the best educational environments I've ever experienced, and that includes my most rigorous UT-Austin honors classes. All of our teachers were local Guatemalans who held bachelor's or advanced degrees and often worked as engineers, lawyers, or technocrats. PLQE also accommodated parents and their young children, retirees, and working professionals. Each student received five hours of Spanish instruction one on one, five days a week.

I spent six weeks there and improved my Spanish from upper elementary (A2) to lower advanced (C1). While I was taking lessons, Guatemala descended into political protests, resulting in the first president in Latin American history, Otto Perez Molina, to step down following a peaceful revolution. Taking advanced lessons with lawyers or social activists helped me develop more nuanced views on important issues of the day.

For around $300 per week, we received 25 hours of instruction and full room and board with a local family. Every afternoon and weekend, there were optional trips covered by our tuition using local transport and guided by one of our teachers to women's cooperatives, K'iche villages, rural *campesino* farms, and sites of natural beauty or historical importance. I sometimes served as a translator for less-experienced students.

The girl deferring Harvard from rural New Hampshire spent a few weeks at PLQE's "Mountain School" outside the city to volunteer and learn K'iche.[257] Consider that one semester of tuition at NYU ($26,500) could fund the equivalent of 88 weeks studying and living at PLQE. You could theoretically live at PLQE for four and a half years at the same price as a full year's NYU tuition and living expenses.

One of my favorite people I've met abroad is Wilder, who was 18 years old, and I was 27 when we spent a week together in 2016 in Swakopmund, Namibia.[258] For whatever reason, Wilder from wooded New England had a fascination with deserts. Namibia is mostly desert, famous for the Skeleton Coast and the setting for

Mad Max: Fury Road. Swakopmund is one of the world's driest cities despite being on the ocean and almost always cloudy. A surreal mist hangs over the town.

Wilder eventually enrolled at Sewanee University while spending time as an outdoor adventure guide. Eventually, he pursued environmental engineering studies related to clean water extraction and preservation. He studied abroad in arid Tunisia before receiving an international Watson fellowship to study in the Netherlands and other countries such as India, Peru, and Australia to explore how different cultures perceive the value of water.[259] Coincidentally, I met another Watson fellow conducting marine ecology conversation work in the Philippines.

One of the things I love most about traveling is that the things that seem to matter most back home are almost completely irrelevant abroad, for example your age, skin color, education level, hometown, your material possessions, what you majored in, where you work, what were your SATs, etc. I seek out people who are curious, conscientious, and make an effort to know themselves and our world. All that matters is who you show up as each day and your openness to new experiences.

Saying yes to something is so much easier when you're not worried about how it will affect your colleague's or classmate's perceptions or your college admissions chances. It's also easier to opt out and say no to that which doesn't interest or serve you. There isn't a pressure to commit to something out of a misplaced sense of obligation. That degree of freedom and autonomy is simply something you can never find while remaining in the same system that you were born into.

People taking gap years can explore their interests and develop their identities away from their parents' prying eyes or hovering blades. The biggest complaint from them and friends of mine like Jan is they feel somewhat out of place relative to their more immature and less socially developed classmates when they eventually enroll in college. In turn, their year or two away helps them excel in college and strike a more manageable work/life balance. Spending time away from one's hometown or country enables you to see the bigger picture and acknowledge concerns beyond a narrow worldview.

When I followed up with travel friends who've taken gap years and subsequently applied for and enrolled at their university, they universally reported that it was beneficial. Around 3 percent of Americans who eventually enroll in college take an intentional gap year, which is, frankly, higher than I would have expected.[260] Surveys suggest that students who take a gap year overwhelmingly report that it contributed to personal growth, increased maturity and self-confidence, improved communication skills, especially cross-culturally, and helped them find their life direction.[261]

I've met people on gap years learning non-college skills like permaculture, yoga and meditation, SCUBA or free diving, kayaking, salsa and other dancing, conservation, world music and art, wilderness survival, storytelling/blogging, etc. Americans age 18 to 30 have access to one-year Working Holiday Visa (WHV) schemes that allow employment in Australia, Ireland, New Zealand, Singapore, South Korea, and Canada. WHVs allow the holder multiple entries and exits and to open a bank account for legal employment. They're entitled to all the rights, benefits, and protections as residents of that country. I know people who have worked on ranches, farms, yoga studios, government agencies, wineries, cafes, and so on. My Dutch girlfriend and I met in New Zealand while she was taking a mid-career break to pursue her WHV.

In college, students who took a gap year tend to have higher grades and graduate on time relative to their non–gap year peers, which contradicts parental concerns that their children will fall behind academically by taking a year off from school.[262] Taking a gap year may diminish the chances of having mental health issues in college that necessitate a leave of absence. Gap years improve retention and graduation rates.[263] Indirectly then, gap years improve one's graduate school prospects. Some universities even offer incentives for deferred enrollment. For example, Duke University began a scholarship program to a few dozen students each year to facilitate structured gap years.[264] When doing your college search, ask the admissions offices what their policy on deferment is and any scholarships available to facilitate gap years.

Of course, during our current pandemic, taking a gap year abroad is difficult, if not impossible. At some point in the hopefully not-so-distant future, and perhaps by the time this book is published, our world will have returned to some semblance of normality. I've loved my year spent in New Zealand's safe haven, but I miss living in the tropical, developing world. I went abroad originally to lend expression to a deep yearning I've felt since going on cruise ships with my mom as a teen.

My mom was especially fearful of me going abroad, even to Scotland in 2009, for a summer university exchange. Part of me resents her living out of fear and imposing those insecurities on me, although I acknowledge that it's a mother's job to worry. It saddens me to know that there are many other people with similar ambitions and come from affluence whose families will not permit them to explore abroad due to a misplaced sense of fear or worries that they're somehow missing out on the "college experience."

I went to Bosnia, Rwanda, and beyond after securing scholarships and setting an ultimatum to my parents: This is going to be my life, so you better get used to it. Only after creating a profitable business while traveling the world did my mom ease up and acknowledge that I'm living my best life and becoming my best self.

I also don't think gap years are something parents should impose on their child. Allow it as a possibility and offer them space and resources to make the option realistic. It shouldn't be a means to an end or an opportunity to bolster one's resume for a future college admissions cycle. Yet, a gap year will improve your future admissions chances. Anticipating a gap year early on in high school could forgo the senior year application process entirely. Applying to college after graduating high school lessens a lot of the stress and peer pressure because anxious classmates and social media posts do not surround you.

My advice for a gap year is to leave it semi-structured or entirely unstructured. Buy a one-way ticket somewhere, book a week's accommodation at a hostel, and figure it out. For anyone reading this who has done their own open-ended travels, you know almost immediately that many people are "on the road" taking similar journeys. You don't stay lonely or alone or without direction for long. That tolerance for adventure is probably not palatable to even the most open-minded families. Instead, it may help to plan a month or two of volunteering or language school at places like PLQE.

I'm not naïve enough to think some parents, and mine included, would ever permit their child to gallivant for a year without a "plan." Isn't it strange, though, that some won't blink an eye at throwing three or four times that amount of money to send them to Zoom University?

I've complimented the handful of families who gained admission at elite universities but forewent enrollment during the COVID-19 pandemic. It's completely irrational that demand for elite universities remains high even during virtual learning. For some of my transfer clients, I ask what in the world they were thinking of paying full-price tuition at an out-of-state or private university only to spend freshman year in their bedroom.

I don't recommend paying for some expensive gap-year program that structures an entire year down to the hour. Some of these paid-for gap year programs are better than others. There are even gap year fairs to connect with programs (gooversea.com). Most programs are quite expensive, and there are, unsurprisingly, consulting firms that charge hefty fees to google what you could otherwise find yourself. One family reported excellent experiences with Winterline Global Skills that teaches life and survival skills over nine to ten months, for example, but as with anything, research your options and become an informed consumer.

I suppose a highly structured program is better than nothing, and for many families, that's the only risk that would be tolerated. I'm agnostic on which program is preferable to another. These gap year firms capitalize on anxious parents who are insecure about sending their child abroad. They take advantage of your relative ignorance about the unknown and charge exorbitant fees for promises of safety and security. In my experiences, especially with language schools in Guatemala, Peru, and Indonesia, you can find perfectly safe, high-quality experiences at lower prices than what these gap year agencies offer.

Call me a purist, but travel needs to have some degree of uncertainty, serendipity, and possibility of failure. Spending time abroad or away from home can be stressful and anxiety inducing. Traveling doesn't have a predefined pathway for what success looks like. Thriving abroad isn't like an AP or SAT exam you can master with sufficient effort and tutoring. But that's the point.

Some balance between planned programs and unstructured time seems ideal to me. When I meet young Europeans or Aussies on my travels, they typically volunteer or study a language for the first month or two before finding other opportunities while on the ground. They also tend to work and travel through WHV schemes at higher rates than Americans. If something terrible happens or you're homesick, the world is so connected—or hopefully will be in a year or two—that you're only a day or two plane ride away from returning home or parents coming to visit.

I'm going out on a limb here by suggesting that a gap year should be outside the helicopter parents' tendencies for total control and meticulous planning. To those parents, for once, consider the possibility of letting your child thrive, that there's more to life than earning A's and padding their resume. Allowing them a little bit of independence might just surprise you when you see what they're capable of.

NYU professor Scott Galloway calls for gap years to become the norm and not the exception. It helps prepare children for the future. He laments, "An increasingly ugly secret of campus life is that a mix of helicopter parenting and social media has rendered many 18-year-olds unfit for college."[265] Many students at elite universities haven't been permitted to develop the soft skills, the autonomy of thought, or the overall maturity required for thriving on college campuses. They're the UT Honors classmates who I bested in scholarship and research competitions because they had taken their access to a high-quality education for granted. My overly coddled peers hadn't sufficiently developed the intrinsic motivation and curiosity required of innovative and thought-provoking research. I earned better grades and had a lot more fun in college than most of my peers from the most privileged families and high schools.

I want to leave this topic with a final vignette and conclude with a thought experiment. I know a select few, whether teenagers or adults, feel like they don't quite fit into conventional society and yearn for something different. They question conventional wisdom and wonder if there is an alternative way of living. I write this primarily with them in mind, not the students who plan their lives from pre-med to residency or whose conviction is to become a Wall Street investment banker.

Following my traumatic Fulbright fellowship in Malaysia and to the protests of my mom, who preferred I lead a "normal life," I booked a one-way ticket to Cancun, Mexico, for a college friend's destination wedding. I had savings, a few skills (SCUBA Divemaster and ESL teaching), and vague notions of starting a college consulting business. Otherwise, I had absolutely no plan. It was the first step toward living my dream life on my terms. I would have it no other way.

On the plane from Dallas to Cancun, I penned a journal entry "The Beginning" on February 25, 2015:

"The last time I departed the US via plane fourteen months ago was under very different circumstances. I headed off to Malaysia for my Fulbright fellowship to begin an experience I thought I wanted. Despite the ability to live abroad and travel subsidized by the US and Malaysian governments, it wasn't what I wanted. Deep down, I knew that yet refused to listen. I am not making that mistake this time. My own contentedness is entirely up to me. No government job, no colleagues, no ex-girlfriend, no school, no one to report to. The temptation to give in to the pull of 'the plan' to lay out things in advance was strong; however, I have conviction in keeping things open-ended. I am the pilot of my own destiny."

In that same entry, I noted how much slower other people seem to grow in conventional systems. Being told what to read and write, what work projects to commit to, and which networking events to attend might work for some or even most people, but it seemed stifling to me. I spent my two months at home following

Malaysia studying and working on personal projects. I reread the ten most influential books at that point in my life, including Nassim Taleb's *Antifragile*, Robert Greene's *Mastery*, and the *Art of Non-Conformity* by Chris Guillebeau. I integrated these three books into a series of hypotheses about what my unconventional future might entail. I still refer to my "synthesis project" once a year to see how my ideas have played out in practice.

Just before flying to Mexico, I wrote, "It is remarkable just how productive I can be when I am not accountable to anyone or being told what to do. I have to imagine that people who work in jobs they don't enjoy are at a disadvantage because they're locked out of their creative potential. If I keep growing at this rate, I am curious to see where I'm at in five years." Even then, not in my wildest dreams did I imagine my level of professional success, the number of deep and meaningful relationships I've made, and the scope of life experiences that my years abroad have brought me, exactly six years after beginning my journey. My wish is that everyone has the opportunity to realize their potential, whatever that might involve.

My first year abroad on my own terms was expectedly rocky. I spent many anxious nights sleepless. I hid my concerns from travel acquaintances and wore a false bravado that suggested everything was okay. I wrote to a close friend in May 2015, a month after starting my business: "There is an interesting fear that's creeping up. Nothing too severe, but this occasional [feeling] that this whole thing will be a total failure. I don't really care about the money side of it, but if it does succeed, it will be the ultimate validation and access to a lifestyle completely of my own choosing."

More than a fear of failure, I dreaded a life resigned to mediocrity. I applied tremendous pressure on myself to juggle a new relationship, constant movement, and Spanish language classes while building Tex Admissions from hostels, bus stops, and homestays with dodgy wifi. Inviting uncertainty and risk into my life during relatively calmer global times helps me adjust when the world falls apart, like during the current pandemic. It isn't accidental that I went to and remained in COVID-free New Zealand and Australia. My lifestyle is an adaptation optimizing for survival.

I view myself in the words of Pennsylvania Wharton professor Adam Grant, author of *Originals*, as a "shaper." I'm a curious, non-conforming rebel who practices "brutal, non-hierarchical honesty." I reject the defaults that society offers and actively explore other possibilities. I check my own **biases for the status quo.** He offers four responses for people we commonly call "black sheep" that have different ideas about their lives from what their family or society expects: "exit, voice, persistence, and neglect. Only exit and voice improve your circumstances."[266]

"Neglect" pushes your concerns aside and inevitably leads to college mental health leaves of absence, professional burnouts, and midlife crises. "Persistence" entails continuing down a false path and doing the same things over and over while expecting different results. Grit and sticking with it isn't admirable if you loathe waking up each day.

I admire activists with skin in the game who use their voices and platforms to fight within systems to enact meaningful reform. I don't doubt that it's possible to maintain a balance between professional ambitions, personal relationships, and getting enough sleep every night in our fast-paced world, but that conventional life isn't for me. I've known since high school that I didn't fit in. My existential loneliness continued throughout university, working in UT admissions, and my Fulbright fellowship. Rather than persist and constantly push back on society's mores and customs, I exited the system.

I've found like-minded people and feel a sense of community among other nonconformists. I prefer to chip away at the Ivory

Tower walls from the outside than making minimal differences working from within, as I outlined in chapter 8.3 about Dashboard. My ideas reach more people in one year through my blogs and YouTube channels than if I spent a lifetime working inside a university. I'm writing this book in part to offer a vocabulary to the misfits and anomalies of all ages and backgrounds who question if there might be another way to do things.

Mahatma Gandhi's life inspires us to be the change we wish to see in the world. It isn't naïve to wish for a society that nourishes human flourishing, where rising tides really do raise all ships. Only by identifying flaws in our all-too-human, deeply broken systems can we carve out our own paths and identify possible solutions.

I carried a copy of Friedrich Nietzsche's (1844–1900) magnum opus *Thus Spoke Zarathustra* with me to Mexico.[267] A few political theory and philosophy college courses touched on him, but it had lain forgotten on my bookshelf. It was and remains the single most challenging book I've ever read. It's hard for me to conceive any book that could be more important to me than *Zarathustra*. I understand better the feelings elicited from religious worshippers when they read *The Bible, Quran,* or the *Mahabharata.* They aren't simply books to Christians, Muslims, or Hindus; they're guides, pinpricks of light in a world of shadow.

Perhaps like a student tackling the Old Testament for the first time, I understood almost nothing on a first read of what Zarathustra was up to when he descended from his cave into varied hamlets and had bizarre dialogues with eagles and corpses. But there seemed to be some timeless wisdom worth digging deeper to discover.

I set aside *Zarathustra* and instead spent a week reading the Sparknotes of all his other works. For the next six months, I hunted down and found in English bookstores in Mexico and Guatemala many of his primary texts like *The Gay Science, The*

Twilight of Idols, and *The Birth of Tragedy*. I don't have an eReader, or at the time, a smartphone. I carried the hardcopies with me and sent them home with my parents when they visited me in Mexico. They brought an anthology for me to continue my studies. Their visit was my dad's first time out of the country in over 20 years.

Nietzsche was a "rising star" in his day, the youngest person to hold the Chair of Classical Philology at the University of Basel in 1869 at 24.[268] Philology was an umbrella term that encompassed the studies of historical texts, in his case, Ancient Greek poetry along with Latin and Hebrew. Before he moved to Basel, he renounced his Prussian citizenship (a part of Germany before the 1871 unification). He lived the rest of his life stateless, something that isn't possible to choose today.

He wrote *Zarathustra* over four periods of ten days each from 1883 to 1885. Reading his thoughts on his own writing process reminded me of the profound creativity I experienced when I wrote 60,000 words of this book in the draft's first two weeks. Focused creativity gives my life purpose. Like him, I took daily long walks and noted in my journal the ideas that appeared.

For Nietzsche, each of his books that came before *Zarathustra* built up to one of the most creative outbursts in human history. Subsequent works like *On the Genealogy of Morals* and *Beyond Good and Evil* attempted to explain to his confused audiences what *Zarathustra* meant by "God is dead." *Zarathustra* turns traditional morality on its head. Religious systems and cultural values that claim to have our best interests in mind are more interested in extracting tithes and owning our sense of right and wrong. Nietzsche called bullshit on organized religion and his day's dominant value systems. He insisted there must be alternative ways of living.

Similarly, I refuse to justify an admissions system that is neither fair nor just. In the college admissions context, universities have made virtues of holistic review, diversity, and academic excellence. Instead, their supposedly pro-social values corrupt society. Elite college admissions oppresses marginalized populations and distorts the interests and character of their mostly affluent student bodies. Like Zarathustra, I've questioned the myths that admissions offices convey and that society believes, ending with skepticism about whether one needs to enroll in college immediately after high school. I've redefined conventional standards of excellence and growth beyond resumes, corporate hierarchies, advanced degrees, or social esteem in my personal and professional life. I am only in competition with my own potential. I haven't had a resume in five years, and I hope never to have one again.

From my early readings, I started to gather that Nietzsche didn't just take a gap year following his permanent departure from his prestigious professorship at Basel at age 35. He wasn't like the German philosopher Immanuel Kant (1724–1804), who lived on a rigid schedule with predictable routines. Residents of Kant's lifelong home in Konigsberg are reported to have set their watches to his afternoon walk through the park. In contrast, Nietzsche wandered Europe at his leisure, living with friends and off a modest pension. His remaining years were the most productive of his life. In Adam Grant's framework, he was an irreverent original who exited the system. He lived a gap life on his terms.

He's perhaps the most misunderstood philosopher of all time. His critics say he advocated nihilism or that we should somehow embrace a lack of meaning in our own lives. Instead, he observed that we live in a world increasingly without traditional sources of meaning such as religion and community. The system, he claimed, was broken.

Our deeply divided and depressed society is a direct extension of the criticisms Nietzsche made about Europe during the Industrial Revolution. Powerful governments and religious institutions fear those who think for themselves. His ideas were dangerous. If sufficient numbers of people opt out of their rules and regulations, how can they exploit our labors or claim ownership to our souls?

He advocated for free thinking. It's up to each of us to find our purposes, our paths, despite whatever obstacles, hardships, or structural oppression life throws our way. Meaning comes from within. Even for his detractors, he's considered one of the most brilliant if deeply flawed people in human history. Since his untimely passing, he's influenced every prominent Western philosopher and many poets, writers, and social scientists.

I read every analysis by the eminent Nietzsche scholar Walter Kaufmann. He rehabilitated Nietzsche's reputation following a disfigurement and corruption of his ideas by Germany's Kaiser Wilhelm I and later by Hitler. Nietzsche's writings were never intended as a political philosophy or a system of governance. Almost every other modern commentary or popular portrayal of his work inevitably gets his philosophy and biography wrong.

I found and studied the works that influenced Nietzsche, such as Stendhal's *The Red and the Black* (1830). Stendhal's protagonist Julien Sorel lays the foundation for Nietzsche's critique of flawed aristocratic virtues. Much of Fyodor Dostoevsky's creative life began around the time that Nietzsche's ended. Stendhal and Dostoevsky wrote poignantly about aristocratic caste systems and social inequalities in their time that also apply to contemporary American meritocracy.

Contemporary author and Man Booker Prize winner Aravind Adiga's book *The White Tiger* (2008) follows the same tradition of Nietzsche and Dostoevsky. The protagonist Balram Halwai ruthlessly breaks from his community and traditional systems of morality to become a successful entrepreneur in India's highly unequal caste society. The 2021 award-winning film adaptation provides a scathing commentary on the impossibility of "pulling oneself up by their bootstraps" using ethical or decent means. Balram is a white tiger, the rarest and most mythical animal in the forest, destined for power and freedom. He is what Nietzsche would call an Overman, a person who constructs value systems outside of conventional norms.

After weaseling his way into a prominent family as one of their drivers, Balram's story concludes with him murdering his boss and stealing a substantial sum of money, resulting in his entire family being killed. He lives at peace in Bangalore under an assumed identity rather than hammer coal bricks for sixteen hours each day in "the Darkness" in his home village, Laxmangarh. Balram rejects the Indian caste system, what he calls "the rooster coop." Roosters trapped in a coop know that they will die next, yet they do nothing to resist. The only way into "the Light" is for Balram to manipulate and conquer any person in his path. Balram's life is analogous to Stendhal's Julien Sorel, who, through cunning and wit, triumphed over French aristocracy, or like Dostoevsky's "underground man" who opted out of conventional society.

Neither Adiga nor Nietzsche advocate for committing crimes or lawlessness. But when society pushes people into corners and leaves them no other options, like a tiger pacing the cage of a zoo, then humans desperate to break out of figurative prisons will sometimes do whatever it takes to live life on their own terms. I'm thankful that I was born into a society where I needn't run roughshod over people or commit crimes or indecent acts to "get out" of my hometown.

I digested Greek plays that featured Dionysus, the god of wine who brings joy to the suffering, to put my own unapologetic love of life's pleasures in context. I studied French existentialists such as Albert Camus and Jean-Paul Sartre, who embrace Nietzsche's observation that life is a struggle and one worth fighting for. Each were heavily influenced by Nietzsche's conception of the "overman" and "the will to power." I read the complete essays of Y Combinator founder and hacker philosopher Paul Graham who follows Nietzsche's irreverent style by nurturing technological innovators who disrupt twenty-first-century marketplaces.

After my year in Latin America, I began 2016 in Southern Africa. I reread almost all of Nietzsche's supporting texts that provide context to *Zarathustra*. When I finally revisited *Zarathustra* following three chaotic, exciting, and dangerous years abroad, the book clicked. I reread *Zarathustra* a third time in 2019, and it drank like water in the desert. The best books fascinate me more than the most exotic travel destinations.

Only after following four years of independent study and living on my own terms, and developing a value system contrary to most social norms, did his philosophy and psychology make sense. His works and those he influenced helped give me a vocabulary and framework to make sense of my life within the world's broader context. It isn't like I read his or any self-help books and decided that's how I would live my life. Living comes first, theorizing second.

Studying Nietzsche in a college environment wouldn't make any sense because he is a practical philosopher. Understanding his life and ideas comes only through exiting the system and living life on your own terms. Academics almost always miss his primary points because they're studying his thoughts in a vacuum. They think and talk about him in the abstract, whereas I feel and carry on his legacy.

My message isn't that everyone should read Nietzsche or the books that have inspired me. Instead, I challenge you to find the authors and vocabularies that help provide context to your feelings and values. Books that tell you how to live will always be less interesting than those that teach you how to think. That's why I'm not writing yet another how-to-apply-to-college book but instead one that questions fundamental college admissions assumptions.

My first book, *Your Ticket to the Forty Acres*, was an initial attempt at sharing my views of the world as I see it. I sprinkled in some controversial ideas but kept the tone composed and inoffensive. *Surviving the College Admissions Madness* begins integrating my unconventional personal life with my professional perspectives. It is a takedown of an unjust admissions system that stifles human thriving and well-being, the two things that concerned Nietzsche most. His life-affirming wish was that every person can maximize their potential.

I'm unconcerned if my calls for reformation equate to heresy against the admissions gods. Copernicus feared that publishing his heliocentric theories would risk excommunication from the Catholic church. Decades later, Galileo took up the Copernican cause of proving that Earth revolves around the Sun. For his contributions, the Roman Inquisition declared him a heretic and sentenced him to a lifetime of house arrest for contradicting the Holy Scripture. Original ideas are dangerous, but changing the world never comes from taking the safe path. I read so many ambitious and idealistic college essays about changing the world. As you grow older, stay true to those intuitions and don't allow society to squeeze out your creativity and hope.

I'm currently working on my memoirs of an unconventional existence tentatively titled *From Texas to Bali* that will carry on where this book leaves off. I take aim at society as a whole instead of focusing narrowly on college admissions. In the scripture of the Bhagavad Gita, I'm following my *dharma* (loosely translated as one's obligations to society in accordance with one's essence and conscience). Lord Krishna said to the conflicted warrior-prince Arjuna that "it is better to strive in one's own *dharma* than to succeed in the *dharma* of another."[269]

If you've made it this far, I thank you for your patience and attention. I hope my book has proven thought-provoking, entertaining, and, at times, exasperating. I want to leave you with my favorite question of all time.

The "Eternal Recurrence of the Same" is a thought experiment and an ethical guide. It helps the inquirer determine if they're on their right path and to what degree they may regret their past behaviors. I reread my journals from previous years when I return home, and it's the central question that guides the examination of my past behavior and beliefs. It helps me determine whether I'm staying true to myself and am on the right path.

Nietzsche asks: Would you wish to relive your life exactly as you have, in an infinite number of lives for all eternity? Would you relive "every pain and every pleasure, every friend and every enemy, every hope and every error, every blade of grass and every ray of sunshine once more, and the whole fabric of things which make up your life?" [270]

His hypothetical stipulates that you cannot change any of your behavior. That entails reliving every regret, harm caused to another, and missed opportunity precisely as it has already occurred. The eternal recurrence of the same differs from karmic reincarnation into another being in a future life in Hindu or Buddhist traditions or some Christian interpretations of predestination. It instead serves as a bellwether for whether you're on your ideal life path, and if not, what steps can you take to right the ship?

What path are you on, and is it true to your character and aptitudes? What regrets might you have in the future for roads not traveled?

Choose wisely. You only live once. And with your decisions forever.

Acknowledgments

My second book has flowed more quickly than the first, thanks largely to a thoughtful and eager support network. I wrote my first book mainly in isolation, wandering around the Caribbean and South America without feedback or input from others.

First and foremost, I want to thank my partner, Judith. We met just before the pandemic and the global lockdowns starting in March 2020. The ideas presented in this book have been floating around for years. She posed the challenge that nudged me over the edge: "What if twenty years from now, all that you've done or written is your first book?"

She supported me when I elected to go into solitude for three weeks in New Zealand's South Island foothills, where I wrote the first pages of this book. I know it isn't easy being with someone who wakes up in the middle of the night to write or pulls the car over to jot down new ideas. Writing a book can be a moody, all-consuming process. I appreciate her patience, kindness, and willingness to read my rough drafts from start to finish despite English being her second language and a relative lack of familiarity with American college admissions. We're both grateful to the New Zealand and Australian governments for allowing us to stay in relative safety during COVID-19. Writing a book is comparatively more manageable when you don't have to worry about getting sick or being separated from your partner.

One lesson I learned from launching my first book is that you cannot produce a high-quality product without the assistance of professional services. Retaining the Auckland-based creative and content production agency Augusto and Corner Store has lessened the stress of book cover design, branding, and crafting the public face of *Admissions Madness*. Thanks to Kimberley Warren, Mariano Segedin, Bronwyn Williams, and the rest of the team for helping me produce a provocative design scheme to match my irreverent message.

Meredith Tennant has done an excellent job catching all of the minor mistakes, errors, and omissions. Editing for detail is a continued improvement area for me, and her feedback helps polish my ideas and present them with precision and clarity. Mohamed Zalabia provided his expertise with the tedious task of making sense of and organizing my endnotes and citations. Paul Sutliff put together a comprehensive index. Andrea Reider helped format the Kindle and paperback versions. My publicist Rob Nissen has helped my message spread as widely as possible and contribute to nationwide college admissions and higher education conversations. Kaylan Madrid manages the social media side and helps put out my video content. Thank you to Nigel Pegrum of Pegasus Studios in Cairns, Australia, for recording and producing the audiobook.

Dozens of students, friends, colleagues, and parents offered feedback. I want to thank Steve Schwartz, David Herrick, Ryu Parish, Caitlin James, Keren Cherian, Savindu Wimalasooriya, Matt Portillo, Joseph Wegener, Aron Qiu, Milan Patel, James Schnoebelen, Ishika Puri, Jeff Giddens, and Kaylan Madrid. Any mistakes, errors, and controversies are my responsibility alone.

Finally, I want to thank my parents Pam and Paul Martin, for allowing me to grow and accepting my unconventional lifestyle.

I've only been home for two months total since January 2017. Each will be the first to tell you that it isn't a parent's dream to have a world-traveling child, but they're happy that I'm happy. I came from a community where a little bit of bad luck can lead to catastrophic consequences. Had they hovered over and micro-managed my childhood, I'm sure I wouldn't have taken such travel big risks or dared to become an entrepreneur and author. I had the great fortune of being born into a loving family with a wonderful grandmother and a supportive older brother. Love you, family, even when we're hemispheres apart.

Appendix:
Glossary of Cognitive Biases
and Reasoning Errors

Definitions adapted from Wikipedia articles on each topic, accessed on February 12, 2021.

Affective or Hedonic Forecasting – A broad category of cognitive biases and psychological effects suggesting that we're not very good at predicting what will bring happiness.

Anchoring Effect – An individual who depends too heavily on an initial piece of information that distorts their subsequent decision making. Anchoring limits one's ability to change course or account for new information that may undermine the initial belief.

Apophenia – The tendency to perceive meaningful connections between unrelated things.

Application and Mission Creep – A gradual or incremental increase beyond the original intentions, i.e., continuing to add applications in November that weren't part of the summer list.

Argument from Incredulity – Logical fallacy where a situation that seems highly improbable or impossible to imagine is in fact true. "I can't believe that university denied this incredible student!"

Availability Cascade – The tendency for crowds to adopt the same simple explanation for a complex situation as that explanation gains popularity, even if the explanation is flawed.

Availability Heuristic – Placing too much emphasis on an example that's readily available and recently accessed, i.e., a student looking at their classmates' admissions outcomes while failing to account for the small or nonrepresentative sample size.

Bandwagon Effect – The tendency for an individual to adopt a behavior or belief because that's what everyone else does, i.e., overemphasis on the Ivy League.

Causal Oversimplification – Attributing a single cause to explain a complex situation, usually in reference to students pointing to "the thing" that "got them in" or was responsible for their rejection. In reality, no admissions decision is ever due to a single cause.

Cherry Picking – Selectively choosing a single instance or example to support an argument while ignoring evidence to the contrary.

Choice Supportive Bias – The tendency to positively weight a previous option or de-emphasize another when the situation changes. "I never wanted to go to that school anyways," or a student who sees their safety school in a renewed light.

Chronological Snobbery – The belief that beliefs or behaviors in the present are superior to those from the past, or that past societies or institutions were less intelligent than the present.

Confirmation Bias – The tendency to search for information that confirms one's beliefs or worldview while excluding evidence that calls their position into question.

Continued Influence Effect – We tend to weigh information we receive first more heavily than subsequent data. Universities recruit students earlier than ever to exploit this tendency.

Courtesy Bias – The tendency to not disclose one's true feelings so as not to offend or to express politeness toward someone asking them a question or responding to a survey.

Crab Mentality – If live crabs in a bucket cooperated, they could make a mountain for others to climb on top of and out to freedom. Some crabs would inevitably get left behind. Instead, each crab pulls the higher ones down so that no crabs escape. It's the selfish tendency to believe, "If I can't have it, neither can you."

Default to Truth – We tend to default to believing what people say, resulting in the inability to detect fraud or reluctance to call out potential lies.

Dunning-Kruger Effect – Coined from social psychologists David Dunning and Justin Kruger who identified the effect. People lowest in ability or knowledge tend to express the most confidence in their beliefs. Online college admissions message boards are a Dunning-Kruger hurricane.

Egocentric Bias – Overreliance on one's personal perspective to make generalized claims about the world or larger systems.

Fading Affect Bias - Memories associated with negative emotions tend to be forgotten more quickly than those associated with positive emotions.

False Dilemma Effect – Mistaking the rejection of one option for an endorsement of another without acknowledging a third possibility. Either I go to school or I don't go ignores that delaying college with a gap year is a valid alternative.

First Mover Problem – Constitutes either an advantage or disadvantage to be the first person or institution to do something. In college admissions, universities are highly reluctant to move first on any topic (e.g., forbidding the SAT or adopting a lottery), so moving first functions as a deterrent to widespread reform.

Fundamental Attribution Error – The tendency to believe that how people act defines who they are without paying sufficient attention to the context or situation. It fuels the sometimes-mistaken belief of "once a cheater, always a cheater."

Furtive Fallacy – When people attribute mistake or malice that results in a disappointing outcome, i.e., rejected students claiming that the university erred in their decision making or disliked them on a personal level.

Group Attribution Error – The tendency to believe that the characteristics of an individual group member reflect the group as a whole, i.e., an exceptional student from one school implying everyone at the school is exceptional.

Hasty Generalization – An error of inductive reasoning where someone mistakenly believes that past trends will result in future outcomes. It creates the tendency to rush to conclusions without considering a sufficient amount of evidence.

Hindsight Bias – The mistaken tendency to believe that past events were more predictable than they were at the time. Stimulates the reaction of "I knew all along that I would get denied." If you knew it with certainty, why waste any time applying at all? Some part of you must have felt you had a chance.

Hostile Attribution Bias – The tendency to interpret a benign or indifferent behavior as hostile, i.e., "the university rejected me because they're evil." In reality, they don't care about you one way or another.

Humor Bias – The tendency for funny memories or information to stick stronger relative to something mundane or banal.

Hyperbolic Discounting – Signals a disconnect between short-term and long-term preferences. Students prefer to gain admission to their dream schools while discounting the long-term potential consequences to their mental health or student debt load.

"I can't stand it here!" Fallacy – A term I've coined to describe the tendency specific to college admissions for some students to want to attend an out-of-state university for no other reason than they can't stand their current situation. This ignores the fact that Texas or California are huge states. They often pay a high cost for wanting to move far away from home.

Illusion of Validity – A cognitive bias where a person overestimates their ability to interpret and predict accurately the outcome when analyzing a set of data. They find patterns in the data that fit the hypothesis or predicted outcomes of a given tool used to assess or acquire the data. Holistic review tools give the illusion of validity because a high four-year graduation rate is misattributed to the utility of the process. In reality, a lottery may produce similar effects, diminishing the confidence admissions counselors place in their predictive abilities.

Illusory Superiority – A cognitive bias where someone overestimates or is overconfident in their skills or knowledge relative to the average. Admissions counselors have the illusion that they're better judges of character and student success than non-admissions counselors.

Incomplete Comparison – A statistics mistake where an individual draws strong conclusions without access to a complete data set.

Inconsistent Comparison – Commonly known as incorrectly comparing apples with oranges. Naviance scatterplots might show overall university outcomes for classmates from your school, but if you're applying to Computer Science, it may not be appropriate to compare your credentials with a dataset composed of students from all majors.

Information Paradox – The counterintuitive notion that the more information we access, the less knowledge we may possess. Acquiring more information, such as reading admission statistics and overconsuming college guides, produces more confusion and anxiety. Sometimes, less is more, or some ignorance might produce bliss.

Insensitivity to the Sample Size – An error of statistical reasoning of drawing strong conclusions from an insufficient dataset.

Most commonly occurs when students make sweeping conclusions about what it takes to get into a given university by comparing the outcomes of them and their 50 friends while failing to account the 100,000 other applicants.

Is/Ought Fallacy– Mistakenly assuming that because something is a certain way, that it should be that way. Conversely, just because you believe something ought to be the case doesn't make it so.

"Just to see if you can get in" Fallacy – A term I've coined to describe the tendency when building your college list to apply for very high reaches where your chances of gaining admission are close to zero, wasting time, money, and emotional distress. See: Lloyd's Fallacy.

Just World Fallacy – The mistaken belief that good things happen to good people and bad people get what they deserve. Sometimes, cheaters gain admissions and honest students are rejected.

Law of the Instrument – A cognitive bias that produces an over-reliance on familiar tools. Students sometimes write their college essays as if they are literary criticism because that's how AP English Language and Literature teaches writing. "To a hammer, everything looks like a nail."

Lloyd's "so you're saying there's a chance" Fallacy – A term I've coined to describe the overweighting of a statistically highly improbable outcome as having more weight. Usually due to wishful thinking or believing oneself to be more exceptional or deserving.

Loss Aversion – The behavioral economics finding that losses hurt more than the good feelings generated from equivalent winnings.

Ludic Fallacy – Coined by Nassim Taleb to describe the misattribution of making complex decisions where some information is unknown as equivalent to decision-making in domains with bounded probabilities. We can calculate the exact odds of a roulette ball landing on Red 32, but college admissions is substantially more complex and defies exact probabilities.

Mere Exposure Effect – Developing a preference for something because it is familiar and not because it is optimal. The aura of an Ivy League degree makes it a popular option for many even if other, lesser-known universities would be a better fit.

Misleading Vividness – Arguing from anecdote by exaggerating a single instance of something as representative of a trend or a greater whole. In college essays, students might hyperbolize a particular setback as indicative of their entire life.

Moral Luck – Concept developed by philosopher Bernard Williams and popularized by Thomas Nagel and Michael Sandel to assign blame or just desserts based on an individual's behavior without accounting for the context or background circumstances. Affluent students from the most-elite high schools perceive their favorable admissions as due entirely to their effort without considering their underlying privilege. Conversely, we're quick to ascribe blame to an adult criminal even if they experienced severe neglect and child abuse and may not have had complete control over their behavior. In common language, we congratulate admissions offers as "you deserve it" when the reality is more complex.

Motivated Reasoning – A form of emotionally based reasoning to justify a position without regard to empirical evidence or objective facts. Really really wanting to gain admission somewhere isn't sufficient to make it happen.

Neglect of Probability – The tendency to overestimate rare occurrences because it may have happened occasionally in the past. For example, a single student gaining admission to MIT with an SAT 1200 doesn't make a future occurrence any more likely. Below-average academic students neglect the long odds of gaining admission to elite universities.

Nirvana Fallacy – Mistakenly comparing the reality of a situation with an idealized version of it, i.e., all your problems are not solved by gaining admission to an Ivy League college.

Optimism Bias – A form of wishful thinking where an individual believes a statistically probable negative event is less likely to occur to them. Believing you have a good chance of elite college admissions doesn't alter the probability. Similar to Lloyd's Fallacy.

Planning Fallacy – The tendency to believe a task will take less time than you imagine. Students routinely underestimate how much time and effort their college applications require even when they have evidence of older siblings or classmates that suggest otherwise. Contributes to procrastination and submitting applications right at the deadline.

Projection Bias – The tendency for present emotional states to cloud one's judgment about future emotional states. We overestimate how much our future selves share our current preferences.

Regression Fallacy – Ascribes a cause where none exists, as when an applicant points to a lack of volunteering hours as the cause for their admissions rejection. There may simply be no discernable reason why you didn't gain admission.

Salience Bias – The predisposition to focus on items that are more prominent or emotionally charged and underweight or ignore something that is unr`emarkable. Admissions counselors tend to overweight novelty, like an applicant gaining admission because they're a mahout elephant trainer.

Self-Serving Bias – A set of biases and cognitive errors that seek to preserve or promote one's self-esteem, or the tendency to perceive and present oneself in an overly favorable light.

Shared Information Bias – The tendency for group members to spend more time and energy discussing information that all members are already familiar with (i.e., shared information), and less time and energy discussing information that only some members are aware of (i.e., unshared information). Usually occurs in parent circles or friend groups that look at the same limited datasets over and over while ignoring the bigger picture.

Social Desirability Bias – The tendency to overreport or emphasize good behavior and downplay negative behavior, i.e., when a student writes glowingly about themselves in an essay while bypassing their flaws.

Special Pleading – Claiming to be an exception without basis. Usually occurs in the appeals or deferral process, where students literally plead for an admissions space.

Stanford Duck Syndrome – Describes the pressures that elite university students feel to appear calm and effortless while struggling underneath the surface. Just as ducks seem placid on the water's surface, their feet churn ceaselessly below.

Status Quo Bias – A preference for the current state of affairs; reluctance to change.

Survivorship Bias – The tendency for only winners or "survivors" to emerge in a data set. Students only see "the 50 Best Harvard Essays" while failing to consider that hundreds of students with mediocre essays still gain admission. Also, online users are more likely to report their successes than failures.

System Justification – An underlying psychological need to accept the status quo while expressing reluctance to reform, even if they would benefit from a change. Students regularly justify an incredibly unfair and inconsistent college admissions system because it's comfortable. Considering alternatives is inconvenient or distressing.

The Better-Than-Average-Fallacy/Placement Bias – The tendency to believe that we're better than average without evidence to justify this belief. Most applicants think their essays are above average when, by definition, half of all applicants have below-average submissions.

Von Restorff Effect – Coined by German psychiatrist and pediatrician Hedwig von Restorff to describe when, presented with multiple items or situations, people tend to remember that which is most different or anomalous. Students recall that one kid who got into MIT with an SAT of 1200 while failing to acknowledge the thousands of 1600s who got denied. Admissions reviewers tend to overweight rare or novel applications among the "sea of sameness."

White Savior Complex – Refers to white people or those from developed countries who feel obliged to help communities of color or communities in developing countries for self-serving reasons, i.e., taking mission trips abroad with the primary purpose of generating eventual college resume and essay content.

Wishful Thinking – Forming beliefs that feel psychologically relieving even if those beliefs are not grounded in reality or evidence. Wanting something really badly won't make it happen.

Zero-Sum Bias – The real or perceived belief that one person's gain is another's loss. College admissions is nominally zero-sum where there are finite spaces available, but this characteristic gets distorted when students falsely blame their classmates for taking their spaces. In reality, pairs of applicants are rarely if ever considered head to head.

Notes

Argument:

1   Thomas Stockham Baker, "'Getting Into College' Has Become a Very Serious Problem," *New York Times*, September 1, 1907, http://timesmachine.nytimes.com/timesmachine/1907/09/01/104707570.html.

2   Fred E.Crossland, "Politics and Policies in College Admissions," *The Phi Delta Kappan* 46, no. 7 (1965): 299–302.

3   James D. Walsh, "The Coming Disruption: Scott Galloway Predicts a Handful of Elite Cyborg Universities Will Soon Monopolize Higher Education," *Intelligencer*, May 11, 2020, https://nymag.com/intelligencer/2020/05/scott-galloway-future-of-college.html.

4   "Regional Accrediting Organizations," Council for Higher Education, accessed February 12, 2021, https://www.chea.org/regional-accrediting-organizations.

5   Kristen, "Admissions Officer Spotlight: John Yi," *Bulldogs' Blogs, Yale University*, August 21, 2016, https://admissions.yale.edu/bulldogs-blogs/kristen/2016/08/21/admissions-officer-spotlight-john-yi.

6   Michael T. Nietzel, "Rice University Will Expand Its Enrollment: Why Other Elites Should Follow Suit," *Forbes*, April 1, 2021, https://www.forbes.com/sites/michaeltnietzel/2021/04/01/rice-university-will-expand-its-enrollment-why-other-elites-should-follow-suit/?sh=3ab7ea-45b6a7.

7   Cady Lang, "Hate Crimes Against Asian Americans Are on the Rise. Many Say More Policing Isn't the Answer," *Time*, February 18, 2017, https://time.com/5938482/asian-american-attacks/.

8   I have excluded some private universities such as Miami, Tulane, and Northeastern, and public universities such as Wisconsin, Maryland, and Ohio State not because they aren't quality educations or competitive process. They have lower-than-average yield rates and aren't generally an applicant's dream school/top choice. They're the kinds of school applicants locked out of the top 50 will choose to enroll at as second choices or adequate backups.

Private universities: Amherst, Boston University, Bowdoin, Brown, Cal Tech, Carnegie Mellon0000, Claremont McKenna, Columbia, Cornell University, Dartmouth, Duke, Emory, Georgetown, Harvard, Johns Hopkins, MIT, New York University, Northwestern, Notre Dame, Pomona, Princeton, Rice, Stanford, Swarthmore, Tufts, University of Chicago, University of Pennsylvania, University of Southern California, Vanderbilt, Wake Forest, Washington University at St. Louis, Wellesley, Williams, Yale.

Public universities: Florida, Georgia Tech, Illinois Champaign-Urbana, Michigan-Ann Arbor, North Carolina-Chapel Hill, UC-Berkeley, UCLA, University of Georgia, UT-Austin, Virginia, Washington-Seattle

9   Scott Jaschik, "'Alarm Bells' on First-Generation, Low-Income Applicants," *Inside Higher Ed*, January 26, 2021, https://www.insidehighered.com/admissions/article/2021/01/26/common-apps-new-data-show-overall-gains-applications-not-first.

10   Caitlin Flanagan, "Private Schools Have Become Truly Obscene," *The Atlantic*, March 26, 2021, https://www.theatlantic.com/magazine/archive/2021/04/private-schools-are-indefensible/618078/.

11   Michael J. Sandel, *The Tyranny of Merit: What's Become of the Common Good?* (New York, NY: Farrar, Straus and Giroux, 2020), 166, Kindle.

12   Daniel Markovits, "How Life Became an Endless, Terrible Competition," *The Atlantic*, September 4, 2019, https://www.theatlantic.com/magazine/archive/2019/09/meritocracys-miserable-winners/594760/.

13   Daniel Markovits, *The Meritocracy Trap: How America's Foundational Myth Feeds Inequality, Dismantles the Middle Class, and Devours the Elite* (London, UK: Penguin Press, 2019), xiv.

14   "Neighborhoods," Opportunity Insights, accessed February 17, 2021, https://opportunityinsights.org/neighborhoods/.

15   Sandel, *The Tyranny of Merit*, 165.

16   I googled my proposed book title only after finishing the manuscript and saw a 2015 *New York Times*op-ed by Frank Bruni with a similar title: "How to Survive the College Admissions Madness." He wrote that piece a year before he published *Where You Go Is Not Who You'll Be: An Antidote to the College Admissions Mania*. Presumably, he could have made a book with a title similar to his op-ed, and he went instead for "antidote to the college admissions mania." I can't claim sole credit for the insight into my book's title. It's more a consequence of making similar observations and consulting some of the same sources, a case of "simultaneous discovery." Education critics have used the language "madness" and "mania" for at least a hundred years, so Bruni isn't the first to invoke such terminology either. I have a trademark pending for Admissions Madness, so I am a first mover on a formal brand and content presence. Oddly, Bruni doesn't hold the trademark or the web domain for Admissions Mania.

17   See "25 by 25 Initiative," Texas A&M University, accessed April 15, 2021, https://engineering.tamu.edu/25by25/index.html, (that built on its 20 by 20 to enroll 25,000 Engineering students by 2025.)

18   https://www.esv.org/Matthew+16/ Accessed January 7, 2021

19   UT Enrollment Management and Student Success, "UT Austin Admission Decisions," YouTube video, 3:36, January 25, 2021, https://www.youtube.com/watch?v=L0CgGNmOVQ0.

20   Markovits, *The Meritocracy Trap*, 49.

Chapter 1

21   UT Admissions Guy, "Apply Texas Essay A Tell Us Your Story Drafting Workshop Part 2," YouTube video, 29:37, June 21, 2020, https://www.YouTube.com/watch?v=v0yKldOTtb4&t=45s; "Getting into Texas Universities: Create your Perfect Apply Texas and UT-Austin Applications ," TEX Admissions, accessed March 30, 2021, https://texadmissions.com/gettingintotexas.

22   It takes a certain mental framework to identify underlying themes in sample essays that might work for you without feeling insecure. I give counsel to my clients on best practices for reviewing samples that provide constructive tips for improvement rather than additional sources of anxiety. I often wonder whether my example posts do more harm than good.

23   Melissa Clinedinst, *2019 State of College Admission* (Arlington, VA: National Association for College Admission Counseling, 2019), 1-27, https://www.nacacnet.org/globalassets/documents/publications/research/2018_soca/soca2019_all.pdf.

24   When I was starting Tex Admissions in 2015, one of the best pieces of advice I received is to read every essay Paul Graham ever wrote. Even though I don't have a startup in the conventional sense, nor do I know anything about computer programming, I spent that year following that advice. Graham's wisdom is timeless because of its straightforward, no-nonsense writing style that makes original connections across different domains. I love reading Graham because his writing appears so effortless it makes me feel inferior. Feeling less-than-someone-else signals to me an opportunity for growth. Paul Graham, "The Age of the Essay," *Paul Graham* (blog), September 2004, http://www.paulgraham.com/essay.html.

25   "About Christopher Hunt," College Essay Mentor, accessed December 8, 2020, https://www.collegeessaymentor.com/about-chris.

26   Alia Wong, "College-Admissions Hysteria Is Not the Norm," *The Atlantic*, April 10, 2019, https://www.theatlantic.com/education/archive/2019/04/harvard-uchicago-elite-colleges-are-anomaly/586627/.

27   "Personal Statement (Essay) Topics," Office of Undergraduate Admissions, Loyola University, New Orleans, accessed November 29, 2020, http://apply.loyno.edu/essay-topics.

28   Thank you Reddit user /u/PuzzleheadedRadish89 for the tip on Kentucky.

29   "Admission Requirements for Freshman Students," Montana State University, accessed November 29, 2020, https://www.montana.edu/admissions/apply/freshman.html.

30   Thank you Reddit user /u/ RandomPerson777666 for the tip.

31 "How to Write the University of Kentucky Essays 2020-2021," *CollegeVine* (blog), August 14, 2020, https://blog.collegevine.com/how-to-write-the-university-of-kentucky-essays-2020-2021/.

32 I removed references to my Rice blog post, but thankfully I saved them elsewhere because I reinserted the content a few weeks later once my clients and I cleared up the misunderstanding.

33 As of November 27, 2020, www.downrightwackyadmissions.com remains available.

34 "Uchicago Supplemental Essay Questions," University of Chicago, accessed December 2, 2020, https://collegeadmissions.uchicago.edu/apply/uchicago-supplemental-essay-questions.

35 Giovanniii23, "What Did we Think About our University of Chicago Supplemental Essays?" Reddit, November 3, 2020, https://www.reddit.com/r/ApplyingToCollege/comments/jn48yl/what_did_we_think_about_our_university_of_chicago/.

36 "Scholarships for Incoming Freshmen," Texas Tech University, accessed December 5, 2020, https://www.depts.ttu.edu/scholarships/incFreshman.php.

37 Sarah Weber, "Georgetown instates test-optional policy for 2020-21 application season," *The Georgetown Voice*, September 27, 2020, https://georgetownvoice.com/2020/09/27/georgetown-instates-test-optional-policy-for-2020-21-application-season/.

38 "Diversity and Multicultural Recruitment," Office of Undergraduate Admissions, Georgetown University, accessed November 24, 2020, https://uadmissions.georgetown.edu/applying/multicultural/.

39 Ashley Robinson, "University of California Drops SAT/ACT Scores: What It Means for You," *PrepScholar* (blog), November 19, 2020, https://blog.prepscholar.com/university-of-california-schools-no-sat-act-score-requirement.

40 "Alcohol, Tobacco, and Other Drugs," New York University, accessed December 3, 2020, https://www.nyu.edu/life/safety-health-wellness/live-well-nyu/priority-areas/ATOD.html; "Sexual Health," New York University, accessed December 3, 2020, https://www.nyu.edu/life/

safety-health-wellness/live-well-nyu/priority-areas/sexualhealth.html;
"Student Conduct: Mission, Values, and Learning Goals," New York
University, accessed December 3, 2020, https://www.nyu.edu/students/
student-information-and-resources/student-community-standards/mis-
sionvaluesgoals.html.

41   I like to think I would have been wiser during my freshman year at
UT and socially distance if there were a global pandemic, especially since
I live with a compromised immune system. But if I'm being totally honest,
I probably wouldn't have remained isolated, although obviously I would
never be foolish enough to write down my *authentic* beliefs for a stranger
to read…

42   "Our Values," Stanford University Human-Centered Artificial Intelligence, accessed November 30, 2020. https://hai.stanford.edu/about/
values.

43   Jack Liu, "I Viewed My College Admissions Files - University of
Michigan Decision Reaction," YouTube video, 10:43, January 5, 2020,
https://www.YouTube.com/watch?v=bki2hKMRIjk&t=442s.

44   "Mission Statement," Kenyon College Athletics, accessed November
28, 2020, https://athletics.kenyon.edu/sports/2012/8/6/GEN_Mission-
Stmt.aspx?tab=missionstatement.

Chapter 2

45   Jessica Lahey, "Why Kids Care More About Achievement Than Helping Others," *The Atlantic*, June 25, 2014,
https://www.theatlantic.com/education/archive/2014/06/
most-kids-believe-that-achievement-trumps-empathy/373378/.

46   David Graves, "2021 EA Decisions and Data," *University of Georgia
Undergraduate Admissions* (blog), November 20, 2020, https://www.
admissions.uga.edu/blog/2021-ea-decisions-and-data/.

47   Caroline Nash, "Logan Powell's road to the Brown Admission
Office," *The Brown Daily Herald*, November 12, 2020, https://www.
browndailyherald.com/2020/11/12/logan-powells-road-brown-
admission-office/.

48   Scott Galloway, *Post Corona: From Crisis to Opportunity* (New York, NY: Portfolio - Penguin Random House, 2020), 128.

49   One service I refuse to provide are "appeals" for rejected students who are requesting reconsideration. Independent consulting is an ethically gray area, and one line I draw is not profiting off highly distressed families looking for the impossible—someone who can assuage their heartbreak and definitely get their kid in. Instead, snake oil salesmen and false prophets surface every spring to fill the appeals void left by more reputable consultants.

50   It's only by sheer luck that I'm an essay coach rather than a test prep specialist. I've never been more grateful for being a mediocre standardized test taker because the test-optional movement is likely to diminish the test prep industry.

51   Dependence on adjunct professors and graduate students are outside the scope of this book. For further reading, consult these pages: Colleen Flaherty, "Barely Getting By: New Report on Adjuncts Says Many Make Less Than $3,500 Per Course and Live in Poverty," *Inside Higher Ed*, April 20, 2020, https://www.insidehighered.com/news/2020/04/20/ new-report-says-many-adjuncts-make-less-3500-course-and-25000- year; Graduate student unionization efforts: "Grad-Student Unions," The Chronicle of Higher Education, accessed November 23, 2020, https:// www.chronicle.com/package/grad-student-unions/.

52   Jeffrey J. Selingo, *Who Gets in and Why: A Year Inside College Admissions* (New York, NY: Scribner, 2020), 40–41, Kindle.

53   Selingo, 15–16.

54   Selingo, 227.

55   Marguerite L. Jackson, "Needed: Some New Rules in the College Admissions Game," *The Phi Delta Kappan* 46, no. 7 (1965): 336–39.

56   https://www2.texasattorneygeneral.gov/opinions/openrecords/ 51paxton/orl/2019/pdf/or201917995.pdf Accessed December 5, 2020

Chapter 3:

57   List of events from the 2018 World Nomad Games: "All Sports," World Nomad Games, 2018, http://worldnomadgames.com/en/sport/.

58   My post about McCombs admissions features a photo of Anthony and I playing chess with unusually weighty pieces. "Advice for UT-Austin McCombs School of Business Applicants," Tex Admission, accessed January 5, 2021, https://texadmissions.com/blog/2018/5/16/advice-for-ut-mccombs-school-of-business-applicants.

59   Search Google Maps Bishkek White House and Manas International Airport—a very straight half-hour drive.

Chapter 4

60   In actuality, Marcus Aurelius died from a plague and not the betrayal of his power-hungry son Commodus.

61   "Need a Free Account?," Waking Up with Sam Harris," accessed November 24, 2020, https://app.wakingup.com/request-free-account.

62   Markovits, The Meritocracy Trap, 35.

63   Ray Dalio, Principles: Life and Work (New York, NY: Simon & Schuster, 2017), 202.

64   See Matthew Walker, Why We Sleep: Unlocking the Power of Sleep and Dreams (New York, NY: Scribner, 2017), for a comprehensive assessment of the role sleep plays in our development and lives.

65   Clinedinst, 2019 State of College Admission, 1-27.

66   Sandel, The Tyranny of Merit, 181.

67   A2cthr0waway, "Ivy Day is the Anniversary of my Suicide Attempt, and this is what I want to tell you," Reddit, March 25, 2020, https://old.reddit.com/r/ApplyingToCollege/comments/fow4w1/ivy_day_is_the_anniversary_of_my_suicide_attempt/.

68   "Teen Homicide, Suicide and Firearm Deaths," Child Trends, May 8, 2019. https://www.childtrends.org/indicators/teen-homicide-suicide-and-firearm-deaths.

69   Gretchen Frazee and Patty Gorena Morales, "Suicide Among Teens and Young Adults Reaches Highest Level Since 2000," PBS, June 18, 2019, https://www.pbs.org/newshour/nation/suicide-among-teens-and-young-adults-reaches-highest-level-since-2000.

70   Hanna Rosin, "The Silicon Valley Suicides," The Atlantic, December

2015, https://www.theatlantic.com/magazine/archive/2015/12/
the-silicon-valley-suicides/413140/.

71   Hanna Rosin, "The Overprotected Kid," *The Atlantic*, April
2014, https://www.theatlantic.com/magazine/archive/2014/04/
hey-parents-leave-those-kids-alone/358631/.

72   Scott Jaschik, "Suicide Note Calls Out Pressure on Students," *Inside
Higher Ed*, February 12, 2018, https://www.insidehighered.com/
admissions/article/2018/02/12/
suicide-note-16-year-old-renews-debate-about-pressure-top-high-schools.

73   Sarah Ketchen Lipson, Emily G. Lattie, and Daniel Eisenberg,
"Increased Rates of Mental Health Service Utilization by US College
Students: 10-year Population-Level Trends (2007–2017)," *Psychiatric
Services* 70, no. 1 (2019): 60-63.

74   Tiger Sun, "Duck Syndrome and a Culture of Misery," *The Stanford
Daily*, January 31, 2018, https://www.stanforddaily.com/2018/01/31/
duck-syndrome-and-a-culture-of-misery/.

75   Julia Lurie, "Everyone's Battle: Confronting College Depression," *Huffpost*, May 25, 2011, https://www.huffpost.com/entry/
everyones-battle-confront_b_813685.

76   Injustice_510, "I'll be dying soon," Reddit, January 12, 2021, https://
old.reddit.com/r/ApplyingToCollege/comments/kvhgyq/ill_be_dying_
soon/. (Accessed January 20, 2021, The post has since been removed).

Chapter 5

77   John R. Reitz, "The Anatomy of College Admissions," *The School
Counselor* 16, no. 1 (1968): 66–68.

78   Rick F. Yacone, "The Confusion in College Admissions Procedures,"
The School Counselor 10, no. 2 (1962): 48–52.

79   Franklin Bowditch Dexter, *On some social distinctions at Harvard
and Yale, before the Revolution* (Worcester, MA: C. Hamilton, 1894):
18–22, https://archive.org/details/onsomesocialdist00dextuoft/page/18/
mode/2up.

80   Holly, "Accepted: The Evolution of College Admission

Requirements," *Trinity Banter*, May 2, 2014, https://commons.trincoll.
edu/edreform/2014/05/accepted-the-evolution-of-college-admission-
requirements/.

81   "Limit College Admissions: Columbia and Princeton Forced to Keep
Down Enrollment," *The New York Times*, January 16, 1924, https://www.
nytimes.com/1924/01/16/archives/limit-college-admissions-columbia-
and-princeton-forced-to-keep-down.html.

82   James. B Conant, "Wanted: American Radicals," Atlantic Monthly,
May 1943: 41-45.

83   Holly, "Accepted."

84   Nathaniel B. Abbott, "College Admissions; Human Factors Deemed
Important in Selecting Candidates,"
The New York Times, May 24, 1960, https://www.nytimes.
com/1960/05/24/archives/college-admissions-human-fac-
tors-deemed-important-in-selecting.html.

85   "DECREASE IS FOUND IN BIAS IN SCHOOLS; American
Jewish Committee Says 'Good Sense of People' Rejects Hate Mongering
EDUCATIONAL GAINS CITED Liberalized College Admissions
Reported -- 'Checkmating of Bigots' in Nation Hailed," *The New York
Times*, October 24, 1953, https://timesmachine.nytimes.com/timesma-
chine/1953/10/24/84428140.html.

86   Olive Evans, "On Getting into College," *The New York Times*,
April 23, 1967, https://timesmachine.nytimes.com/timesma-
chine/1967/04/23/83655916.html.

87   If you've ever attended a college fair at your high school or a university in the state of Texas, you were attending a TACRAO event. When
I worked in admissions, TACRAO coordinates the scheduling of which
high schools received fairs and on what days and times. It is a good example of coordination between high schools to accommodate colleges so that
university admissions representatives can optimize their time and students
are less likely to be missed out by a counselor who is double booked on a
college fair.

88   "COLLEGE CAPACITY HELD INADEQUATE; Admissions
Deans Hear of 'Gloomy Prospect' Ahead," *The New York Times*, April 21,

1965, https://www.nytimes.com/1965/04/21/archives/college-capacity-held-inadequate-admissions-deans-hear-of-gloomy.html.

89   Evans.

90   William Borders, "IVY'S ADMISSIONS IRK PREP SCHOOLS; Colleges' Hunt for Diversity Protested by Headmasters," *The New York Times*, April 30, 1967, https://www.nytimes.com/1967/04/30/archives/ivys-admissions-irk-prep-schools-colleges-hunt-for-diversity.html.

91   Evan Jenkins, "Colleges Shift to Hard Sell In Recruiting of Students," *The New York Times*, March 31, 1974, https://www.nytimes.com/1974/03/31/archives/colleges-shift-to-hard-sell-in-recruiting-of-students-a-new.html.

92   "College Admission: Confronting the Tensions Between Student and Parent," *The New York Times*, April 10, 1979, https://www.nytimes.com/1979/04/10/archives/college-admission-confronting-the-tensions-between-student-and.html.

93   "College Admission."

94   Anna Diamond, "South Korea's Testing Fixation," *The Atlantic*, November 17, 2016, https://www.theatlantic.com/education/archive/2016/11/south-korean-seniors-have-been-preparing-for-today-since-kindergarten/508031/.

95   Markovits, *The Meritocracy Trap*, 129.

96   Michael J. Seth, "Democratization, Prosperity, and Educational Change," in *Education Fever: Society, Politics, and the Pursuit of Schooling in South Korea* (Honolulu, HI: University of Hawai'i Press, 2002): 224-56.

97   Ju-min Park, "South Korean Children Finish Last in Happiness Survey," *Reuters*, November 4, 2014, https://www.reuters.com/article/us-southkorea-children-idUSKBN0IO0OA20141104.

98   Liang Choon Wang, "The Effect of High-Stakes Testing on Suicidal Ideation of Teenagers with Reference-Dependent Preferences," *Journal of Population Economics* 29 (2016): 345–64.

99   Gregory Warner and Lulu Garcia-Navarro, "Brazil in Black and White," *npr*, August 14, 2017, https://www.npr.org/transcripts/542840797.

100 "Abitur: Should Every German State have the Same High School Leaving Exam?," *The Local de*, 26 July 2019, https://www.thelocal. de/20190726/should-germany-get-rid-of-abitur-lottery-and-opt-for-nationwide-high-school-leaving-diploma.

101 John Round, Colin C. Williams, and Peter Rodgers, "Corruption in the Post-Soviet Workplace: The Experiences of Recent Graduates in Contemporary Ukraine," *Work, Employment & Society* 22, no. 1 (2008): 149–66.

102 Elena Denisova-Schmidt, *Anti-Corruption Policies Revisited* (London, University College London, 2015), https://anticorrp.eu/wp-content/ uploads/2015/03/Russia.pdf.

103 Nataliya Rumyantseva and Elena Denisova-Schmidt, "Institutional Corruption in Russian Universities," *International Higher Education* 82 (2015): 18-19.

104 Fred E. Crossland, "Politics and Policies in College Admissions," *The Phi Delta Kappan* 46, no. 7 (1965): 299–302.

105 Jonathan A. Lewin, "Application Joins Common Herd: Harvard Replaces Unique Form with Standardized Queries," *The Harvard Crimson*, September 12, 1994, https://www.thecrimson.com/article/1994/9/12/ application-joins-common-herd-pthe-harvard/.

Chapter 6:

106 Ben Lindbergh, "The Evolution of MLB Scouting Is a Threat to the Profession Itself," *The Ringer*, March 8, 2019, https://www.theringer.com/ mlb/2019/3/8/18255453/cincinnati-reds-scouting-reports-series-part-3.

107 Selingo, *Who Gets in and Why*, 10–11.

108 "Jennifer Glynn, *Persistence: The Success of Students Who Transfer from Community Colleges to Selective Four-Year Institutions: Executive Summary* (Lansdowne, VA: Jack Kent Cooke Foundation, January 2019), https://www.jkcf.org/wp-content/uploads/2019/01/Persistence-Executive-Summary-Jack-Kent-Cooke-Foundation.pdf.

109 "Statistics," ICAI, accessed February 19, 2021, https://www.academicintegrity.org/statistics/.

110 Markovits, *The Meritocracy Trap*, xxii

111 Cork Gaines, "Crazy Stat Shows Just How Common Doping Was In Cycling When Lance Armstrong Was Winning The Tour De France," *Business Insider Australia*, January 3, 2015, https://www.businessinsider.com.au/lance-armstrong-doping-tour-de-france-2015-1?r=US&IR=T.

112 Jennifer Levitz and Melissa Korn, "The Trick High-Schoolers Are Using to Boost Their Grades," *The Wall Street Journal*, June 18, 2019, https://www.wsj.com/articles/a-way-for-high-school-students-to-boost-their-gpas-take-classes-at-other-high-schools-11560850201?page=7.

113 "Friend who was a rampant cheater got into Harvard rea," Reddit, accessed January 18, 2021 https://old.reddit.com/r/ApplyingToCollege/comments/kfdk2c/friend_who_was_a_rampant_cheater_got_into_harvard/ (Post deleted); You can browse these posts to see many other instances here: https://old.reddit.com/r/ApplyingToCollege/search?q=cheater&restrict_sr=on.

114 James M. Lang, *Cheating Lessons: Learning from Academic Dishonesty* (Cambridge, MA: Harvard University Press, 2013).

115 Mollie K. Galloway, "Review: A Learning Opportunity," *The Review of Politics* 76, no. 3 (2014): 533–35.

116 Sara Dorn and Susan Edelman, "The Disgraceful Cheating Scandal at One of America's Best High Schools," *New York Post*, January 27, 2018, https://nypost.com/2018/01/27/cheating-still-rampant-at-disgraced-stuyvesant-school/.

117 Class of 2018 database of feeder schools can be found at https://polarislist.com/.

118 Erica L. Green and Katie Benner, "Louisiana School Made Headlines for Sending Black Kids to Elite Colleges. Here's the Reality," *The New York Times*, November 30, 2018, https://www.nytimes.com/2018/11/30/us/tm-landry-college-prep-black-students.html.

119 http://www.tmlandrycollegeprep.org/Memorandum percent20re percent20TM percent20Landry.pdf Accessed February 21, 2021.

120 Empowerly, " Let's talk about Lying and Admissions: By a Former Stanford Admissions Officer," Reddit, February 5, 2021, https://old.reddit.com/r/ApplyingToCollege/comments/lddhlo/lets_talk_about_lying_and_admissions_by_a_former/.

121 Parts of this and the next two sections are adapted from Section II of my *Your Ticket to the Forty Acres*.

122 Selingo, *Who Gets in and Why*, 105.

123 Anemona Hartocollis, Amy Harmon and Mitch Smith, "'Lopping,' 'Tips' and the 'Z-List': Bias Lawsuit Explores Harvard's Admissions Secrets," *The New York Times*, July 29, 2018, https://www.nytimes.com/2018/07/29/us/harvard-admissions-asian-americans.html.

124 Peter Schmidt, "In Admissions Decisions, the Deciders' Own Background Plays a Big Role," *The Chronicle of Higher Education*, April 12, 2016, http://www.chronicle.com/article/In-Admission-Decisions-the/236088.

125 Selingo, *Who Gets in and Why*, 105.

126 Selingo, 189.

127 Selingo, 63.

128 Derek Thompson, "Meritocracy Is Killing High-School Sports," *The Atlantic*, August 30, 2019, https://www.theatlantic.com/ideas/archive/2019/08/meritocracy-killing-high-school-sports/597121/; https://www.theatlantic.com/ideas/archive/2018/11/income-inequality-explains-decline-youth-sports/574975/ Linda Flanagan, "What's Lost When Only Rich Kids Play Sports," *The Atlantic*, September 28, 2017, https://www.theatlantic.com/education/archive/2017/09/whats-lost-when-only-rich-kids-play-sports/541317/; Derek Thompson, "The Cult of Rich-Kid Sports," *The Atlantic*, October 2, 2019, https://www.theatlantic.com/ideas/archive/2019/10/harvard-university-and-scandal-sports-recruitment/599248/.

129 Selingo, *Who Gets in and Why*, 151.

130 Richard W. Moll, "An Admissions Man Says It Isn't So Hard," *The New York Times*, January 7, 1979, https://www.nytimes.com/1979/01/07/archives/an-admissions-man-says-it-isnt-so-hard.html.

131 Moll concludes his article with sage wisdom: "A host of fine institutions out there have room for you and want you. If you realize that hardest-college-to-get is not necessarily the best college, then there is no harm in playing the game of trying for it. But be willing to expend considerable time and energy. Blow your horn—but in tune and with clarity. Relax

through this journey. And laugh a little. Don't let yourself become what you are not. You should he looking for a college for you, not for someone you are pretending to be."

132 Margaret Ferguson, "The Letter of Recommendation as Strange Work," *PMLA* 127, no. 4 (2012): 954–62.

133 Consult this essay from NACAC that shares other best recommendation letter practices: Jim Paterson, "Toward a Better Letter," *NACAC*, accessed January 10, 2021, https://www.nacacnet.org/news--publications/journal-of-college-admission/toward-a-better-letter/.

134 Andrew Simmons, "The Art of the College Recommendation Letter," *The Atlantic*, February 24, 2014, https://www.theatlantic.com/education/archive/2014/02/the-art-of-the-college-recommendation-letter/284019/.

135 Jon Boeckenstedt, "Letters of Recommendation: An Unfair Part of College Admissions," *The Washington Post*, March 3, 2016, https://www.washingtonpost.com/news/grade-point/wp/2016/03/03/letters-of-recommendation-an-unfair-part-of-college-admissions/.

136 Patrick Akos and Jennifer Kretchmar, "Gender and Ethnic Bias in Letters of Recommendation: Considerations for School Counselors," *Professional School Counseling* 20, no. 1 (2016): 102–14.

137 Scott Jaschik, "Expectations, Race and College Success," *Inside Higher Ed*, October 24, 2017, https://www.insidehighered.com/news/2017/10/24/study-finds-high-school-teachers-have-differing-expectations-black-and-white.

138 This Prep Scholar blog post is the closest I could find along with offering helpful tips. Rebecca Safier, "The Complete List of Colleges That Require Interviews," *Prep Scholar*, September 15, 2020, https://blog.prepscholar.com/full-list-of-colleges-that-require-interviews.

139 Jennifer Gross, "The Truth about College Interviews," National Association for College Admission Counseling, accessed January 17, 2021, https://www.d121.org/cms/lib/IL02214492/Centricity/Domain/106/The percent20Truth percent20about percent20College percent20Interviews.pdf.

140 Military Academies like Navy or the Air Force are an exception because they're also evaluating a candidate's fitness for service and sincerity

about completing their commitments following graduation. Auditions for performing and musical arts programs also seem essential to assess one's talents, but they're ripe with their own set of issues beyond the scope of this book.

141 Hayley Glatter, "The Futility of College Interviews," *The Atlantic*, December 29, 2017, https://www.theatlantic.com/education/archive/2017/12/the-futility-of-college-interviews/549359/.

142 Malcolm Gladwell, "The New-Boy Network," *The New Yorker*, May 21, 2000, https://www.newyorker.com/magazine/2000/05/29/the-new-boy-network.

143 Jason Dana, "The Utter Uselessness of Job Interviews," *The New York Times*, April 8, 2017, https://www.nytimes.com/2017/04/08/opinion/sunday/the-utter-uselessness-of-job-interviews.html.

144 Jason Dana, Robyn Dawes, and Nathanial Peterson, "Belief in the Unstructured Interview: The Persistence of an Illusion," *Judgment and Decision Making* 8, no. 5 (2013): 512-20.

145 Selingo, *Who Gets in and Why*, 195.

Chapter 7

146 Zack Friedman, "Student Loan Debt Statistics In 2020: A Record $1.6 Trillion," *Forbes*, February 3, 2020, https://www.forbes.com/sites/zackfriedman/2020/02/03/student-loan-debt-statistics/#309aff74281f; Daniel Kurt, "Student Loan Debt: 2020 Statistics and Outlook," *Investopedia*, March 16, 2021, https://www.investopedia.com/student-loan-debt-2019-statistics-and-outlook-4772007.

147 Kadija Yilla and David Wessel, "Five Facts about Student Loans," *Brookings*, November 12, 2019, https://www.brookings.edu/blog/up-front/2019/11/12/five-facts-about-student-loans/.

148 Abigail Johnson Hess, "College Grads Expect to Pay off Student Debt in 6 Years—This is How Long it Will Actually Take," *CNBC*, June 19, 2019, https://www.cnbc.com/2019/05/23/cengage-how-long-it-takes-college-grads-to-pay-off-student-debt.html.

149 Eva-Marie Ayala, "Only about half of all Texas students graduate from college within six years," *The Dallas Morning News*, September 12, 2018, https://www.dallasnews.com/news/education/2018/09/12/only-about-half-of-all-texas-students-graduate-from-college-within-six-years/.

150 "Fast Facts: Graduation Rates," Institute of Education Sciences, National Center for Education Statistics, accessed January 12, 2021 https://nces.ed.gov/fastfacts/display.asp?id=40.

151 "Fact Sheet: Focusing Higher Education on Student Success," US Department of Education, July 27, 2015, https://www.ed.gov/news/press-releases/fact-sheet-focusing-higher-education-student-success.

152 Jason N. Houle, "Disparities in Debt: Parents' Socioeconomic Resources and Young Adult Student Loan Debt," *Sociology of Education* 87, no. 1 (2014): 53-69.

153 "Office of Financial Aid," Rice University, accessed January 18, 2021, https://financialaid.rice.edu/.

154 Terri Williams, "10 Ways Student Debt Can Derail Your Life," Investopedia, March 18, 2021, https://www.investopedia.com/articles/personal-finance/100515/10-ways-student-debt-can-destroy-your-life.asp.

155 Victoria Wang, "Killer Loans—College Debt Triggers Depression and Suicide," *Salon*, June 1, 2019, https://www.salon.com/2019/06/01/killer-loans-college-debt-triggers-depression-and-suicide_partner/.

156 Christopher Ingraham, "7 Ways $1.6 Trillion in Student Loan Debt Affects the U.S. Economy," *The Washington Post*, June 25, 2019, https://www.washingtonpost.com/business/2019/06/25/heres-what-trillion-student-loan-debt-is-doing-us-economy.

157 Ian Bogost, "America Will Sacrifice Anything for the College Experience," *The Atlantic*, October 20, 2020, https://www.theatlantic.com/technology/archive/2020/10/college-was-never-about-education/616777/.

158 BlueLightSpcl, "Recent seniors and current college students," Reddit, June 10, 2020, https://www.reddit.com/r/ApplyingToCollege/comments/h0kx9r/recent_seniors_and_current_college_students_how/ftolizr/.

159 John M. Grohol, "15 Common Cognitive Distortions," *PsychCentral*, May 17, 2016, https://psychcentral.com/lib/15-common-cognitive-distortions/.

160 Greg Lukianoff and Jonathan Haidt, *The Coddling of the American Mind: How Good Intentions and Bad Ideas Are Setting Up a Generation for Failure* (New York, NY: Penguin Press, 2018).

161 "Third Stage of Grief: Bargaining," *eCondolence*, accessed January 20, 2021, http://www.econdolence.com/learn/articles/third-stage-of-grief-bargaining/.

162

Chapter 8

Selingo, *Who Gets in and Why*, 31.

163 Scott Carlson, "How Enrollment Challenges Can Spur Change," *The Chronicle of Higher Education*, January 21, 2018, https://www.chronicle.com/article/how-enrollment-challenges-can-spur-change/.

164 Edward B. Fiske, "The Marketing of the Colleges," *the Atlantic*, October 1979, https://www.theatlantic.com/magazine/archive/1979/10/the-marketing-of-the-colleges/376296/.

165 Douglas Belkin, "For Sale: SAT-Takers' Names. Colleges Buy Student Data and Boost Exclusivity," *The Wall Street Journal*, November 5, 2019, https://www.wsj.com/articles/for-sale-sat-takers-names-colleges-buy-student-data-and-boost-exclusivity-11572976621?mod=article_inline.

166 Melissa Ezarik, "Report: COVID-19 Prompts Colleges to Invest in Digital Marketing," *University Business*, June 12, 2020, https://university-business.com/report-covid-19-prompts-colleges-to-invest-in-digital-marketing/.

167 Belkin, "For Sale."

168 List of universities by four-year graduation rate: "Highest 4-Year Graduation Rates," US News, accessed January 14, 2021, https://www.usnews.com/best-colleges/rankings/highest-grad-rate.

169 "I just got an email from Providence College and the subject was 'Re: Your College Acceptance,'" Reddit, accessed February 11, 2021, https:// old.reddit.com/r/ApplyingToCollege/comments/lumyd5/i_just_got_an_ email_from_providence_college_and/ (post deleted).

170 Grace Shan, "USC's Decision to Send AirPods to New Scholarship Admits is Insulting," *Daily Trojan*, March 2, 2021, https://dailytrojan.com/2021/03/02/ uscs-decision-to-send-airpods-to-new-scholarship-admits-is-insulting/.

171 Harriet Ryan, Matt Hamilton, and Paul Pringle, "Must Reads: A USC Doctor was Accused of Bad Behavior with Young Women for Years. The university Let Him Continue Treating Students," *Los Angeles Times*, May 16, 2018, https://www.latimes.com/local/california/la-me-usc-doctor-misconduct-complaints-20180515-story.html.

172 Doha Madani, "USC Agrees to $1.1 Billion in Settlement with Hundreds of Women Alleging Abuse by Gynecologist," *NBC News*, March 26, 2021, https://www.nbcnews.com/news/us-news/usc-agrees-1-1-billion-settlement-hundreds-women-alleging-abuse-n1262075.

173 "I just got an email from Providence College."

174 Megan Reeves, "Never mind: 'Big Mistake' Cited as USF St. Pete Takes Back 430 Admission Letters," *Tampa Bay Times*, January 22, 2019, https://www.tampabay.com/education/never-mind-big-mistake-cited-as-usf-st-pete-takes-back-430-admission-letters-20190122/.

175 Nick Anderson, "John Hopkins Mistakenly Says 'Yes' to Hundreds of Rejected Applicants," *The Washington Post*, December 16, 2014, https:// www.washingtonpost.com/local/education/johns-hopkins-mistakenly-says-yes-to-hundreds-of-rejected-applicants/2014/12/16/20b5f9f4-8575-11e4-b9b7-b8632ae73d25_story.html.

176 Gale Holland and Seema Mehta, "UC San Diego Admissions Gaffe Dashes Students' Hopes–Again," *Los Angeles Times*, April 1, 2009, https://www.latimes.com/archives/la-xpm-2009-apr-01-me-ucsd-reject1-story.html.

177 California State Auditor Report: Elaine M. Howle and Doug Cordiner, *The University of California: Its Admissions and Financial*

Decisions Have Disadvantaged California Resident Students—Report 2015-107 (California State Auditor, March 29, 2016), https://www.auditor.ca.gov/pdfs/reports/2015-107.pdf; University of California response: "UC Report Strongly Disputes Assertions in State Audit, Demonstrates How it Puts California Students First," University of California, March 29, 2016, https://www.universityofcalifornia.edu/news/straight-talk-report.

178 The most straightforward policy recommendation to increase access and educational quality is for state legislatures to prioritize funding public education, which have been on the decline in almost all states over the past two decades.

179 Kaylee Harter, "Shifting Population: Chinese Students Drive International Enrollment Increase," *The Lantern*, April 15, 2019, https://www.thelantern.com/2019/04/shifting-population-chinese-students-drive-international-enrollment-increase/.

180 Christopher Avery, Andrew Fairbanks, and Richard Zeckhauser, *The Early Admissions Game: Joining the Elite* (Cambridge, MA: Harvard University Press, 2003). The book provides a detailed history of early admissions deadlines. It provides a data-driven analysis of early deadline practices of the 1990s.

181 Selingo, *Who Gets in and Why*, 119.

182 James Fallows, "The Early-Decision Racket," *The Atlantic*, September 2001, https://www.theatlantic.com/magazine/archive/2001/09/the-early-decision-racket/302280/.

183 "Yale's Surprise Decision to Keep Early Admissions May Undercut Efforts of Other Ivies to Recruit Highly Qualified Blacks and Low-Income Whites," *The Journal of Blacks in Higher Education* 54 (2006): 14–15.

184 Heather Antecol and Janet Kiholm Smith, "The Early Decision Option in College Admission and Its Impact on Student Diversity," *The Journal of Law & Economics* 55, no. 1 (2012): 217–249.

185 Abril Castro, "Early Decision Harms Students of Color and Low-Income Students," *Center for American Progress*, November 4, 2019, https://www.americanprogress.org/issues/race/news/2019/11/04/476789/early-decision-harms-students-color-low-income-students/; Harold O.

Levy, "Colleges Should Abandon Early Admissions," *Inside Higher Ed*, January 12, 2017, https://www.insidehighered.com/views/2017/01/12/discrimination-inherent-early-admissions-programs-essay.

186 "2020 Ivy League Admissions Statistics," Ivy Coach, accessed February 9, 2021, https://www.ivycoach.com/2020-ivy-league-admissions-statistics/.

187 "Waitlist Statistics," College Transitions, accessed February 18, 2021, https://www.collegetransitions.com/dataverse/waitlist-statistics.

188 Hannah Muniz, "College Waitlist: What Are Your Chances of Getting in?" *Prep Scholar*, September 6, 2020, https://blog.prepscholar.com/college-waitlist.

189 "Regents Make UT Austin Even More Affordable," University of Texas News, July 9, 2019, https://news.utexas.edu/2019/07/09/regents-make-ut-austin-even-more-affordable-2/.

190 Randy Diehl, *Final Report of the Task Force on Undergraduate Graduation Rates* (Austin, TX: The University of Texas at Austin, 2012), https://ue.ucsc.edu/documents/past-projects/success/utaustin-graduation-report.pdf.

191 Selingo, *Who Gets in and Why*, 222.

192 Selingo, 224.

193 HB 588 was a compromise between urban and rural legislators to promote racial and geographic diversity at Texas public universities by guaranteeing admission to students graduating in the top 10 percent of their senior class from any Texas school. SB 175 in 2009 later allowed an exception for UT-Austin to admit 75 percent of their incoming class automatically because almost all spaces were previously occupied by top 10 percent applicants. LOS was an effort to increase financial aid opportunities for the state's most underserved rural and urban schools.

194 "David Laude Appointed Graduation Rate Champion at The University of Texas at Austin," College of Natural Sciences, May 8, 2012, https://cns.utexas.edu/news/laude-senior-vice-provost.

195 Paul Tough, "Who Gets to Graduate?" *The New York Times* Magazine, May 15, 2014, https://www.nytimes.com/2014/05/18/magazine/who-gets-to-graduate.html.

196 What may have been the case in 2014 wasn't what happened the year it unrolled in 2013, although I have reasons to believe that the Dashboard regime continued until the 2017 Texas Advance Commitment reforms.

Chapter 9

197 Amy Stuart Wells, Lauren Fox, and Diana Cordova-Cobo, "How Racially Diverse Schools and Classrooms Can Benefit All Students," *The Century Foundation*, February 9, 2016, https://tcf.org/content/report/how-racially-diverse-schools-and-classrooms-can-benefit-all-students/.

198 Flanagan, "Private Schools Have Become Truly Obscene."

199 Kriston McIntosh et al., "Examining the Black-White Wealth Gap," *Brookings*, February 27, 2020, https://www.brookings.edu/blog/up-front/2020/02/27/examining-the-black-white-wealth-gap/.

200 "Percent Change in Employment," Opportunity Insights, accessed February 18, 2021, https://tracktherecovery.org/?nosplash=true.

201 Davide Scigliuzzo, "The Rich Are Minting Money in the Pandemic Like Never Before," *Bloomberg Wealth*, January 17, 2021, https://www.bloomberg.com/news/articles/2021-01-17/the-rich-are-minting-money-in-the-pandemic-like-never-before.

202 Tommy Beer, "Report: American Billionaires Have Added More Than $1 Trillion In Wealth During Pandemic," *Forbes*, January 26, 2021, https://www.forbes.com/sites/tommybeer/2021/01/26/report-american-billionaires-have-added-more-than-1-trillion-in-wealth-during-pandemic/?sh=2b4eb1b82564.

203 Beverly Daniel Tatum, "Segregation Worse in Schools 60 Years after Brown v. Board of Education," *The Seattle Times*, September 14, 2017, https://www.seattletimes.com/opinion/segregation-worse-in-schools-60-years-after-brown-v-board-of-education/.

204 Kevin Robert Martin, "Dispelling Myths: Race, Privilege, and Affirmative Action," in *Your Ticket to the Forty Acres: The Unofficial Guide for UT Undergraduate Admissions* (Washington, DC: Amazon Digital Services LLC - KDP Print US, 2017), https://texadmissions.com/race.

205 Markovits, *The Meritocracy Trap*, xvii

206 Anna Kirkland and Ben B. Hansen, "'How Do I Bring Diversity?' Race and Class in the College Admissions Essay," *Law & Society Review* 45, no. 1 (2011): 103–138.

207 James Warren, "The Rhetoric of College Application Essays: Removing Obstacles for Low Income and Minority Students," *American Secondary Education* 42, no. 1 (2013): 43–56.

208 Jeanita W. Richardson, "Demystifying and Deconstructing the College Application Process," *The Journal of Negro Education* 77, no. 4 (2008): 382–97.

209 Dallas County Promise (website), Dallas College Foundation, accessed December 3, 2020, https://dallascountypromise.org/.

210 My Kiva Lender Profile: https://www.kiva.org/lender/kevinrobertmartin.

211 Anecdotally, very few African American students email me or complete my free admissions questionnaire. I've had one African American client ever, a high-income student attending a private high school.

212 Kirkland and Hansen, "How Do I Bring Diversity?"

213 Hannah Natanson, "Harvard Rescinds Acceptances for At Least Ten Students for Obscene Memes," *The Harvard Crimson*, June 5, 2017, https://www.thecrimson.com/article/2017/6/5/2021-offers-rescinded-memes/.

214 "Asian Africans," Wikimedia Foundation, last modified March 5, 2021, 08:34, https://en.wikipedia.org/wiki/Asian_Africans.

215 Empowerly-Admissions, "STOP pushing 'sob stories,'" Reddit, June 13, 2020, https://old.reddit.com/r/ApplyingToCollege/comments/h8ezgq/stop_pushing_sob_stories/.

216 Other excellent *This American Life* Peabody-award winning episodes are the series about race and education are episodes 561 and 562 "The Problem We All Live With" about white parents in a St. Louis school district resistant to recent efforts at integration. Another is episode 550 "Three Miles" about the divide between private and public school kids living near each other. *This American Life* producer Chana Joffe-Walt produced one of my favorite series ever, *Nice White Parents*, whose themes are similar to my book. Times may change, but history often repeats itself.

217 I searched my email inbox and was unable to find my essay. I would have loved the opportunity to read and share what I can only imagine was a very cringey draft.

218 Markovits, *The Meritocracy Trap*, 26.

219 Ember Smith and Richard V. Reeves, "SAT Math Scores Mirror and Maintain Racial Inequity," *Brookings*, December 1, 2020, https://www.brookings.edu/blog/up-front/2020/12/01/sat-math-scores-mirror-and-maintain-racial-inequity/.

220 Markovits, *The Meritocracy Trap*, 65.

Chapter 10

221 Markovits, *The Meritocracy Trap*, 138.

222 "GDP (Current US$) 2019," The World Bank, accessed April 16, 2021, https://data.worldbank.org/indicator/NY.GDP.MKTP.CD?most_recent_value_desc=true&year_high_desc=true.

223 Galloway, *Post Corona*, 136.

224 Markovits, *The Meritocracy Trap*, 39.

225 Markovits, 137.

226 Galloway, *Post Corona*, 180.

227 Markovits, *The Meritocracy Trap*, 49.

228 Markovits, 146.

229 Markovits, 144.

230 Sandel, *The Tyranny of Merit*, 177.

231 American Inequality (website), Jeremy Ney, accessed January 18, 2021, https://americaninequality.substack.com/.

232 Pavel Grigoriev and Markéta Pechholdová, "Health Convergence Between East and West Germany as Reflected in Long-Term Cause-Specific Mortality Trends: To What Extent was it Due to Reunification?" *European Journal of Population* 33, no. 5 (2017): 701-31.

233 Theo Wayt, "Lifespan Now More Associated with College Degree than Race: Princeton Economists," *The Academic Times*, March 8, 2021, https://academictimes.com/lifespan-now-more-associated-with-college-degree-than-race-princeton-economists/.

234 "Quick Facts: Union County, Florida," The United States Census Bureau, accessed on January 18, 2021, https://www.census.gov/quickfacts/unioncountyflorida.

235 Katie Jones, "Ranked: The Social Mobility of 82 Countries," *Visual Capitalist*, February 7, 2020, https://www.visualcapitalist.com/ranked-the-social-mobility-of-82-countries/.

236 "2020 General Election," Union County, updated November 6, 2020, https://enr.electionsfl.org/UNI/Summary/2825/.

237 Markovits, *The Meritocracy Trap*, 72–73, 229.

238 Markovits, 277.

239 Sandel, *The Tyranny of Merit*, 23.

240 Sandel, 125.

241 Sandel, 68.

242 Josh Rovner, "Juvenile Life Without Parole: An Overview," *The Sentencing Project*, April 13, 2021, https://www.sentencingproject.org/publications/juvenile-life-without-parole/.

243 Sandel, *The Tyranny of Merit*, 24–25.

244 Audrey Spensley, "U. Offers Admission To 6.1 Percent of Applicants in its Most Selective Year Yet," *The Daily Princetonian*, March 30, 2017, https://www.dailyprincetonian.com/article/2017/03/u-offers-admission-to-6-1-percent.

245 Peter Stone, "Access to Higher Education by the Luck of the Draw," *Comparative Education Review* 57, no. 3 (2013): 577–99.

246 "Students Selected by a Lottery Begin College in Capital," *The New York Times*, September 15, 1968, https://nyti.ms/3p6RhMT.

247 Jeffrey Selingo, "The Best Way to Fix College Admissions are Probably Illegal," *The Atlantic*, April 27, 2018, https://www.theatlantic.com/education/archive/2018/04/college-admissions-antitrust/559088/.

248 Barry Schwartz, "Top Colleges Should Select Randomly from a Pool of 'Good Enough,'" *The Chronicle of Higher Education*, February 25, 2005, https://www.swarthmore.edu/SocSci/bschwar1/Chronicle%20of%20Higher%20Education%202-25-05.pdf.

249 Barry Schwartz, "Do College Admissions by Lottery," *The New York Times*, September 25, 2015, https://www.nytimes.com/

roomfordebate/2015/03/31/how-to-improve-the-college-admissions-process/do-college-admissions-by-lottery.

250 Barry Schwartz, "Do College Admissions by Lottery," *Behavioral Scientist*, June 4, 2019, https://behavioralscientist.org/do-college-admissions-by-lottery/.

251 Arthur C. Brooks, "A College Degree is no Guarantee of a Good Life," *The Atlantic*, July 2, 2020, https://www.theatlantic.com/family/archive/2020/07/will-going-college-make-you-happier/613729/.

252 Markovits, *The Meritocracy Trap*, 182.

253 "The Successful College Dropout Is Rare. The Majority of Startup Executives Have Advanced Degrees," Kauffman Fellows, accessed January 17, 2021, https://www.kauffmanfellows.org/journal_posts/startup_degrees.

254 "Diversity of the Students Who Choose WGU," Western Governors University, accessed January 16, 2021, https://www.wgu.edu/about/students-graduates/student-diversity.html.

255 Sue Shellenbarger, "Delaying College to Fill in the Gaps," *The Wall Street Journal*, December 29, 2010, https://www.wsj.com/articles/SB10001424052970203513204576047723922275698.

256 "About PLQ," Hermandad Educativa: Proyecto Linguistico Quetzalteco, accessed February 26, 2021, https://plqe.org/about-us/.

257 "About the Mountain School," Escuela De La Montana, accessed February 26, 2021, https://escuelamontana.org/about/.

258 One of my favorite memories with Wilder was playing chess each afternoon at the café. A young guy sat down at the table next to us and watched our amateurish attempts at clever strategy. He thanked us for letting him watch and stepped away following checkmate. An older gentleman at the table to our other side asked, "Hey, did you know that kid who was watching you play? He's our chess national champion of the whole country."

259 Luke Gair, "Wilder Mccoy Named Sewanee's 49th Thomas J. Watson Fellow," *The Sewanee Purple*, April 12, 2020, https://thesewaneepurple.org/2020/04/12/wilder-mccoy-named-sewanees-49th-thomas-j-watson-fellow/.

260 Kevin Eagan et al., *The American Freshman: National Norms Fall 2015* (Los Angeles, CA: UCLA Higher Education Research Institute, 2015), https://heri.ucla.edu/monographs/TheAmericanFreshman2015.pdf.

261 Nina Hoe, *American Gap Association: National Alumni Survey Report* (Philadelphia , PA: Temple University, Institute of Survey Research, 2015), https://americangap.org/assets/2015%20NAS%20Report.pdf.

262 "Bob Clagett on Taking a Gap Year," *College Admission Book*, March 20, 2013, https://collegeadmissionbook.com/blog/bob-clagett-taking-gap-year.

263 Joe O'Shea, "A Gap Year Could Be the Answer to the Student Mental Health Crisis," *Quartz*, September 14, 2016, https://qz.com/704435/a-gap-year-could-be-the-answer-to-the-student-mental-health-crisis/.

264 Melissa Korn, "Welcome to College. Now Take a Year Off," *The Wall Street Journal*, December 25, 2018, https://www.wsj.com/articles/welcome-to-college-now-take-a-year-off-11545742801?page=18.

265 Galloway, *Post Corona*, 151.

266 Douglas A Wick, "Quit Before Leaving – How to Handle Dissatisfying Situations," *Strategic Discipline* (blog), January 22, 2018, https://strategicdiscipline.positioningsystems.com/blog-0/quit-before-leaving-how-to-handle-dissatisfying-situations-0.

267 Walter Kaufman's translation. If you ever reach Nietzsche's primary texts, only go with Kaufmann's translations where possible.

268 "Philosopher Friedrich Nietzsche Biography," Pantheon, accessed February 25, 2021, https://pantheon.world/profile/person/Friedrich_Nietzsche/.

269 Eknath Easwaran, *The Bhagavad Gita (Easwaran's Classics of Indian Spirituality)* (Tomales, CA: Nilgiri Press, 2009), 102, Kindle.

270 There are two formulations he proposes, both from *The Gay Science*, the book that immediately preceded *Thus Spoke Zarathustra*.

"Whoever thou mayest be, beloved stranger, whom I meet here for the first time, avail thyself of this happy hour and of the stillness around us, and above us, and let me tell thee something of the thought which has suddenly risen before me like a star which would fain shed down its rays upon thee and every one, as befits the nature of light. – Fellow man! Your whole life, like a sandglass, will always be reversed and will ever run out again, – a long minute of time will elapse until all those conditions out of which you were evolved return in the wheel of the cosmic process. And then you will find every pain and every pleasure, every friend and every enemy, every hope and every error, every blade of grass and every ray of sunshine once more, and the whole fabric of things which make up your life. This ring in which you are but a grain will glitter afresh forever. And in every one of these cycles of human life there will be one hour where, for the first time one man, and then many, will perceive the mighty thought of the eternal recurrence of all things:– and for mankind this is always the hour of Noon"

"What, if some day or night a demon were to steal after you into your loneliest loneliness and say to you: 'This life as you now live it and have lived it, you will have to live once more and innumerable times more; and there will be nothing new in it, but every pain and every joy and every thought and sigh and everything unutterably small or great in your life will have to return to you, all in the same succession and sequence' ... Would you not throw yourself down and gnash your teeth and curse the demon who spoke thus? Or have you once experienced a tremendous moment when you would have answered him: 'You are a god and never have I heard anything more divine."

Index

Made in the USA
Coppell, TX
17 December 2021

69177511R00289